ALL QUIET IN THE WEST

ALL QUIET
IN THE WESTERN SUBURBS

WORLD WAR ONE IN CHISWICK AND NEARBY DISTRICTS

JOHN H GRIGG

YOUCAXTON PUBLICATIONS
OXFORD & SHREWSBURY

ISBN 978-1-912419-31-9
Printed and bound in Great Britain.
Published by YouCaxton Publications 2018

YouCaxton Publications
enquiries@youcaxton.co.uk

Contents

Preface

The idea for this book came from my history studies of local newspapers in Chiswick Library. I was recording items from the Chiswick Times and the Acton Gazette year by year from the 1890s, and when I reached 1914 found a wealth of material about the First World War. There were hundreds of letters from servicemen. Some were written direct to the papers but most were to relatives, friends, former employers, churches and clubs and were sent on to the Chiswick Times for publication. There were also reports from local journalists based upon interviews...

The Rev. R.A. Oldfield, vicar of St Mary Magdalene Church in Chiswick, received many letters from former members of his London Diocesan Church Lads' Brigade who were serving in the forces. They were mainly on the Western Front but also in other parts of world. The letters to the Rev. Oldfield were published in the Chiswick Times nearly every week during the war. The Church Lads' Brigade at St Mary's was a thriving organization. Of particular importance was their band. They had a football team and the brigade had outings to seaside resorts and other places. Thomas King, secretary of the Chiswick Working Men's Club, also forwarded numerous letters he received from club members.

Most of this book consists of the letters from the servicemen. I have also included an abridged article that appeared in the Brentford and Chiswick Local History magazine about the beginning of the war, and short reports about events when the war ended. There is a lot more – munition workers, women, and conscientious objectors – that could be the subject of another book. It is the first time nearly all the letter writers had been abroad, and there is evidence of historic and traditional racial prejudice – particularly in some letters from India, Egypt and Palestine.

Some letters write of little more than the weather, or just give news about other 'Chiswick lads' and you wonder how much has been censored. We now know that more than sixteen million people died in World War One. Have those letters that questioned the war been suppressed and what can be learnt from the letters? That the men were fighting for a just cause against an evil enemy? Or were all combatants duped into loyalty by rulers of nations in a struggle for power in Europe and across the world?

Nevertheless there are descriptions of the horrors of war and life in the trenches – how they prepare food and live with constant enemy shelling – they have numerous nick names for the different types of enemy bombs and shells. These are accounts direct from the men in the ranks and give some insight into how they sustained themselves in the midst of the horrors of war, with thoughts of loved ones, music, and happier times at home.

I would like to thank Linda Shampan, Bob Fowke and Rodney Walshaw for their help in producing this book and Labour Heritage for their sponsorship.

John H Grigg. June 2018.

1. When the War Began

The First World War may have started in August 1914 but for many years local papers in the west of London had reported anxieties at local political, church and society meetings. At some meetings there were warnings that our navy must keep pace with Germany; at others there were calls for peace and friendlier relations with Germany. Local fears reflected those at national level.

But by 1914 Germany was seen as an enemy, war seemed inevitable, and stories of spies and plans for German invasion were rife in the newspapers which were the only means of communication – apart from word of mouth, rumour, letters and postcards.

Spies and Secret Agents

Albert Holden, a post-card photographer of Goldsmith Road in Acton was preparing to take a photograph of Southsea Castle in May, three months before war broke out, when he was arrested by two soldiers under the command of an officer. He was taken to the castle and kept for three hours while the plates were developed and examined. He was released and told he was fortunate 'as the Isle of Wight, Portsmouth and Southsea are full of German spies.' Mr. Fenton, the Chiswick Fire Brigade Superintendent, was similarly detained on the Isle of Wight when he had foolishly snapped a torpedo boat coming into the harbour.

A Belgian soldier who had fought the Germans and had escaped to England was quartered in Grove Park Road, Chiswick. He was arrested by a London Defence Corps private for making a sketch of Tower Bridge. The matter went to court and the case was dismissed after the Belgian Consulate spoke up for the accused. Another man was arrested at Brentford Docks in possession of 'plans' that in fact were harmless water colour sketches.

This spy mania spread to fears that German agents were secretly preparing for an invasion, and at an Acton District Council meeting the Surveyor was asked if he would inspect the district to discover whether any concrete foundations had been prepared for German guns. The surveyor said the council had no power to do so and it was a matter for the military.

There was a sensation at Acton Wells when, acting upon information received, a large body of police raided the premises of C. Roder & Co., the London factory of a German music publishing company, and arrested 23 German workers. Most of the firm's 200 employees were English. The information received was that the concrete roof was two feet thick and commanded a wide view over the Great Western Railway line and junctions.

When questioned by a press representative the firm referred the reporter to the architects of the building who said the suggestion that the roof could be used as a platform for guns was absurd. He showed a photograph of the saw toothed roof, which was composed mostly of glass, any concrete being only two inches thick.

Pigeon fancying was a popular pastime. John Klewhein, a Bavarian who had been in England since 1898 and had an English wife, lived in Hamilton Road in Brentford and kept pigeons. The suspicion was that they could be used to send messages to Germany. It was explained that the birds were hatched in Brentford and if let out wouldn't fly anywhere. Despite that he was fined £5 and the birds were ordered to be destroyed.

In Bath Road Hounslow smoke was seen near a van and at once was thought to be the work German spies. The Fire Brigade were called and it proved to be nothing more than fumes from a cartload of manure.

The anti-German mania ran to demands that the public house near Acton Town Station called 'The Crown Prince of Prussia' be changed to 'The Crown Prince of Russia' and that Brandenburgh Road be renamed. It was later renamed Burlington Road. In

Isleworth German sausage was transformed into breakfast sausage. But the mania lead to a tragic result in Acton.

Military Guards were placed on the Great Western Railway. 19-year-old William Ellis, who was apparently stealing walnuts from a garden and was challenged by a special constable, ran away along the railway. He was called to halt by one of the armed soldiers. He refused and was shot in a nearby brickfield. He died the following day in Acton Cottage Hospital. A verdict of 'justifiable homicide' was returned and the soldier was commended in the coroner's court for doing his duty so promptly.

Aliens Interned

Once war was declared on August 4th all unnaturalised Germans, Austrians and Hungarians had to register at Police Stations. 75 year old Henry Bettcher of Heathfield Gardens in Chiswick, who had lived in England for 36 years, was prosecuted for not registering. He told Acton Justices that he had once been told by a judge that he was a British subject eligible for Jury service and it was not necessary for him to be naturalised. He was fined £10, an amount he could not pay. As he was led towards the cells an English friend paid the fine and Mr. Bettcher was released. So distressed was he by the proceedings that he collapsed and died the following Sunday.

There were other cases reported in the local papers, including an Englishwoman who had married a German and didn't realise that she had therefore 'chosen' German nationality. Registered Aliens were watched by the police and several were arrested and fined for travelling more than five miles from their registered addresses.

In October 1914 the Home Office ordered the internment of all un-naturalised aliens of enemy countries. One local woman whose German husband had been arrested and taken away had difficulty in finding him. Laden with food and other items that her husband might need, she went to Olympia, which had been commandeered as a detention centre. She was directed to Newbury and then to place after place, until she found him at the Aldershot detention camp.

Panic in the High Road

When war was declared there was, like everywhere else, panic in Chiswick. There was a rush on the shops and several ran out of supplies. One problem was getting stocks from wholesalers whose horses had been requisitioned by the government. In Brentford 150 horses were commandeered for the army from the council, hauliers, breweries and laundries, and a number of men were out of work as a result.

There was a run on the banks as customers withdrew deposits. A local bank manager said customers were asking for gold, but when it was explained that it was in the national interest to reserve gold, most took bank notes with a small proportion of gold and silver. Another bank manager said everyone was paid out in gold but many brought their deposits back later, repenting their hasty action

The government extended the bank holiday to get control of the situation, and when they opened again banks were generally insisting on seven days' notice for deposit withdrawals in order to stop any further depletion of gold reserves.

Reactions to the War

Excited crowds gathered at level crossings and bridges. A large number of people spent whole nights on the bridge near Brentford Station to cheer the troops as they passed by. Normal timetables were suspended to allow trains carrying troops, horses and guns to get to Southampton.

German goods were boycotted and J Bosence, Jeweller of Chiswick High Road, was wrongly reported to the police as a German. He could, he said, trace his family back to 1066 in Cornwall. Another High Road trader, Harry Hallier, a baker, put an advert in the *Chiswick Times* offering a £10 reward to anyone providing information leading to prosecution of anyone saying he was a German.

Some responded by volunteering help for the war effort. Mrs. Dorey, president of the Brentford Needlework Guild, after an appeal from Queen Mary, set to work making flannel shirts, socks, sweaters, cardigans for the troops and night shirts for hospitals. Another women's group, the Brentford Women's Working Association, which met every Thursday afternoon in Brentford Library, had by the middle of September sent 128 flannel shirts and pairs of socks for the 8th Middlesex Battalion B Company.

Stranded in Europe

August was the middle of the holiday season. There were stories of tourists in Switzerland endlessly delayed in returning to England, but the people really in trouble were those caught behind enemy lines. John McLaren, working in Germany, and Mr. Haynes, working in Vienna, had problems getting back to London. Miss Waycott, a Red Cross Nurse working in Brussels, was trapped when the German army occupied the town.

Joining the Army

At first there was no great rush to join the army and a local vicar wrote to the *Chiswick Times* to say he was nauseated by the spectacle of be-flannelled young men enjoying cricket, tennis and river punting while others gave their lives in Belgium and France.

Men who had been in the regular army and were reservists were called up straight away. 150 London United Tramways Company employees were on the reserve and the company lost a tenth of its work force. Over 200 naval reservists in Brentford were directed to report to Chatham and elsewhere.

A large number of reservists at Brentford Gasworks and the Royal Brewery were called up and both places announced that the men's places would be kept open until the war ended – expected then to be by Christmas. The Gas Works would pay half wages for subsistence of their families, and the brewery undertook to look after their families while the men were away.

In September a huge recruiting rally in Acton Park attended by about 2,500 people resulted in 20 volunteers, but all but five were rejected on health and other grounds. Similar rallies in Homefields Park, Chiswick Town Hall and Chiswick Empire did a little better. Not many joined up at these rallies, but maybe they had an influence because men started to join up individually, and when reports arrived from the Expeditionary Force in France recruitment picked up. Servicemen's letters appeared in the local newspapers. The false war of spies, secret German guns and the High Street panic faded once the deaths and casualties appeared. English casualties arrived at Chiswick Hospital and wounded Belgian soldiers at Devon Nook, a converted house in Chiswick. It was reported that the Duke of Northumberland had placed a part of Syon House and grounds at the government's disposal for convalescent wounded.

The *Chiswick Times* printed the names of close on 1,500 Chiswick men who had responded to the call by the end of November. This included reservists, and those who volunteered for 'Kitchener's Army' or the Territorials.

The Middlesex Regiment

Most local men joined either the regular army (Kitchener's Army) or the Middlesex Regiment (Duke of Cambridge Own), known as the 'Die Hards'.

The 10th Middlesex Territorial Battalion was based at Stamford Brook in Chiswick and the 8th Battalion in Hounslow. By the end of August 80 extra men had joined the Middlesex 8th Territorial Battalion at the drill in Brentford. The 10th Middlesex started the war with 700 men. Most of them were quickly sent with the 8th Battalion to Sheerness to assist in guarding the Medway and Thames defences. Crowds gathered to see them off. They marched off to Hammersmith where a special train awaited. Then they went to Sittingbourne for training where, by all accounts, they had a high old time. On 30th October the 10th sailed for India to release a regular army battalion for the war in France and remained there until the end of the war.

The 8th Battalion went to Gibraltar and then to France in March 1915 and later in the year they amalgamated with the Middlesex 7th Hornsey battalion. A second 8th battalion went to Egypt in August 1915 and then to France in June 1916 where the whole battalion went into quarantine for typhus. Records say the second 8th was then disbanded. A third 8th battalion remained in reserve in England.

Meanwhile, back in Stamford Brook a reserve 10th battalion was being raised that was over 1,000 strong by the end of 1914. This reserve in 1915 became part of the 53rd Welsh Division and sailed for Gallipoli in July 1915 where heavy losses were suffered. Later that year the division was evacuated to Egypt and was engaged against the Turks in Egypt and Palestine until the war's end. A third 10th Middlesex Battalion joined the South African Brigade in France in 1917 and a fourth Battalion remained in reserve in England.

The War

When 1914 ended there was still hope that it would be over in a few months. We now know that it was not so. Parish war memorials honour 750,000 United Kingdom men who died in action or from disease and other causes in the struggle for power in Europe.

Sources: Chiswick Times, Acton Gazette, Middlesex Independent, Middlesex Regiment Records.

2. Stranded in Europe in 1914

7 August 1914. *Chiswick Times*
Chiswick Scouts in Belgium.

The Chiswick (All Saints) Scout troop were at the International Scout Camp near Brussels, when a message was received by District Scoutmaster, Mr. H. S. Martin that Germany had presented an ultimatum to Belgium and the scouts should leave Belgium as quickly as possible. Then the British Legation warned that communication with the coast might cease at any moment.

Mr. Martin had a vehicle and by speeding and cutting across fields, he drove to and back from Brussels and ascertained a train was leaving shortly after noon for Ostend to connect with a boat to England. Tents and equipment were rapidly dismantled and after a hurried meal, they departed from the Belgian scouts amid cries of 'Vive l'Angleterre' and 'Vive la Belgique!'

Troops, women and children were hurrying in all directions and there was pandemonium in Brussels where shops were closing and soldiers were commandeering every available horse, leaving a spectacle of endless carts left stranded without horses. They witnessed shops owned by Germans attacked and looted by angry crowds.

They managed to board a crowded train with minutes to spare, but at Ostend the vessel already had 1,400 on board. No more were allowed and hundreds were left in despair as it steamed out. The scouts acted with admirable coolness and discipline. A corner of the quay was occupied as a temporary camp. Mr. Martin spoke to the Belgian authorities and the news was 'no further boat today – perhaps one tomorrow.' A room at the quay station was made available. Food supplies bought in the town. Water was the main difficulty – at 6d for a small bottle.

Through the night, there was the continuous tramp of soldiers being dispatched as quickly as possible. The Belgians are courageously determined to defend their hearth and home but the questions asked by the crowds in the streets was 'Is England coming to help us?' 'How soon will the English come?'

2,000 were waiting when there were signs of a boat at 8.30am on Tuesday. Things looked ugly in the fight for the gangway and soldiers with fixed bayonets were sent down but the crowd was too great for them. Small children were in danger and two mites were eventually handed over to the scouts to take care for. The fights were indescribable but the deck was eventually reached and at 10am the boat steamed out of the harbour amidst a volley of cheers. The sea passage to Dover was made through a channel of war vessels and cheers were exchanged between passengers and the sailors manning the warships. At Dover, guns were mounted on all the forts. The never-to-be-forgotten journey ended at Charing Cross at 5.30pm.

14 August 1914. *Acton Gazette*
Acton Lady's Adventure – Stranded in Switzerland.

Miss Fountain of 45 Hillcrest Road Acton, was in Zermatt, when the first news of the war reached them after a hard day's climbing.

'The village was in great excitement and the Swiss Army had been mobilised. We treated the situation lightly until on Sunday night a copy of the *Daily Mail* told that Germany was already at war and England's decision was in the balance. Home through Germany was closed so our return tickets were useless. We decided to leave for a frontier town near France.

Next morning people were crowding into the 7.40 train to Visp to proceed to Geneva, Lausanne etc. We got the 9am train packed with Americans, English and French and all kinds of luggage – ice axes etc. All talked over the situation, the Americans being particularly anxious to reach the coast and possibly steamers. The heat was intense and we finally reached Lausanne at 11.30pm – dead tired and with nowhere to stay but a hotel porter hailed us and we found ourselves in a comfortable pension – where we were destined to stay for three weeks.

The next morning, we went to the Consul's office and there, to our surprise, were nearly all the English and American people we had met on holiday. Some had been there two or three days. The French frontier was closed. Our money was short and the telegraph did not work for a week. We spent time in crowds waiting for passports, asking the Consul about special trains, making shirts for soldiers, and being horribly bored. The only advice we were given was 'to wait patiently.'

We had no news from England and nobody at home knew where we were. We wrote letters that had to be sent via Genoa, wondering if we would get home before the letters arrived. When one lady received an English newspaper, excitement ran high, and tears were not far from many eyes as we read of the stirring scenes that had been going on in London. After 10 days, we heard the French frontier was open again and that 200 people per day would be allowed to cross and take what trains were available and travel with soldiers.

French mobilisation went on for over a fortnight and at first only the most daring set off into what was truly the unknown. We heard nothing of what was going on the railway and whether or not the intrepid starters ever reached their goal, Paris. All promised to write but no news came.

On the Wednesday of the third week, with money nearly exhausted, against the Consul's advice, as trains were still scarce and crowds of refugees vast, we determined to venture on, not knowing the dangers we might encounter. We laid in provisions for three days. At 6.30am we were on our way to Valorbe, the Swiss frontier town. We were only allowed to book stage by stage to Paris there being no through-trains.

At Valorbe, the fun commenced – a mad rush from our train to the French one – the Americans coming in an easy first in the science of 'shove'. There was only room for 110 people and there were 250 of us. Soldiers turned out all of us with no seats. There was no other train for six hours. Those of us who spoke French, chatted to the Swiss soldiers, who were very kind and guarded our luggage as we took a 3-hour walk among the lovely Jura hills. There was a holiday spirit when we returned, the Swiss soldiers being glad of the break in monotony during the inaction of their enforced times on duty.

At last, a French train came in – an hour before we were due to start. So we took it to Pontalier, the French frontier town where our passports were examined and we were searched before leaving the station. In answer to my question, it was explained they were looking for papers or explosives. German spies carried the latter very often.

The next train was at 6.30am the following morning. A hotel was hastily found. The Maire gave a permit to leave and on Thursday, we set off again to Dole where we spent three hours talking to English soldiers. We took letters from two of them to post to wives in London. We took off again at 1.30pm – rich Americans and poor English travellers alike crowded into 3rd Class carriages.

At Dijon, a train for Paris was waiting and then commenced the hottest and weariest 12 hours I ever spent. Paris was reached at 3.30pm and we took a taxi from Gare du Lyons to Gare du Nord. There amongst many of the weary stranded, we waited till 7.30pm for a train to Boulogne, six more hours of travelling – a triumphal journey when soldiers in the station at Boulogne found it was the English train. Passports were again examined, names and addresses taken and after two hours, we started. Our way across was guarded by warships on either side.

Finally, we took the train to Charing Cross and arrived at 7.30, too thankful to be safe in Old England once more, to mind how tired we were.

4 September 1914. *Chiswick Times*
Dan Mason's Escape from the Continent.

A very long train journey from Lausanne to Paris, where there was a scene of devastation. Any shop bearing a German name had been sacked. The state of trade was worse than in England. Shops and cafés closed. People waiting outside shops. No motor buses because they had all gone to war.

His papers were not properly in order, but first at Gare du Nord he rowed with an official until he got sick of him and at Boulogne he waited in the quay for 6 hours and slipped aboard as there was a row about a German chap.

25 September 1914. *Chiswick Times*
Chiswick Chemist in Germany.

John McLaren of the Chiswick Polish Company is still in Germany. Several Germans have arrived from England and there is a promise that when England releases the Germans, the English would be allowed to return to England. He finds it comfortable there and most people are quite polite.

'Of course, I have to listen to a lot of uncomplimentary things about England, but I generally do not comment, so nothing in the shape of personal insult results.

The early enthusiasm has died away and the people are not taking such a cheerful view of Germany's position. English firms are being boycotted, notably 'Sunlight' and 'Dunlop Rubber' but I expect this will die out as soon as the war is over.

The town is entirely dependent on overseas trade and the great majority of warehouses are closed. But owing to fine organisation, few people are in want of food and cover. The theatres are still open and last night I heard a very fine recording of Lohengrin.'

16 November 1914. *Chiswick Times*
16-year old son of Mr. G.W. Haynes, 39 Southfield Rd, Bedford Park, Chiswick was arrested in Vienna. He writes a letter to his father:

'Soon after war was declared, Englishmen in Austria-Hungary were held as political prisoners. We were invited to report to police stations and my employer sent me with a letter to the Commissioner asking him to allow me to go back to England.'

At first, he was in a cell with criminals but, after a request, was put among political prisoners with four other Englishmen. French and Russia prisoners were in adjoining cells. They were removed to Karlstein Castle after being marched to the railway station, guarded by Bosnian soldiers with fixed bayonets, foot police and mounted police. 'We Englishmen whistled popular airs until stopped by a police sergeant.' At Karlstein Castle Haynes was put among 44 people in one room – nineteen English, two French and the rest Russian.

'We slept well enough that night on straw of poor quality. Subsequently we did not sleep well and had terrible colds. It was extremely cold"

The day after they arrived they had black coffee without sugar and a hunk of bread for breakfast. They strolled the courtyard and climbed the castle tower for a view of the beautiful country. At 12 o'clock, they had soup and 4oz of bread and meat 'that was so fat that most of us threw it away'. The Englishmen started to play cricket, coats for wickets, thick branches for bats and a chunk of wood for a ball. 'The side I was on knocked up 25 runs.'

Quite unexpectedly, he was released with a Frenchman and sent back to Vienna.

'I was a prisoner for 12 days and I pity, from the bottom of my heart, those unlucky persons who must stay until the war is over. My employer made an application and promised to be responsible for my actions and through this I was released.'

20 November 1914. *Acton Gazette & Express*
**Miss M. Waycott, of Derwentwater Road, Acton, has returned
from Belgium, where she was engaged as a Red Cross Nurse.**

She was one of twenty sent by Mr. Alfred de Rothschild to
Brussels on 9 August. On arrival, they were given an enthusiastic
welcome by the people and slept at a convent. She and another
nurse were sent to the Brussels residence of Baron Janssen in
Avenue Louise that had been converted into an up-to-date
hospital.

'Belgian Red Cross ladies had been working hard there before
we arrived. Our first patients were badly wounded Belgian soldiers.
One, shot behind the ear, had lain for ten hours before being
found. Patients were brought in on stretchers covered in straw
and what with the blood, dust and dirt we wondered how we
would get them clean.

Ten days after our arrival, the Germans entered Brussels. We
had no idea what would happen. Belgian flags began to disappear
from every house and shop. Our patients had become P.O.Ws
and those fit enough were taken away.

The Post Office was closed so we had no news, letters or
newspapers from home except German notices posted on street
corners, giving news of German victories. For eight days, we
heard firing day and night.

One night, 12 more patients were brought in – 10 Germans
& 2 Belgians. We wondered how the Germans would like being
brought to a Belgian house and nursed by English nurses – but
they seemed only too glad. When they left they wrote to Baron
Janssen thanking him for the kindness they had received.

We had to keep the Germans at one end of the ward and
the Belgians at the other, but they were all treated the same and
were given three meals a day and plenty of beer & stout. One of
the Belgians had been shot through the spine. The bullet was
extracted but he died a few hours later.

On 22 September we were told all English nurses and doctors were to leave Brussels by order of the Germans. We were to go to Denmark – a neutral country. After a fortnight waiting in the house of a Belgian gentleman 150 nurses, 11 doctors and dressers assembled at the station. We had all taken our seats when we were told to get off as we could not be taken that day. The next day, we were ordered to be at a doctor's house by 9am and after waiting two hours, a German general came.

He asked if we were all there and, on hearing one nurse refused to leave, he sent a soldier for her. While we were waiting outside the station, she arrived escorted by two soldiers. A German officer called our names and as we answered we were allowed onto the platform. The train had been used to bring German troops. The carriages were very narrow with hard wooden seats and backs. The smell was appalling. An armed soldier was put into each carriage. We, unfortunately, had two. They took corner seats and we four nurses had one between us. We were told the windows had to be kept shut and we were not allowed to leave the train that simply crawled along stopping for 15 or 20 minutes every hour or so.

The guards smoked and turned out from their pockets china and glass ornaments that we gathered they had looted from Louvain. They would get out at every station. We had to keep the window closed and the blinds down. They told people that English were on the train and men opened the doors to laugh and jeer at us. The soldiers were given coffee, soup, cigars, chocolate and bread, but we were not allowed to buy anything. Fortunately we had provided ourselves with some food.

We passed several troop trains and our 'friends' drew our attention to the enormous guns that they said were for London and added 'You will give us some wine where we come.' It was a truly awful night and the guards never ceased smoking. At one station we were ordered off the train. Our travel cases were searched and we were relieved of scissors, forceps, fountain pens and knives. The train continued at 5 mph and at last, after 32 hours, we reached Cologne where we were taken to a dining hall, where we had supper. Soldiers were stationed outside. Crowds assembled in the street and the German national anthem was played for our benefit.

Afterwards we left Cologne and to our relief soldiers were not to be with us in the carriage, although they were still on the train and every half hour one would come into the carriage. Sleep was impossible and there was no light in the carriage that night. Just as it was getting daylight, a soldier stayed with us for an hour – we later learned we were passing the Kiel Canal.

At 8am, we reached Munster where we could get some breakfast – large enamel bowls of coffee, sausages and rolls. The soldiers were amused to see us drinking coffee out of their bowls, but we were hungry and thirsty and only too glad to get it.

At another station, we were allowed to get out for a walk for an hour – a short one because armed soldiers guarded each end of the train. We could get a wash from a tap by the side of the railway, so we got a wash – the first for two days.

Late that afternoon, enamel bowls of soup and meat were brought to the train. We were all very cold and only too glad to get something hot. We reached Hamburg at midnight. We were told supper was ready but had only ten minutes to get it and as the waiters served the soldiers first, we came off very badly. There were many people on the station, when we arrived, and from the looks they gave us, I think we would have had a bad time, had we not been so well guarded. The soldiers took great care to stand between us and the crowd.

We spent another night on the train, soldiers continually in and out, and every time the train stopped we heard so much commotion that sometimes we wondered what was going to happen to us. The next afternoon, we reached the Danish frontier and, to our joy, our 48 guards left us. We were thankful to see the back of them, and to have the blinds up and the window open, and to know we were in a neutral country. At 6pm, we left the train after being in it for four days and three nights. The Danish people were kindness itself and at every station, they brought us fruit, etc.

At Copenhagen, we were met by the English Consul, and stayed for a week while arrangements were made for our return to England. We were invited to go over the two magnificent hospitals there and also the Finsen Light Institute. We left Copenhagen at 7am and reached Christiana at 10pm where some Norwegian Red Cross nurses came to meet us. We left Christiana at 11.30pm in a sleeping car and reached Bergen at 11.30am

Many English people in Bergen had heard of our arrival and came to the station in their cars and kindly drove us around until our boat left at 1pm on Saturday and reached Newcastle on Monday evening.'

3. The Western Front 1914

The British Expeditionary Force (BEF) arrived in the Mons area of Belgium. They were driven back 200 miles by the German armies. After halting the advance the BEF advanced 50 miles to Aisne in France and bitter fighting followed to hold the town of Ypres.

7 August 1914. *Chiswick Times*
The first war report in the *Chiswick Times* came from driver W. G. Turner, from his home at 20 Glebe Street on leave after being wounded.

'We landed at Boulogne and went straight to the front – some place between Mons and Charleroi. Waiting in a cornfield. German guns found their range guided by an aeroplane. I came out of that bit safely. We were trying to get to the wounded and I was riding the off horse of one of the ambulance wagons, when a shell exploded killing the near horse. I was knocked off my horse and as I fell a shrapnel bullet got me in the right leg. You feel a burning sensation like a red hot needle; you don't know what to do for the minute.

With others, I was placed in the trenches from which our chaps were firing. When it was dark, we were taken to a nearby convent. Then, four days by train to Rouen and hospital ship to Southampton.'

'And you hope to go back?' asked the *Chiswick Times*. 'Yes. It was a fight where we were, it was slaughter.'

18 September 1914. *Chiswick Times*
A Richmond dairyman, George Kay, was home after a leg injury from shrapnel.

He was at stables near Mons. They were shelled and the stables caught fire so they retired but a shell burst high and struck several down and he was hit.

'The stable fire was spreading and I was told to cut the horses loose. Then I ran through rifle fire for 300-400 yards till out of range – through barbed wire and a hedge. I struggled through more hedges to a railway line where I found a man of the Royal Irish – an awful sight with six shrapnel wounds – calling for water. I carried him for half a mile and found water and stuck with him although I was weak and he was heavy.

Half way across a turnip field I slipped and fell and looked back and saw the stables on fire, mountains high. Thank God we were out of that – worse than bullets. I met one of my own regiment. We found a door and we used it with the help of two Frenchmen to carry the Irishman and came under shell fire again. Finally we handed him over to a company of Cameronian Highlanders.

I think I marched many miles and at last got a horse to Mons. I was put on a train for Havre, then a Red Cross ship for Southampton. I expect to be back in Germany in about two weeks. I'm sure things can't last long now. They have a lot of men, but what's the good of them against our shooting? Now I have seen my wife and child, mother and dad I will go back with a good heart.'

He was with his brother-in-law at the stables and has not heard of him since.

2 October 1914. *Chiswick Times*
Chiswick Councillor Street received a letter marked 'passed by Censor' from Lieutenant H. J. C. Hawkins, former captain of Ealing Park Cricket Club.

'Just got a day's rest. Very busy getting the wounded through. Yesterday we got shelled. Four horses were blown in half. The heads of two of them was all I could find. Germans are using 10" siege guns brought to use in sieging Paris. I was knocked over by a shell that burst 15 yards from me. The drivers of the wagons were blown off their boxes, some badly wounded but none killed.

We see nothing but stinking old horses and dead Germans in ditches and the mess they leave behind them is awful. The third day of a huge battle is in progress, the Germans having fallen back on a position of great strength. But we shall have them soon I think. I think this is the end of all things. At least I hope so.

For three weeks I have had no sleep, except for two hours for one night in three, perhaps. So I must have a dozen winks now. Good-bye.'

9 October 1914. *Chiswick Times*
Bandsman Pearson of the Northamptonshire Regiment was brought up in Twickenham and went to school in Isleworth.

As bands 'are of no use in wartime', he was attached to regiments as a stretcher bearer. At Mons he covered the retreat of the 5th Division. There is an army rule, that the first man stretcher bearers come to, be he friend or foe, he has to be carried to safety. At Meaux, after taking a wounded Irish Guardsman to a field hospital, he and four others had been left behind and were taken prisoner by the Germans.

'Next we were pushed into a barn which had two open doors, guarded by sentries. The Germans had a riotous time with loot captured from the village and got under the influence of drink. At 2am, we crept out, and crawled five miles, until we reached French lines, and rejoined the British army. Two days later, under fire, I was carrying a German officer to one of our hospitals, when a bullet struck my left foot. I carried on until another bullet hit below the knee. I remembered nothing until I found myself in a temporary hospital at Vendresse. We were in range of German guns and were removed to St Nazaire by rail in long cattle trucks, well fitted out with 12 stretchers. The journey took 3 days and 2 nights, but we were well treated by the French en route. Then, by the 'Carisbrook Castle' to Southampton.' In two weeks, he will report back to Northampton.

He experienced some hard times. Rare opportunities for washing and shaving and sometimes he had to subsist on a biscuit or two for 2 or 3 days. Food was plentiful but there was difficulty in getting it to the men who were fighting.

16 October 1914. *Chiswick Times*
Probation Nurse Miss M. E. Curtis writes from L'Hôpital Militaire, le Musée des Beaux Arts, Limoges, France.

'We crossed from Folkestone to Dieppe on September 19th, where they tried to retain some of us because there are so many wounded there. We got to Paris the same night and were there for a week to deal with ID cards and other formalities.

At Limoges, the museum has been converted into a hospital and we had to scrub and clean. On Monday we got in 86 patients, only two of whom are English. As I am interpreter as well as probationer, I have a good deal to do.

I am on night duty with a nurse in one of the surgical wards with 20 beds. We had five operations yesterday. The work is more interesting than an ordinary probationer, as being so few of us I have to help in giving hypodermics etc, in fact doing an ordinary nurse's work.

The men are so grateful and nice to us and when we arrived and walked from the station the townspeople formed into two rows and kept their hats off until we passed. Paris was very quiet and the people all looked so sad. The restaurant keepers gave us presents to bring to the wounded and gave us our meals as cheaply as possible.

Most of the medical cases are pneumonia, bronchitis, rheumatisms and typhoid and as soon as diagnosed, are sent off to the fever hospitals. I must go and get ready for the morning's work. It is 4am and the sleepless ones can be washed and settle down again.'

23 October 1914. *Acton Gazette & Express*

Mr. F. J. Barker, 128 Shakespeare Road, Acton, sends in a letter from his son, Bombardier E. J. Barker of H Battery Royal Horse Artillery.

'The 9th Lancers in the next place to us lost 40 killed and wounded. We have had a very hard time of it as the enemy held good positions on the other side of the river Aisne, near Soissons. They meet their doom shortly as the allies are forcing them to retire. Another big battle is to come – short and sweet I have no doubt. I have no doubt Germany will cease to exist on the map after this little bit of business. Our chaps are well and eager, as I am.'

5 October 1914. *Chiswick Times*

Private F. W. Fulton of the 1st Bedford's writes to his wife in Chiswick.

'We have borne some of the heaviest fighting and our numbers have been greatly lessened. We have lost many officers, three in my company in a few days, the last being killed on the spot a few yards from me. The same shot also injured a lieutenant, whom I helped carry to the doctor.

The rifle fire of the Germans cannot be compared with ours, and the slaughter is sometimes awful when they advance in their well-known 'Lumps.'

The most disheartening thing we have to put up with is being shot at by an enemy we cannot see. A few days back, we twice rushed to a village but had to clear out owing to the heavy shell fire. Part of a house under which our troops were standing was knocked down on top of them as they were reading letters that had just come in.

I have been really astonished at the bravery of our officers. I particularly noticed a major of ours who stood in the open directing troops who were taking cover from heavy shell fire. He stopped a piece of shell and is now among the wounded.'

19 October 1914. *Chiswick Times*
Private A. Webdale, 2ⁿᵈ Battalion Royal Scots, writes to his parents at 57 Clifton Gardens, Chiswick.

'I am writing to let you know I arrived safely at Southampton; have been invalided home through getting wounded in my neck with shrapnel shell. It all happened in an advance that we made at ____ (censored) driving the enemy back about a mile and a half, which we stuck to under very fierce fire, losing a great number of heroes.

I am still happy to think I have got off so lucky after accounting for a good few Germans. I am afraid General French's contemptible little army (as the Kaiser calls it) has given him all he wants, but he has got a lot to get yet.

23 October 1914. *Chiswick Times*
Chiswick soldier's pet rat.

Corporal Johnson of Chiswick, who was wounded at the Battle of the Rivers, had a white rat given to him at Boulogne by a French girl in exchange for a piece of his overcoat as a souvenir. He kept the rat in his right hand pocket all the time he was in action and fed it from his rations. He was badly wounded in the right arm and took his little white friend with him to Netley hospital where a nurse looked after it. Since he left hospital and came home to Chiswick he had been offered £1 for it. 'This little companion was with me all the time I was in action and I wouldn't take £20 for it!'

30 October 1914. *Chiswick Times*
Gunner A. W. Digby's story.

Gunner A. W. Digby of 33, Chiswick Lane of the 'L' Battery of Royal Horse Artillery left Aldershot on 10ᵗʰ August and went from Boulogne straight to the firing line. They had no idea they were so close to the greatly superior enemy forces at Mons until they came under artillery fire and were attacked by infantry. They retired unseen and enemy shelling of the empty position continued for two hours.

After the battle of Mons they covered the allied forces' retreat to Compiegne. Through this retirement, they fought by day and retreated by night. A common occurrence to see men asleep in their saddles.

On the eve of the great advance, because means of communication were cut, they did not know a strong body of French cavalry had retired during the night and their position occupied by German infantry with ten field guns.

As mist cleared, the German guns opened fire making retirement impossible because nearly all the horses were killed. They got three of their guns into action but two were knocked out. The remaining gun served so well that all but one of the enemy guns were silenced. The three men who worked the last gun have been recommended for the Victoria Cross and the one remaining officer has been presented with the Legion of Honour.

A relieving force captured the German position taking 200 prisoners. L. Battery were left behind when the Allied advance started and only about forty have returned to tell how the guns were worked until the very last.

30 October 1914. *Chiswick Times.*
Private Goode, 40 Corney Rd, Chiswick with the East Surrey Regiment returns home wounded.

They were ordered to scout a wood and it came to hand-to-hand fighting. He was clubbed in the jaw with a rifle butt and knocked unconscious. He regained consciousness in the trenches with his regiment and lay there for four days. His regiment lost 262 men and 4 officers

Asked if he was anxious to go back, he said if called, he will be there. The sights he had seen and the experiences he had gone through were so unnerving. 'Even now, I am amongst the Germans in my sleep. It was heart-breaking to see women and children walking roads with their feet red raw.'

6 November 1914. *Chiswick Times*
Wounded soldiers arrive at Chiswick Hospital.

Fifteen British soldiers and one Belgian were conveyed by five cars from Herbert Hospital in Woolwich and received by medical men and the matron, Miss Sutherland. The children's ward at the top floor was made available and the children moved to the conservatory. All the men were 'walking wounded'. Several were interviewed by a *Chiswick Times* reporter.

Private Stone. 1st Battalion Gloucestershire Regiment. Wounded at Ypres.

He witnessed Captain Shipway being hit. Struck by a bullet and fell from his horse, 'a very popular and generous officer. We lost 52 men that day, the first on which we came under shell fire. The Germans outnumbered us by 10 to 1, and had they known we could never have got away, but diddled 'em fine. We sent out a sergeant and six men as a patrol. We have not seen them since.'

Alexander Maclaren. Northumberland Fusiliers. Wounded at the Battle of the Rivers. He has great respect for the Germans' firing ability when they are entrenched, but not so much for their firing on the charge. 'They don't like the bayonet – that's the time to hear them squeal. I have seen them throw their hands up when we have been going to fire, but we are tired of that game and they have to throw down their arms and come out or we will still go for them.'

He was wounded on 14th October, when they had held a position in a turnip field for some time under heavy shell fire. In the night, the Germans retired about 1,000 yards. 'Then we got the order to retire – it was a wrong order because a ditch meant we had to go through a gate singly and shrapnel from shells picked off two out of every three men. They got me in the leg.

After I got to hospital I heard that our men, with the Royal Irish, and the Scots, had a bayonet charge and drove the enemy back two miles.' There was a gleam in his eye as though he hated missing the chance of using cold steel. During the Mons retreat, they never knew the Germans were never more than half hours' march from them the whole time.

'The places are now so well trenched that you can walk from the bottom to the top of a hill, without being seen and it is only when men get careless that they are hit.' He has a bullet, taken from his bully beef tin, when he had a narrow escape. He had other souvenirs including a German belt with the words '*Gott mit uns*'.

Private Hills. 1st Battalion, Shropshire Light Infantry. He got hit in the trenches near Armentieres. They had been one hour in, two hours off for a week. They lay down and slept where they could. 'One morning we found the German trenches only 50 yards away, occupied by 300 of them. The Germans charged when our small party went out and the Germans got it pretty hot. Our artillery shelled them out of those trenches.'

Private Walker. The Shropshires. He was billeted in a church when it got hit.

Private Bramwell. Also of the Shropshires. He was in a party sent out to enfilade the Germans, that is, sweep the enemy line with gunfire. – a corporal and five men. The corporal was killed as they came out of a ditch. 'The Germans were coming in a body for us – too many and I advised our return. I had accounted for four of them when one got me. My chum said "I've got him" and I saw the man who had shot me fall dead. The Germans are brave men and they can shoot. In the night they dig trenches within 25 yards and would by next morning be ready for us.'

He said the worst thing was the dreadful stench from the German dead piled up in front of the trenches and used as additional protection. 'So bad was this we retired 500 yards to give the enemy opportunity to bury their dead, but the line of the English was so thin that they were unable to do it.'

Bramwell lay for eight hours with an arm wound and then crawled for four miles before he could reach a safe hospital. 'We kill ten of theirs to one of ours, though they are using the same formation as us now. They used to come on like bees out of a hive but have given up that game. The French did the same at the beginning but they too are learning to skirmish in open order. This is the fiercest battle in history. Even Mons was foolery compared and South Africa was 'skittles' to it.'

<u>Private Rutherford.</u> 3rd Battalion Black Watch, a 21-year-old Scotsman. He has a serious wrist injury that must have been caused by an explosive bullet. He and others are certain the Germans are using these cowardly weapons. A chum of his had half his head blown off. No ordinary bullet could have done that.

All of them are very sanguine as to the ultimate success and do not believe the war can be of very long duration. They do not think it can go on for another year or more. 'We have seen the slaughter of the enemy and he cannot last out many months more. The German artillery is not superior to ours but the Germans seem to know the ranges, 'Taubes' *(Taubes were the first German mass produced aeroplanes)* are very useful for them in that respect.'

We hope they prove right. Chiswick is proud to be their resting place. They show natural cheerfulness – and a little sarcasm. 'We never saw any ham and eggs in the trenches and wonder how near the front those who said they did actually got.'

6 November 1914. *Chiswick Times*
Belgian wounded soldiers at Devon Nook in Chiswick.

They are getting a lot of attention and help. Two girls from a Hammersmith laundry came along to offer any help and now give some hours cleaning vegetables each evening. Food is being donated as well as books and Belgian newspapers. There is a list of about 50 people helping at Devon Nook.

<u>Dirmana Conte.</u> 18 years old of the 13th Regiment of the line, a bank clerk who enlisted without his mother's knowledge, was leg wounded at Caen, tells several stories. On one occasion, a German

ambulance advanced, they ceased firing, but the ambulance was then unmasked and from it 4 machine guns opened fire.

Sergeant Major Marin, says he was wounded by Germans who advanced with a French flag.

Joseph Colot and Leon Colonne were both wounded at Caen.

Emile Dannon was wounded at Nieuport in the coast battle, was in trenches 'for the whole of the time,' and was under fire for 25 hours at one time. They fought from Liege to Namur. Asked as to the truth of German atrocities, he said some were of such a nature he could not describe them. On one occasion, a mother defending her pretty daughters from the Germans, had her arms cut off, whilst he had seen wounded Belgians killed by the Germans.

Francois Bosschaert. 9th Regiment. Also wounded at Nieuport.

13 November 1914. *Chiswick Times*

The Rev. A. E. Oldfield, Vicar of St Mary Magdalene's Church in Chiswick, ran the Chiswick branch of the London Diocesan Church Lads' Brigade (LDCLB), a boys and young men's Club. He receives letters from 'Old Boys' who had joined up.

Private F. Sheppard. 45th Company, Army Service Corps.

'An enemy aeroplane had to descend the other day, after one of our boys put a bullet through its petrol tank. On 5th November, we burnt a dummy of Kaiser Bill.'

Private Percy Grieve.

'A man dressed in a Scots Greys officers uniform, came up to the London Scottish C.O. and said "Follow me and I'll put you in a good position." The C.O's suspicions were aroused and he put a bullet through the bogus officer's head. He was a German having obtained the uniform of a dead British officer. A dozen Germans who must have lost their way stumbled into our camp and after a fight they gave themselves up.'

Private Dawkins. London Scottish.

'About twenty of us were cut off but held off the Germans, who were about a hundred strong. There was hand-to-hand combat and I bayoneted one and shot others. I escaped bayoneting as I lay on the ground by turning and wriggling.'

20 November 1914. *Chiswick Times*
Private G. Elsley, writes from the 1ˢᵗ Hampshire Regiment.

He has been through the campaign since Mons. The Germans lately have been trying to break through. Troops cheerful apart from cold and wet in the trenches. 'A terrible war and I hope it will soon be over. Our casualties are many but the Germans' must be terrible. They simply flock up in bundles. Poor people's homes are pillaged & burnt.'

20 November 1914. *Chiswick Times*
Private Sullivan writes to his wife at 13, Balfern Grove.

'I had a very narrow shave. Our convoy was hit going through a town and two of our chaps were killed and six injured. The town was shelled and was on fire. All people had left but we managed to rescue a dog and a canary. There is wanton destruction by the Germans as they are driven away. It was the prettiest town with a beautiful cathedral, which they seemed to be aiming at. Not very much time to ourselves as a big battle is going on.'

20 November 1914. *Chiswick Times*
Account of 'Germans at Louvain' given by M. Glaas, a Belgian refugee, who is a guest of Dr & Mrs. W. T. Harris, Bourne Place, Chiswick.

He was a resident of Louvain, which was occupied by German soldiers and there was a rumour that French troops were about to attack. They fled into cellars 'women and children nearly terrified to death.' The Germans set fire to a number of houses and the church. The following day, the town was panic-stricken. Shops and wine cellars were looted.

A German officer and soldier went to every house to say all people must leave because the town was to be bombarded. The roads were thronged. They came across several dead bodies of civilians – appalling sights.

'At Rotselaer, we were stopped by Germans and women and children were separated from the men. The cries of the children were heart-rending. The men were taken back to Louvain which was in ruins. The men were packed into cattle trucks – a few who protested were beaten with rifle butts' – the trucks had little air, no food or water, in a 'poisonous atmosphere.'

The train took them on a 20-hour journey to Cologne. At every station, abuse was hurled at them. At one station, a mob tried to get at them, having been told they had been caught murdering women and children. On the way, 'twenty of our party went mad'. The following day, they were taken back to the station. 'On the way, the crowd were much quieter and appeared to be almost ashamed of their own soldiers.' They were entrained, bound back for Belgium. Eighteen were forced into compartments intended to carry eight. The train stopped for the night near Verviers. One man, who tried to escape, was shot down and brought back to the train on a stretcher. Another died when he threw himself from the train. Another drowned when he jumped from the train into a canal.

They got off the train in the heart of the country, told by a German officer that they were free. For want of food, they tore up vegetables from the fields. They tramped to Malines under escort. During the night, a shot was fired and one man, in a panic, rouse from sleep, screamed 'The Germans are coming' – he threw himself in the canal & drowned. They finally reached Ghent where M. Glaas was re-united with his wife & daughter.

20 November 1914. *Acton Gazette & Express*
Bombardier J. J. Earp, Royal Field Artillery, writes to his father at 39 Elthorne Avenue, Hanwell.

'I think the army opposing us must be pretty well beaten. Our infantry are capturing prisoners wholesale, the majority of them young lads of 16 and 17 year or old men.

I would like you to be here to watch us bargaining for goods. I went into a shop for soap and they handed me matches. French matches are awful. We call them 'stinkers'. You have to wait till they are half burned out before you can light your pipe or cigarette.

Our position is fairly well protected from shrapnel, but should one of their 'Jack Johnsons' burst near us, I should not guarantee our story to be much longer. Big shells – we call them 'coal boxes' – are not so dangerous as their lighter guns and field howitzers with shrapnel. The noise from the explosion is terrific and they make a big hole in the ground which makes them appear more deadly than they really are.

The country here is rather flat. There are a lot of small woods about. There are also several small villages and once the Germans entrench in them they do not like removing. In a place a little way back, they had a mounted machine gun and played 'Old Harry' with our infantry. In another village they used a church spire as an observation station and were directing the fire of their big guns from it.

It is a touching sight to see the refugees leaving their homes and belongings, nothing but what they have on, not troubling to pack anything or lock their doors. Big towns we pass through are practically deserted – no traffic, shops with shutters up, and people standing about in groups terror-stricken.

20 November 1914. *Acton Gazette & Express*
A letter from Private W. Terry, 11 Gladstone Rd, Acton Green, serving with the Rifle Brigade.

He gives an account of the life of a soldier after leaving the trenches for a rest:

'We came out of the trenches at night, when it was raining hard; we were smothered in mud; hadn't had a wash for weeks or a shave (excepting some narrow shaves of a different kind) and marched a few miles to our billet. We found some very decent cottages, the people having gone away. Our food has been extraordinarily good and on the night we cooked some bacon before going to bed. I volunteered to cook for the section and started with bread and butter and bacon for breakfast; roast meat, potatoes, cabbage and onions for dinner; while for tea we had the usual bread and butter, with lettuce we had commandeered from a field. In the trenches we manage to make tea, but cannot always get hot meals. There is, however, more corned beef than we can eat.'

4 December 1914. *Acton Gazette & Express*
A letter from Corporal S. Westbrook, 1ˢᵗ Middlesex Regiment, to his home at 2, Packington Rd, Acton.

'I was in charge of a trench section at Fromelle, near Lille, when one morning the sentry called me to look over the top of the trench. A young German boy, not more than seventeen years of age, walked towards us, with his arms above his head. In one had he held a photograph. He exclaimed: 'Don't shoot meester'. I motioned him to come on and found the photo to be of an elderly woman with six children. I took him to an officer who could speak German and he told him the photo was of his mother and sisters and brothers and his father being dead, he had been the sole support at home. He added he had been made to join the army six weeks before and because he did not wish to fight for the Kaiser he had surrendered.'

11 December 1914. *Acton Gazette & Express*
Lance-Corporal Wilcox of the 3ʳᵈ King's Own Hussars writes to his father at 273 Acton Lane.

'Thanks for your letter. Just finished 72 hours in the trenches. Two or three killed. Very cold and my feet frozen. Shells coming over all day. We watch them burst and crouch down when they burst too near. The Germans at night send fireballs over our lines to see if we make any movement. The aeroplanes do splendid work and the Germans waste a good many shells trying to bring them down.'

11 December 1914. *Chiswick Times*
Letter from 2nd Lt. George Cursons, Middlesex Regiment to his father at Grove Road.

'The food is not scarce but monotonous. The only thing warm is tea. Germans seem to know our meal times for as soon as we start feeding, up roll the shells. On the way to some dug-outs, one or two poor devils got hit by random bullets. Shelling started again. There are shrapnel shells and 'Johnsons'. Johnsons are harmless but make a large hole 4 to 6 feet in depth. One bursting on the parapet completely buried us. Things eased up and I went back to get some tea.

12 or 14 miles on wicked roads into reserve for two days' rest. Some of the men had been days in the trenches. Not there long before returning to support the London Scottish. German high explosives are quite the thing. All that was left of a farmhouse was a cloud of red dust and a few sticks and stones. Whole villages have been treated like that.

You must think I am very miserable. I can get up quite a good moan but I have never enjoyed life more.'

11 December 1914. *Chiswick Times*
Private J. Townsend of the 7th Division Motor Transport writes to a friend in Chiswick.

'We are in the thickest fighting and our convoy has had narrow escapes but has always come out without a scratch. Well, I don't think the war has started yet and you will read of a few surprises to come on both sides. The people here are very good to us. The roads are very rough – about as wide as Brentford's Half Acre.

I have had many nights getting our cars out of ditches, while there are shells bursting like lightening. It makes you feel as if your number is up. Rough weather. Snowing all day yesterday. We had snow ball fights. Britons vs. Germans' among ourselves. '

11 December 1914. *Chiswick Times*
Letter from Driver R. Tyler, 25ᵗʰ Brigade Royal Field Artillery with the Ammunitions Column of the 1ˢᵗ Division.

'Snow cleared off and very wet underfoot. Woolen clothes and tobacco received from 'The Queen and ladies of the Empire'. Our Colonel has told us our brigade has been one of the hardest worked of the artillery. We were used for drawing on the Germans in the Mons retreat and were the first to start driving them back. On one occasion, we were three miles in front of our infantry, causing great loss to the Germans. We had the honour of being the first brigade to cross the River Aisne.'

11 December 1914. *Chiswick Times*
Letter from Corporal Laurie, Cyclists Section 19ᵗʰ Infantry Brigade, a former Chiswick policeman, to Sub-Divisional Inspector Copping.

He is grateful for the cigarettes that he shared with 'my scouts'. Now in charge of two detachments of the Brigade's Cyclists Scouts.

'My job is to go ahead of the brigade to find out numbers and disposition of the enemy – very risky but exciting. The Indian troops are behaving admirably considering they are not used to modern warfare. I was in their trenches making sketches of German positions. They were going about with utmost sangfroid despite Jack Johnsons flying about in all directions. I was also in the Middlesex Regiment's trenches and they were making themselves miniature dug out homes underground. Amazing how a Tommy adapts to any circumstances.

We had snow and hard frost. Boys in trenches suffered, not being able to move about, and some were carried away on stretchers with severe frostbite. Out of thirty shells fired at our billets, only two burst, as if the Germans are using old ammunition. Frequently this town has been shelled and not one shell has burst – a poor look-out for Germany.

The King and Prince of Wales have visited. Give my regards to all sergeants and men at Chiswick Police Station.'

11 December 1914. *Chiswick Times*
Another letter from Driver Tyler.

'The King was here yesterday and presented the V.C. to B. T. Hurlock. Fighting for Ypres was hell at first. Ypres is completely ruined – churches as well as hospitals. We were the only column supplying the whole division, when the Prussian Guard charged us. These were about 60 yards from our guns. One of our batteries drove them back and fired twelve wagons of shells in an hour and the guns got red hot.

Three of us took ammunition to the infantry at 2am, a terrible journey, driving over dead Germans and some of our own. Shells and bullets flying at us. I honestly thought it was my last day.

In the Mons retreat we were twice reported captured. We were with the Munster Fusiliers when they were captured and also with 'L' Battery when they lost nearly all their men. We saw the remains of them on the side of the road.

It was no fault of our troops that the Germans got as far as they did. It broke our hearts to keep coming back. The Irish Guards refused to leave one point until they lost nearly all their men. Sometimes our wounded have to walk five miles to hospital – painful to see them helping one another along. It was worse when we first came here as we saw our fellows walking while German prisoners rode in the ambulances.

We have seen with our own eyes some of our wounded left behind who have been bayoneted or their wrists cut open by the Germans. Of course, all Germans are not the same. Give their famous guards their due. They are good, brave, fair, fighters, but found our infantry and artillery more than they could face.

One of our greatest needs are boots. I have not known dry feet for a month. I don't know if all the bootmakers are on strike but if I don't get a pair soon I shall have to lay up.

18 December 1914. *Chiswick Times*

241 men of Rev. A .E. Oldfield's Parish have joined the colours.

Drummer Charles F. Smith is in the Canadian Grenadier Guards band in Toronto. 'Best wishes from one your old choir and brigade boys.'

Private G. Elsley of the Hants Regiment, 11th Brigade 4th Division writes:

'Wet trenches awful. Now fitted out with fur jackets that are alright provided it does not rain. Things quiet except for 'Johnny Sniper' and we have lost some men. Dare not show one's self in daylight. We play the same games. The King visited on the 3rd and got a good reception. Shall make the best of things at Christmas.'

23 December 1914. *Chiswick Times*

Corporal W. Lewis, dispatch rider, writes to his home in Richmond.

He left Aldershot and embarked for Havre from Southampton on 13th August 1914.

'We were dumped in large sheds by the quay – not allowed out without special permission, which I gained to get a safety razor. At night we left by road and train via St Quentin to a small town called Wassigny.

Day riding was a treat, but at night sentries and barriers were everywhere. Barriers could be barbed wire, carts, chains, ropes or trees with sentries with fixed bayonets. Many of our chaps hit the barriers causing damage to themselves and their machines.

Another complication was that the noise from the machine made it practically impossible to hear a sentry's challenge. Several dispatch riders were shot at. On one occasion, I heard a challenge and stopped to find ten rifles levelled at me. After several incidents, special orders were issued and things settled down.

We went on to Maubeuge and I had my nearest shave from capture. I was sent with important dispatches to our 5th Cavalry Division, my directions being that they were somewhere around Harmignies or Hautchin. I inquired of villagers beyond Hautchin for news of English soldiers, but without result. I turned back and found divisional HQ in another village. It seemed the Germans were on the outskirts of Hautchin and if I had gone on, I should have run straight into them.

We moved HQ to Bonnet and were stationed there during the battle of Mons, delivering to various troops during the day. At night, I had to take down and reassemble another fellow's gearbox and then retreat. That rider is now a P.O.W. There was another retreat and I was sent to escort a lorry to Landrelier. You must understand there was no field telegraph and dispatch riders had to do all the work keeping the various corps linked up.

For two nights, ten dispatch riders were hard at it, keeping the retiring army fed with orders. At Landrecies, our office was in the Town Hall and I was sent out with a dispatch for General Lomax, commanding the 1st Division, with more vague directions being told I would find him somewhere near Hantmont. I eventually found him at Lemont Fontain, miles away.

When I got back to Landrecies, the Germans were in possession of our HQ. Scrapping at every street corner. I found myself in the thick of a scrum and it was in this, that I got a severe cut over the right thumb and forefinger. Whether from a sword or a bullet I do not know. I could not get it dressed in the village where our medical corps were, because the Germans were shelling it and they had to clear out. So I put a field dressing on the right hand and drove the motor bike with one hand to La Grand Fayte and reported to the C.O.

This resulted in me being sent to St Quentin with one arm in a sling – still on the motor bike. St Quentin was in a panic owing to the Germans being on the outskirts. I had to abandon the bike and got the hospital train just in time to Rouen, where the wound was treated and I was hospitalised in the Hospice Generale.

After four days, the order came to evacuate Rouen. Serious cases were shipped to England and the less serious to an unknown destination. This did not suit me, so I tried to report for duty but the medico would not pass me. Still he was a sport, and said that if I was missing at roll call, he would not inquire what had happened to me.

So I was missing at roll call. I heard there were some motor cycle men in town. They did not know where 1st Army HQ was, but directed me to General HQ and I entrained for Le Mons. My arm was still in a sling. After three days at Le Mons, I got a bike and set off with 26 other riders for General HQ at Meux. From there, after inquiries, I got to 1st Army HQ and told the C.O. what I had done. He told me I was wrong but that he was very glad to see me. I rested a few days and my hand healed.

Then I was promoted to artificer – no more riding but I am responsible for the running order of some 25 motor cycles. I have a travelling workshop with benches and vices and if any bike is abandoned, I go out in a lorry to retrieve it.'

From Aisne, he worked round to Belgium and his workshop has been under shell-fire on several occasions. Once, a piece of shrapnel came through the lorry. He brought it home on his leave together with a helmet of the 239th Regiment and a German knapsack – a substantial cowhide affair. He has now returned to the front.

23 December 1914. *Chiswick Times*

Letters to Major J. H. Clarke, commanding officer of St Michaels Church Cadets, Bedford Park, Chiswick.

Lance-Corporal Carter. 'C' Company 1ˢᵗ Middlesex Regiment:

'I have had some thrilling times with the old Die Hards, especially when the Germans sent us over their so called Jack Johnsons. They are very dangerous, but we have got so used to them that we sit in the trenches singing and laughing at them. The Germans cannot make us out. They hate us because they know we do not care a fig for them. Sometimes of a night-time they sing to make themselves happy, but I believe they are down-hearted at the same time. They fear our little bit of steel. I know that much.

I begin to think and hope that this war will soon be over, but I am sorry to say that I shall not be home for the band supper. I think wonders will have to happen first. I am pleased to hear you had your colours consecrated and I only wish I had been there to see it.

Wishing you all a bright and merry Christmas and a prosperous New Year.'

Lance Corporal C. Mitchell. 1ˢᵗ East Surrey Regiment.

'I have received your very welcome parcel. Trying weather lately and to put on a dry and new pair of socks seems to put a new life into us. Rather quiet lately. Only a few snipers who make us keep our little heads down.

I fully think that the enemy is now beaten and I hope to return and say they are a ruined nation. I am beginning to think I shall pull through: I have had so many narrow escapes. On 26ᵗʰ August I had a rifle shot go through my hat and a piece of shell hit me on the left leg only making a bruise. A month ago I was on a road with a party when the Germans sent about a dozen Jack Johnsons within a few yards of us. Fortunately no-one was hit. The same night, I was put in charge of a trench with about fourteen men. The Germans shelled us all the following day. One officer and a man were killed and eight men wounded. I think after all these experiences, I deserve to pull through.

Time is very precious, so I close by wishing you a very merry Christmas and a happy New Year'.

23 December 1914. *Chiswick Times*
Letter from Private J. J. James, Royal Naval Reserve, serving on a hospital ship.

'We have transported nearly 2,000 wounded soldiers, chiefly French. We have been for a good run but owing to the censor we are not allowed to say where we have been. Wounded are brought here by trains and motors straight from the firing line. We do not see the battle but hear the guns. It is heart-aching to see the poor helpless and dirty creatures whose language we do not know.

A 22-year old Belgian could speak English and had been hacked with a sword and carried 3 or 4 pieces of bone in his pocket. He may have an arm amputated. His home has been destroyed and he does not know where his mother and father are.'

23 December 1914. *Chiswick Times*
Gunner J. W. Paletine, Surrey Regiments, writes to his home in Richmond.

He joined a battery at the Battle of the Aisne and was in action for 33 days, firing both day and night.

'Everyone should be proud of the Surrey Regiments, as in cricket so in the fighting line, they are not satisfied until honours have been won. I am very sorry to say a great number were killed here, even the colonel, who at the time of his death was firing a Maxim gun.

During the evening of the 16th we proceeded beyond Ypres. The enemy made repeated attacks but with utter failure. My battery took part in the largest artillery duel the world has ever known. Nothing could be heard but the roar of the guns. We got through with very few casualties. The Germans must have suffered terrible loss, dead could be seen everywhere, the sight being too awful to mention. The Kaiser, finding it impossible to take the town, ordered its destruction. Not one house remains inhabitable: a 12th Century church was blown to atoms. Other towns and villages that we passed through have suffered the same way.

Refugees, old and young, could be seen tracking along with few belongings knowing only too well what 17 inch shells have done – large enough to bury a cottage. At present, we are not doing much and are hoping to get back for a rest.'

4. India

The 10ᵗʰ Middlesex Territorial Battalion went to India to relieve a regular army for transfer to France and the battalion stayed there for the duration. Many letters home describe the excitement of the voyage to India and the wonderment of the country and experiences there. There is evidence of the historical racial attitudes to the local population.

23 October 1914. *Chiswick Gazette*
Our Territorials – 'going to India'.

The honour of being sent to India has been bestowed on the 10ᵗʰ Middlesex Foreign Service Battalion, who have been training at Sittingbourne since the mobilisation of the 'terriers', to relieve troops there for the front. Although many who were anxious to get to the front are disappointed, the general feeling is one of satisfaction at being sent on foreign service.

'Our battalion is at full strength at over a thousand men & NCOs. Only 800 can be taken abroad, this being the strength of the corps which we are to relieve. Two hundred will therefore return to the reserve battalion at Stamford Brook. This will be a relief for some who did not want to go to India. Some of the 200 have already said goodbye to friends and relatives and will now not be going to India.'

48 hours' leave had been granted and many last farewells were seen at Victoria where special fast trains had been chartered to bring the men back to Sittingbourne. Only the men were allowed on the platforms and there was a constant demonstration of cheering, waving, and singing of patriotic songs. A very hearty sendoff indeed for the '10ᵗʰ' to be repeated, we trust, when the time comes for the return.

Preparations for leaving are in full swing, the quartermaster coping wonderfully. Shops in the town are busy supplying the men with all essentials – tobacco and cigarettes being sold in large quantities.

Many have been fortunate to have 'smokes' given as farewell presents. If there is one thing, more than any other, that a 'terrier' enjoys, it is a 'good old smoke', wherever he may be. Squad drill continues.

'Exactly when we leave England is not known, but when we receive orders, it will be done in quick time. Much has been said of the way young men have responded to the call. We have yet to prove our ability but, with the splendid training received, we feel sure the 10th Middlesex is a battalion to be justly proud of. It is early days to think of a return, but it will be a very effective battalion that marches through Chiswick and Acton when it does come back.

1 January 1915. *Chiswick Times*
10th Middlesex in India. Letter from Private H. F. Price, son of Mr. & Mrs. Price of Chiswick High Rd.

'Sunday 1st November 1914

Our last parade at Sittingbourne was on October 29th in full marching order with our sun-helmets on. Everyone was outside their houses to cheer us to the station.

Monday 2nd November 1914

Coming into Southampton, received cheers on every street corner and the children seemed to think we were off to the front. This is a Canadian northern liner, sailing between Bristol and Quebec. Half the battalion is in the 3rd class and the rest in the 2nd. Sergeants and officers have the 1st class state rooms. The routine is Reveille 6am, breakfast 7am, parade 10am, dinner 12 noon, parade 2.30pm, tea 4.30pm, lights out 9.15pm.

We came up with several other troopships, formed into two lines with five boats in each and moved off down the channel with a 2nd class light cruiser leading the way.

4th November 1914

Saw the Eddystone lighthouse and the last of the mother country. We have an hour on guard and two off during the day, and 4 on & 8 off during the night.

It came up rough about midnight and I could only walk about by hanging on to the rails. Sea began to pour in through the portholes that had been left open down below. I had the experience of closing them, having to go through several inches of water in some places. You cannot get to sleep easily when the boat is rolling about a lot. The tables in our mess room had been laid overnight but by morning everything had made its way to the floor.

Only about 200 were not sea-sick and assembled for church parade. We stand only with difficulty and just as psalms finished an extra big lurch put nearly all of us in our seats. A huge crash came from the kitchen as if all the plates had shot from one side to the other. All started to laugh except the captain who was conducting the service. We watched the Atlantic billows rolling into the Bay of Biscay.

It calmed down and by Tuesday 4.30pm Gibraltar was seen. A torpedo boat came out to meet us and a French battleship guarded us into Gibraltar. The weather is of the balmy kind now and we don't need much clothing. The food is good, but we object to tea sometimes – bread, cheese and pickles. We have porridge, bread, butter and coffee for breakfast with sausages and potatoes or haddocks. For dinner, always soup, a joint of beef, mutton and two vegetables. We, lucky 10th, have the best boat of the whole ten troopships.

On Friday morning, we arrived at Malta but no orders had been received so we went on our way. The Mediterranean blue is beautiful. The decks are covered with awnings to keep the sun off. Sports were organised after leaving Malta. One competition involved eating a bun as quickly as possible.

We are doing 20 knots an hour – 450 miles a day, and eighteen British transports have joined us, escorted by two French cruisers. Some fellows slept on deck and on Saturday there was a tropical rain storm – worse than you ever get in England. Vaccination starts this afternoon.

This Sunday, we saw the revolving searchlight, over the entrance to the Suez Canal.

100 yards inside the canal a naval officer came on board. Other boats, with pressmen, wanted to get on board, but our officers would not let them, nor would give any information. A hosepipe is ready for any natives who try to get in the port-holes. We have about eight coaling barges each side of the ship and the coolies are constantly calling on Allah – they are of every language and tribe – all black by the constant coaling of vessels. We can see an innumerable number of pyramids and about 100 camels. Above several houses, are adverts for Dewars' Whiskey, Swiss Milk, Lipton pears, etc

13ᵗʰ November 1914

We weighed anchor and set off along the canal seeing just sand as far as the eye can see on either side. The wind blows up the sand into a little fog and portholes have to be kept shut.

At the end of the canal, at Port Tewfik, native craft swarmed round the boat with goods to sell. Words had no effect but the hosepipe did. Two old deep barges took us ashore for a route march and then back to the ship.

We remained at Port Tewfik for several days. I went for a sail in a lifeboat – the worst part being climbing 20 feet down a rope ladder which wobbled all the time. A convoy of Indian troops appeared. On the Monday, we arrived at Aden, which somewhat resembled Gibraltar and looks to be well fortified.

On Tuesday, a convoy carrying Australian and New Zealand troops came in and several of the men rowed round our ship and greetings were exchanged. Some had not had a cigarette since leaving Australia six weeks earlier and our fellows threw them some. They went away merrily after giving us one of their war songs.

After we left Aden, we passed another 30 ships from Australia. There are a good many colonials coming to England. We are about 500 miles from Bombay. I shall be going to a nonconformist service this evening in the 1st class café, by fellow members of the 10th. These services are very good, considering one of the fellows preaches. We arrived at Bombay today (Tuesday) at 5am. Dawn broke at 6am – it was glorious. We are standing by for disembarkation.

8 January 1915. *Chiswick Times*
10th Middlesex in India. Letter from Private Grubb.

'On the boat we were rigged out with a blue suit similar to a lounge suit, with a dented hat and a pair of canvas slippers. We must not shave our upper lips as the Indians don't think much of a man minus a moustache.

4th November 1914

We get the most important news by wireless. There are hundreds of porpoises in the Mediterranean, and they follow the ship for miles jumping out of the water every few yards.

6th November 1914

Two French destroyers came up yesterday. Some of our chaps sang the 'Marseillaise' after a style, and they fired a blank salute which caused some of our chaps to rush up on deck, thinking their last day had come. We reached Malta at about 9pm and after stopping about 10 minutes to hand over mails passed on.

8th November 1914

A concert. Church Parade. 10/- paid to each man. Saw heaps of flying fish this afternoon, about 9 inches long, silver coloured and fly for 20 – 50 yards, a foot above the water.

10th November 1914

Our boat was coaled at Port Said by about 100 Arabs, carrying small baskets. They wear nothing on their feet and walk and walk over coal like we would on carpet. They bargain with our chaps, demanding 3d or 4d for silver rings, the majority possessing half a dozen on their fingers. The police dress like sailors, only with red stripes and they beat the Arabs with canes. Heaps of boys keep their parents by diving for pennies. We were not allowed ashore and were prohibited from buying from or selling anything to the Turks or Arabs

12th November 1914

Last night while we were in bed, a sergeant came round to say the colonel had a cablegram from Stamford Brook saying that rumours that the Middlesex Regiment had been sunk were untrue and all were safe and well. We have fire and collision drills occasionally. Half the battalion went ashore yesterday and the band was treated to cigars and drinks by the French Consul. We were expected to go today, but the tug and lighters did not turn up.

15th November 1914

The usual concert last night. Went ashore today and had a route march from the port to the town of Suez. There were gaudy coloured ramshackle buildings, dirty Arabs, smart Egyptian policemen and a few Europeans – mostly French.

The policemen are armed with swords, bayonets and canes and the children and Arab traders took good care to keep out of their way. The Egyptians hate the Arabs and say "Me no Arab. Me Egyptian".

The women cover their faces and wear ornaments on the bridges of their noses. What beauty they have to hide, I do not know; perhaps it is ugliness. The men dress in a kind of skirt and squat on the ground and jabber. There is not much distinction between the pavement and road. We can buy a paper called the 'Egyptian Mail' for 2d. The news is two or three days old.

There are three destroyers in the harbour looking after about fifty liners and transports, also German prizes of war. They play powerful searchlights at night. We are now in the Red Sea, going about 10 miles an hour to keep together.

21st November 1914

The cruiser and an armed transport did some practice firing at a moving target yesterday. Two chaps are down with sunstroke and pit helmets must be worn. Fancy Dress carnival this evening.

23rd November 1914

Reached Aden today. Not much of a place. There are many mountain eagles that dip into the sea for food. The natives are jet black and many have their heads shaven – even the boys. Some can speak English sufficient to bargain and swear at anyone.

27th November 1914

We left Aden and passed 28 transports, probably taking Indians to the Front. We must have passed 150,000 to 200,000 troops on their way to Europe.

30th November 1914

Reached Bombay and have four days' train journey to Calcutta.

9th December 1914

We have reached Fort William in Calcutta on the Indian Peninsular Railway and then the Nagpur Bengal Railway. A great city, immense buildings, fine shops and a university. The Dalhousie Barracks has a room big enough to hold a whole battalion. The wireless station has a range of 5,000 miles. I came across several Chiswick chaps in the battalion. Some companies have gone up to the hills for field training and we expect to go in a month or two. There is a regimental institute with a library, billiards, games etc. The Calcutta YMCA gave us a welcome with concert and spread, and the Bengal Governor General made a short speech.

8 January 1915. *Chiswick Times*
10th Middlesex in India. Letter from Private H.E. Price.

'You see only about a score of women on your journey across India. The men seem to keep them locked up. Those you do see are quite ugly and are always getting water or carrying things on their heads. The native villages are of mud or cane huts and the better class of houses have a garden attached. Children are more upright, well built, happy and clean, although darker than any English children. They go naked in most cases, but are so dark it does not matter much. The Indians of every caste are very modest. We are looked up to everywhere by the natives and the police do not let them come near us on the station.

On Thursday we had a short march round the country after tea. Water lilies were out in bloom in many ponds and you think how poor the ones in Kew Gardens are. At Khagpurgh Junction, 100 miles from Calcutta, we drew our dinners on plates and had to walk about 50 yards to the shade to eat it. Hawks swooped down and picked up 5 or 6 dinners with their claws before you could say 'Jack Robinson'. We are having a fine time. Weather is grand, blue sky and sunshine all the time.'

10th Middlesex in India. *Chiswick Times*
Letter from Private Arandell.

'You remember the horse trams that ran from Kew to Richmond? With the seats back to back? We had half that space on the train. Fifteen packed in with baggage and rifles. You can take it we roughed it. When we got to Fort William it was a town in itself, more than twice as large as White City. A bed of corrugated iron – my body was all wrinkles and stripes in the morning. Now been issued with pillow slips and mattress covers and a bale of coconut fibre to put in the covers – instead of feathers. It took two hours to pick – as good as picking oakum. At first, we thought the regulars watched us and criticised but now are impressed by the way we march and say we are the smartest terriers they have seen in India. They are Royal Fusiliers from Hounslow. They left for the front this morning.

15 January 1915. *Chiswick Times*
10th Middlesex in India. Lance Corporal D. Chadwick, 10th Middlesex writes to his parents at 15 Chiswick Common Rd:

'At Port Said, the Arabs coaled the ship. People talk about slaves in England – it is nothing in comparison. It took them 10 hours and never stopped. They get 2/- a man. These Arabs are a murderous lot and would think nothing of killing a man for 2d. It is a common sight to see boys and girls walk about nearly naked – a lot of them naked – you get used to it. The only English they know is 'Baksheesh' (meaning money). That is the first word a child is taught and little children in their mother's arms ask for money as you walk along.

We arrived at Fort William in Calcutta on the 4th. The natives are very cunning and have to be kept under. The more you curse and swear at them, the more they respect you. If you want a native you simply shout 'Boy!' When you are walking down a road and some Indians are coming along, you don't step out of their way. They get out of yours.

I have three servants – a Nappi Wallah (barber) who shaves and cuts my hair when I like for 2d a week. A Dhobi Wallah, who does my washing for 4d a week. And a boot boy, who cleans my buttons and polishes my boots for 2d a week. You can imagine us walking along the Calcutta High Road with big cigars stuck in our mouths, little lords, everybody stepping out of our way. A cigar is a halfpenny here that would cost 3d or 4d in England. Bananas are twenty a penny.

We are only staying here till April. Then, if the war is over, we shall come home. If not, we shall come home on leave, and then off to France on lines of communication.

Three things keep you awake here: mosquitoes, jackals and hyenas.'

22 January 1915. *Chiswick Times*
10th Middlesex in India. Letter from Private T. T. Harris to his father at 2 Clovelly Road, Ealing.

'Fort William is as large as the two Ealing parks put together: We have our own power and light station, bakery, dairy, bazaar, post office, institute and a wireless station with ten pylons. There are six gates, and to get inside, you have to pass over three drawbridges and through three gates. There are two moats. The ramparts must have once bristled with cannon. I have heard the fort is 2,000 years old. Now there are modern guns, but the real defences of Calcutta are 30 or 40 miles away, half of our battalion is stationed at two of these forts and we shall have our turn presently.

Our bazaar is run by natives. You sit down before you begin to bargain and the shopman often gives you a cheroot or a cigar. In the New Market, Calcutta, you get fruit at a third or half the price asked. We got 10 oranges and a small pineapple for six annas (6d). The bazaar provides everything. I have made two friends in the bazaar. One is highly educated, though he keeps a shop, the other speaks less English, but has a wonderful smile and laughs and earns 20 rupees a month (25/-). They are Hindoos and their intense reverence is wonderful and are delighted that I knew one of their stories of the god, Rama.

Our barrack is one of seven in the fort. We are on the first floor – 15,000 square feet accommodating 170 men. Below are native quarters and store warehouses. Dalhousie barracks has three larger floors and easily houses 600 men.

We parade from 6.45 to 8.00am and from 9.30 to 11. We cannot leave the fort before 4pm except on Saturdays and Sundays, and also on Thursdays in commemoration of the Mutiny which ended on that day. I have visited the zoo, not as good as ours, however the grounds and flowers are lovely and butterflies are everywhere.

On January 6th, the company are going to help garrison a Fort at Chingri Khal, 40 miles down the River Hooghly. It is a desolate spot among paddy fields and near the jungle – noted for mosquitoes and snakes. We shall have a month there.

The Calcutta Club have lent us their swimming baths on Tuesdays & Thursdays from 3-5.

Our Church Parades are different from those at home. We go armed with rifles, bayonets and 20 rounds of ammunition. It is a mutiny relic, as at that time defenceless soldiers were shot while at the church. Cologne is said to be a city of a thousand smells.

Calcutta runs it close. The native tobacco, smoked in water pipes, has a very heavy unpleasant odour. The leaf is mixed with molasses and other things.

I have never felt so well in all my life. I feel I am growing in chest and arms and all my muscles are being developed. Five hours drill a week does much Lord Kitchener's test is a 15 miles march with rifle, ammunition and equipment, with no halt, followed by 2,000 yards skirmishing and then an obstacle course which includes a 10 foot wall climb.'

22 January 1915. *Chiswick Times*
10th Middlesex in India. Letter from Private W.J. Brocks who was a Town Hall official before the war.

'We are not supposed to go out into the native villages, because for one thing there are diseases knocking about and for another, they are very treacherous and likely to do you in.

On Sunday, a dozen of us went out on one of our exploring expeditions. After catching a couple of snakes – one 10 feet long, we came across a native village concealed in the jungle. These villages are surrounded by trees and shrubs and the natives live in low mud huts. I and two or three others wanted to go into this village. The natives came out and stared at us and invited us in. We kept a lookout as to where we were going and how to get out if they were troublesome. We went through a gate and, if that had been shut, we could have been caught like rats in a trap.

We got into a sort of square and the native that spoke to us ordered that planks and chairs be brought for us to sit down. There were only two who could speak English.

We asked if they had any cocoanuts and they brought about thirty and wouldn't take any money for them. The chief showed us round, and then came halfway back with us.

In the afternoon some of the fellows went again and were told if they went again on Monday, they would be given some eggs. They brought back 50 the next day, so we touched lucky. I daresay no other white men have been inside that village until the war broke out.

The rumour that the 10th Middlesex were to be recalled to the front is not correct, though I should like to see the front before it is over.'

5 February 1915. *Chiswick Gazette*
10th Middlesex in India. Private T .T. Harris writes to his father from Chingri Khaj.

'Arrived here at 2pm having left Fort William at 9am. Travelled on the Eastern Bengal State Railway to Diamond Harbour and then on a single track line. There are only two and a half 10th Middlesex companies here and fifty of the Royal Garrison Artillery and native servants. The fort is by the side of the two mile wide Hoogly River. All round is a moat and sandbags and barbed wire defences. 6" guns command the river and also some field and machine guns.

We live in reed huts with raised floors and a bamboo thatched roof. They are like the native huts you pay 6d to enter at Shepherds Bush. There are sixteen to a hut and there is one lantern. It looks awfully romantic to see us squatted around it in tailor fashion.

We sleep on a mat with two blankets and two sheets and a mosquito net slung from the rafters. Each hut has four doors. Jackals prowl around at night when it is very cold. When we go to wash we have to cross the railway line and the moat to arrive at a pretty dirty pond with a T-shaped landing-stage to reach the water. We miss our church services. We have a church parade when a parson turns up. There was a long covenant service at the Wesleyan Church last week. When kneeling at the altar, it was very impressive and peace-giving.'

12 February 1915. *Chiswick Times*
10ᵗʰ Middlesex in India. Letter from Private H. Price.

'I went for a walk and saw a native wooden idol of a woman with other subjects built above her. It is a rule that we never go near any sacred objects because the natives don't like it. The carved idol by the River Hooghly, considered sacred, was about five feet high. This shows the natives are not all Christians by a long way yet.

On a small path, natives invariably give way to a soldier. The women shoot round corners or hide themselves until you are past. It's really quite comical. When I got back from my walk, orders were out to move us to Jaffapore for a musketry course.'

26 February 1915. *Chiswick Gazette*
10ᵗʰ Middlesex in India. A member of 'H' Company, 10ᵗʰ Battalion, writes from Fort William:

'There is plenty of sport – football and cricket'. Their cricket XI lost to Calcutta C.C. On 1ˢᵗ January they took part in a Proclamation Parade to celebrate Queen Victoria assuming the title of 'Empress of India'.

'I am afraid I have to make a grumble or two. It was 16 days before we received any pay – then 10 days before we were paid again. This means we get into debt and have to pay a rupee a week for messing.

A day's rations are:

Breakfast - tea (no milk) & bread; dinner – stew; bread for tea.

How is any man to do his firing and drills on this food?

All the chaps are very dissatisfied and look forward to going to the front.'

Letters from Private T. T. Harris of 10ᵗʰ Middlesex.
'From Chingri Khal, 11 January 1915

We are moving to Barrackpore Station. At Chingri Khal, there are many beautiful birds – and kites that swoop to carry away your dinner. I lost an egg, and one fellow had a spoon stolen by one of those scavengers. There are vultures and the most beautiful birds are the small green fly-catchers.

From Ishapore, 19 January 1915

We went from Chingri Khal to Barrackpore – fine barrack accommodation – cleaner, lighter and more interesting than Fort William. Then 24 of 'H' Company went 3 or 4 miles to Ishapore. They guard the Government rifle and shell factory that employs over 500 natives. The guards work in pairs. My cousin and I work together as one relief. We do the rounds once an hour and watch the safe. We can sit on a box under a tree and smoke and chat. It is very lonely at night, with jackals, bats & owls for company.'

From Jaffapore, 25 January 1915

The road there was full of ruts and ridges. Jaffapore is simply a rifle range. Barest necessities. Water comes from Barrackpore, allowing one wash a day. There are five brick buildings but everyone sleeps under canvass.

Yesterday we had permission to go to Barrackpore to fetch some of our kit and had the luxury of a shower bath while they were there. We had a sing-song on the way back and got to the hymns. It made us feel very happy and near to home and to our own church and to Him whom we worship there.'

'Today I have seen an old Actonian who is with the 9th Middlesex.'

5 March 1915. *Acton Gazette.*

10th Middlesex in India. A soldier writes.

'After two months the climate is getting hotter and the malaria-carrying mosquito is to be feared. A few men are in hospital and the New Year was marred by the death of one soldier. A cross has been erected in his memory.

Various duties have been allotted – church orderlies, clerks, librarians etc. The chief work is guarding one of the largest forts in the world. An important duty is guarding important machinery at Kidderpore docks.

At Barrackpore and Chingri Khal, lonely guard work has the weird Indian touch with at night the hideous noises of jackals and pariah dogs, which can unnerve the best of men, while the native is not to be trusted and will steal anything. Although a mud hut here may be safer than a trench in France, it may not be as comfortable with insects and lizards in every corner and jackals coming into huts sniffing for food. But the 10th Terrier has adapted to circumstances & the pale London look has gone.

Good progress is being made with shooting. Musketry training by NCOs is vigorous and a few marksmen and first class shots have been recorded. Parades are at 6.30am and several evening parades have taken place at the Maidan just outside the fort. Scout and communication sections do most of their training on the plain and have attained high standards in Morse, Semaphore and, at night, lamp signaling. The machine gun sections have added mules to their ranks for the transport of ammunition and gun parts. Loading up the animals, who are not very willing, often provides humorous scenes.

Beside facilities for football, cricket, tennis, fives etc, there are 'sport parades' to the excellent gymnasium in the fort and the swimming baths in the town. We are clad in light khaki drills and shorts and the rig-out made for a smart Proclamation Parade. Regimental colours are worn in our 'topees'. Walking outdoors is with trousers instead of shorts and a blue service cap with badge attached.

We are allowed out after 4pm. The beautiful Eden Gardens are quite close, where pleasant evenings can be spent listening to music and watching beautiful sunsets. These evenings remind us of Hyde Park, the great difference being the lack of feminine companionship – a greater attraction than that of music.

The YMCA organises trips to some of the world's most important temples. The camera has been a great friend and many albums have been sent to friends in England. There is difficulty in getting good meals owing to much dry weather. We constantly get fruit salads and pancakes and would welcome a good plate of beef and cabbage. Fruit and eggs are cheap and the majority of our salary is spent on these delicacies. But such is a soldier's life in a foreign country.

One great pleasure of the week is the arrival of post from home. Everyone wants to know 'if there is something for me'. Excitement runs high when the orderly corporal brings up the letters – often at midnight. Our lads do not think only of themselves but are anxious for friends at home.

Services are held on Sundays. There are Roman Catholic and Church of England churches in the fort and a Wesleyan church for non-conformists in the town. Calcutta folk have invited many of us into their homes.

German prisoners have been in the fort lately – mainly well-to-do business men. Our NCOs have had trips escorting these men to other places and these trips are much sought after for seeing interesting scenes of India. We are pleased to hear of the doings at Stamford Brook. Everyone's heart is in the good old HQ's. We feel confident we have done our bit even through not actually in the firing line.'

12 March 1915. *Chiswick Times*
10th Middlesex in India. Private Jack Fensom, former member of Chiswick Fire Brigade.

'We could see flames and all turned out. It was a scramble getting through the jungle. We set to work, but they only had native pitchers, which we had to hand one to one another from a native pond. We were there to one o'clock in the morning. It was caused by one of the natives going to sleep and knocking over his hubble bubble. I wished the Chiswick Fire Brigade had been out here. They would have put it out in half the time. When we arrived some of the natives were praying before it and the women were crying. Poor devils! I expect they feel it just as we do at home.'

12 March 1915. *Chiswick Times*
Letters to Rev. A.E. Oldfield.

Drummer Will Bailey. 10th Middlesex in India.

'Thank you for the Chiswick Times and I am surprised to see young Fred has joined the Royal Engineers. I have been at camp for thirteen days with the East India Railway Volunteers taking part in manoeuvres. Camping is better than in England where the weather is not so good, but a bit uncomfortable when you find a snake in your tent and wake up at night and find half a dozen jackals rummaging round your tent.'

Drummer Alf Wilkinson. 10th Middlesex in India.

'Been on detachment as a bugler in Baradpore and Jeffrepore. Good stations but bad for musketry work. I miss the annual bible class tea and magic lantern show at St Mary's.'

Drummer F.R. Lock. 10th Middlesex in India.

'Plenty of training – not so bad now we have our khaki drill clothes. Some of us have been up country for musketry, but I would rather do it in the old homeland because the light is so strong and so is the sun, that it is hard to find the bull's eye at 500 yards. Route marches every week and a 12 mile march all through different native places.'

(All three drummers were for many years in St Mary's band.)

26 March 1915. *Chiswick Times*
10th Middlesex in India.
Letter to Mr. A. Edwards, 125 High Road, Chiswick from Private C. Knight, who is at Fort William, Calcutta.

'The really hot weather begins at the end of March and the rainy season towards the end of June. The country is pretty, but not prettier than English countryside. Calcutta is a very large town. The European quarter is quite like the West End in miniature, without so much crowd and noise. It is close to the river, and the docks are a mile or two away. The river is deep and broad enough for average-size ocean steamers to pass up and down.

The English population here are all 'big pots', who drive about in motors and carriages, hence the swell appearance. The chauffeurs and coachmen are, of course, all natives. There is a native volunteer band – as good as many English town bands – who play in the gardens each evening. We have electric light and trams in Calcutta. The native policemen are very smart in their white uniforms with brass buttons, red turbans and leather belts. The railways are very similar to those in England.

The country is much greener than you would expect, considering the hot sunshine and small amount of rain. This is owing, I think, to the heavy early morning dews. The principal vegetation is palms, banyan trees, also coconut palms and banana.'

2 April 1915. *Chiswick Gazette*
10th Middlesex in India. Letter to his mother and sister, at 68 Chatsworth Gardens, Acton Hill from Sgt. A.S. Kell.

'The Viceroy is visiting Calcutta to unveil statues on the Maidan. All those ceremonies are carried out with much glitter and popping off of guns to impress the natives.

The 1st & 2nd of March are great days for the natives. The 1st March being the beginning of the New Year according to the old style of reckoning. Groups sang and thumped tom-toms all night and next day too. They have a peculiar custom of throwing brightly coloured paint at each other's clothes. You meet crowds of them with their white garments covered with patches of red and purple, and sometimes their heads are smeared with the stuff.

The trams are in the continental style – open all through, with seats running from one side. They are run in pairs. The first car for Europeans chiefly, though some of the better class of natives use them – and the second car is for the rabble, usually packed in like sheep. A good service for 6 Pie (1½d) you get a quarter of an hour's ride and the highest fare seems to be 2 Annas (2d).

Sometimes the car is stopped to allow the conductor to get down and wash his face and feet at a stand-pipe – a thing that natives are continually doing. There are sometimes as many as four conductors on the car but I never discovered one yet who could understand a single word of English.

The Zoo at Alipore, 2½ miles away, is about the best place to spend a few hours. Only 1d to go in, except on Sundays when Europeans patronise it and it is then a Rupee (1/4d).'

2 April 1915. *Chiswick Gazette*
10th Middlesex in India. Letter from Lance-Corporal Fowler, E. Company.

'Drummer Revell died after a short illness and he was buried the following day with military honours in the military cemetery. A gun carriage covered with the Union Jack on which rested his drum and bugle. The Colonel and three hundred of the regiment turned out. Three volleys and the Last Post was played. The memory of so popular and valuable a man will live long.

Come to the Cookhouse Door has not been a call so eagerly responded to. The food has been poor stuff – especially when we all pay extra a week for it. Steps are being taken to alter things. Good food will result in good soldiers and is important to keep us fit if we are recalled for service in Europe, which is the hope of all of us out here.

Dazzling light makes musketry tests more difficult than at Bisley. Although our best shots drop a few points, our battalion has a very good average.

Photography is popular as is design work in wool, sketching and painting. Of an evening, popular melodies on instruments of all kinds fill the air, generally having a crowd of chorus boys to help matters while the mouth organ, so popular in the trenches, is often to be heard. Practical jokes are popular and are likely to continue while the beds are collapsible.'

9 April 1915. *Chiswick Times*

Thomas King, secretary, Chiswick Working Men's Club has received several letters:

Private R.A. Wilkie. 10th Battalion Middlesex wrote from Jaffapore Camp, near Barrackpore, India.

'The heat goes a long way against active service. I think a regular soldier's life out here must be a very lazy one. F. Company and the machine gun section pitched 150 tents beside the railway line just outside the Kiul station. There were the usual 'wet' and 'dry' canteens and a first rate boxing ring.

The first parade was physical exercises and then dispatched with mules fording a river and we ascended a steep stony hill – not easy with a maxim on your shoulder. We did this for a fortnight except for two days trench digging and two when the rain kept us in. I have never seen rain like this. Before we could dig run-offs round our tents, we were under water.'

16 April 1915. *Acton Gazette*

10th Middlesex in India.

'Nearly four months have passed since that dawn of a September morning when, looking through portholes, we of the 10th Middlesex got our first glimpse of India – Bombay – and, let it be said, a very pleasing sight. It is hard at first to realise that we have been here so long, but an analysis of things done will show that only an extended stay could permit of their accomplishment.

Immediately after arriving at Calcutta, companies had to be sent away on detached duties, such as guarding river points, ammunition factories etc. Chingri Khal and Khala Tana, two of the river posts, are set in rather nice surroundings on the bank of the Hoogli, and the strict night guards, often at isolated places, are productive of those qualities of watchfulness and dependence so essential in a sentry, to say nothing of the 'hardening' effects of living under active conditions.

Although in the past the 10th Middlesex were not a battalion of Bisley shots, they always passed with credit their compulsory musketry tests. We only hope the Huns will give us an opportunity of proving that the Territorials of Acton and Chiswick can shoot. Neither would there be any argument if the 10th got going with the bayonet. The machine-gunners, signalers and scouts, have worked with earnest energy to fit themselves for the test in France or Germany, which we hope will yet come.

The dentists of Acton and Chiswick will have a field day when we get home, for the meat of India is something to create sad reflections. Of course, in a hot climate, meat has to be cooked and eaten soon after killing and this probably accounts for its toughness, but one sometimes wonders at the apparent longevity of the beast. When does a calf become a cow, or a lamb a sheep? 'Too old at forty' ought to apply to animals, in India at any rate.

The general health of the 10th Middlesex is fortunately good, cases of serious illness being small. The men do everything to uphold the prestige of the British Army in this beautiful country but naturally they are most keen on getting their chance at the front (which rightly or wrongly is their interpretation of 'active service') and will hope so till the end of the war.'

14 May 1915. *Acton Gazette*

Messrs. Eastman & Son Ltd of Acton Vale have recently received letters from three of their employees who are with the 10th Middlesex Territorial Battalion at Fort William, Calcutta, from which we give these extracts:

Corporal H. .L. Amess.

'I think that most of us have learnt a lot from what we have seen out here, and we shall always look back with pleasure to our trip here. I myself have been very lucky, catching one or two jobs which meant travelling to another part of this vast country.

Food is not so bad out here, but what made me mention it last time was one of our fellows writing home to a local paper and saying we were living a life of ease and comfort. Milk is one of the worst things to drink here; so is water, unless it has been boiled. It is now impossible to keep cool even doing nothing, and when one comes off parade they have to change everything. Our battalion is reckoned to be the smartest Territorial battalion in India, and it ought to be, for we are being treated as regulars as far as discipline goes, I am pleased to say; one must not move on parade, or even go on parade with a pair of toe-capped boots; so you see we shall be proper soldiers by the time they have finished with us. Parades now consist of physical training, and bayonet fighting, intermixed with a little company drill and rifle exercises to prevent us getting stale.

All we hope for now is that we shall see some fighting, for otherwise we shall feel as though the 'Tenth' have been left out in the cold, even though people tell us we are doing our share by looking after India.'

Drummer W. G. Wood.

'In the best of health. We have just finished our training which ended up with what is called Kitchener's test - field work and night marches, and it is a bit stiff for a warm country like this. When you have been running across fields and rough ground for 14 hours a day for 3 days, you are just about fed up with soldiering I can tell you. After being wet through all day, it is a change to put some dry clothes on.

To keep us fit, now the training is finished, we are made to go in for sport of some kind or the other. The football season has just started and we get plenty of football. The matches start at 5.30pm which must sound very funny to you at home. It is too hot in the daytime for anything. The natives are very keen on football and hockey, and they have some very smart teams out here; and don't they look funny playing without any boots on! They will walk for miles to see a good match and the noise they kick up sounds very funny. I must now close thanking the firm once again for their kindness.'

Drummer E. Walduck.

'Everything is all right, except the food. Most of our money goes in food. We get such enormous appetites. The weather is getting hotter every day and they have started the punkahs. Ours is the only electrically-driven punkah in the Indian Army. The others are manipulated by hand. We have also been served with mosquito nets, now the mosquito season is over and we don't want them. Life here is a bit dull. We can't go very far from the fort and most of the interesting spots are out of bounds. The only chance we get of seeing something of Indian life is when we go for a route march (about 15 miles) every Saturday round Calcutta.

We haven't long been back from Sonapur on manoeuvres. It was a stiff three days, but very instructive and rather interesting. If we live through this Indian summer, we'll all deserve iron crosses! It's only spring now and it's 98 degrees in the shade. It's been raining this last week or two and when it rains here it rains, and no error. The roads are nearly knee-deep in mud instead of being choked with dust.'

21 May 1915. *Chiswick Times*
10th Middlesex in India. Calcutta to Darjeeling by Private R. Guthrie.

'The train starts at 1.45pm from Sealdah station, and proceeds through the flat country of Bengal, past rice fields, forests of bamboo, and a general mixture of tropical jungle, no signs of life anywhere except a hut here and there. The heat is very great, and it is like being in a furnace in the carriages as the train proceeds, the hot damp air being blown in through the windows. To shut the windows is to make the carriage hotter and utterly unbearable.

The fiery ball of the sun sinks over the tall palm trees, making them stand out in great relief against the sky and casting weird shadows round about. The train is stopped in the heart of a thick forest, and the strange noises heard in the dark make one feel it is safer to be near the lights and occupants of the train. The train moves on, and late at night reaches the limit of its present gauge (6ft). All baggage is transferred to a still smaller gauge (4ft) and after much noise of whistles blowing, natives shouting, and bells ringing, the train starts on the second stage of its 820 miles journey.

All night we go bumping along on a badly-laid track, and dawn comes, still showing the country of rice or paddy fields, but it is now that one sees a very slight change in the natives, who look perhaps a little wilder, but showing a slight Mongolian descent in their faces, narrower eyes and higher and more prominent cheek bones. Their bodies are better formed and more muscular, and the women in some cases wear a few more inches of clothing. Also the foliage is slightly altered, looking more like that found in European countries. I have forgotten one item. The State of Bengal ends at the Ganges, which is crossed by the Sara Bridge, one and a half miles long, just recently opened by the Viceroy, and the river swarms with native bathers of all castes, who wallow in the mud.

As the train proceeds we have risen 500 feet but still the heat is very great, and about 10am we stop again and change into a smaller railway, the Darjeeling Light Railway. Here we are about 30 miles from the foot of the Himalayas and have to prepare to change into warmer clothing. This railway has a gauge of 3ft, and the carriages are very similar to those of the Volk's Railway at Brighton – open – and very small engines, which are enormously powerful, having very small wheels with a piston drive of about 8 inches to the stroke.

The train moves off, and we notice a complete change in the natives. Tibetans proper, of very small stature, rather grotesque to look at, but living better lives than the Bengalee, cleaner and healthier. They seem to be more industrious, their houses are well made of bamboo and stand well above the ground, and everything is in better order. The country has now completely changed to a dense forest of semi-tropical foliage – tall forests of teak, elm etc interlaced by a tangled mass of undergrowth, ferns, creepers etc. At times we leave this country completely beneath us, and we are able to look out for miles away over the country. Trees of all kinds and shades are everywhere. This country must be covered with snow for three months and as it melts, large streams are formed down the mountainside. In the train we pass over small dried-up water gullies, which must have an enormous amount of water passing over them at the winter break-up. I see them winding away down for many hundreds of feet into the lower regions of the forest.

Still higher we climb; often the train stops, owing to the steepness, and we are ordered to get out to relieve the weight as we have some extra trucks on board. In many places the engine is almost opposite the last carriage, so complete is the circle. We now begin to feel the change of atmosphere, which is colder and keener, and the mountainside not so densely covered. Here and there we pass small hamlets, built on the side of the mountain. The people look, and are, immensely strong and agile, the hard mountain life no doubt accounting for this. They look the picture of happiness and energy, swarthy-skinned, the men wearing long pigtails, and their hair jet black; the women quaintly dressed and wearing large grotesque earrings, which during their years of wearing have drawn their ears to awful fantastic shapes.

Unlike the Hindoos and all plainsmen, the Chinese and Tibetans treat their women well, never keeping them from the strangers' gaze, and they always seem happy and proud when noticed by the white strangers; but they are always on the make. It is hard for me to explain the great difference between the two great peoples.

From the start on this light railway we stop every 3 or 4 miles for water, which is drawn from a well in the mountainside. On again, we come to a station (Kurseong) which shows us to be 6,950ft high and overlooking a part of the railway.

Now, owing to the last part of the journey being so steep, the train has to make several shunts on the line on small ledges.

The strange part of this railway is that very little has had to be done for a base for the lines. A roadway seems to have been made long before the line was thought of, saving a great deal of labour and trouble of upkeep, small bridges of a few yards in length being the chief engineering difficulties.

It is now dark and our engine is carrying a pail of lighted oil rag, which as we career through gullies, must look very weird from the lower altitudes. Owing to a breakdown, we are travelling at a fair speed, and at times, we spin round corners at an alarming angle, and I begin to contemplate the horrible bump we shall get if we topple over. At last our train journey comes to an end, late at night, and from Darjeeling station we march to Jalapahar Hill.

Owing to the steep ascent and the rarity of the air we are soon out of breath and stop. The silence and darkness has a strange effect on us. The pathway leads up the side of a hill in a zigzag course and a Ghurkha guide shows us the way for the first time. Next morning we awake and see the sun shining on the Kanchanjancha mountains, making the snowfields shine in all colours, truly a wonderful sight.

Today I have been down to Darjeeling proper. In the market a fair is being held, Chinese from the far interior bringing skins of all kinds, tea, spices, grain, silks, etc. Tibetans from the mountain passes selling everything one can think of, and fairly cheap. A month ago, the winter was just going and then, as every year, these strange peoples come over the mountains to sell or barter their wares. I have my 'giddy optic' on a leopard skin and a kukri, a short native sword (but having little cash I must try bartering), also a fur hat will come in useful if I can get any luck. As I walk through this market place I look around me at the stolid faces, the look of which no Westerner has ever yet fathomed.

These peoples are extremely keen traders. There is no kidding them like the Hindoo. 'Pay my price of leave it' is their attitude.

Here at this hill station we have one boy to each room holding ten men. Our boy comes from the interior of China and is the limit in the 'sleight of hand and general lifting trade'. Not having been paid our salaries for ten days, he is providing us with wood, coke, butter, and at times a cup full of tea.

We are allowed 1lb of wood and coke per day but he supplements this. He lives in the town and when asked where he lifts the articles from he says 'All rightee Tuans, you have employ me and food all plenty in villages. You havee no pice, it to come, all food made for to eat.' Quite a logical way of putting it, eh? He reminds me of a bad bus accident; his face looks as if it has been well jumped on, then boiled and slipped out of the mould, and run over. I shall try and get a photo of him, bless him.'

2 July 1915. *Chiswick Times*
Letter to Mr. Thomas A. King, Hon. Sec. of the Chiswick Working Men's Club.

Mr. R. A. Wilkinson with the 10th Middlesex in Calcutta:

'I read with great interest Frank Baynes' letter in the Chiswick Times by last mail. We get all the local news through this medium. I also read of the riots at Singapore and the part played by Percy Bever. Some more fortunate of the boys recommended by the medical officer, have had a change of scenery and temperature at Jalapahar, a hill station in the neighbourhood of Darjeeling, and within 100 miles of Mt. Everest. We get glowing accounts from them of the glorious scenery and I am sure, from photographs some of the boys obtained, that it deserves every word of praise bestowed on it. It is glorious and my one wish is to get a glance at it before we leave.

About a month back, we sent a party to the Persian Gulf. They are attached to the 2nd Norfolks. This is the first detachment we have sent to the firing line. Imagine the send-off they got. It was very touching, and I can safely say that every man left behind would have jumped at the chance of being one of the party. I had a line from one of the boys yesterday describing their trip to Bombay in the train, and from there on to Karachi and Basra. They were again upset internally by the sea trip. A rumour is current today that they have been in action and come through without a casualty.

I must mention our football teams. The first team are competing in the Calcutta League (1ˢᵗ Div.) and so far have been beaten only once, by the E.B.S. Railway. On that occasion, we suffered defeat by one goal after attacking for three fourths of the game. Last evening the return fixture was played and the result reversed. You will see that both teams are in strong positions at the head of the respective tables, and barring accidents should win both leagues. We have a team entered for the All India Cup, and they should go a long way. Four of our men were selected to represent 'England vs Rest' to be played during the present month.'

17 September 1915. *Acton Gazette*
The 10ᵗʰ in Calcutta. Food problem.

Private Cecil George. 1-10ᵗʰ Middlesex, Calcutta. Of Myrtle Rd, Acton, writes complaining about the food and how they have to supplement it from their pay. All kinds of sport are encouraged but only in early morning before it is too hot.

15 October 1915. *Chiswick Times*
News from Calcutta.

Private R A. Wilkie. 1-18ᵗʰ Middlesex Regiment, writes from Fort William, Calcutta.

'I wonder what Chiswick's casualty list would have been if we had been 'lucky'? I am quite content with our present position, though we would all have jumped at the chance before we were sent here. India might be warm, but just now Flanders is the warmer of the two. Thank you for prompting the boys to write to me, but I am sorry to say it has met with no response.

Many thanks to the boys mentioned in your letter for their kind remembrances, which I heartily reciprocate. They will doubtless be pleased to learn I shall soon have an opportunity of a hearty handshake all round. As my time (six years) with this battalion expires in about six weeks, and I am taking my discharge from our depot in Stamford Brook to find pastures new for the exercise of my machine gun knowledge.

Just now we are experiencing the hottest month of the Indian summer. What it is like I must leave to your imagination. A vigorous evening's dancing or a good afternoon's cricket would leave one a lot more comfortable than five minutes in our sun. I shall leave without many regrets.'

25 February 1916. *Acton Gazette*
Letter from Lucknow from an Acton soldier.

Private Cecil George. 1/10th Middlesex Territorials – they have left Calcutta and are now at Lucknow.

'In the native quarters, there are high narrow smelly buildings, nearly meeting at the top. From the verandas native women, smoking their cheap cigarettes, leered down upon us. The alleys and byways were crowded with curious men of all types; some had most repulsive faces, and one could well imagine the cruelties their fathers committed during the Mutiny. How little did we think two years ago that we should be visiting these scenes of historic interest?

The following afternoon three of us hired a gharry for some hours and visited parts of Lucknow. First, we entered a native temple – brilliant chandeliers, paintings of rajahs, and models of elaborate tombs. At the gates of the Residency, we hired a guide, who showed us the points of attack and defence during the siege of 1857, and where notable men fell fighting at their posts. All around the grounds are pillars marking the places where prominent buildings had stood. We saw the house where our major's uncle lived – a doctor, who rendered much service to the wounded in those awful days. The marks of cannon balls were on all the ruins.

We were shown also the dark cellar where the women and children took refuge, and at the top, near the ceiling, was a large hole through which food was passed to them. A great cannon hole gaped at us, and we saw the marks of it on the opposite wall. The graveyard told its own tale of horror, of the death of little children, young wives and soldiers. Out of 3,900 soldiers and civilians, only about 900 were alive when relief came.

What a tale! I could have spent hours there, reading histories, examining relics etc, but time was pressing so we journeyed on in our gharry, next seeing a museum full of wonderful idols and hideous native paintings.'

26 May 1916. *Chiswick Times*
National Reservists in India.

Letter from Bandsman J. McCann, now attached to a force in India, writing to a Richmond friend. His battalion, to which a number of Richmond National Reservist belong, left Agra at 7 o'clock in the morning of 11th April. Reveille sounded at 4am and the men boarded a train which they rode, with brief intervals for exercise at stations, for 36 hours. At Derehadun, where they stopped for the night, reveille sounded at 2.30am, and at 3.45am they were on the march, with the band playing.

'We travelled through forests and villages, and after about 15 miles marching we arrived at a place called Jumnipoor at 9 o'clock, a five hours march. We halted once on the way for a drink of tea and some bread & butter, but the bread was as hard as if it were a week old. We bivouacked on the grass for 36 hours and in the meantime I had a bathe in the Jumna, a river flowing from the Himalaya mountains.

The next reveille went at 2.45am, and after breakfast of hot tea and two eggs, we were marching at 3.45, the band leading the battalion. I have seen lots of monkeys. The roads are awful for marching. After another 15 miles, we arrived at 9 o'clock at Kelsa camp, where we bivouacked for 30 hours and slept on a rug and two blankets, alongside a forest this time. When I arrived at this place I was nearly knocked. My feet had four water blisters, but I had them pricked at once so as to be all right for the next march.

We struck camp again on Thursday morning, reveille sounding at 2.45am. After breakfast our beds were strapped up and put into wagons drawn by yaks, which are really oxen. We marched at 3.45am. We are climbing the mountains this time, and the road or pass is about 18ft wide. On the right are high mountains, and on the left, a steep ravine or what you might call an awful precipice. A very good road for marching. This time we had to climb a mountain – it was a climb and no mistake. At 9 we arrived at a place called Saiah, knocked up completely. After a couple of hours rest, I had a very nice cold bath and felt as fresh as ever, but feet very tender.'

He writes how the path to the top of the mountain – 3,000 ft. – described as a spiral, and a narrow way on the edge of a precipice, along which the men marched in single file, and in some places they really had to climb. The last of the men got in about 12 o'clock.

'We are at one of the hill stations on the North West Frontier, near Afghanistan. I have seen some life in the four months I have been away from home. Where we are now, the climate is beautiful.'

19 July 1918. *Acton Gazette and Express*
Private Jeffreys, formerly a booking clerk at Acton (NLR) Station, reports from the Middlesex Regiment at Outram Barracks, Lucknow..

'I have just witnessed a 'Rami Sami', where natives from all parts assemble every 10 years to wash at a sacred well. Some of them had broken their caste, and were undergoing various forms of punishment. One was lying on a bed of nails, another swinging head downwards from a rope over a fire, and another enduring the pangs of starvation. Altogether it was an extraordinary spectacle.'

11 August 1916. *Chiswick Times*
Letter to Rev. Oldfield.

Drummer W. Bailey. India.

He is recuperating at a hill depot after temperatures of 114 to 116 in the shade at Lucknow. 'We try to keep cool by propping up 'tatties' in doorways. They are made of the fine roots of trees bound together to form a screen. We arrived at the Hill Depot at five in the morning after a 20 mile march from the nearest railway station and after two miles it started to rain.'

29 September 1916. *Chiswick Times*
Letter to Rev. Oldfield.

Bombardier R. S J. Hamilton. In hospital in India.

He has had a bad time with enteric. 'We are having a fine time at present and I don't suppose we shall be here long now (in hospital). I expect to come home to England and will never be sent back on account of having enteric fever.'

24 November 1918. *Chiswick Times*
Letter to Rev. Oldfield.

Bombardier R .S. J. Hamilton. India.

'Getting on fine and splendid weather. Mesopotamia was bad and I would not like to go back there and would like to get back to France or to home. Had a good talk with Higgins in hospital. We hear it is bad in London – a lot of air raids, all the lights out and bad to walk in darkness in the streets. I'm sorry to hear of Fred Smith's death and that Dick Vine has lost his sight.'

5. The War at Sea

1914. The British navy defeated a German flotilla off the Falklands Islands, and in the Indian Ocean the German ship *Emden*, which had been attacking British merchant vessels, was forced aground by the Australian cruiser *Sydney*. There were engagements between the British and German navies in the North Sea.

In May 1915 the *Lusitania*, a British passenger liner, which also had a cargo of arms, was sunk by a German submarine.

In 1916 the Battle of Jutland took place – the only major sea battle between the two navies during the war.

2 October 1914. *Chiswick Times*

Seaman Edward Scott, home now at 4 Dorchester Grove, Chiswick with his wife and three small children, had been serving on board HMS Cressy.

'At first, time was monotonous. We were within ten miles of Heligoland and took on some one hundred German prisoners from the water from the German Cruiser Mainz after the battle of Heligoland Bight. They told us there had been a mutiny on board and their officers fired on them, when they were in the water.

On 22nd September, in the evening, we had a call from HMS Aboukir, calling for help. When we got to her, she had keeled over to about 70 or 80 degrees. It was 10 or 15 minutes before she went down. Whilst we were rescuing survivors, the Hogue, which had also arrived, was hit by a torpedo and went down in less than 10 minutes.

Then half an hour later, we were hit twice. The German submarine surfaced about 500 yards away and our chief gunner fired at her. A third torpedo missed us but we were going down. Our skipper gave the order 'every man for himself'.

I divested myself of my clothes and swam for about fifteen minutes until I came across a plank. I grabbed it with the joy of a long lost friend and hung on. Another man came and hung on the other end. The waves were terrific and I thought I might give up, but then I saw the picture of the wife and kiddies, and that seemed to give me new life. My pal, poor chap, was done. After half an hour he let go his hold. I had kept saying "Keep steady, old man." I think he must have been wounded.'

Scott was in the water 3 or 4 hours until he caught sight of the Lowestoft trawler, which saved so many men. 'She was more welcome than the finest liner.' He shouted and waved until the trawler saw him. He was one of 150 to 200 men picked up. All were in the same plight as regards clothes and the trawler's captain and crew of six had few spare clothes.

'I don't think I ever appreciated tea as much as I did that which we had on that trawler. We were huddled together like sardines and that kept us a bit warm. Our greatest fear was that another submarine might be about.' They were taken off the trawler by the torpedo boat Lennox and landed at Harwich. ''All I had on was a seaman's jumper, and there were others more lightly clad than I.'

Scott had been injured about the body and legs and had lost some artificial teeth. The *Chiswick Times* appealed for a reader to pay for new teeth 'to help Scott the more easily to negotiate ship's biscuits.' He leaves for Harwich next Monday.

13 November 1914. *Chiswick Times*
Letter to Rev. Oldfield.

Fred Buckley, stoker, HMS Ostrich.

'Not seen anything of the Germans. I should like to know when the war is going to finish, sir, it is getting monotonous.'

4 December 1914. *Acton Gazette & Express*

A letter from crew member of HMS Edinburgh escorting 70,000 Indian soldiers from India to Port Said.

'Not a man or ship lost although one man fell overboard but was safely rescued. At one time we had as many as 53 ships to bring over. We had a bump at the Turks behind the Island of Perim in the Red Sea, bombarding and completely destroying their forts at Sheilah-Seya. They opened fire on our troops. The Indian troops attacked and drove them out. Our casualties were 4 killed and 11 wounded.

23 December 1914. *Chiswick Times*

Letter from Private J.J. James, Royal Naval Reserve, serving on a hospital ship.

'We have transported nearly 2,000 wounded soldiers, chiefly French. We have been for a good run but owing to the censor we are not allowed to say where we have been. Wounded are brought here by trains and motors straight from the firing line. We do not see the battle but hear the guns. It is heart-aching to see the poor helpless and dirty creatures whose language we do not know.

A 22-year old Belgian could speak English and had been hacked with a sword and carried 3 or 4 pieces of bone in his pocket. He may have an arm amputated. His home has been destroyed and he does not know where his mother and father are.'

8 January 1915. *Chiswick Times*

Letter to Rev. A.E. Oldfield.

Surgeon Davies, writing from Hospital Transport Ship, Guildford Castle.

'Not much time to ourselves, dressing over a hundred a day in our ward alone. A Welsh Regiment Major, although wounded, refused to go home and went back to the firing line.'

8 January 1915. *Chiswick Gazette*
Actonians on the Falkland Isles – a letter from Mr. & Mrs. E.G. Creece.

Before the arrival of the British fleet, the islands were undefended. The islanders flocked to the hills to watch the sea battle. The wireless station, erected by an Actonian, had a message from the fleet to prepare to receive the wounded. The convent nuns gave up their abode and Mrs.Creece and others set up the temporary hospital. The dead were interned in one big grave and a memorial will be erected.

29 January 1915. *Chiswick Times*
Police Constable E. Badcock, now serving on HMS Challenger in the coastal waters of the Cameroons.

'We have done splendid work in the German Cameroons, but very little mentioned in the papers as these minor colonial affairs are nothing to what is happening in Europe.

We swept for mines fifteen miles up the Cameroon River under fire the whole of the time. We came to the bar where the Germans had sunk ten ships to block the harbour entrance. We blew up some of them to make a Channel. We and another ship entered the harbour because of our shallow draught. More opposition and after 24 hours the capital of the German Cameroons surrendered and most Germans went inland. There is still fighting but I believe it will soon end.'

26 March 1915. *Chiswick Times*
Letter to Rev. Oldfield.

A.S. Brand Ordinary Seaman. HMS Indomitable.

'H. Heighes who I saw aboard the Erin is quite well and wishes to be remembered to you and all the lads. Glad to see the local territorials are back in England to prepare for the front. Best regards to Miss W for sending the Chiswick Times.'

9 April 1915. *Chiswick Times*
Letter to Rev. Oldfield.

A.J. Punter. Able Bodied Seaman. H.M.S. -----

'Pleased to receive the books and magazines that are handed round to my messmates. The ship is darkened when it gets dark. Still patrolling but have not met any of the enemy.'

16 April 1915. *Chiswick Times*
Letter to Rev. Oldfield.

T.J.Cook. Leading Stoker.

'I receive the Chiswick Times every week. Quite a treat to hear a bit about the old place. Hope that all the lads that are keeping the flag flying are keeping fit and that we may all meet one of these fine days. '

30 April 1915. *Chiswick Times*
Letters to Rev. Oldfield.

C. Humphreys. Boy. Late HMS Ocean. Malta Hospital.

'Our ship sank while firing on Turkish forts in the Dardanelles. We did not lose many lives, but your box is gone. When we got hit, three destroyers came alongside and I jumped and slightly sprained an ankle. Don't think I am down-hearted because I am as happy as a sandboy.'

R.M. Osborne. Stoker. HMS -----.

'We have bombarded several places, causing considerable damage and loss of life and killed about 200 Germans and blown up a magazine and light railway at Vanga (German East Africa). At Refugi river we battled up the Koenisburg, a German light cruiser, so that she can do no harm. We also aided troops to capture a large island called Mafia, from which the Germans were getting food and supplies.

We want a chance to come home and have a smack at the Germans there. We want revenge for two men killed and 21 captured from this trip. We have had a very hard time – not much rest and always on alert. Before coming here, we were engaged with the ----- and Breslau, a German dreadnought and cruiser, but they got into the Dardanelles two hours in front of us, so when we arrived, we were fired at by Turkish forts and warned to keep outside. We were ten hours in front of the fleet so it would do no good trying to force an entrance.'

He tells of all the places his ship has visited since leaving home before the war – Rome, Pompeii, Corfu, Alexandria and Jerusalem among them. He is keeping a diary which he thinks will make interesting reading later on. He doesn't think the war will last another year.

7 May 1915. *Acton Gazette*
The Lusitania sunk. – Two Acton brothers among the passengers. *Chiswick Times* report.

With great regret we have to record the loss of a well-known Acton resident in the Lusitania disaster. Two brothers, both of them Acton men, were returning to England, and set out from New York in the company of an American friend. One of the brothers was drowned and the other, after an experience truly terrible, was among the saved.

Albert Norriss Perry, 51 Grafton Road, was we regret to state, drowned. He was last seen standing by the entrance to the saloon, and was then wearing a life-belt. He was a powerful swimmer, but this did not avail him. His body was picked up a few days after the disaster and is being brought to Acton for the funeral tomorrow. He had been for 12 years employed by Messrs. D. Napier & Son, motor manufacturers of Acton Vale. He leaves a wife and a little girl of 15 months.

Albert's younger brother Frederick J. Perry, had also been in the employ of Messrs. Napiers and had been travelling for his firm in the United States. Without a life-belt, he dived from the port side of the Lusitania while she was sinking. In doing so, he struck a boat and broke his collar bone. Trying to get into a life boat, which had several stokers in it, he was thrust back into the water, one of the crew shouting that there was no room for him. He clung on to one of the ropes looped round the boat, and in this position he remained in the water for two hours.

At Queenstown, where he was afterwards conveyed when the boat-load and he were picked up by a steamer, he lay in the hospital, whither he was eventually traced by another brother, Mr. Harry Perry, who brought him home to Acton, arriving there between 8 and 9am on Wednesday. In the course of the day, Mr. Perry was thoroughly overhauled by his medical man and later on Wednesday he was able to give a Gazette representative the following account of the disaster:

Mr. F.J. Perry's Story

'My brother and I were returning from the States. Before we left New York we read in the papers the notice issued by the German Ambassador, and as everybody else did, we pooh-poohed the idea of the vessel being torpedoed. There was a general discussion of the matter throughout the whole of the morning. There was a great crowd at New York to see us all off, and as the ship began to move away the splendid Welsh choir, which had been touring the States, sang to their friends on shore. That and all the following days up to the day of the disaster were beautifully sunny. We had a very good voyage over.

On the Thursday evening we had the usual weekly concert amongst the first class passengers and after a splendid entertainment by the Welsh Choir, the chairman, one of the directors of Messrs. Vickers, made a splendid appeal for the Liverpool Sailors' Orphanage, and referred to the dangers through which we were passing. He said that he was quite sure that every man, from the captain down to the stokers, would be willing to lay down their lives for the passengers if need be. This resulted in a record collection at these concerts for the Liverpool Orphanage.

On the following morning, quite early, before anyone was about, the fog horn was sounding and it continued sounding right up to 12 noon. It certainly was misty, but in view of the danger zone we were in, it seemed a trifle absurd to blow the foghorn furiously as they were doing. At noon it cleared, the sun shone beautifully and one could see for miles. The south coast of Ireland was well in sight. At one o'clock the lunch bugle was sounded. My brother, and an American friend who was travelling with us for his health, and who intended to return with my brother on the Lusitania next Saturday (as my brother was taking up a permanent position with the Pierce Arrow Co) were lunching with me and as we were finished quite early, we went up several decks to the lounge for a smoke. It was then ten minutes to two.

Torpedoed

Shortly after two o'clock, just before the people began to get up into the saloon, there was a terrific impact, marked not so much by the noise, as the force of the explosion. It shook the vessel from stern to stern, as though we had struck a rock or collided with another vessel. We immediately realised that we had been hit by a torpedo. Our American friend was not with us at the time, but my brother and I walked through the lounge to get down to the boat deck. We were met at the entrance to the lounge with a fearful volume of smoke and steam, caused by the explosion, which apparently had reduced the speed of the ship very suddenly. Before we could realise the position, there was a second shock, which came within a minute or so of the first. By this time, there were many people coming up the stairs from the lower decks. We managed to get out onto the boat deck, which was very crowded, considering the majority of the people had been in the dining saloon. Most of the people appeared to have come from the second saloon over the communicating bridge.

My brother and I got separated, nor did I see our American friend, Mr. Brown, who had gone down into the library after dinner to write his last letters before landing. I walked to the starboard side and helped people to get into the boats. One boat was being lowered, but when it was nearly halfway down, one end seemed suddenly to stop and the other end continued, with the result that the people – between 50 or 70 of them – were simply shot out, like coals out of a sack, into the water. The boat then followed them down to the water, stern foremost, and thus immediately began to fill with water. The bows seemed to be held fast by the ropes, which were still over the davits. The boat thus lay useless alongside the ship.

Another boat further along towards the captain's bridge was lowered a few seconds afterwards, and when nearly down to the water, it appeared as though it was going to behave as the first had done, but righted itself and reached the water safely. There were not more than half-a-dozen people out of the previous boat within reach of this second one. They were told to catch hold of the second boat, but I did not see if any managed to get in, or if I did see, I don't remember it. I remember that one of the difficulties of lowering the first boat was that an iron ring had jammed round a staple and one of the crew could not release it.

I jumped into one boat to help in releasing the ropes, preparatory to filling it with the women, when I heard a cry, 'All out of the boat.' Looking round, I saw an officer on the very top deck of all, but could not hear his orders distinctly. Immediately we jumped out of the boat deck, and then it appeared that the ship was simply righting herself, probably through the water finding its own level; and I suppose the water-tight doors were closed. I then saw my brother for the last time, away towards the captain's bridge and near the lounge entrance. I notice he was, like myself, fully dressed, but had on a lifebelt of the kind supplied in each cabin. I asked him where he obtained it and he said 'Inside the main entrance'. I looked in and found there were a large number of saloon passengers there, all with belts on, including some of the ship's officers. Not seeing any belt lying about and not caring to run the risk of going down to my cabin and being caught like a rat if the ship went down, I went on deck.

Then the ship made another lurch to starboard, the side on which it had been torpedoed. With this, I made for the boat deck again. I obtained one of the white cork life belts, but gave this up later to a little boy of about eight, who was coming along the deck, and put him into a boat. The ship was now sinking fast. It appeared to me, we should never get a boat away, and that even if we reached the water, the ropes would not be detached. I decided to wait until the water reached a certain porthole, and when it was a case of 'every man for himself', to dive overboard. This I did, from the port side, which was of course very high in the air. I dived striking the boat, which had previously emptied the people into the water. After an awful struggle in the water – too awful to describe – I came to the top fighting for something to get hold of. After a few seconds, I saw a boat near me, and immediately made a plunge forward to get hold of it, but was as quickly pushed off by some stokers who declared, 'There's no room for a single person.'

I was thus back again in the water, but made a second effort to get hold of the small ropes looped round all the boats. I gripped so tightly that you can see the marks on my fingers now. Thus I was pulled along by the boat for some considerable time. When I felt I was giving out, I put my arm through the loop so as to get a better support. I was taken out of the water about 4.30am having been in it for 2 hours, according to the time at which my watch had stopped. I was rescued by a small fishing boat, and the fishermen were very kind, giving me some hot tea. After waiting about an hour, we were taken off by a paddle steamer, and arrived in at Queenstown at 9.20pm. We were very kindly treated there and I was taken to the hospital.

I should like to say that there was no panic at all. When I saw the people on the boat deck, everyone seemed to be struck with grief rather than fear. Ladies and children were crying, but not screaming. This was really marvellous to me, considering the time that people had been thinking what might happen to them.

No, I cannot say whether the little boy I spoke of was saved or lost. Nor do I know if a gentleman I knew, Mr. Nedbury, a Surrey man, was saved, but I do not see his name in the list of survivors. I did not see the ship go down, but I think it had gone when I came to the surface. I seemed to be an awful time fighting in the water; but after I had risen the second time, I seemed to know that I had got to strike out. I can only just swim, and I could not have reached the boat if it had been any distance away.

My elder brother Norriss is an excellent swimmer. I never saw him again after he was at the lounge entrance. I have heard today that his body has been recovered and is being sent to Acton for the funeral, which will take place at St Dunstan's and Acton cemetery on Saturday afternoon. I returned from Queenstown only today. I have been lying in the Queen's Hospital Queenstown, with a broken collar-bone, bruised legs and arms, and a bad back. My brother Harry though he had no address to work upon, came over to Queenstown to find me, and brought me back at 3 o'clock yesterday afternoon and we arrived at Euston at 6 o'clock this morning.

I have been examined by a local doctor and am fortunate to get off so lightly. It is appalling to realise the exceptionally large number of women and children who have been brutally sent to their death by a country calling itself civilised.'

15 May 1915. *Chiswick Times*
Letter to Rev. Oldfield.

George Mockler. Able Bodied Seaman. HMS ---- off Africa.

'Many thanks for the Chiswick Times which I received on May Day; I was delighted to receive it. It has been very lonely wandering from country to country, travelling over half the globe, and missing more and more as time goes on those who are near and dear to you.

Having read the letter of Private Nightingale, it makes me feel as if I should like to take his place, or anyone else's in the firing line, and I am sure I voice the opinion of the whole ship's company; but then, if someone did not patrol the High Seas, England would to a certain extent, be prevented from receiving the large supplies of commerce etc thus making food and everything else much dearer; so therefore we must put up with the state of affairs at present.

We all hope to be in the North Sea when the German fleet comes out. I was awfully pleased to see how many of the brigade had distinguished themselves during this war, and I am sure every former member, when the opportunity comes, will not let it slip by him, but will take it at once and do his very utmost to serve God, King and country. Since last writing to you, we have travelled over 5,000 miles.'

11 June 1915. *Chiswick Times*
Letters to Rev. Oldfield.

Herbert Jones. Ordinary Seaman. H.M.S ---- care of G.P.O.

'Well, Sir, I have got the news that my father and brother have joined so that makes us all complete and we are all 'merry and bright'. I can't make out what keeps men at home in times like this, but still I see Chiswick is doing great, much to my delight and I am sure the boys at the front think so, and we also know that we have plenty of vacancies for the men who have not joined up yet. Thanks very much for the Chiswick Times (sent by a friend).'

Charles Reffold. Ordinary Seaman. H.M.S ----- c/o GPO.

'I see from the Chiswick Times there are a lot of our lads and that they are fit as a fiddle, just the same as me at present. I read in the paper that there has been a big recruiting week and I sincerely hope it have been a success. We are still waiting for those German sausage hounds to come out of their bunks. There are a few Chiswick lads on board my ship and they look upon the Chiswick Times as an appreciated gift.'

18 June 1915. *Chiswick Times*
Letter to Rev. Oldfield.

A.J.Punter. Able Seaman. H.M.S. ----- c/o GPO:

'.........just a line to let you know that we have had some excitement at last concerning the 'subs'. We were ordered to sea immediately one day to hunt for a suspicious ship, and during the day we ran across a sailing ship on fire. We left that to a trawler and proceeded. Well, about 7.30 we sighted a trawler, who told us that they had a trawler's crew on board who had been sunk by a submarine, and also that another trawler had been sunk, but they never had time to pick up the crew as the submarine threatened to sink them. We arrived at the spot after steaming 30 knots for an hour, and saw the trawler's crew – nine in all – in a small boat hardly big enough for five. Well, we got them aboard and tried to save the boat, but we could not stop, so we sank the boat and proceeded. I had a yarn with one of the trawler's crew, and he told me it was a submarine painted all white with no number; she sank the trawler by gunfire. She fired three rounds at 40 yards, but missed, though the remainder finished the trawler – six rounds in all – and she sank stern first. We are waiting for another day like that, and we all hope that we get the submarine next.'

25 June 1915. *Chiswick Times*
Letter to Rev. Oldfield.

Stoker R.M Osborne. H.M.S --------.

'We've been at it again out here. We thought the Germans might feel a bit feverish after the rain, and it does rain here, so we gave them a few 'pills' but they don't seem to care for them. You see, they (the pills) are rather bad for the digestion, although taken properly they are guaranteed to cure all ills in one dose. We are still on the prowl for the enemy's ships, should any be sulking, but things are a bit quiet. Many thanks for the Chiswick

Times. I must ask you to thank Mrs. W.J.H. for her kind thought, I have been puzzling as to who she is. There are several Chiswick chaps aboard here, and I pass the Chiswick Times on to them. Remember me kindly to all the lads and workers. Hoping to see you when the war is over.'

9 July 1915. *Chiswick Times*
Letter to Rev. Oldfield.

<u>A.J. Punter</u> Able Seaman. HMS ----- at sea.

'I was very glad to hear about the band winning the 'staff' and the 'pace stick' and wish them every success. I wish they would send us out to the Dardanelles, but there, our chance will come some day I suppose. I have been on the sick list a week with my throat, but am glad to say I am well again now.'

16 July 1915. *Chiswick Times*
Letter to Rev. Oldfield.

<u>W.B. Pocock.</u> Able Bodied Seaman.

'I have seen Wiseman a few times since I've been out here and been pulling his leg as our skiff beat theirs in a race and brought about £200 to our ship from his ship It was a good race.'

13 August 1915. *Chiswick Times*
Letter to Mr. Thomas A. King, Hon. Sec. of the Chiswick Working Men's Club.

<u>Stoker C.A. Daykin.</u> Naval Barracks, Chatham.

He writes he has been waiting for orders and will not be sorry to get away. Speaking of the miners' strike, he says 'I thought it was going to last a long time, but it was a good thing it did not, for it meant a lot of lives to be lost. If the miners did keep out, it meant the soldiers going down to Wales & that would have meant a lot of lives going west.'

20 August 1915. *Chiswick Times*
Letter to Rev. Oldfield.

<u>Able Bodied Seaman. George Mockler,</u> HMS --- at sea.

'The last action we took part in was the final smashing up of the German cruiser Koenigsberg, on 11th July. Well I am getting pretty tired of cruising now. We have travelled since leaving England a distance of just under 60,000 miles, and that is only 12 months....'

8 October 1915. *Chiswick Times*
Letter to Rev. Oldfield.

<u>Able Seaman. A .J. Punter.</u> HMS Excellent, 'E' Block 19 Mess, Whale Island, Portsmouth.

'Have arrived at the gunnery school and expect to be here some time. Sleeping in a bed. Quite a change from a hammock.'

22 October 1915. *Chiswick Times*
Letter to Rev. Oldfield.

<u>First Class Stoker R. Osborne.</u> H.M.S. -----.

'After our final action with the German cruiser in East Africa we have been very busy. Very cold here now after being in the tropics.'

November 1915. *Chiswick Times*
Letter to Rev. Oldfield.

<u>Bugler H .V.Jones.</u> HMS -----.

'Very cruel weather. I am on watch tonight and your muffler will take a fancy to my neck for four hours. I have heard that my father has been discharged from the army with rheumatics and his brother is with the 10th Middlesex'

26 November 1915. *Chiswick Times*
Letter to Rev. Oldfield.

Stoker R. M. Osborne. H.M.S. -----.

'Being kept pretty busy as we have aircraft to guard against. At times when anything particular is on the buzz at night the suspense seems awful but getting used to it now. One of our chaps has a one stringed violin, and we had a fine sing song the other night. I've got the parcel with a pipe, dominoes and mittens.'

31 December 1915. *Chiswick Times*
News from Nowhere. Chiswick soldier's voyage to un-named port.

Mr. Baines letter to Thomas A. King, Hon Secretary of Chiswick Working Men's Church Club.

'We reached Alexandria from Marseilles after five days. Some lucky NCOs and men were allowed ashore. The heat was terrific. Orders came through, and much to our disappointment we were not staying in Egypt. On the 23rd we left port sailing to goodness knows where. Our course was erratic perhaps dodging submarines. Anyhow we arrived 'here' on November 27th, and are still on the boat - not allowed yet to say where we are. We will be glad to get ashore and have a square meal. For ten days we have lived on bully beef, biscuits and jam. Lifeboat drill took place every day so we did not live in fear of torpedoes. There was a concert party and an exhibition of shooting at a barrel in the sea.

From the boat the town looks extremely pretty at night with a mass of twinkling coloured lights and snowcapped mountains in the back ground. But, my word, it is cold, and it is much as one can do to keep one's self warm. We are in for a bad time if this weather continues. We all thought we should spend this winter in a warmer country than either France or Belgium.'

7 January 1916. *Chiswick Times*

An Old Eton Street Boy's letters

<u>Private Harry Skinner.</u> Royal Marine. H.M. Gunboat Spey.

He expresses thanks for the gramophone that has arrived in good condition and is enjoyed by the whole crew.

14 January 1916. *Chiswick Times*

Letters to Rev. Oldfield.

<u>Stoker F. Buckley.</u> H.M.S -----, c/o G.P.O.

'Sorry not to have written before, but owing to a lot of sea time we don't get much chance, and it's no good trying to write at sea, because we get too much of the bouncing motion in this destroyer. We are still on the same job, patrolling, but see 'nowt'.'

<u>First Class Stoker, R. M. Osborne.</u> E.1 ward, R.W. Hospital, Haslar, Gosport.

'No doubt you will be surprised to hear I am in England. Arrived here on Friday in the hospital ship from Malta, after having malaria and typhoid fever. I have been up now for three days, after 13 weeks in bed. I had a visitor today. Rifleman Punton came to see me. This hospital is quite close to him. He is still doing very well, and in the best of health. We had a fine talk about the different actions we'd taken part in, and how the boys were getting on in the different places.'

<u>A..J. Punter.</u> Able Bodied Seaman. Somewhere in England.

'I finished my qualifying for seaman gunner about five weeks ago, and got recommended for gun layer. I think I told you I was big drummer in the band here, so I shall be keeping in form with the sticks. Will you kindly thank the lady who sends me the Chiswick Times every week as I don't know her address or would write. I went to the hospital to see Bob Osborne. He is getting on fine. Also met George Mockler and we had a pleasant time together.'

4 February 1916. *Chiswick Times*
Letters to Rev. Oldfield.

A.S. Brand. Able Bodied Seaman. HMS --- c/o GPO.

'Your most welcome parcel to hand. I am still receiving Chiswick Times, but do not know who sends it so kindly, would you please give them my best thanks. I see that Fred Hudson is lost with the Navy – poor fellows; I have had some pleasant times with him at Margate.'

First Class Stoker. R.M. Osborne. Haslar.

'I am still improving, but will not be out of here for a few weeks yet. I saw Alf Punter last week. My brother Charlie and his wife came to see me Sunday. He is still doing very well and expecting promotion to wardroom rank very shortly. Please thank Mrs. W.J.H. for sending the Chiswick Times.'

14 April 1916. *Chiswick Times*
Letter to Rev. Oldfield.

Stoker F. Buckley. HMS -----

'We have hardly been in harbour owing to submarines poking around. It has been an awful winter in the North Sea and I am glad it is over. We have had to stick it in all weathers. I have not written to Miss W. I hope she is patient.'

12 May 1916. *Acton Gazette*
The vicar of St Dunstans, East Acton, Rev. W.M. Le Patoural.
Account in the Parish Magazine of experiences on HMS Defence,
1ˢᵗ Cruiser Squadron.

In a gale his cabin shelves soon emptied all of their contents, and drawers had to be tied up. A rope held him securely in bed on Sunday night.

He conducts prayers every morning and then decodes secret signals till noon. Some afternoons he is free and then censors letters 'which keeps one pretty busy if 900 men write home on the same day.' Then there are prayers at 9pm. There are large congregations at Sunday services. He has a small organ and a few string instruments.

To see the fleet at sea is an unforgettable sight. 'What has impressed me most?' The noise of continual hammering with steel sledge-hammers. The everlasting traffic past my curtain (there are no doors in wartime). Then there is the paint. Painters and paint pots everywhere. One soon acquires the knack of passing along corridors without touching anything. We are very very smart – except the clothes that touch the paint.'

26 May 1916. *Chiswick Times*
Letters to Rev. Oldfield.

Second Class Boy A.J.E. Lovrey. Devonport.

'Just a few lines to tell you I am in the navy. We sleep in hammocks and it is very nice too, until someone comes and lets you come down. Then it is all wrong. I have found what I learnt in the brigade has been very good for me, and I don't get shouted at the same as other boys do. Our barracks are on the edge of the harbour and we see the warships go out and come in. This envelope is borrowed from one of my mates. Harry Edgar did not pass, so I came by myself.'

A.J. Punter. Able Seaman. HMS Excellent.

'I am at the gunnery school. I have just finished qualifying for range finder operator. I got through A1 and am now a second class range taker. The idea of it is to work the range finder on a ship to find the distance the attacking ships are away. Well sir our band is still going strong here. I would be very glad sir, if you would send me some of the old band flute marches for us to learn. I am sure they would be much appreciated by myself and the members of the band.'

9 June 1916. *Acton Gazette*
Rev. Wallace M. Le Patourel lost on HMS *Defence*.

At the sea battle of Jutland the Royal Navy lost 14 ships and over 6,000 men. The German Navy lost 11 ships and 2,500 men. HMS Defence was an armoured cruiser.

The sad news quickly spread in Acton. Three weeks ago he had visited the parish and conducted the weekly war intercession service on May 16th, which to many sounded like a last goodbye. He had been a temporary chaplain to the fleet for nine weeks. Before being at Acton for eight and a half years he had been the curate at Holy Trinity, Chelsea for sixteen years. He was a lover of music and the sea and frequently took holidays on the water. It was only on orders from medical advisors to take a complete change that he decided to accept a temporary naval chaplaincy. When he joined the Defence he found one of his choir boys, Cecil Gosling, on board. By the loss of both lives St. Dunstan's has suffered a double bereavement.

After returning to his ship after May 16th he wrote saying the parish was in the capable hands of Rev. Boustead and he looked forward to his return. A later letter published in the parish magazine said how much he had enjoyed the last service at St Dunstan's. 'We are at sea again. The short holiday seems like a dream. I am afraid it will be seven or eight months before I get any more leave.'

Numerous tributes appeared in the *Acton Gazette.*

16 June 1916. *Chiswick Times*
Chiswick man in the naval battle – experiences on the Royal Oak

The Chiswick sailor's letter was published in the *Daily News* – a thrilling account of the North Sea battle.

'We have been in the thick of the fighting and have gained a name for ourselves, as this ship sank two battle cruisers and two destroyers, without receiving a single scratch herself. During the action I managed to slip up on deck and watch the course of the fight. One German cruiser was attacking us. She fired a salvo which fell 50 yards short. She must then have made a mistake in her range and altered it, as the next salvo fell 50 yards clean over us. Before she could send off the 3rd round we fired and our shots hit her smash amidships – about 8 tons of high explosives and lyddite – which split her in half and sent her to the bottom in ten minutes.

All round you could see the battle cruisers belching salvo after salvo on the Germans. The noise was simply terrific and the whole sky was illuminated like day by the gunfire. Don't believe all the pessimistic reports in the papers, as things are much better than you think.'

30 June 1916. *Chiswick Times*
Letters to Rev. Oldfield.

A.J. Punter. Able Seaman HMS -------.

'My last ship, HMS Ardent, sunk in action. An unlucky ship. I think of the brave lads. We were all chums. Fancy after being together for nearly three years, almost like brothers, for them to come to this sad end. There were three survivors, the captain and two able seamen. But they gave the Germans a good smack in the eye before they went.'

E.H. Hughes. Able Bodied Seaman. HMS ------.

'It was a very exciting battle on May 31st. We were in the thick of it. Ready to have another go at them if they like to come out. I came across Perce Pocock at a boxing competition on one of the ships. He asks after Artie Brand whose ship was well in the thick of the action. We hope to meet the Germans again; it was only the mist which saved them last time.'

22 September 1916. *Acton Gazette*
Sub-Lieut. W.H. Bailey of 19 Clovelly Road, Ealing. Two years with the Merchant Fleet.

He was appointed to a transport in the North Sea in August 1914, and was looking forward to some excitement but the only 'spice' was missing a floating mine by thirty yards.

In February 1915 he was ordered to join a ship in New York, but his voyage across the 'pond' in the S.S. Philadelphia was delayed by a 'patriotic (!) coal strike of Britishers 'when their country was at war.' During the voyage across he shared a cabin with Billy Armstrong, a comedian 'now Charlie Chaplin's right-hand man.' He remembers the hustle and bustle of the New York customs and meeting the British Government official who said he had missed his ship, and on March 22nd he was ordered to San Francisco to join a British Transport.

He waited a fortnight in San Francisco and had time to find out the American people's view of the war, the Frisco population being largely pro-German. Although it is natural for Americans of German descent to be for their fatherland, a few could not understand why the Kaiser 'ruthlessly' broke the Belgian neutrality.

'It was a pity that President Wilson said "We are too proud to fight". This is not really the case. They cannot fight because they are such a cosmopolitan nation that whichever side they are on, they would probably have a million men against them causing a revolution at their own door. There is one thing they have learned from Britain's folly of unpreparedness, that is, "In time of peace prepare for war", and upon this they are acting whole-heartedly, not because they are afraid of the Hun, but of a little nation to the Westward of them. If we must say they are a peace-at-any-price nation, it is because they, at present, lack military power.'

He left for China and after 23 days was sailing up the Yang-tse-Kiang River 700 miles to Hankow, where he found out that the Chinese of the interior were influenced by German missionaries who spread false reports regarding Britain.

His ship went on to Shanghai and Hong Kong where the number of Britishers who had given up good positions, and even paid their own passage home to fight for their King was remarkable. He asked many educated Chinamen their views on the war and found their reply was nearly always the same. "Berlin finish; German ships afraid to sail on water; plenty British ships go, plenty come. Germany no good."

His ship set sail for Frisco and for the next one or two weeks there was nothing but 'the everlasting smile of the Pacific Ocean.' Then they left with a cargo for Japan and at Kobe found themselves among a large fleet of Japanese warships. He describes Japan as a go-ahead little nation with a vast population of sturdy youngsters and picturesque scenery. He felt an overwhelming fear that 'this little nation', which is getting more and more European every day, is becoming 'The Yellow Peril', and certainly if we go on decimating one another at home, the yellow race will soon overrun the world.

After leaving Japan his ship ran aground, and was stuck for a month before being towed to a dry dock in Shanghai for some repairs that took three weeks. Then they sailed for Hong Kong and called at some small Japanese ports before returning to San Francisco where an OHMS letter awaited him with an instruction to proceed by the quickest route to New York to board a British Transport ship. He left the next morning by the Chicago express, and then spent ten days sightseeing in New York before sailing in an oil tanker carrying benzene bound for Devonport Docks. On arrival he was granted ten days leave.

It was the habit and etiquette of mercantile marine officers not to go ashore in uniform. Hence, one old lady 'of ample proportions' wanted to know why he was not in khaki. He replied 'You seem to forget that there is a mercantile marine.' He was also stopped by a recruiting sergeant who, when told he was in the mercantile marine, remarked 'What the ------ has that got to do with the war?'

'We of the merchant service, who brave submarine warfare and mine sown seas, who bring foodstuffs, munitions and men from colonies to fight for you, are entirely forgotten by some of you; everyone is so engrossed by khaki and recruiting that some of Britain's finest and best men do their work silently, and in return get cursed for not being in the army – a true example of "the dog that bites the hand that feeds it." It is a great pity that the papers have to suppress the actual number of merchant vessels and men that have been lost since the war.'

(Statistics concerning British merchant ships lost vary but more than one estimate states 2,500 merchant ships and 15,000 merchant seamen were lost.)

He was glad when he set sail again and felt the freedom of the sea. He left Merseyside with a cargo for the troops at Port Said and then proceeded to India. He had time to study some of the idols and pagodas, the one at Maulman [Moulmein] reminding him of Kipling's poem. They made back to Port Said where they stayed for a week, and were able to ask several soldiers who had fought in the Dardanelles, who was to blame for the failure – the generals, officers or men? Their reply was 'We all did our best; it's the country to blame, for not heeding Lord Roberts' call, and, consequently, only being able to send a handful of men out to reinforce us.'

They next went to Hamilton Roads, Virginia, USA and on to Baltimore for 5,000 tons of coal. In all ports in the States they were compelled to keep a very strict watch against 'German treachery'. His ship delivered the cargo to (not stated) and then went to Buenos Aires for ballast, where their time was made enjoyable by the chaplain of the Seamen's Mission, the Rev. H.W. Brady. He had done a great deal of work rounding up R.N.R. men, enrolling 7,000 volunteers out of a population of 30,000 Britishers, and getting them safely off to the Motherland, beside many other valuable services.

From Buenos Aires they proceeded south and through the Straits of Magellan to Valparaiso in Chile, and then home through the Panama Canal. Within two days of the British coast they were seen and chased by a German submarine, but through their wireless operator the assistance of two destroyers was obtained and on their approach the submarine immediately disappeared. He arrived safely in Great Britain and this time, in spite of etiquette, he polished his buttons and went ashore in uniform.

22 September 1916. *Chiswick Times*
Letter to Rev. Oldfield.

Private E. Ward. Somewhere at sea.

'Very glad to hear of the old boy's doings and of Corporal Garside's D.C.M. It just shows what the boys are made of and I feel proud that I was in your brigade. I am very sorry for the old lads that have fallen and also for Dick Vine losing his sight. I also have bad news. My uncle, Sapper J Pilbean, has been killed in France. I hope to be together soon in the old club, and we will have some games.'

6 October 1916. *Chiswick Times*
Letter to Rev. Oldfield.

A.J. Punter. Able Seaman. HMS-----   They had a glorious send off when the ship was launched, especially from the workmen. Thousands lined the banks. Their band struck up 'Should old acquaintance be forgot.'

3 November 1916. *Chiswick Times*
Letters to Rev. Oldfield.

Stoker Fred Buckley. HMS ------.

'I must say that since I joined the navy, four and a half years ago, I have never felt better. I always used to be ill before, but am never ill now. It must be the rough and ready life. Every day I come up out of the stoke, hot, wet through with perspiration, straight onto the upper deck into the cold wind and stinging spray, and never feel any ill-effects. We are patrolling with clockwork regularity. Twenty seven months of war seem to have gone very quick. I read Mr. Asquith's and Lloyd George's speeches that the war will go on until we win, and I take it to be another two years.'

F. Brereton. Royal Navy.

'I like this kind of life. We have three afternoons to ourselves a week, and a concert once a fortnight. The food is good and there is plenty of it. We sleep in hammocks, which are very comfortable.

Last Wednesday we had a look over the battleships, which proved to be very interesting. We have a fortnight's leave at Christmas I and my chum Robert Lloyd will come round to see you. I met Robert Mockler down here, so we are three lads together.'

10 November 1916. *Chiswick Times*
Letters to Rev. Oldfield.

1st Class Stoker R.M. Osborne. HMS ----- .

'We are in harbour through stress of weather. Heavy gales and bitterly cold. At sea yesterday we had a terrible job to keep our feet, hanging on to anything we could". He has lost his two St Mary's Brigade medals and asks for replacements. 'I am very proud of them, and always liked to show them and talk of the splendid times we had at camp and various outings.'

17 November 1916. *Chiswick Times*
Letter to Rev. Oldfield.

A.J. Punter. Able Bodied Seaman. H.M.S. ----- .

'You will see by the censor stamp that once again we are in the first line of defence. So we shall soon be at the old game – waiting. The weather had been awful – rain and wind.'

1 December 1916. *Chiswick Times*
Letter to Rev. Oldfield.

Stoker W. Watson. HMS -----.

'Thanks for the postcard which was dated 28th September, so you can guess I'm in an out-of-the-way place. We are miles from 'Blighty' to borrow a soldier's word, and it is very warm here. Many thanks for the offer of woollens; we don't wear more clothes than we can help. When there is no wind it is enough to suffocate you. There is a marine band on board that gives a concert nearly every night. I often think of the old times when our lads got up a concert party – 'The Troubadours' and Mr. Bell trained them. Some good days then. I always read the letters in the Chiswick Times from the old boys. I don't think there are many of them in civvies now, except those on Government work.'

8 December 1916. *Chiswick Times*
Letter to Rev. Oldfield.

Seaman Refford. HMS -----

'Very cold weather like the polar regions. My brother is in Egypt again. We shall not be home for Christmas, but all the same it will not make any difference, for I haven't had one home yet, but we will be just as happy keeping the Huns away from England while our old folks have a good time.'

22 December 1916. *Chiswick Times*
Letter to Rev. Oldfield.

First Class Stoker R. Osborne. HMS -----.

'We have been having some very busy times lately and have found several bits of fun – and have not been busy for nothing. We expect to be on board in harbour on Christmas Day. This will be the third Christmas I have spent at sea, but have been nearer home each time. Wishing you and all the boys at home and abroad a merry Christmas and a prosperous New Year.'

29 December 1916. *Chiswick Times*
Letter to Rev. Oldfield.

A.J. Punter. Able Bodied Seaman. HMS -----

'Hoping Christmas will be spent in harbour. Cold .....Plenty of snow ..... Plenty of gunnery, getting ready for the next 'stink' .... I am close to G. Wiseman's ship and sent him a fleet letter yesterday. I am in the band playing the big drum. So I won't forget how to use the sticks when the war is over, and all the old lads get together, and we have one of the old-time church parades.'

2 February 1917. *Chiswick Times*
Letters to Rev. Oldfield.

<u>Victor Jones.</u> Able Bodied Seaman. HMS ----.

'Still going strong. I had a decent time at Xmas. Our bell noisily rang the old year out. I missed my mother's Christmas pudding but it's on the way to me. Thanks very much for the papers.'

<u>R.M. Osborne.</u> 1st Class Stoker. HMS ---.

'At work on another patrol when we return to (English) harbour. We see the harbour lights and towns exactly as they were before the war. Rough sea nearly washed me overboard and I was only saved by clutching the pump on the upper deck.'

9 March 1917. *Chiswick Times*
Letter to Rev. Oldfield.

<u>A.J. Punter.</u> Able Bodied Seaman. HMS ----.

'I am still enjoying the best of health. We get plenty of football (when ashore). We have a fine team on this ship, and we have made a good name with it. We were not up in time to enter for the cup, so we decided to have a go at the winners, and gave them a good match although we lost, but by only one goal. Well sir, I find a great difference in this ship after destroyers, but I suppose I shall get used to her in time. She is 'some' ship.'

23 March 1917. *Chiswick Times*
Letter to Rev. Oldfield.

<u>1st Class Stoker W. Watson.</u> HMS ----.

'Pleased to say that I am in a cooler climate than when I last wrote. Some long trips lately but have not run against any Gott Straffes yet. We have had a few spasms or exciting moments. But we must not grumble as the weather and sea is calm to what we have been having. The boys say this is a pleasure trip we are having, but I wouldn't like to pay for the coal we are burning, between 500 & 1600 tons a trip. We have some big coal ship days.'

30 March 1917. *Chiswick Times*
Letter to Rev. Oldfield.

Boy A.E.J. Loosey. HMS -----.

'Well sir, as you see, I am now on the briny. I would rather prefer sea life as it is far better. We cook our own meals so we now know what we are eating. I hope all the boys at the front are still shaking their fists at the Huns, because we are doing our bit to them. If you have Bob Mockler's and Frank Brand's addresses would you mind sending them to me as I would like to hear how my old chums are getting along.'

20 April 1917. *Chiswick Times*
Letter to Rev. Oldfield.

1ˢᵗ Class Stoker R.M. Osborne. HMS -----.

'I have heard from Alf Punter and he is still well and sends kindest regards to all.

We have had several small actions, and have come out top each time. We have blown up several mines. Weather terribly cold and several severe snow storms. I should be pleased if you could send me the brigade medals to replace those I lost to show my chums who belonged to various brigades as boys (but none like the L.D.C.L.B, I guess). I have seen some of their decorations and we all try to oust one another as to which brigade is the best. None of us will give in, and each has some startling adventures to relate of times spent in camp.'

4 May 1917. *Chiswick Times*
Letter to Rev. Oldfield.

W.B. Wilkinson. Able Bodied Seaman. HMS -----.

'Thanks very much for your welcome letter. I have seen several of our boys out here at different times. The first chap was Will Wells at ---- last year, and after that, Bert Sparks at -----, whilst I was on a most enjoyable four days leave visiting the Sphinx and the wonderful mosques etc. Some little time back I met George Allen here. He was on seven days leave after being on the desert a few months. I expect you already know that Sid is on our patrol ship HMS ---- and I saw him again at church this morning.'

25 May 1917. *Chiswick Times*
Letter to Rev. Oldfield.

Private S. Buchanan. Somewhere at sea.

'No doubt you will remember me as one of your old Brigade boys, and when I receive the Chiswick Times from home each week I always look for the letters from my old chums, and I thought I would like to write to you as well. I have been aboard this ship two months now, and the rest of the time, 15 months, since I joined up, in barracks. I think our boys in France are doing well now. What a time it will be when it is all over and all the old boys meet again.'

1 June 1917. *Chiswick Times*
Letter to Rev. Oldfield.

A.J. Punter. Able Bodied Seaman. HMS -----.

'Sorry not written before, but had an accident with my fingers and have been unable to hold anything. They are better now. Still hard at gunnery, getting ready for 'The Day'. The seamen aboard here have started a drum and fife band and I have again the pleasure of being big drummer. I wish Ralph were here to be bandmaster. By the way, have you any old pieces of flute music, such as 'Royal Windsor' as they would come in very handy when we are on the march, and would be highly appreciated by myself and the remainder of the band.'

1 June 1917. *Chiswick Times*
Chiswick Working Men's Club. Old Boys on active service.

Wal Kemp writes from HMS -----.

'I was sorry to see in the Chiswick Times that George G had been killed. I think of the old days of the minstrel troupe and how many are being killed so young. It makes us sick to hear how our mates at home, who they look forward to helping, come out on strike. I was on a ship escorting a boat of soldiers across the channel. My ship was built at Thorneycrofts so I feel quite at home. On coast patrol we average about 3,000 miles a month. I have volunteered for submarines and expect to leave my ship soon.'

15 June 1917. *Chiswick Times*
Letter to Rev. Oldfield.

R.M. Osborne. 1st Class Stoker. HMS -----.

'Thank you for sending me a second brigade medal to replace one lost. I am in the best of health again. I had rather a severe attack of fever last week again, which lasted five days. We are out on the 'strafe' again now, but there doesn't seem anything much coming our way this time. I was very sorry to hear Tom Bean had been killed. Please express my sympathy to his people. (a spasm on deck, sir, will finish this letter later, Bob.)'

'Nothing exciting, only a mine. And now that's gone, I'll start again. I was very sorry I could not call and see you again as I promised. I was recalled and had to leave on Friday night. I sincerely hope no more of our boys have been killed and hope we shall all meet at home very soon.'

6 July 1917. *Chiswick Times*
Die Hards on the Tyndareus.

Private T. Roffe, Middlesex Regiment, writes about when he was on board the *Tyndareus* when it was struck by a mine off the Cape of Good Hope.

'We arrived at Cape Town on 5th February 1917 and a march was arranged by Lt-Col John Ward and the town turned out to greet us. When we returned to the ship we saw 'nigger gangs' loading cargo and we started out for Durban on the 6th February,

sooner than expected. At 6.15pm there was a terrific explosion –
a mine or a bomb shipped on at Cape Town. The signal to take
to the life boats was sounded when the ship was well down at
the bows. There was excitement but no panic and we lined up
and sang songs. Wireless distress signals brought two steamers
near at hand within three quarters of an hour which renewed
courage as did the words spoken by the colonel.

My lifeboat made it to a steamer and we clambered up rope
ladders. We were given meals of bully beef and potatoes and slept
the best we could on the steel floors with lifebelts for pillows. Our
equipment was lost and we were not well clad. In the morning
we were surprised to see Tyndareus still afloat and efforts were
being made to attach tow ropes. Our steamer put full ahead
for Cape Town where we were transferred to lighters to take us
ashore and we were re-equipped. We were forbidden to speak to
inhabitants about the episode. We went by train to Simonstown
and found the Tyndareus still afloat and we were taken alongside
and boarded and most of our equipment was rescued.

On Saturday the 11th February the inhabitants provided us
with entertainment and tea at the town hall. Speeches were made
and all trouble was forgotten. On the 16th the battalion returned
to Cape Town, packed into carriages like sardines, where some
of us formed a guard of honour for the opening of parliament.

*Tyndareus was launched in 1916. After being damaged by a
mine she was repaired at Simonstown and returned to commercial
service in 1920. She was employed as a troop and supply ship in
the Second World War and continued commercially until 1960
when she was broken up for scrap in Hong Kong. The event off Cape
Town was widely reported emphasising the resilience, bravery and
orderly way in which the 'die hards' assembled and sang while
waiting to be boarded onto the lifeboats. The ship's crew seemed to
have remained on board and assisted in saving the ship.*

7 September 1917. *Chiswick Times*
Letters to Rev. Oldfield.

Boy Harry E. Spratt. HMS -----.

'I have joined the navy and I like it very much. I have been here nearly a week, have been vaccinated and have passed my swimming test, which is about eighth lengths. They say down here that when we have done ten weeks training we go to sea and I hope it is true. Well, sir, being in the brigade for four years has learnt me a lot, so I am going to try and get up in the ship while I am here.'

Boy Robert H. Mockton. HMS --—.

'I am still getting along fine with my navy life. You see that I have again been shifted this time to a sea-going ship. I see by the CT that E. Lovey has been in hospital, but I hope he is now quite well and able to join his ship again. So George Still, a Chiswick boy, has joined the navy. He always wanted to. It seems that Chiswick is very strong on the navy, but I am sure it is the best place. It is better on this ship than in the Egmont barracks, as I see plenty of life travelling from one place to another. Some time back when I was at Malta, E. Maidlow was about ten yards from me for about a month, and I did not know until his ship had just gone to sea, so of course I missed him.'

A.J.Hunter, Able Bodied Seaman. HMS -----.

'I am A.1. I am now back on a destroyer. The ----- was too big for me, Sir, after being so used to a destroyer, but now that I am back I feel contented. We get more running than the big ships, but it all helps to pass the time away more quickly. We have been hard at it these two weeks, only two nights in harbour, but we are now in for a short spell. You might let me know where Tom Cook is and send m his address.'

5 October 1917. *Chiswick Times*
Letter to Rev. Oldfield.

W.H. Wilkinson. Able Bodied Seaman. HMS -----.

'The only time our monotony is broken is when we have a spell in harbour and then we play water polo, cricket and football and I can assure you the ships' teams are hot stuff and are willing to play anybody. We have only a small ship's company of 75 to pick from, and we have surprised all the army teams we have played. The navy team won the cup last season, beating the pick of the army teams by 6 – 1.'

19 October 1917. *Chiswick Times*
Letter to Rev. Oldfield.

Stoker F. Buckley. HMS -----.

'We have had a rise of pay now and get, without the extra mess allowance, 9d a day extra. When I last saw you my money was £3-5s per month; now it is £4-12s. I get 2d a day retainer as well as I have finished my time. I have had my wife here at our base for a month so you can guess I am very happy.'

2 November 1917. *Chiswick Times*
Letter to Rev. Oldfield.

1ˢᵗ Class Stoker R. Osborne. HMS -----.

'I am still in the best of health. We are having some awful weather here just now. We had a spasm yesterday which lasted four hours but our luck was out and all we got was a good wetting. Our mess deck was all flooded out, so you can imagine how happy it was. It is a little better today; the sun was shining but the sea is still very high owing to the strong wind blowing. We are expecting to return to harbour today for a few hours' spell, and we shall be very glad too, if only to get a meal without having to hang on to everything for fear of losing it. We lost everything in the way of dinner on Friday. It shot under the lockers, so we went on biscuit a little sooner than expected.'

9 November 1917. *Chiswick Times*
Letter to Rev. Oldfield.

1st class boy F. Brereton. HMS -----.

'I have not dropped on any boys yet, but I am expecting to see Artie Brand soon, and I suppose he has been home lately or I should have seen him before. I hope that the air raids have stopped. I still hear about the old place by the CT, which comes in very handy at our little spare time, including the 'dog' watches.'

30 November 1917. *Chiswick Times*
Letter to Rev. Oldfield.

1st Class Boy F. Brereton. HMS -----.

'I have not dropped on any boys yet, but I am expecting to see Artie Brand soon, and I suppose he has been home lately. I hope that the air raids have stopped. I still hear about the old place by the CT which comes in very handy at our little spare time, including the 'dog' watches.'

7 December 1917. *Chiswick Times*
Letters to Rev. Oldfield.

Boy Telegraphist A.J.E. Lovrey. HMS -----.

'As you can see, I have arrived out here safe. Sir, I am pleased to say that I have come across two Chiswick lads out here. They are two brothers, one on HMS ----- and one on HMS -----. Their name is Wilkinson and they live in Glebe Street. Do you mind asking Miss W. if she minds sending my book, the 'Boy's Friend' along to the above address. I miss my reading of it.'

1st Class Stoker Sid Wilkinson. HMS -----.

'I have come across my brother Will. I see him every fortnight. Much to my surprise, I ran across Bill Smith, the old brigade fellow, and he said he was having a good look round for some of the other chaps but I was the only one he had come across. I must ring off now as I have got the middle watch, and it is piped down as I am very sleepy. Best wishes to the Band of Hope.'

4 January 1918. *Chiswick Times*
Letters to Rev. Oldfield.

1st Class Boy F. Brereton. HMS ------.

'Had time to write when the boson piped "make and mend." I had a surprise when George Still joined the ship. I met Artie Brand just before I went on leave and he has heard from his brother who has been slightly wounded. He might run across Reachill Howell who is on HMS -----. It is proper parky up here for we wash down the decks and it has turned into ice before we can sweep it down.'

Stoker Fred Buckley. HMS ------.

'On Boxing Day we were still patrolling the same old waters since 1914 on the lookout for U boats. I expect a long leave in January or February. I haven't got the 'hook' yet, being a 'Tickler' in the R.N. I haven't tried for such; I'd rather have me 'blank' than the 'hook' I think.'

1 February 1918. *Chiswick Times*
Letter to Rev. Oldfield.

1st Class Stoker W Watson. HMS -----.

'I used to think it was rough on the Royal Sovereign round to Margate; some of the boys were sick then, but I have a different opinion now of what a rough sea is like. One night we got it lovely. Down below it washed up the plates, and a chum of mine got washed down the bilges and broke his leg. We had a lively time trying to keep the fires going. All the coal was being washed from one end of the hold to the other and we had to catch it as it passed us. We wanted sea boots to keep the home fires burning. Some of the lads starting singing "Life on the Ocean Waves" to cheer us up. We will pull through OK. I can see my brother with the triangle. I can see us having some music next time I get home.'

22 February 1918. *Chiswick Times*
Letter to Rev. Oldfield.

1st Class Stoker R. Osborne.

'I am in hospital having had an operation for an injury caused by a dropped spanner in the engine room.'

8 March 1918. *Chiswick Times*
Letter to Rev. Oldfield.

Signaller Harry Greenham. Egypt.

'My ship was torpedoed on the way to Egypt and the men sang hymns while the nurses were safely got off. "Abandon Ship" came two minutes before she went down. I owe my life to the lifebelt I had on at the time because I can't swim a yard and was picked up after two hours.'

5 April 1918. *Chiswick Times*
Letter to Rev. Oldfield.

H V Jones. HMS -----.

'In the pink. Back from a few days leave in Chiswick where my younger brother, Jim, I saw eagerly playing the flute in the band. I met an old brigade pal who is in the tank corps and has damaged his leg.'

6. Gibraltar and Malta

Both were naval bases for the British fleet and staging posts for troop ships. There was a military hospital in Malta.

23 December 1914. *Chiswick Times*
Corporal J. Hewer, 'A' Company, 8th Middlesex, writes from 5th Barracks, Gibraltar.

'I am in the best of health guarding the German and Turkish prisoners, who at times have made attempts to escape. Our orders are to shoot on sight.

The rainy season is on and at times we get a good drenching. It is very cold at night, but each man has four blankets and two sheets. In our spare time, we go sight-seeing over the Rock and in the caves and it is very interesting to chat with gunners in charge of the big guns.

It is a common sight to see the fleet bringing in a captured boat. We have got the harbour full of them and occasionally we get a new batch of prisoners. They are well cared for and I think would sooner be here than fighting against us. There are some very decent fellows amongst them. I was talking to a few today and they knew Richmond and Twickenham very well. We are not allowed to tell them anything about the Rock and have to be very strict as regards discipline.

Friday 28 November is the anniversary of the siege of the Rock. All soldiers, where possible, were given a holiday, so our officers got up some sports in the morning.'

1 January 1915. *Chiswick Times*

10ᵗʰ Middlesex in Gibraltar – letter from Colonel Garner in response to Mrs. Fane de Salis, wife of County Alderman de Salis, concerning charges made to the Territorials for shirts and socks collected locally and sent out for the men.

The Colonel explains that it is usual company practice to make a weekly deduction from each man's pay to provide a fund to make good barracks damages etc. However, the deduction is not being levied and the fund is furnished by the sale of the socks, shirts etc to the men. In cases when it is expressly stipulated that items are not to be sold in this way, they are issued free.

26 March 1915. *Chiswick Times*

Letter to Rev. Oldfield.

Private Alfred R. Cox. Royal Army Medical Corps in Malta.

'We are tired of inactivity and have doubts of ever going to France on account of developments in the Dardanelles. We knew what was coming off in the Dardanelles months ago. I'm looking forward to playing the organ again at the church. Was going to play at the barracks church services but much to my disappointment was shifted to another place.'

4 February 1916. *Chiswick Times*

Letter to Chiswick Working Man's Church Club.

Private C.J. Kilbey. Ricasoli Hospital, Malta.

'We are allowed out to the village of Vittarioso and to Valetta town across the harbour, and everything is very interesting to us – the people, shops, and not least, the milkmen, with their herds of goats in every street. I have heard from no-one in the battalion and have no idea where they are except a vague one they are in Egypt.'

24 March 1916. *Chiswick Times*
Letter to Rev. Oldfield.

Private S. Pine. Convalescent camp, Malta.

'I was in the London Diocesan Church Lads Brigade (LDCLB) for two years and after that played for St Mary Magdalene's football team for two years, and I could not have any better pleasure that I did with the boys of St Mary's, for they were good sportsmen, and they have done their duty by answering their country's call, and if everybody could take an example from them there would be no need to call upon the young fellows the same way as they have got to do at the present day. Pleased to hear that Arthur Reffold was back in England safe, and that Bert Chandler is also.'

14 April 1916. *Chiswick Times*
Letter to Mr. T.A. King. Chiswick Working Men's Club.

Private C.J. Kilbey. Malta.

'I am still at the convalescent camp at Tuffisha. The bandages taken off after four months and although weak I am much better. Expect to be sent home at the end of April. The weather is beautiful with blinding sun and nice blue sky every day; just an ideal climate for recuperating, but there's no place like old England for that, I think. You can guess the weather when I tell you we have open air concerts by the Red Cross professional party and Miss Lena Ashwell's YMCA party; also cricket matches on a matting wicket. The footballers have to wait till after tea, because of the heat before they can play. I hope soon that the boys in France will put the final touch on the Kaiser, and we'll all be home again. Of course, there's no doubt about it, he's got to go under.'

18 August 1916. *Chiswick Times*
Letter to Rev. Oldfield.

Sapper H. Jales. Malta.

'I am now convalescing after a spell in hospital. My legs still give trouble but with plenty of sea bathing I thinks they will improve.

The place for bathing reminds me of being back with lads at the Riverside camp. The Western Front advance should alter things for them out East.'

20 October 1916. *Chiswick Times*
Letter to Rev. Oldfield.

Rifleman A. Wilkinson. Malta.

'I have got over my malaria and was fortunate in going straight into a hospital ship. Pleased to hear the 'Zepps' are having a rough time. Things were getting very lively when I left in ------. We were shelled out of our camp, but, luckily we had only one casualty – their shells being very poor.'

1 March 1918. *Chiswick Times*
Letter to Rev. Oldfield.

Private A. Beame. In hospital in Malta.

'I am much better and have been put in charge of a Maltese work party. They are hardworking and much better than 'Johnny Greek'. I've met only two Chiswick chaps since I joined in September 1914.' He has served in France, Egypt and Salonica.

7. Western Front 1915

By the beginning of 1915 series of defensive trenches dug by both sides made breakthroughs virtually impossible.

The German Army endeavoured to recapture Ypres and used gas for the first time. The British Expeditionary Force (BEF) broke through the German lines at Neuve Chapelle and Vimy in March but were repulsed. In the autumn the British used gas in a breakthrough at Loos but that too was contained by the German Army.

The towns of Hartlepool, Scarborough and Whitby had been shelled by the German navy in December 1914 killing 137 people.

Letters from the front describe the horrors of the war. There are attempts at cheerfulness and they often say how fit and healthy an army life is. The importance of cigarettes and music is a recurring theme as is the condemnation of striking coal miners at home.

<u>1 January 1915.</u> *Chiswick Times*
Corporal Lawrie, cyclist section, 19th Infantry Brigade, and former Chiswick Station policeman, writes to Sub-Divisional Inspector Copping.

'Thank you for the Christmas presents. We just heard of the bombardment of Scarborough, Whitby and Hartlepool and although very sorry for the poor people who lost their lives, nearly everyone here thinks it is a good thing to happen, as it will make people at home realise that this war is a more serious thing than some people think and that Germany is not finished yet, although we hear of great Russian victories with which you have to take a pinch of salt.

This town I am in got a very severe shelling the other night. 116 civilians have been killed since the Germans were driven out of it. The weather is dreadful; continuous rain and the boys in the trenches are having a rough time between mud, rain etc.

All regiments in my brigade are now at full strength again and personally, I think we are waiting for the spring before we make a general advance. I believe with Kitchener's army thrown into the balance, we'll start a sweeping movement and the Germans won't be very long out of Germany.'

1 January 1915. *Chiswick Times*
Letter received by Rev. A.E. Oldfield, vicar of St Mary Magdalene Church from one of his old boys' club men.

Private R.J. Vine. 'A' Company, 10th Battalion, West Yorkshire Regiment, Wartham Camp, Dorset.

'We can do a 20 miles march with rifles and although we do six hours drill a day I still think the army is a lazy life. The difficult part is shaving. I have tried shaving, with some success, with tea, ginger beer and cold water. A man named Dixon had three children killed and one injured in the Hartlepool affair and has left for home. His case is as bad as any; he has all our sympathy.'

1 January 1915. *Chiswick Gazette*
Driver A. Newton, HQ staff, 29th Brigade, Royal Field Artillery, writes to his wife at Colville Road, South Acton:

'We are having black nights. Almost impossible to see anything a foot in front of us. We were taking up ammunition and just as we were getting near the gun pits, the Germans turned the searchlight on us and they shelled us. One wagon turned over. I got away with mine and then went back and got the other one out under heavy fire but had no casualties. It is very wet but officers and men are sticking it without complaint. The officers are having it just as rough as the men, but they all muck in and help one another.

We pulled a dead German out of the canal the other day. The top of his head was blown off. I suppose his pals had no time to bury him and so chucked him in the water. We found three pears tied up in a handkerchief and a silver spoon in his mess tin.'

8 January 1915. *Chiswick Times.*

Letters to Rev. A.E. Oldfield.

Private G. Elsley, Hampshire Regiment.

'On Christmas Day not a shot was fired. We and the Germans seemed to understand each other. Peace on earth, goodwill to all men, was carried out between our lines and the German's. We sang a song and then they sang; some have splendid voices. Compliments were yelled across to each other; several of them understand English. Cold and frosty and a bit of snow and there was heavy fighting on our left on Xmas Day.'

Donald Avens, writing to his sister at 19 Oxford Rd, Chiswick. from the 4th General Hospital in Plymouth:

'It is only my feet, although of course I cannot walk yet. Came over from Havre by hospital ship carrying 1,700 sick and wounded. Nurses were like angels over there. Three days before I left the battalion, one of our chaps had his head clean blown off a few feet away from Ted and myself.'

Surgeon Davies, writing from Hospital Transport Ship, Guildford Castle.

'Not much time to ourselves, dressing over a hundred a day in our ward alone. A Welsh Regiment Major, although wounded, refused to go home and went back to the firing line.'

Private Wilkin. Queen's Westminster's.

'I was at a Xmas Day Communion Service attended by seventy in a barn cleared of straw. The roof had been damaged by shell fire. Some men covered in mud from the trenches. There were a few shots during the service which was the most impressive I have attended.'

8 January 1915. *Chiswick Gazette*

Life saved by prayer book.

On bidding her farewell, Drummer Court was given a prayer book by his fiancée, to carry in his left breast pocket. At the battle of the Marne, finding the book pressed too heavily, he transferred it to his left trouser pocket. Shortly afterwards, a shrapnel burst nearby, killed six and wounding fourteen, but Court was unhurt. Later, he found a hole in his trousers and saw that the ivory back of the prayer book was torn, and in the leather bag where he kept the book lay a bullet.

As a thanks offering for his preservation, the drummer desired to present the prayer book, leather bag and bullet to be kept in St George's Church and a petition has been presented to the Commissary Court of London by the Vicar and church wardens for the fixing of an oak box and glass front, in which the items can be kept.

8 January 1915. *The South London Press*
A Christmas Truce. Clapham man describes amazing scenes at the front.

Corporal R. Ridley of E Company, Queens Westminster, whose home is in the Clapham Road, writing from the trenches on December 27th, describes a remarkable truce that took place between the Germans and the British at Christmas.:-

'We have had, as no doubt you have seen by the papers, had a good deal of time in the trenches, and also a number of casualties. Only on Christmas Eve a pal of mine received a shot in the cheek which came out at the back of his neck, outside my dugout.

At night (Christmas Eve) we sang songs and then we heard clapping and "Encore" from the trenches opposite. We lighted candles and stuck then on entrenching tools and they copied us. We then held lighted matches and stood up on the parapets. They did likewise and so we said, "Hang it all! If they don't fire at that we'll get out in front. This we did and struck matches and smoked cigarettes, danced, sang, etc, and they sang and clapped. To light up the scene a building in the German lines had been set alight by our artillery earlier in the day. They then shouted "Happy Christmas! Football tomorrow!" Little did we think what the morrow would bring forth.

Christmas Day. – When I got up I found our chaps walking about out of the trenches, and further, the Germans were doing likewise, as if we were only separated from joining hands by the trenches.

I visited a few burnt out buildings nearby. The damage done to big farm houses is appalling. The habitants will have a shock when they come home. We helped some Germans bury a few of their snipers we had killed and held a service over them. They thanked us and we went our respective ways to our trenches. We were not satisfied, so we went out on our own and called them out, and we exchanged cigars, cigarettes, buttons, hats, etc and shook hands as though we had been friends reunited after years of parting.

Then, to crown it all, a German came rushing out with a camera. After shaking hands he took my photo with each arm through a German's arm. We made a truce on our own, and if it was left to the soldiers we could finish the war today.

Hoping you are all quite well and spent as happy a Christmas as we did – if not as novel, and cold, and muddy.'

22 January 1915. *Chiswick Times*
Sergeant W.H. Barnes, 7 Holly Road, who has had ten years service in 6th Dragoon Guards, writes to the *Chiswick Times*.

'A private and I were out looking for a lost comrade and we became cut off and had either to make a dash for it or surrender. My comrade said: 'I am not going to surrender.' We dashed at a number of German cavalry, got two of them and were securing two horses, when my chum was hit in the neck and killed. I was hit in the neck and the bullet came out through my face. I lay as though dead and the Germans went through my pockets and took 2½d. I can tell you, they are dirty dogs.

I was found by a French peasant and taken on a barrow to a priest's house. I was unconscious from Monday to Friday. I had lost the sight of one eye. They gave me civilian clothes and although the village was not vacated by the Germans until the following Sunday I escaped their notice by feigning to be deaf and dumb.

I made myself useful by bringing in the French wounded. I got to Compiegne and then on to Paris.

In Paris I met two of my own troop – 'Don't you know me?' but they only nudged each other. Then another chap came up and said 'Why it's old Barney'. 'Get out' said the other chap, 'he's been dead three weeks'. It was me right enough, although I must have looked a bit of a sight.'

29 January 1915. *Chiswick Times*
Training with Kitchener's Army – Private E.J. Hagel, West Yorkshire Regiment, 10th Service Battalion reports from Wareham in Dorset.

'I Joined on 4th September and am training at Wareham, Dorset. Rain drips through tents. There are 10,000 troops there. Drill, marching, trench digging, battle training with blank ammunition.'

29 January 1915. *Chiswick Times*
Letter from Rifleman F.E. Clarke, 16th London Regiment, Queen's Westminsters to his brother, Mr. Nelson Clarke, The Dairies, Hillrise, Richmond.

'I was in the trenches, 1st to 21st January and when relieved struck lucky being billeted in a barber's shop, run by a lady. All cooking is done for us and we are shaved by a lady in the morning. She tells me she is coming to London in February or March to find a house she intends to occupy after the war. She has been very good to us, and made us all comfortable.

In the trenches our position is by a flooded river, near a village occupied by the enemy. Their trenches are 60 yards away and sniping was extremely warm. The Germans used to fire from buildings in the village until our guns in the rear paid them a call. The German artillery amused itself wasting twelve shells on an empty house a hundred yards to our rear, mistakenly thinking we were occupying it.

We get a good supply of woodbines, but they get rather monotonous, so if you can send out a few players occasionally they will just keep me going. Butter and tinned stuff is always acceptable – easy to carry about and it does not matter if you drop tins in the mud.'

12 February 1915. *Chiswick Times*
Gunner E.G. Hutton, Royal Home Artillery, had come from Canada to enlist, writes to his aunt.

'I volunteered with five others to work a new gun which throws bombs into the German trenches. I want to get some of my own back, as my two friends have gone under. You say 'Don't be too venturesome' but the chance is too good to lose. If I go under, tell them at home that I tried to do my duty.'

19 February 1915. *Chiswick Times*
Letters to Rev. Oldfield.

Private Arthur Hill. 2nd Battalion, Grenadier Guards.

'A touching incident in front of our trench. A German officer had been wounded in a charge and lay in front of our trench. He crawled but could not manage to get to our trench. One of our stretcher bearers got up out of our trench and called out to the Germans asking if they would shoot if he went to pull the German in. But they made no answer. So our chaps shouted across and told them to fetch him and they would not shoot, so two Germans came over and fetched him in. The Germans said 'Thank you English' and our chaps gave them a cheer which was taken up by the Germans.

It shows how a British Tommy will not take the word of a German, but a German knows that if a Britisher gives his word he will stick to it. We have a church service once a week. Every man attends as our first thoughts are of home and God when we go into the trenches.'

Private Walter Burch. 4th Battalion, Royal Fusiliers.

He is a stretcher bearer. 'The Germans put two 'Jack Johnsons' into a house used as a dressing station a thousand yards behind the line. Three of our chaps were buried alive. We could hear their cries and got them out. We dug them out and they were a mass of wounds, one having a severely damaged lung, where a beam had been lying on him.

Shell fire makes a chap feel nervous. You can hear them whistling in the air and the noise increases near the end of their journey. Then you hear a louder noise that you know is the burst. Best thing is to lie flat and trust to luck. All our stretcher bearers do 24 hours in the trench to bandage the wounded and render first aid.'

Gunner W. Alexander. Royal Field Artillery.

He is grateful for receiving the *Chiswick Times*. 'Yesterday the Germans gave us a two hour bombardment that wounded a few of our fellows and broke our telephone wires. I went out to mend one but was driven back by a shrapnel shell. I managed to do it up later.'

Reverend Oldfield has heard that William Ward and George Revell, who are prisoners of war, have received the parcels and money he sent.

19 February 1915. *Chiswick Times*
Extracts from the diary of Sergeant H.G. Boxall, lately a clerk at the local Labour Exchange, serving with the Royal Army Medical Corps attached to the Leinster regiment.

1st October 1914

Had been entrenched at Aisne for eleven days. First very nerving experience of shell fire. Plenty of sniping on both sides. 32 casualties.

2nd October – 6th October 1914

Rested for a few days. Five of us in a 'comfortable little flat' – originally the home of three pigs, but comfy with the help of clean straw.

10th October 1914

Forced marches every day. Wet weather and sleeping on the side of the road. Still cheerful.

11th October 1914

Entrained. Slept soundly in a horse box until arriving in a siding at Calais. Seems whole town came down to meet us. Food, wine and coffee pressed upon us. Left Calais at 9pm, singing 'Tipperary' and the Marseillaise.

15th-16th October 1914

In motor lorries towards the front. Severe engagement plainly audible in the distance. It is said the enemy on the run. Came to a bridge over the River Lys and a dog, evidently tied there by the Germans to give the alarm, started barking wildly and we came under heavy rifle and machine gun fire. Our 18-pounders shelled their position and then away went our wild Irishmen and took the bridge. The poor dog was found simply riddled. Then street fighting until the village cleared of enemy. We captured 14 prisoners. Our casualties 22 men and one officer.

18th October 1914

Enemy appear to be strongly entrenched and we are digging in. Dressing station established half a mile in rear.

19th October 1914

Subjected to heavy bombardment. Our house struck once but our small party has escaped. Our wounded coming in very fast. Some poor fellows frightfully torn about, mainly by shell fragments. This is not warfare, it is simply wholesale slaughter. A shell bursts and possibly 20 or 30 chaps are knocked out.

The wounded coming in tell us the Germans have been charging our lines en masse repeatedly and have been driven back each time by 15 rounds rapid fire and machine guns. Our casualties very heavy and we are working as hard as we can with the help of half-a-dozen French women who have stayed despite the heavy bombardment.

20th October 1914

Shelling continues and ambulance wagons can't get to us to take casualties down the line. Good fairies must be keeping guard as we have escaped being hit although a house opposite is burning merrily apparently hit by an incendiary shell.

21st October 1914

Been at it for 30 hours. Hardly any sleep. Dressing station now moved to an inn nearer the firing line. One room, an operating theatre – another two, temporary wards. Very heavy firing and fighting and more cases coming in.

22nd October 1914

Three 'coal boxes' hit the building. How we got out with two patients who could not walk beats me. Got to the next village being swept by rifle fire and shells where we handed them over. We went back to try to recover equipment but the inn was in flames. Little was recovered and all personal kit lost. All we have is what we stand up in.

23rd October 1914

Managed to get two hours sleep. Reports are that our troops have held the line against great odds. In some places, the German dead are lying piled up like a wall in front of our trenches. This has been a terrible three days for everyone. There are 453 left out of our battalion of 986. Some of the German wounded say their losses have been terrible and it was impossible to get past the deadly rapid fire of our troops.

The sky torn with the flashes of guns and bursting of shells. Seven poor devils knocked out by a shell that burst on top of us. After this, we are crawling along the ditches on either side of the road. What is left of our battalion has moved out for a few days rest in reserve

24th October 1914

Arrived at a village and are billeted at a farm. The hayloft is to be our home from home for a few days. On the march here I found myself dropping off to sleep, though still trudging along. What a relief to be behind the firing line for a bit; it is just like heaven after the last few days. Just going to drop on some straw to sleep. Too knocked out to wait for anything to eat. It has been raining all night and we are just drenched.

26 February 1915. *Chiswick Times*
Private F. Culver, East Surrey Regiment, writes to his father at King St, Richmond.

'In training at Sandgate, and there is a rumour that we are going to Aldershot and are going to march there which would be an interesting 4 or 5 days. We have a comfortable billet in a house where the good lady looks after us like a mother.

Battalion training includes entrenching at night. Each company is allotted so many hours. They may dig all day and then fill them up again the next day. The trenching ground is on top of a very high hill – Tolsford Hill. No lights are allowed at night. There are different kinds of trenches – firing line, supports, communicating etc. The spade has been mightier than the sword! Return journeys in the dark are great fun, climbing fences, avoiding rabbit holes and unfilled trenches, and we sing – revised versions of well-known songs. We practise bridge building with barrels, ropes, poles and planks. The bridges have floating spars.

We also build rafts by removing the wheels from wagons. We have been to the rifle ranges where the targets represent the head and shoulders of a man in khaki. They come up in different places for about 10 seconds. Other practises are at a man running.

Sham fighting has been practised through woods, over ditches and hedges. Attacking or defending positions such as farm houses – the whole ending with a bayonet charge when everyone is expected to go mad.

Also, 'retirements' when the enemy has been reinforced and proved to be too strong. In retiring under fire, a company or platoon is usually left behind to cover the remainder of the force. Portions of the firing line retire alternately. Rapid firing is taken up to deceive the enemy as to the number of men left behind. A steady retirement can give the enemy something to remember although a great many lives may be lost.

We have done several route marches with the brigade that is made up of the East & West Surreys and East & West Kents. We march for about twenty miles – 6,000 strong – with transport wagons, stretcher bearers, mule packs etc.

The Kent Education Committee has arranged French and map-reading classes. Lectures also on history mostly dealing with Germany.'

5 March 1915. *Chiswick Times*
Private Frank A Baynes. Reports from the Royal Army Medical Corps (T) 85th Field Ambulance 28th Division. BEF.

'Some Scottish regiments are here now. Even when badly wounded, they are bright and merry. The food is very good, the best fed soldiers in the world. We have dealt with 3,000 cases of sick and wounded since January. Our section, next week, will be on indoor duty so we shall miss our moonlight trips picking up the wounded.

We have played football against French and Belgium soldiers. They could not beat our boys but want to play us again.'

5 March 1915. *Chiswick Times*
Letter to Rev. A.E. Oldfield.

Private George Elsley. Hants Regiment.

'Some Canadians are attached to us – a fine set of men. They were soon trying to snipe at the Germans. Consequently one of them got killed. The Saxons are trying a new game, shouting across to us, hoping to see our heads pop up for a target. Six months of warfare taught me something. Just behind our trench are ruined houses and a crucifix. The shelled houses have only walls remaining, but the 12 foot high crucifix has only been hit twice by bullets.'

12 March 1915. *Chiswick Times*
Corporal Fowkes' story.

'At Mons I was in the mounted charge of the 2nd Cavalry Brigade at some artillery to take off fire from the infantry. We diverted the fire but failed to capture the guns. We dismounted and as we were retiring, I heard a cry of 'Corporal, Corporal'. I went back to pick up a wounded recruit, but shrapnel exploded over us and killed him in my arms.

We remounted and an officer led the way along a railway cutting under fire. On coming out of the cutting my horse was shot and rolled down the bank on top of me, injuring my spine and stomach, dislocating my right knee and smashing an ankle. At some stage I was shot in the head. The Germans came up, bayoneted the wounded, stripped them and me, and left me for dead. I lay there unconscious till next day when I was carried by a Belgian doctor to a village. To my horror I found I was totally blind and lay in a delirious condition for 19 days.

I have a good constitution, of an elephant. When I joined the army for the South African War the surgeon who passed me said don't drink and don't smoke. Don't suppose I smoked six cigarettes in a year and never touched alcohol, until I found them giving me brandy when I came round in the Belgian village.

The Germans captured the village and I became a Prisoner of War. I received electrical treatment at a hospital in Mons and then came the welcome news that I and others were to be exchanged. At Liege, we were put on a train for Flushing. In the train, the Germans were gentlemanly absolutely – an orderly to each carriage. Ours could speak English, and he was a jolly decent chap.

We had a rough journey to Folkestone, and then to Queen Alexandra's Hospital at Millbank. I was still blind and the treatment differed from that in Belgium. My left arm was immersed in water, and a wet pad placed on my right arm. Electricity was passed through my body.

Can you imagine my joy on 22nd February when I woke and could distinguish the electric lights? I would rather have lost two legs than my sight. The doctors ordered electrical treatment again and within ten minutes I could see. When wounded I was covered with blood and unconscious, and that is why the Germans imagined me to be dead.'

12 March 1915. *Chiswick Times*
Letters to Rev. A.E. Oldfield.

Private A. Hill. 2nd Battalion, Grenadier Guards.

'At present, on rest from the trenches. I visited a cathedral in a French town (not allowed to mention which) and listened to the choir and the very good sweet sounding organ. French churches are very gaudy, though the windows and architecture are very good. The best I visited was about 12 kilometres from the firing line and the roof was so high I could not see the top.

It would make you smile to see the way we have of making a mug of water boil. The trenches are very dry and it is nothing to light a fire with one stick of wood. Another way is to save all your grease, put it into a tobacco tin, make a wick with a small piece of rag or sacking, push this well into the centre, then set it alight. This is sufficient to boil at least three mess tins.'

Gunner R. Hamilton. Royal Field Artillery. BEF.

'I received your parcel and when I was opening it three Jack Johnsons came over but did not catch our billet. We are alright and hope we shall remain safe.

We were playing football when three shells came over and I thought they could see us. However I am still on my feet. I shared the parcel with my pals so we shall be having a nice cup of cocoa. Remember me to the lads and I am looking out for some of them.'

19 March 1915. *Chiswick Times*
Letters from the son of a well-known Chiswick resident.
24ᵗʰ February 1915
'Sitting in a dug-out only 75 yards away from the Germans.
Fearfully tired as had 24 hours guard duty before leaving for the
front line – means I only had 1½ hours sleep the night before
last. Did three two-hour sentry posts during the night, the other
time spent filling sandbags and building sleeping and resting
places in the trench. Any amount of firing going on – bullets
whizzing over our heads or hitting the sandbags in front all the
time. Artillery shells whizzing over continually. Heads have to
be kept down. Beastly cold, snowing and raining nearly all the
time. Fearful mud and dirt.'
25ᵗʰ February 1915
'Got back from the firing line – a treat to sleep on a truss of straw.'
3ʳᵈ March 1915
'Were relieved in the trenches just before dawn and had quite
a time. A brilliant moon and the enemy spotted us and gave us
a fusillade. We were of course marching in single file. Expected
machine gun fire did not come. The place where we are resting
is in ruins, blown to atoms, furniture and contents strewn all
over the place. Almost the entire population has gone although
a few returning. We are well within range of enemy shells and
never know when they are coming.

Today, ordered to stay in billets (a barn) otherwise the
Germans may see the place is occupied and try to shell us out.
Impossible to get anything here, no cigarettes or tobacco for love
nor money. We are paid one franc a day, the balance of course
accumulating. Please send over papers and magazines as nothing
to read when off duty.

We are not allowed to keep a diary in case it should get into
enemy hands – so keep my letters for me to read again when I
get home. I should be glad to have another tin of that coffee

and milk, cigarettes, Three Castles tobacco, boxes of matches, milk chocolate. They charge an awful price for chocolate here and it's not very good.'

19 March 1915. *Chiswick Times*
Letters to Rev. Oldfield.

Private Frank Cooper. Mechanical Transport, Army Service Corps.

'We have to sleep on ammunition boxes. Poles support tarpaulin nailed to the sides of lorries and we have to find them the best we can. One day a goalkeeper missed his goalposts – purloined for use as supports. Woke up one morning and found the tea I had left had turned to ice.'

Stretcher Bearer A. Collard. East Lancs Regiment.

'What are the shirkers doing? Music halls and going home to grand beds. Do they give a thought for their brothers fighting their battles? They have excuses. We want them to come and help crush the foe. Just let them look how these cowards treat the men, women and especially children in France and Belgium. Some of them may fall, but rather die than be a shirker.'

26 March 1915. *Chiswick Times*
Letters to Rev. Oldfield.

Thanks expressed for the *Chiswick Times* that is sent to them.

Private E.F. Bryant. 3rd Royal Fusiliers.

'I have been in hospital with frost bite and will be glad to get back to the firing line which is very hard work in the trenches, as the water was up to our waists and it was also cold, but the boys and myself stuck it till the end of our 72 hours, when we got relieved. Very bad walking home, as our feet were so cold and frost-bitten, having been in the water for so long. We are getting hold of the Germans all right. As soon as they see us coming along with our rifle and bayonet, they run for all they are worth. If I catch one, I shall make up for losing my best chum.'

Bandsman W. Burch. 4th Royal Fusiliers.

'I am pleased to hear C. Clark has got home. Things are very lively and our casualties have been fairly heavy lately. But the present position is much better. Our troops hold a big hill all round and we are able to get our wounded out of the trenches in the daytime. Just on the right of our position, the Germans bombarded our trenches for about an hour – an awful sight from where we were watching. They took the trenches, but not for long. You know what our chaps are. They said they would have them back and they did, by the following morning.

I have seen a Chiswick Chap out here. His name is Wood.'

Driver Jack Clarke. Royal Garrison Artillery. BEF.

'I get my Chiswick Times from Mrs. F. It is quite a treat to read one another's letters. Well done, St. Mary Magdalene. The weather has improved. I hope the junior corps are still going strong and I hope before long to be back in the old homeland.'

26 March 1915. *Chiswick Times*

Letter from one of the First Canadian Contingent 'Somewhere in France'.

8th March 1915

'I wanted to be with my company in the trenches, but was kept on at HQ on duty from 8am to 10pm. The worst part was the shelling of the town by the Germans. You can hear the wretched things coming – the 'swish-sh-sh' then the explosion and the rattle of tiles, slates, back windows etc when they strike a building. Hardly any casualties, but one chap was killed and another wounded not two yards from the doorway where I was standing.'

9th March 1915

'At 5.30am, we were roused and have been 'standing to' – that is, ready to march into action, at a moment's notice. We were told take cover, and Jack & I dashed for the nearest house. He was just behind me and, I'm sorry to say, was wounded in the head – thankfully it is only a slight wound and I think he will soon be out of hospital.'

12th March 1915

'We waited till 6.30pm and most of the battalion went to the trenches, but my company had to do duty in supplying the firing line and doing fatigue work like preparing barbed wire, taking rations and water to the trenches. We only go up with supplies at night time, and sleep in the day.

Last night eight of us took sheets of corrugated iron for dug-outs. Heavy work – about a mile to the trenches. The last part through ploughed fields up to your knees in mud and over single planked bridges crossing ditches in the pitch dark. We had a narrow squeak on the first journey when the Germans sent up one of their star shells – a fire ball which illuminated brilliantly a large area and lasted about five seconds. We were right in front of their trenches, about 300 yards away, with absolutely no cover. They spotted us and opened fire with machine guns and rifles. We flung ourselves flat – my face, clothes and boots in about 4 inches of mud & water, and the beggars did not get one of us. The bullets swept right over us, so it was a close shave. Later we took up rations and ammunition.'

26 March 1915. *Chiswick Times*
Mr. T.A. King, secretary of the Chiswick Working Men's Club received a letter from an old member.

Gunner C.A. Faulkner. 37th Howitzer Battery, 8th Brigade, 5th Division.

'Have been posted to this battery that has won two V.C.s – Bombardier Luke & Driver Drain. Luke couldn't be a more modest little chap. A captain who got wounded received the D.S.O and there are five Distinguished Conduct Medals (D.C.M.s) amongst the non-coms, gunners and drivers.

A fine morning, after a severe frost and we gave the Germans a sharp reveille with our lyddite and shrapnel and soon afterwards they returned the compliment. All the civilians on these farms are ordered to get out back from the front. They pack up their wagons and get on the road so they get shelled by the Germans, but they seem quite indifferent to it now.

We pass the evening merrily and have all the latest on the mouth organ. Nothing is more welcome than a line from chums at home. My favourite shag is 3½d an ounce, and an ounce or two, with some A.G. cigarette papers would be gratefully received.'

1 April 1915. *Chiswick Times*

A letter from a wounded Richmond man to his wife in Hounslow.

'You ought to have seen me when I came in. I couldn't lift my leg and although I was in pain, I had to laugh at the dirt that was on me. When the orderly came to attend to me, I believe he thought I was an Indian. The sisters are so good to us and do all they can to make us comfortable.

In Belgium we knocked on a door for water and found a woman with eight children and two she had taken in whose husband was a P.O.W. The floor was bare ground, the roof leaked, there was no furniture – nothing more than a big shed. We clubbed up three frames for her and now she has a little stall on a pram, selling chocolate and apples. We came across another 'old girl' crying. Her house was blown up and she did not know where her husband and children were. We are getting used to it now. When I think of England and home, I thank God I am an Englishman.'

2 April 1915. *Chiswick Gazette*

With a camera at the Front. Report by an anonymous photographer.

He had to obtain a permit from the Belgium War Office and was told he had to apply to Army Generals in Command and he was told he would be placed under arrest and his apparatus destroyed if he took pictures. It was clear that pictures had to be taken without permission and he would give all generals and HQ staff a wide berth.

He first went to Diest, which was much harassed by the German cavalry in advance of the German main army where he visited a Red Cross Hospital, where there were many German wounded soldiers, and he chatted with a German Baron and officer, who asked him where the English soldiers were trying to get to, trying to get him to divulge which part of the front the British Army was occupying. The German officer said there was no harm in telling him since he was a prisoner with a bullet in his lung and a shattered leg and could not move even if invited to escape. 'I had no idea where our troops were or even if they had left England. I photographed him being attended to by a Belgium nurse before I left.' The next morning the town was overwhelmed by the Germans and the wounded prisoners set free. 'How useful any information would have been to that officer!'

'I got behind the Belgian line and snapped them as they lay defending the city whose destruction by the Germans caused world-wide horror. 160 Belgium lancers, waiting under cover half a kilometre to the rear, came up and charged the enemy position. Only 38 returned to the cover of houses.

Countless numbers of refugees were pouring up the road terrified and carrying what little possessions they could. This slowly moving mass, the shells bursting over their homes in the town behind, and the flames and smoke rising in ever-increasing volume, made a heartrending sight I shall never forget.'

9 April 1915. *Chiswick Times*
Thomas King, secretary Chiswick Working Men's Club has received several letters.

Private Frank A. Baynes, 16th Lancers

From somewhere in Belgium. 'Glorious weather but cold. We are to be here for some time unless a big advance comes shortly.'

Sgt. A.W. Taylor, 16th Lancers

'I'm now away from the firing line, resting. We were playing football 500 yards away from the billet, when it burnt down. All horses were saved except one and we lost all our kit. These farms burn quickly.'

Corporal S. Larwood. 1st Battalion Sherwood Foresters.

In a letter to his relatives, he wrote that six of them went as near as from 10 to 18 yards from German trenches to find out what they were doing. They were spotted when retiring and came under fire. He dived over the parapet into the trench.

'Some of the Germans know English well – 50 or 60 yards away, one shouted 'Surrender, you English fools, surrender!' He got a shower of bricks. In one German trench, a gramophone is on the go nearly every night.

I was wounded when we came under very heavy shell and rifle fire on 24th January. The Captain ordered a move to the other end of the trench. We had to dart across an opening one by one. Three of us were hit by a shell burst and, as being bandaged up, another shell fell amongst us. When the Germans attacked, they got it hot.'

He is now in Torquay hospital where 'all is going on well.'

9 April 1915. *Chiswick Times*
Letters to Rev. A.E. Oldfield

Corporal G. Barnes. BEF.

'What I like best of all, is to listen to the birds throughout the day, giving us a nice little song over the trenches. It sounds so sweet, as we don't get much music. I have got two stripes and hope I shall get more.'

Driver A.S. Smith. Transport Section, 13th London Regiment.

'Our regiment suffered rather heavily in that last big battle. The Germans shelled the field where the transport was billeted and we had orders to get out. Luckily we did, because a dozen Jack Johnsons came down where we had been standing. There is a strange sight in the village – a knocked about church has horses in the vestry and wagons down the aisle.

9 April 1915. *Chiswick Times*
Lt. John Skinner, 1ˢᵗ Canadian Division, letter to his mother, Marlborough Road, Gunnersbury.

'A few days ago a shell came over and killed my sergeant and four men. We had our first dose of the trenches and on the whole enjoyed it although in spots one sank up to one's knees. It is safe in the trenches – getting in and out is when the casualties occur. We go in at night but in bright moonlight and we had it pretty warm in spots.

The Germans are only 40 yards away and shout in perfectly good English: 'Now, then, you Canadian fellows, why don't you charge?' Being so close to the Germans makes some funny situations at times. The other night, another regiment had to stop work on wire entanglements when German fire got too hot. In the morning, they found the job finished. The Germans had done it for a joke.

One of our officers was chucking grenades into the German trenches and they were signalling the shots like they do at Bisley with a little flag – until he got a 'bull' and the signalling stopped. If one has the least bit of a sense of humour, there is pots of fun to be had simply from listening to the Tommies.'

9 April 1915. *Acton Gazette*
Letter from Geoffrey Lamb to the Rev. W.M. Le Patourel, Vicar of St. Dunstans, East Acton.

'My dear Vicar. It is now seven weeks since we saw the last of the English coast. We went into the trenches, and that was an eye-opener for me. The communication trench goes through a church yard. The church is an absolute ruin. We reached the firing line and I saw my first battle. It was the night and when dawn came there were dead all around. Those in the rear of the trenches we buried, but those in the front are still lying where they fell! There is no truce for burial; consequently it is impossible to remove the bodies in the firing zone.

We came out of the trenches that night, and had a long march to the base, a very tiring experience after very little sleep, and with such a weight of kit and ammunition to carry. We are near a cathedral and go to services when possible.'

16 April 1915. *Chiswick Times*
Letters to Rev. Oldfield.

Several send thanks for receiving parcels and copies of the *Chiswick Times* and report how they meet up with other men from Chiswick.

Sapper J. Jennings. BEF.

'I was looking for letters in the Chiswick Times this week but saw none. Remember me to all the 'bhoys'.

Trooper F. Sheppard. BEF.

'We are still awaiting orders to go into action. We have played the 7th ------ at football and won 3 – 1. We looked like mudlarks and our chaplain, a very nice chap, complimented us for playing in such mud. We are staying near one of the most finest beautiful French churches that I have seen since I came out.'

Private G. Elsley. BEF.

'Thank you for the Chiswick Times and the parcel. My chums are glad to have a drop of milk in their tea now and again. The weather is simply grand and you would not know it was war till a Jack Johnson comes flying over. I found a gunner's grave nearby and am doing it up with turf to make it look nice. Am doing cyclist orderly, cobble roads and shell holes – like a switchback & cannot see anything at night.'

Sergeant W.A. Giles. BEF.

'I have another Chiswick fellow in my squadron. Some of our graves are being tended by civilians – rough little crosses being replaced by elegant crosses. The graves are in the middle of a ploughed field and have been fenced off and each grave planted with evergreens and flowers. One old lady said her son had been killed in action and she hoped someone was doing the same for him.'

<u>Private W. Anderson</u>. East Surrey Regiment

Complains about men at home going on strike. 'What would they do if Tommy laid down his arms to strike for another penny? Our lads take it without a murmur and always laughing and joking.'

30 April 1915. *Chiswick Times*
Canadians at Ypres. Letter from the son of a well-known Chiswick resident.

'I wonder if you got the four letters I wrote. When we left the trenches a week ago, I gave two to my own officer and one each to two others. My officer and one of the others have been killed, and the other may have been. On Thursday, we were not sorry to get out of the town (Ypres). The whole battalion of a thousand was billeted in a five-storey factory. A perfect death trap if a German shell got it.

My company marched off to a fine barn, one and a half miles to the north. Balfour and I fixed up a comfortable corner and went out for a game of football. Suddenly terrific German shell fire started up two miles away to the north, where the French held trenches. We took no notice at first and carried on playing. The shelling moved to the North East, where our own trenches were some five or six miles away. Then they were shelling Ypres and we began to take an interest in the doings.

Large yellow patches of vapour hung over where the French trenches lay – the wind came from that direction and we began to feel the effects of it and our eyes and throats began to sting – breathing in a funny-smelling ammonia – very pungent. Even then, we were only more or less disinterested, passing remarks such as 'poor devils, they are getting it thick over there' and wondering how our Canadian 5th Battalion, who relieved us on Monday, were getting on.

The order came 'Stand to!' Within three minutes, platoons lined up, rifles loaded, one round in the breach and five in the magazine,

150 rounds in our equipment and 50 extra in bandolier. We moved a couple of fields towards Ypres. Then we closed in because German shells were landing among us. 400 yards back, we opened out again in a ploughed field and began to entrench ourselves.

When in drills the sergeants used to curse us for not working hard enough, we used to say 'wait till it's necessary and then see.' In ten minutes I had enough cover for myself banked up round my head and shoulders that would have taken half an hour on parade. We advanced to another line of trenches. By this time, it was getting dark. Casualties were occurring all the time. Then we were ordered to swing to the left where the Germans were in a wood.

I never reached the wood but the fellows drove the Germans out alright. A bullet went in at the left of my abdomen and passed four inches along and came out again on the right side. I thought I was all in. My chum Balfour bandaged me. I wonder if he came through. He hated leaving me but was obliged to.

I waited wearily until the stretcher bearers found me. Being a stomach wound I dared not drink water and I was getting awfully thirsty. Shells were bursting all round. They carried me to a horse ambulance some way off; then a rough ride to the field dressing station, where the wound was dressed, still lying on the stretcher. A long wait for being taken by two motor ambulances.

That must have been midday Friday. Then by train and another motor ambulance to the Casino at Wimereux – 1.30am Saturday. Then for the first time for three months, I was undressed and got into a bed. We are very comfortable here in the hospital building where students take their exams.

I lost everything on the battlefield. Even my belt with my two knives, which they had to take off to get to my wound. I got to England without a thing. Can you send some cigarettes? I haven't a halfpenny to send out to buy any with.'

There were further letters from him – presumably passed on by the officers who were killed.

'The day before yesterday, we went for a walk around the town, imagining it was fairly safe. Suddenly big shells fell all round. We were in a café having coffee and pastries. Women and children rushed in from the streets like mad people. The old girl in the café rolled down the shutters, closed the door and turned us out into the street. Men and soldiers were running from place to place. It was an awful sight – people and horses blown to pieces. In the main square, the beautiful Cathedral and Cloth Hall were blown to pieces. My friend and I found cover in the square down three steps, a kind of semi-basement.

Some fellows had just come through an action the previous night. They were pretty well a bundle of nerves. They were just outside their HQ when a shell hit. The poor beggars did scoot, those who were not hit. The shelling has been incessant – day and night. Strange how callous one gets to the real danger of shells.'

A postcard marked '1am, 26th April'.

'Have arrived at the General Hospital, Oxford. Am doing well. Good that the bullet went right through.'

30 April 1915. *Chiswick Times*
Letter from C. Carter, member of the Chiswick Cadet band, to Cadet-Major, J.H. Clarke.

'The weather is getting A.1 – no more standing in water up to our waists. We wait for Mr. Fritz to try his dirty work on us. We have a lot of old scores to rub off, and rub off we will. Tell the band I shall soon be home, at least I hope so, if God spares me. How I long to stroll along Chiswick High Road. I really think July will see the finish.'

30 April 1915. *Chiswick Gazette*
A report from Private Arthur L. Drury, of 'Redcroft' Horn Lane, Acton.

'Last Friday one of our companies went into the trenches and we went up to do fatigues. We marched to a village which is smashed to atoms. We had to carry hurdles, stakes, barbed wire, etc, to the trenches, and we went along a road parallel to the trenches and quite open. There were a lot of bullets flying about. We got our confidence from the Guards to whom we are attached temporarily – the Scots, Irish, Grenadier and Coldstreams – and they are the finest soldiers that ever lived. Next day we went into the reserve trenches doing fatigues – flooring the trenches with bricks.

On Sunday afternoon we went into the firing line about 350 yards from the Germans. They were a very quiet lot, and did not do much shooting unless we started. Every now and then flares would go up to see if the enemy had any working parties out in front of the trenches. I didn't feel particularly cold, although there was a thick frost in the morning. Next day we marched back to the school where we are billeted, and next afternoon straight back into the firing line known as the 'duck's bill', owing to the shape of the line, and we were on the point, only 50 yards from the Germans, and had to speak in whispers because of listening patrols which they send out at night.

We had some pretty hot shots opposite us – they smashed three of the Guards' periscopes. At night, as there were no dug-outs, we had no sleep. One advantage about being so close to the Germans is that they dare not shell our firing trench, because of their own, but to counteract this, there is the bomb throwing business.

You can hear the thud of the mortar being used and can see the bomb turning over and over in the air. Then the cry goes up 'bomb up' or 'bomb right' and you all scuttle round the opposite transverse. The Guards all seemed to think it a good sport, and always make a rule of returning two bombs for every one of the Germans. I think it was through being mixed in with the Guards that we soon became so confident. Early in the morning, before the German lines can be distinguished, these chaps walk about on top of the trenches and go into the fields behind and get vegetables and wood for their braziers. Then they put up dummy periscopes and signal the shots to the Germans with a spade – bull or 'washout.'

In spite of bombardments nobody was injured. We were relieved in the evening, and went to a brewery at the back of our trenches, where we slept in the cellars. As I write now, there is one of our aeroplanes that I can see a long way off, with shells bursting all round it. In spite of this, I think these men have one of the safest jobs going. I should think I've seen the Germans fire over 200 shells at various aeroplanes and they have not hit or brought down a single one.

Altogether I think I have enjoyed our little trip so far. We have only had five wounded, two rather seriously, but three were stray shots and one other was a shell splinter. It does not do to think of the bad side at this game. A sergeant of the Guards was trembling like a child when they started shelling us. He told us he'd seen such fearful sights from shell fire and that, combined with the fearful noise, had broken his nerve.'

A report in *Fall In,* the Middlesex Battalion magazine, describes a gas attack in May 1915. The *Acton Gazette* reprinted the article in August 1916.

The Battalion left England in March 1915, going into billets near Ypres. They were speedily in action. At this period the Germans were using asphyxiating gas and its effect on unprotected soldiers was almost too terrible to describe. On April 24th the 8th with other troops were ordered to stem the German onslaught at the point where the French and Canadian lines joined. They were to hold the trenches on the Gravinstafel Ridge near St. Julian which they did until attacked by gas.

Sir John French wrote that the whole of the line held by the French Division was rendered incapable by the gas attack. Smoke and fumes hid everything from sight and hundreds of men were thrown into a comatose or dying condition. The whole position had to be abandoned.

Lieut-Col William Garner, commanding the 4/8th Middlesex Regt, who was himself wounded, gave an account of the fighting saying after the Germans gassed out the French the Middlesex were sent up in support of a British battalion that had also been driven out of trenches by gas. On the 25th the 8th counter-attacked and recaptured the trenches, losing five officers killed and three wounded besides 100 men. "Our men did not give way; they stood firm as they have always done. I am proud to have commanded such men."

In this battle and the subsequent May 24th action, the 8th lost nearly half its strength, killed, wounded or missing. A number were invalided home suffering from gas poisoning.

Captain T. F. Chipp was lying wounded in hospital when he heard his company had returned to the trenches. He insisted on being stretchered to where his men were fighting and continued to command them. He had the spirit of a true 'Die-Hard'.

7 May 1915. *Chiswick Times*
Letters from the Front.

We printed last week, letters received by a Chiswick resident from his son who was wounded in the fighting round Ypres. Earlier letters received were the following:

'We fell in at 7.30pm on the 15th, and my section, with others, were detailed to carry ammunition to the front line trenches. The transports cannot get nearer than three miles from the front. The roads are absolutely full of holes, nearly all full of water and big enough some of them to put a cart in, from the German shells. It is heavy work carting ammunition. We have two of us to a box. There are carrying cords each side of the box, which almost cut off one's fingers and we had changed hands very many times. It is of course pitch dark. No lights of any kind, naturally, can be used. Even on the roadway there are old trenches to cross, sometimes by a single plank, and when there is no water in them we scramble down and up and again.

Then when we got off the road, there is a good mile to walk over ground at the rear of our trenches, where generally the pairs carrying the boxes have to walk one behind the other along ridges about a foot wide between the shell holes. One or the other frequently slips and goes into a hole, occasionally up to his knees in water. All this time at the rear of the trenches, there is nothing to protect you from the view of the enemy except the darkness, and they and our people are throwing up fire balls all the time, so it is not by any means what one could call a pleasant or safe job. At one spot we have to scramble over a heap of ruins of buildings, all loose bricks and tiles, at another place through a hole in a wall made by a shell, so you can appreciate that, as they say in Canada, it is some tough stunt.

The most disagreeable part however, is the continued shelling. Rifle and machine gun fire, although not by any means pleasant, is not so bad as the shells the enemy are firing at quite close range – you hear the bang, swish, burst in quick succession. At night we see the lash of the burst and at day the smoke – we get both shrapnel and lyddite chucked at us – and it has come too close for some of our fellows.'

The second letter says:

'I am just commencing a letter to you this afternoon, having just had breakfast. I am lying down in a dug out (it is not high enough to sit upright in) underground. We are in a pretty tough place this time.

I will commence telling you how we have been getting on since we left our rest billets on Wednesday the 14th. We fell in in full marching order, carrying our own tinned rations, water, and everything we possessed, including of course such little extras as we had purchased at one o'clock pm. My pack was a fearful weight. We marched along, and the colonel gave my company an address, saying we were in for the toughest job we had yet had, and hoping we would come through all right. Then we boarded L.G.O.C. (London General Omnibus Company) motor omnibuses, which took us about 5 or 6 miles. Then started our march about 3pm.

By George, it was some heavy march! We were going steadily on and on, and did not reach our present whereabouts till 11pm at night. We had been up since 5 in the morning. Can you imagine how fagged we were? The last three halts we had, almost everyone went down flat in the road to have a rest. At the early stages of the march at the halts, I was careful to take off my pack, because in my canteen I had an open tin of condensed milk and one of 'café au lait', but in the end I did not worry about the stuff spilling; a nice mess I found in my canteen! At last the weary march was over. Thank goodness the Germans had not planned an attack for that night – I fear they would have found the Canadians easy meat – as I heard one describe us over the trenches once – on that occasion.

Well my company is acting as reserve this time so we did not go to the front-line trenches, but crawled into our underground holes about 400 yards behind. Not to rest long, however! After an hour's sleep we were hauled out (I was half asleep for the first few minutes) to draw rations. Then, at 3.30am we had to 'stand to' till daybreak, after which, thank goodness, we were through till next night. It is a weird sort of position we are in now. We dare not show even our head outside our dug-out during daylight. We are underground the whole day long. The German artillery have the exact range of every spot all round here, and are shelling us day and night. Apparently, however, they do not know the exact locality of our reserve dug-outs, and if we were to show ourselves then aeroplanes would spot us, and we should get hell. Well, all day yesterday we simply slept and slept and slept. It was quite a treat for the bursting shells to wake you up and to feel you could go to sleep again. At last, however, dusk came and it was time to do our 'day's' work all night.'

Working men's church club members. A further batch of letters from members of Chiswick Working Men's Church Club, received by Mr. T.A. King, Hon. Sec, who has kindly sent us the following extracts.

Gunner C.A. Faulkner, 37th Howitzer Battery, 5th Division, writes from 'Somewhere in France.'

'The German aeroplanes are very active now the weather is finer. We were relieved from a position defending Ypres – about a mile out – and we had three days' 'rest', as they call it, at Popperinge, where on Friday evening a German aeroplane passed over at 5 o'clock, and dropped three bombs, killing ten of our soldiers and wounding thirty others – civilians and soldiers. Our battery passed through the place afterwards, and the poor people were terror-stricken. We are now back in this position to the --- of Ypres town, which was a beautiful town with a fine cathedral some time ago, but one can't say much for its beauty now, as the place is continually shelled. This part has been occupied by the French and Belgians all through the war, and I leave you to guess the condition of the place.

We are working very hard from 5.30 reveille to late at night, making cover for our guns and ammunition wagons, building some sort of stable coverings for our horses and collecting all the timber for the horses to stand on, otherwise they would soon be troubled with greasy hocks............ Of course all our movements of troops have to be at night. Very pleasant indeed for our poor feet on these terrible cobble roads, especially if you suffer from corns. The men are passing along now, singing their favourite songs. One battalion passed along with mouth organs and some tin drums for a band and it sounded very well too.

Please thank the kind members for their fine box of shag, which I am sorry to say is all gone.... The nice parcels of delicacies some of the chaps receive make me feel terribly hungry. I shall have to try the Chiswick tradesmen, I think.'

Driver A.R. Hoskins, Royal Field Artillery, in a letter to Mr. King says:

'As you see, I am still in the land of the living, but I really wonder at it, for in this place you have every chance of getting killed, what with the fight for food, having to do with horses that have not been taught manners, and the conditions of the weather. Then there is the riding school. The place is a death trap. They do not intend that you shall be ordinary riders, but trick riders, riding without use of hands and lying flat on the horse's back. I have come a cropper while I was trying to execute this last order. The saddle and all came with me, and I can tell you that it has done me no good. In fact, I think to sign on the club would not be a bad plan. They have sent all our best-behaved cattle to the front, and have given us some remounts to mind, and they are keeping us busy. They seem to think they must put their feet in the manger, before they commence to eat, and to kick you out of the stall as soon as you have fed them.

Things at ----- are far different from those we enjoyed at Mill Hill Barracks, where cleanliness was the first thought. I have hopes presently of being able to give you an account of life in another barracks in England. There were about 300 left here during last week. They mostly went to Woolwich and they will shortly leave for the front.

Private J. Barnes, in a letter dated April 9th:

'We have been rather busy out here. I am sure our regiment will do their best to uphold the traditions of our race, and it has never been known for any of our regiments to do their work other than fearlessly. We all hope to come back to England safely. Anyway it is up to England to win this war, and win it we shall do. I feel sure about that.'

In conclusion, he says he will be pleased to accept any cigarettes sent out, on behalf of himself and his section.

7 May 1915. *Chiswick Times*

Private A.W. Hall, 8th Middlesex Territorials, killed at Hill 60.

The news comes from his brother Fred, who is in the same battalion. Letters recently received by his parents.

16th April 'I have had a chance of shooting the Huns. I have been in the trenches and know now exactly what a regular soldier's life is like. When we went into the trenches we fought side by side with the Middlesex regulars, and fine soldiers they are. Fred and I are always in the same town, and we always share our parcels of 'fags'. We always show our letters from home to one another. It doesn't make much difference to our fellows – mud or water they keep smiling. I don't go into the trenches with my company now, but have to learn the way in and out and then go back to headquarters, and when any of the officers want to go up, have to take them, and the same with the rations. We don't get any rest, and it is a responsible job to get 200 men in safely. Last time I took in reliefs I had one man wounded out of 198, but it was only a slight wound. All the scouts in the battalion have these kinds of jobs now.'

His brother Fred, who is in the quartermaster's stores of the 8th Middlesex, writes, dated *18th April*:

'We arrived here yesterday morning at 7 o'clock and our guns started bombarding the town the Germans are occupying and we captured about 2,000 prisoners and a hill. The guns have not finished yet and it is 12am. Our battalion came out of the trenches on Friday night and arrived at their billets at 4am and had to 'stand to' until 7 o'clock, and then marched nine miles. They were completely knocked up. About 9.30 last night, the 'Alarm' went and all the troops in the town turned out, and we had to 'stand by' for further orders. They carry the old name of 'Die Hards' well. I don't go into the trenches myself, but carry the food to within 200 yards of the trenches, and two shells burst within 150 yards of us the other night. The house we are billeted in has been partly blown to pieces. The shells are going over us now and the guns are at work.'

20ᵗʰ *April*   'On Sunday we had it all right, our heavy guns bombarding the German trenches, and on Monday the Germans gave it us hot, but we were moving from the town at the time, and saw five shells burst quite close. Our new billet was in pigsties, but we moved from them and bivouacked in an orchard, and are quite comfortable. I have run against a lot of men from Twickenham I knew before the war broke out.'

7 May 1915. *Chiswick Times*

The death is reported, but not officially confirmed of Private W. Brown, of the 8ᵗʰ Middlesex Regiment, one of the assistant masters at the Council School, Teddington.

Private W. Brown wrote to Mr. G.H. Orton at Teddington, dated April 18ᵗʰ:

°Perhaps you would like a short description of our last parade to the trenches. We were billeted in a barn (very salubrious with pigs and cows beneath, scenting the night air during our slumbers). We parade at 5.45pm laden with food, tins of meat, bread, tea, sugar, bacon, cheese, water and dried pea soup, as much as we can carry. Roll call. Off we go, and march six miles. Around us in horseshoe fashion fireworks, like star shells illuminate the sky. We halt once or twice. At length we reach a village about the size of Whitton. It is now one desolation – one mass of intertwining debris. Here we add to our weight by carrying for another two miles, gallon jars of water, sacks of charcoal and coke, or packs of fifty sandbags. Each man with a full pack, with rifle and other extras, has about a half hundredweight. We are pack horses, I can tell you.

In single file we proceed, dodging shell holes filled with water. Sometimes we slip and flounder in them and come up smiling. Bullets from the trenches, whizzing and whistling above, around and below. Nearly every time, someone gets wounded – going in or coming out. After doing a mile and three quarters we come to the communication trench leading to the firing trench. Here I come a cropper. I slipped gracefully and dignified into an old trench five feet deep and filled with water. Craddock (St Stephen's) pulled me out, and dripping with slime and water, I arrived in the firing trench. The night was cold. We relieved the 3rd Middlesex. As the stars went up we popped our heads and saw as clearly as in the daylight the German trench, running horseshoe fashion 20 yards away. Commenced filling sandbags. In places the trench was only one sandbag thick, and the bullets came through. All the time we worked the bullets cracked and whizzed above us. By dawn we had made our part of the traverse absolutely bullet proof.

'Ah! The dawn came with rosy blush; a skylark soared aloft between the trenches as if eager to split its tiny throat and poured forth in divine ecstasy its song of matins. We breakfasted. In a small tobacco tin we put our fat, add a little rifle rag, set fire to it, and in 20 minutes the water boils, and then we sup the cup that cheers. Still we fill sandbags.

No-one sleeps at night. No one enters the dug-outs either. All are on the alert for sounds of a charge or digging for sacking purposes. An officer comes round to see that all are alert. During the three days we were in the traverse, we filled enough sacks to make a semi-circle wall four feet high. Each set of occupiers of the trench must leave it better for their occupation. Suddenly the Germans fire at the same spot in the same sandbag, rip it up of course, and another one must be placed there. Who said the Germans cannot shoot? Head up one minute and hospital or grave follows. Our officer threw hand grenades into their trenches and they retaliated. Our casualties were heavy, especially in the 'B' and 'C' companies. Last night we expected an attack. At midnight we were relieved by the 2nd Cheshires and at 3am the attack came, and was repulsed with heavy losses. Since then heavy artillery bombardment has taken place.'

21 May 1915. *Acton Gazette*

Death & Glory. Two Acton brothers give their lives for their country.

A South Acton family has given two sons for our country. Both died on Sunday 9th May, 'fighting bravely to the last'.

Corporal William H. Belsten was aged 24. He was attached to the 13th County of London (Kensington) Regiment. In civilian life he was an assistant master at St Paul's School, Brentford. In September last he enlisted and by February was at the front, and passed through the struggle of Neuve Chapelle.

His brother Walter, a year younger and a private in enlisted on 5th August last, up to which time he had worked as a carpenter. By 18th November, he was in the trenches, and in one terrible struggle he was the only man left out of his section. Both were Acton boys, and had lived all their years with their parents, Mr.& Mrs. W.H. Belsten of 8 Colville Road, South Acton.

On Friday last, Mr. & Mrs. Belsten received unofficial intimation that both had been killed in the same action somewhere in France on Sunday 9th May; and this news was officially confirmed early this week. The first news came from a friend, one of seven men left out of a whole platoon. The letter read:

'Dear Mrs. Belsten, It is with the deepest regret that I am writing to tell you of the death of your two sons, both of whom were killed in action on Sunday May 9th. I am writing now to express, not my own personal sympathy only, but that of the seven men left in the platoon to which your brave sons were attached. We send you our poor, but heartfelt sympathies in the great blow which you all have to bear. Your sons died bravely fighting to the last, and the memory of their courage and bravery we shall never cease to remember. I pray that God in His never-failing goodness will give you His great consolation. The Kensington Battalion did their duty well. The casualties for obvious reasons I cannot give you yet; but you will undoubtedly see by the papers.'

The last letters

On May 8th, the day before his death, William wrote:

'I am still in the pink, and am writing this back in the billets after our victory. We never expected to be here now. Yesterday, everything was ready for the great attack, and in the usual run our battalion would have made a lasting name for itself, for we were given the most important position along the line, and our platoon was leading the attack. Our job was to take three lines of trenches, and then a farm, and then dig ourselves in...... If I am alive after the battle, I will tell you all about it.

We have been in the firing line for the past four days. It is an absolute miracle that up till now, not one of our chaps has been hit. Not far from us, the Germans rumbled a working party, and turned a machine gun on them – 6 were killed and 14 wounded. Another regiment had a patrol out – 6 men and a corporal. The Germans spotted them, and about 20 crept out, got behind them and clubbed five, and stabbed the other two. Three wounded got back to tell the tale.

We never know from one minute to the next when we shall be called home. I have told you all this because I want you to pray for us even more during the next few days. It is a comfort which I shall never be able to describe, to feel and know that so many are sending up their prayers on our behalf. God knows we have very little time ourselves..... For some reason the attack has been put off, but when it does, the whole Empire will ring with the news, and Neuve Chapelle will never be forgotten. And now I must say 'Au Revoir', not 'Good-bye' for I have a sort of feeling that, as at Neuve Chapelle, and in fact since I have been out here, I shall somehow come through all right.'

Walter wrote on the same day:

'We are preparing for a big move, and no doubt, will be right in the middle of it by the time you receive this... ......I have written to the Vicar (the Rev. W.A. Macleod) asking for prayers, for we have no strength except in God. How weak we are without Him! I was able to attend Holy Communion this morning, though I have been very busy for the past few days......... Don't worry; for God will keep us safe from all evil. May He comfort you and bless you. We shall very likely get a bit of leave if this move comes off successfully, so I am looking forward to seeing you soon.'

A friend says of both William and Walter Belsten: 'they were both church workers at All Saints' South Acton and dear Christian young fellows; eager and willing in God's service. It has been an awful shock to us. Only last Wednesday a letter was read to the C.E.M.S (of which they were members) asking our prayers.'

The Gazette understands that the action which claimed these two noble lives was led by Major Stafford, a brother of Rev. R.G. Stafford, curate at All Saints Church, South Acton. On Sunday evening at All Saints; appropriate and sympathetic reference to the bereavement sustained by the parish was made in the course of a sermon by the Rev. Austin Thompson of St Peter's Church, Ealing. Mr. and Mrs. Belsten and family desire to return their sincere thanks to all the numerous friends who have sent letters and messages of sympathy in their great bereavement.

4 June 1915. *Acton Gazette*
Writing to his father, Mr. A.M. Drury, of 'Redcroft', Horn Lane, Acton, Private Arthur L. Drury says:

'We've been in the trenches for the last 12 days, and don't look like coming out yet either. We've done four days in firing line, and the rest in reserve. As you surmise, we are in the big scrap; in fact we were told it was the greatest battle the world has ever known. Last Sunday week, it started. We were in the reserve trenches. The bombardment started at 6am, and lasted three hours in our part of the line.

You can't imagine what the noise is like – we had to put cotton wool in our ears or the drums would have burst. There were, I was told, over 300 guns engaged, firing as hard as they could, and the same number of shells bursting, so you can guess there was some row. Of course, we know very little of what happened, as the scrap has continued since, and there have been bombardments every day and night. The other night we saw a wonderful sight. It was about 1.30 when a green flare went up on our left. Immediately both sides started sending up their white flares right along the line as the green light was evidently a signal of some sort. We were in support on rather higher ground, and could see about 10 miles of the line and these hundreds of flares (which described a large course in the air and fell near the enemy's line) made a wonderful sight.

Then the guns started – flashes all round the horizon – and the flashes of the bursting shells over the trenches made a bright flickering light all over the country. When this died off a bit, and the noise of the guns was less, we could hear the crackling of the infantry firing rapid in the trenches, and rattle of the machine guns. It was the most wonderful sight I've ever seen or am ever likely to see. The noise, too, is one which can never be found under any other conditions.

At the present moment, we are in support; there are no trenches here, as it is more or less marshland, but the lines consist of breastwork of sandbags. Just behind our lines are some ruined houses, and we have slept the last two nights in these; no windows or doors and we have no blankets; so it's none too warm. The place is one mass of mud, as it's been raining continuously for about four days. You can guess what it's like in the trenches, when I say that being marshy, we've got several wells in our trench, and the water, which we use for cooking, is only two feet below the surface.

We are getting pretty rotten time in the trenches. We stand to arms between 7 & 8pm in case of attack at dusk, and then do one hour on and one off until 2.30am, when it begins to get light, and we stand to arms until 4am. The hour off duty too, is usually spent in putting up fresh sandbags, fetching rations, water etc. During the day too, we fill sandbags etc so we don't get much time off. Until the night before last, I didn't have more than 15 hours sleep in 10 days, and I don't know how I managed to keep on night after night, but half-an-hour's sleep snatched now and again refreshed me wonderfully. However, I'm all right again now. We saw a regular regiment do a charge on our left a day or two ago. It was beautiful to see. The Germans ran out of their trenches like a lot of rabbits. The prisoners they've taken here are mostly old men and boys. A rotten over-fed looking crowd they are.

15 May 1915. *Chiswick Times*
Letters to the Rev. Oldfield.

Trumpeter R. Squair. British Expeditionary Force.

'I regret to hear that Llew Davies is killed. I myself nearly added to the list last Friday, but I happened to be one of the lucky ones. I only felt the heat of the burst. The shell went off between me and an infantryman, he being wounded and I never got a scratch; nor was my horse hit. We are getting on very well here – slow, but sure – the same old thing each day. The Germans open fire on us with about 10 or 11 rounds of shrapnel and we congratulate them with about 100, and they soon stop arguing with us then. I have been looking out for some of the Chiswick men, but have only come across one.

I have got a German helmet, and am after another; if I get it I will send it home to you. The boys go after them for keepsakes. We had a lot of prisoners go by yesterday. I don't know if they understand me, but I told them they were unlucky; the only thing they can win is the Iron Cross.'

Lance Corporal E. Wiles. BEF.

'I am glad the boys are joining the colours. I have been looking out for anybody I know who comes from Chiswick. There is one in my company. His name is Barnes, from Dale Street, and we keep each other company.'

Private G. Anstiss ('Syko'). BEF.

'I think we have got them beat now. They have to poison us with gas now, but we are sure to win, as everything we have done is human – that is more than they can say, sir. Thank you for your kindness in thinking of one of your old boys .... Mrs. H. sends me the 'Chiswick Times'. Thank you, Sir.'

Gunner W. Alexander. BEF.

'I enjoy reading the 'Chiswick Times' and read it at times when I should be doing my work and, of course, get a telling off by our signaling instructor. There is not much fighting around here at present, but a lot of fighting goes on our left about nightfall and about two hours after daylight every day. I wish the boys of the old Brigade every success.'

Trumpeter W. Jones. Royal Field Artillery. BEF.

'Am quite well; the weather is keeping lovely. Would be all right if it were a holiday. Things have been very exciting lately. Get plenty of souvenirs from the German guns. You can hear them coming buzzing over, then a big bang. Then off we go for pieces of shell.'

Parcels for the BEF

If under 12oz, parcels for troops abroad are sent cheapest by letter post, the rate for which is 1d per ounce. Rev. A.E. Oldfield asks us to mention this, as many poor people appear to have paid for parcels rate – 3lb: s, 7lb: 1s 4d, 11lb: 1s 7d – for quite light articles, such as having brushes and buttons.

A rumour corrected

The statement that Private Arthur Llewellyn Davies was killed by gas is quite untrue and the rumour has caused much annoyance to his relatives. Davies was killed by shrapnel when taking rations to the trenches.

4 June 1915. *Chiswick Times*

Letters to Thomas King, Secretary, Chiswick Working Men's Church Club.

<u>Frank Baynes</u>. Belgium. Royal Army Medical Corps.

He is on three weeks rest in glorious weather. 'Three nights ago the Germans brought their awful gases into action again. We saw some nasty sights. When you see poor fellows struggling for breath it seems worse than when they are severely wounded. Respirators are proving a great help. The feeling out here is very bitter against the Germans for using the gas, and everyone seems to think we should retaliate on the same lines, and very quickly too.

We had to go to a dangerous position to fetch some wounded. A shell hit one of the ambulances but we and the patients got away alright. Our work of stretcher bearing has to cease at two o'clock in the morning, as it is light then and we could be easily seen from the German lines.'

Ypres has not a whole building left standing. The Germans still shell the town and we have to go through the town with wounded on roads that are almost impassable.'

He enquires about the club, concerts, band performances and cricket matches. Some Wills cigarettes would be most welcome.

Private A. Perkes. Army Service Corps. Writes to his father at 25 Westcroft Square, Chiswick.

'You no doubt know we took a lot of ground, and that the French have done remarkably well. Our guns have not ceased since the 9th May. .....We are all in high spirits ..... France may be a nice place, but I am quite content to remain in England for good after this 'Cookes Tour.' I sleep on my lorry's seat. No cushions and sixteen inches wide. I do most of the cooking for six of us on an oil drum with the top cut off to make a lid. The drum is in a trench with two round tins for chimney pots and a side of petrol can for a shelf in the oven. Wet mud on the top and sides keeps the heat in. We guarantee to cook anything, from a pudding to a large joint. A petrol can cut in half is a frying pan and another makes a pot for boiling water.

Yesterday there were seven aeroplanes of ours up ..... The Germans waste ammunition trying to bring them down. Our column is attached to the French army, and goes where it is required.

They are wicked swine using gas bombs and sinking the Lusitania ..... America's attitude – too proud to go to war! Too cowardly and mean in my opinion. ..... Last Monday a lot of Jocks got too far advanced and had to surrender. The Huns took their arms away and told them to go back to their own lines. As they turned to go they turned machine guns on them and shot them down like dogs. I think we should do the same horrible things to them.

I think the war will finish before the winter ..... In spite of the gas bombs, we are whacking them.'

Private G.G. Wilkinson, 57 Glebe Street. Reports from the 10th Royal Hussars.

He lies wounded in a Northern France hospital and praises the Red Cross nurses. 'If there is such a thing as precedence in honour we think our devoted sisters should hold that exalted position ..... Their splendid work, kindness and careful attention, without any consideration of themselves through long hours of duty ..... It is a credit to their noble womanhood ..... The awful nature of some of the wounds ..... Their constant dressing which cannot be done without great pain must put an increased strain on the nerves of these ladies known to us as sisters.'

11 June 1915. *Chiswick Gazette*
Sergeant G. Davis writes from the 2nd Battalion, Middlesex Regiment (The Diehards).

'After being billeted, all non-commissioned officers were called for by their captains, and the great secret was revealed to us as to why we had had so much exercise. The Germans were going to get a mighty wallop, and the place chosen to strike at and capture was Neuve Chapelle. Maps and aeroplane photos were shown, and the parts we were to take in this great enterprise were allotted to us.

After we were told that we should have 400 guns at our back, we thought that it would be a walk-over. When we had explained to our sections what was going to be done, they were almost crazy with joy. 'Now we can smarten the parade up,' they said.

At 11pm, we marched off and about 1am we halted by the roadside to partake of tea, bacon and bread – the last meal for many a brave lad. After the meal was finished, we went to our positions. Marching in Indian file, we looked in the darkness like long black snakes; not a sound was heard and not a light shown, as slowly but surely we got there.

At last we reached the lines of breastworks close up together, which had been prepared some time before. Boom! Boom! It is 7.30. The artillery have found the range. Then the most terrible bombardment in history commences. Guns of all calibers are used. The noise is awful and it seems as if the earth is being beaten by some gigantic steam hammer. We watch the shells exploding over and in the Huns' trenches; we go mad with excitement.'

Go on, the Diehards.

Our bomb-throwers in the first trench start cake-walking and swinging their hand grenades, Indian club fashion, at the same time singing 'Allemands come out and fight' to the tune of the Marseillaise. At 8.10, the first line advances, and as they leave their trench we shout: 'Go on, the Midds! Go on, the Diehards!' They are met by terrible machine gun fire. 'Get ready, the second line,' Over they go, and get more cheering.

'Don't forget Mons, lads! Good luck!'

A handshake as one chum passes another, 'Good luck, Jim, take care of yourself.' They meet the same fate as the first, only a few getting up to a trench facing the Huns.

'Get ready, the third line, Advance!' I, having seen where our men lay thickest, determined to make my advantage in a different direction, so broke through a thick hedge on my right, jumping at it, my half platoon following me, 'Follow me, Number 2!'

Maxim Jammed

I ran as fast as the spongy ground would allow me. I made a right incline and reached an old trench of ours, which was full of Devons. I ran up the trench to an opening which led to a communication trench. Here I saw poor Lieutenant McFarlane, the tallest and most popular officer of ours killed. He led the bomb-throwers and made too good a target. The communication trench was full of water, but what is water after what we had experienced in the trenches? 'Come on Number 2, through here,' and we join up in the trench facing the enemy. We reached there without one of Number 2 platoon getting hit. 'Now then boys, give them hell, plug into them!' Our maxim is jammed.

'For God's sake, pass down to the Devons to bring their machine gun here quick.' The lock of our gun was examined and rectified, and just as the Devons came with their gun we got ours into action. The Devons were led by a colour-sergeant, who was bowled over as soon as he sighted the gun. All their men went down. The Germans could not find ours, and we had found out where they were situated. Then they got a peppering.

'Mons, the Battle cry!'

At last the order comes down: 'Packs off!' 'Now then boys, we are for it, Get ready, the third line!' A whistle sounds, and over the parapet we go. 'Go on, Die Hards! Don't forget Mons! Whirroo!' The sight that met our eyes almost staggered us, our poor first and second line lying in all positions. Then we saw red, we reached the barbed wire, trampled on it, cut and hacked it, the barbs cutting us in all places. We were beaten back.

'Rally boys, and at it again.' This time we won the trick, the trench was ours. 'Stop using your bayonets, take them prisoners.'

A more terror-stricken lot of men one never saw. Afterwards, the trench was cleared and the prisoners placed under escort.

Not to be killed

The next day, they gave us Jack Johnsons, coal-boxes, high explosives and shrapnel for 13 hours. At 8am, I was munching a biscuit with a man of my section. About 18 inches separated us, and a piece of shrapnel about four inches square came down between us. If it had struck our heads we should have been killed on the spot. I remarked: 'Harrison, old chap, we are not to be killed.'

11 June 1915. *Chiswick Times*
Letters to Rev. Oldfield.

Private W. Lawrence. BEF.

'.................... I have been down at --- for a week and am having a bit of a rest after eleven weeks hard work up the line, but I do not think I will be here much longer as they are sending some away every day, and my turn will come soon...............You will not have many boys to take to camp this year, if you go, but I expect next year you will have a record company, if all the old boys are spared. I am very glad that Chiswick men have done their share in this war, and also that St Mary's Company choir have upheld the reputation of St Mary's.................. and I am sure the training I got while in your company has done me a lot of good since I joined.'

Driver Jack Clarke. BEF.

'We have had very warm and exciting incidents in this neighbourhood lately, but all is fairly quiet now. I still get the 'Chiswick Times' from Mrs. E— which is a treat.......... Things are fairly successful all along our front and since the first time the gas was used we have had two more samples, but respirators are splendid and enable us to carry on for a long period before the fumes reach the nostrils and mouth. It is pitiful and yet terrible to see the destruction of such a beautiful place as ---- all in debris, and the once fine churches, factories, schools and houses all on the ground, either burnt or blown down. One danger is taking ammunitions etc up to the guns............. We have been hard at it for two months and get relieved tomorrow.'

Private C. Wrathall. Aldershot.

'I don't know when I shall be going to the front but I am one of the next draft and hope it won't be long as I am getting tired of the same thing day after day for nine months............ I am glad to say I am not for the 'gravel crushers' as I am in the machine gun section and expect to pass out in a day or two. I was surprised to see Fred Bailey is out at the front as I have been looking for him in the R.E.'

Private A. Hill. BEF.

'We are at present having a rest. The delicacies came in time for tea, so you can guess we had a fine spread. The chaps at the present are playing at leap-frog. Last night with the help of several mouth organs, we were having some dancing; so you see we are enjoying ourselves all right............. No doubt you have heard of our loss; we having lost our company officer, also several other officers. We being in support had orders to go into the firing line, but I think the Germans had us in the line, for as soon as we started they turned the maxim gun on us. Jolly hard cheese for us. It was a rush and keep your head down.'

Private G. Elsley. BEF.

'Weather is grand and I can get about on a cycle here, being under cover from the enemy. They are always shelling the village I have to pass through, so you can guess I nip through pretty quick. We have had some hard times round our quarter, but they have calmed down a bit....Saw a Zeppelin pass some way off – too far away for our guard to reach.'

18 June 1915. *Chiswick Times*
Letters to Rev. Oldfield.

Gunner R.S.J. Hamilton. B.E.F.

'............ we are having grand weather now and I hope you are getting the same. We have been having it very quiet just now, and I hope we shall make another start. Well sir, they have given us two respirators to each man to prevent the poison gases getting to the men's chests. It is very bad to get those gases down us................ We get plenty of bathing now as we do not get much firing. We are only doing about six rounds of fire each day now and so we go down for a bathe. The Germans do not send many shells into ---- now. The Chiswick Times comes every week through the kindness of a friend. It is great reading the old paper and so I don't mind the shells coming over while I am reading it......'

Gunner Walter Woodhead. 'Somewhere in France.'

'............ I am glad to hear the boys are getting on alright. We have been on the move these last few days. We are now right behind the firing line. We were very lucky when we were in action. We never had one casualty in our battery. ...... Well, sir, what is your opinion of the war? I myself do not think it will be over for some long time yet.'

Trooper Frank Sheppard. BEF.

'I am sorry I have not written before, but the reason is I have been too busy. I had a nasty accident and have been in hospital a few days but left on Sunday 30th May. I was sent from the battery to the ammunition column for more ammunition and it was very dark, about midnight and when half way on my journey the Germans started shelling the main high road, so you can guess I set off at a good pace so as not to get caught, but going so fast and being very dark, I never saw a very large hole the shells had ripped in the road, and in I went, motor and all on top of me, and the next thing I remember was that I was lying on a stretcher at one of the field hospitals, a bit shaken up and bruised. They sent me from there down country for treatment, but glad to say I feel a great deal better today. I might say the message was delivered quite safe, but by whom I cannot say............Today our division came out of action after eight weeks very hard times.'

[Following letter, dated 11 June]

'Many thanks for your letter dated 9th June. I am pleased to say I am a lot better now. I am having things a bit easy just at present as our division is resting. I saw in the Chiswick Times which Miss C sends me, that poor old Lew Davies had been killed. It is very hard, but it is for a good cause. We have been issued with a very good respirator for the next time they use the gas; they will not find it all their own way as it was before.'

Private A. Hill. BEF.

'For the past fortnight we have been indulging in a well-earned rest. I made the most of this while the chance lasted. Eventually we were called upon to go and hold a position hitherto held by the French who were relieved by troops of ours........The boys took the news that they were again for the trenches in a spirit that they are noted for. We started from our billets at 9 o'clock. As soon as we began to move the boys started into a popular refrain. We kept up the singing and laughing to within sound of rifle fire. The order was the passed down the line 'all singing to cease'. By the time we reached the trenches it was near midnight. We entered and traversed a communication trench that seemed to have no ending. After an hour's travelling we did eventually reach the end of the trench. It was far too dark to see what kind of trench we had ventured into. Imagine my surprise then, when I had a look round and saw that we were in a trench that I have never before seen the equal of. To describe some of the dug-outs would be to call them trench palaces. One particular dug-out was the masterpiece of construction, having a door, window, and even a good quality and quantity of furniture. The one that I and my friend occupied was strewn with straw, with a screen at the entrance for protection against rain, wind or sun. We were in this trench some 18 hours. We then moved up to the front line of trenches. During the 48 hours we were there we only experienced a few small shells, called 'whiz-bangs' and a few stray shots.'

Killed in Action:

We regret to state that amongst the <u>Rev. A.E. Oldfield's</u> old boys killed are:

- <u>Sergeant Ernest Edwin Moss</u>, 2nd Battalion, Royal Fusiliers on 14 May

- <u>Private Edmund F. Bryant, 3rd Battalion, Royal Fusiliers</u>

- <u>Lance-corporal Clement</u> <u>John Amullar</u>, 2nd Battalion, Royal Fusiliers, on 28 May

<u>Sapper Jack Jennings</u> has been wounded.

<u>18 June 1915.</u> *Chiswick Times*
Private S. Archibold, 2nd London Div. (Cyclists). Writes from Towchester Hospital to his mother at 406, Chiswick High Road.

'This is a lovely place here, and is kept by a lady who is a jolly good sort. You ask me for experiences......... I can tell you one or two. We were in with the Irish Guards at the time. They are funny chaps, like most Irishmen; splendid fighters, though. Well, one of the Guards suddenly yelled out, 'Oh begorrah! They've kilt me!' and started feeling all over his body to find where he had been hit. Then he called out 'All right sergeant, I'm not hit.' But he was, though – a bullet had just scratched a piece of skin off the bridge of his nose – a close shave for him. He looked very funny, I can tell you, feeling for broken bones.

Another incident shows how long the Germans will keep their rifles trained on a certain spot. A chap put his mess tin on the breastworks. The German knew he would want it for breakfast, and waited for him to take it down. The chap didn't hurry in doing so, and the bullet went clean through the mess tin, and his arm as well. But he won't do it again. I had a piece of shrapnel that went through the leg of a chap who was standing next me. When a shell comes over we run for cover and if there isn't any, we have to flop down on our stomachs and trust that it won't hit us. This chap flopped down by my side when the shell burst and a piece went through his thigh, over my legs and buried itself in the sandbags, where I found it, so I thought myself jolly lucky. Still - these things happen every day and in a little time you take no notice.'

18 June 1915. *Chiswick Gazette*
Lieut. Tweedy Smith writes to his family in Ealing – Collecting the Dead

'When I wrote last Sunday, we were 'standing to' which we continued to do day and night until Tuesday. We were billeted about four miles behind the lines, waiting for an attack. We were in reserve and did nothing in particular.

On Tuesday morning I was selected as 'liaison' officer to go to headquarters to wait for any orders and to make myself generally useful. In the middle of the morning I received orders for two companies of the Queen's to go up to the trenches at once. I cycled back to the colonel, and within an hour, we were slogging up the busy main road in the broiling hot sun.

On the way up, I passed my old friend Stammers resting outside a cottage. He lives at Acton. The last time we met was at the Law Society before the war, and although I could not stop to speak we chatted together for a few minutes as we were marching. It was awfully cheerful to see him again. He is in the motor machine gun section and is having an exciting time although he only arrived in the country ten days ago. Whenever a part of the line is pressed, he jumps on his motor bike with his machine guns, and rushes up there, and when he has had enough of it with shelling, or the Bosches have got their fill of bullets, he rides back again ready to dash to any other portion of the line. He was in good form. I expect he enjoys it better than law, which is more than I do.

We got up about 3 o'clock and halted just behind the firing line while our company commander went forward to get orders. Meanwhile I reconnoitered the position from a neighbouring artillery observing station from which I could see the German fire trenches, with their communications. I watched the shelling of an isolated farm which the enemy still held in spite of it being a ruin. It bristled with machine guns, so that every time our infantry assaulted it, they were repulsed. We were in the centre of the country, where some of the heavy fighting of the past fortnight has taken place. It is even flatter than Flanders usually is, and it is so low-lying that it is impossible to dig trenches proper here; after two feet down, water is struck. All the fortifications are breastworks, which are more vulnerable to artillery fire. It is the usual type of populous country, many red-bricked houses and well-to-do farms scattered all over the landscape. We have halted under cover of some tumble-down houses, and the Germans are 800 yards away. Shells are flying over our heads.

In this respect things have altered since the winter. Then the artillery used to open fire at regular intervals, say at 11 in the morning, then after lunch for an hour at 3, and again after tea. During this time our gunners exchange compliments for half an hour or so and then shut up for a bit. They used to rest and would not allow shelling to interfere with their lunches. Now things are different......We have got superiority of artillery fire here. The guns boom the whole time, they never cease, at every second a gun speaks. Day and night it goes on, but although it never seems to stop and one gets used to the unceasing screeching, one is occasionally reminded of it by an extra-unusually loud report. On the other hand, the Germans fire comparatively infrequently, only firing when there is an attack going on or a good target is presented to them. It is evident that plenty of shells are needed to keep the pot a-boiling.

We move on a bit further to get the men into dug-outs, as an attack is just going to begin. We are just in front of a battery which begins a hellish noise, to which the Germans reply, trying to find out exactly where it is. With all their searching, they do not manage to spot it; then they drop a few shells around us, three of which fall uncomfortably near. We have 3 or 4 men wounded, and I got a shower of debris on my back which shook me up a bit, but no damage done. After a couple of hours of this, a digging party is sent out to collect the wounded and bury the dead. All night long the stretcher bearers work hard at trundling wounded along on the wheeled stretchers. At dusk, I split my platoon up into working parties and take them out to search for the dead and collect their effects and equipment and bury them. It is a ghastly job.

It was reserved for the morrow to learn what an advance really means to the advancers. Although our superior artillery must give the Germans hell and cause tremendous havoc in their ranks, yet an advance is not all on our side, as you shall read. Remember that, however heavy our casualties are the Germans must be heavier. It is not so much the ground gained that counts, but which side knocks out the most men.

We were awakened at dawn after a couple of hours heavy sleep in spite of the bombardment. Another officer told me that Johnson – an awfully good sort and one of the favourites of the mess, also a very handsome fellow with curly hair – had been wounded in the night with some of his men. We had had supper together just before one o'clock, and he had jokingly said that it would be hard luck if any of us got knocked out before having a 'go' at the beggars. However we did not think anything very much of it, as a man is considered lucky if he gets wounded in this business. As we were going up, we saw poor old Johnny being brought down on a stretcher. He was dead. He had received shrapnel in his back while getting out of a trench to bring in some wounded. Two men with him were severely wounded, one has since died.

When we arrived at the trenches at dawn, we could make out the extent of the damage done to the front line trenches, which we could not gauge a few hours previously. Every section of breastwork had been blown in by the accurate shooting of the German artillery. Our old front line from which we advanced was in an indescribable mess. Dug-outs blown in, breastworks down, rifles, ammunition, bombs, spades, stretchers, hundreds of tins of bully beef – there had evidently not been time to distribute the day's rations before clearing out of the trenches – everything in an indescribable litter. Our men had been pounded in their breastworks, and when they had advanced by climbing over the top of the parapet, they were peppered with machine guns; half way between the two trenches, the infantry had found it impossible to get along, and had built up a fire position in a little long dip of about four inches in the ground. There one could see a long line of dead men with their rifles pointing towards the enemy. And in spite of all this, our infantry took the German trenches. Men scramble for the slightest piece of cover when they are under such a fire.

We begin to collect all this litter and pick up the dead, which are strewn about the field.........As the sun begins to rise and it gets clearer, there is danger that a vigilant observer may spot us, so we have to knock off work about six in the morning. We had been working for 7 or 8 hours and been up since very early on the previous morning, so you may imagine we were very tired when we marched back to the ruined village of -----------. We found it deserted, and I found a couple of houses not quite so ruined as the rest in which to quarter my platoon. By 8 o'clock, the officers had breakfasted in the largest and only house that had not been hit. My campaigning experience made me choose a cupboard in the centre of the house for a shakedown; it was protected by two brick walls on nearly all sides, which was a great comfort. In spite of the continuous firing by the heavy batteries by the side of the house and just behind it, which shook the house to its foundations every time they let off, I managed to get a couple of hours' sleep before the Germans started shelling the village. Then I thought discretion the better part of valour, and took shelter on the leeward side of the house. I managed to get another good sleep in a somewhat safer room in the afternoon. I also had the luxury of a mail bag for my feet and some straw for my hips. While I was with my platoon after tea, making arrangements for the night's work, a shell landed on top of the house, knocking down a heap of bricks, slates and debris on us. We rushed out of the house, getting nothing more than bricks on our heads and shoulders. I was surprised how little real solid bricks hurt when you have other things to think about. After waiting in a cellar for a short time, we paraded in the village street while the shells, some of them lyddite, were bursting about us. Luckily no-one was hit except one man in my platoon, so we moved off back to work.

Before it was dusk, I had marshalled my men in working parties at the end of a communication trench opposite the German lines. The field was strewn with dead and we got out to try to get as much work done as possible before it was completely dark. I had no sooner got my men working, when rifle fire rang out; one man dropped dead and one was wounded high up through the left leg. I lay down in the open while some of my men crept back to the trench. Soon the Germans stopped firing on us, and I got the working parties going again. We were then permitted to carry on for over half an hour, while we could stroll about the open, working hard at covering up these dead men. Then apparently the Germans thought we ought to have finished, so they gave us another burst of rifle fire. We lay down and waited while the bullets flew over our heads. As we did not budge they apparently telephoned back to their batteries for some shrapnel shells burst over us. We stuck it for about 10 minutes and then I ordered the retirement into our own trench. It was not any good being made into mutton together with the other fellows lying out there. I managed to get the men to crawl back instead of running. It was quite exciting crawling from cover to cover, from shell hole to shell hole and running along ladders over disused trenches full of water, while the Bosches had free shots at us.

We had to wait half an hour at the top of the communication trench, while the shelling went on before we could move. Shrapnel has a distinctly unpleasant sound, it buzzes and pings so. It would not stop, so I got the platoon down to the end, and counted up the men under cover of some ruined houses near a road. It was dark, and you can imagine my anxiety when I found there were six missing. After a lot more waiting, the shelling ceased and I got into billets about 11pm. The missing men turned up later, having been mixed up with another platoon. That night I slept soundly.

Next day was spent quietly visiting some heavy batteries, and being fine. I made a reconnaissance from the attic of the tallest house in the village. Part of our work during the rest time of the day consisted in sorting all the papers etc of the dead officers. I went through a small proportion of the officers who have been put out of action during the past fortnight in these parts. As you may imagine it was a most pathetic business.

As dusk drew near, we went forward, but before we got up to the front line, the Germans started an attack, to which our artillery immediately replied with an intense bombardment. We got the men under cover and then I had a good view of the show. Remember this was a German attack and when we looked towards their lines it looked as if they were attacking with gas. Every soldier now wears a respirator and they look funny when they are not in use; they are worn around the hat-band over the cap badge. On examining the position with glasses, we could see that it was a curtain of shrapnel and shells over the German lines. The bombardment was so intense, that our shells were dropping in every section of trench and a huge greyish-yellow cloud hung over them, caused by the bursting shells. We moved into reserve trenches and waited for three hours. Although we were sitting in front of a battery we only got about half a dozen shells anywhere near us.

After the show quieted down a bit, we returned to our ruined houses, but my day's work was not finished, even then. One of my corporals was attacked with colic, which doubled him up in such agony, that it distressed me very much. It was the result of sitting in a damp trench. I rushed round the village to find a doctor, but none was nearer than the nearest dressing station, three quarters of a mile away, where I had to take this writhing man. It was midnight and the shrapnel was bursting around the batteries past which I had to go – most unhealthy it was until I got inside. There were a couple of padres waiting to comfort the wounded as they came down; one was a Roman Catholic and one a Church of England. They both shared a fuggy little room with the young doctor who attended my corporal. It was the weirdest consultation I have ever attended. We could hardly hear ourselves speak for the shells bursting around, and the noise of the guns. I did not get a shake down until one that night, and we were on the road at five in the morning on the way back to real billets. We are now standing to at half an hour's notice. There are rumours of a big show tonight.

There has been an attack every night during the past week, but today things have been quiet and I suppose that it is the calm before the storm.'

18 June 1915. *Chiswick Times*
Letter from one of 1ˢᵗ Battalion Royal Fusiliers.

'After nearly 10 months in the trenches in France and Belgium, I write a few words to the 'Times' asking our friends at home if they still feel safe – those who will not join us, and help to push the Hun out or, better still, wipe him out? I have seen a few things considering I have been on the Marne, Aisne, at Armentieres, Ypres, Soissons and Villers Cotterettes, and other little shuffles.

I have seen the results of gas and a lot of the atrocities perpetrated by the Huns, and I ask all to help and send us plenty, and to spare, of gas shells, high explosives, and anything, in fact, that will rub them out.

As I write, 'Jack Johnsons' are pushing bits of my trench in, only 25 yards away to my right and shaking dirt on me.'

18 June 1915. *Chiswick Times*

Letters received by Mr. Thomas A. King, Hon. Sec of the Chiswick Working Men's Church Club.

Private Frank A. Baynes. Letter dated 18 June.

'We had a 15 miles march to get here but did it in fairly easy stages. The roads out here are not at all pleasant to march on, as the greater portion is made of cobble stones and are somewhat rough at intervals. Perhaps it is as well that they are, as I am afraid they wouldn't last long if they were made on the lines of London roads.

We expect to go back to active work again soon and in a way I shall be pleased when we do, as one gets tired of endless fatigues etc. Our daily routine is: Reveille 5.30am, parade 6.30am, fatigues until breakfast time, 8am, fatigues again at 9.30am till dinner time, 1 o'clock. Each day at 2.30 we have a respirator parade. At this parade we have to march and double round, wearing our respirators to accustom ourselves to breathing through the mouth, which should be filled with the cotton waste of which the respirator is made. This is somewhat difficult at first, and after running round two or three times one feels very uncomfortable and longs to get the thing off. Of course one gets accustomed to it after a time, but I shall be glad when we get the helmets, which are much better, and are now being issued to the army.

Two of our sections are running hospitals – one for officers only and the other for the men. The other section does the majority of the fatigues such as sanitary duties, so you see we are kept fairly busy throughout the day. Fortunately we are being blessed with very fine weather just now and as we are out in the open all day we are developing enormous appetites. The general health of the boys is excellent and everyone is getting quite tanned.

In orders the other morning, the Army Order regarding the shaving of the upper lip was read out, so now the boys have got to grow a moustache. I can't imagine myself with one, and am afraid that when I return to England it will have to come off. You will be pleased to hear that another of our 'Old Boys', Freddy Barnes, has enlisted. He has joined the Royal Flying Corps. We have formed an excellent concert party in our corps, and they have given us some excellent shows. They also visited another brigade and were very well received...... You will be pleased to hear that my brother Will is going on well, and hopes to be in England soon.'

25 June 1915. *Chiswick Times*
Letters to Rev. Oldfield.
Bandsman W. Burch. BEF.

'We came out of the big fight I told you about on the ----------
at dawn. We took three lines of trenches and about 200 prisoners, including 3 officers. Our artillery started bombarding about ------
and knocked their trenches to pieces. We had our dressing station almost in the firing line and used a dug-out for the purpose. It was only pure luck that it was not knocked in as they shelled us continually after our troops had taken the trenches.... You could see nothing but black smoke and pieces flying in the air. You ought to have seen our troops jump out of the trench to charge. Our regiment was in the third line. The men were absolutely mad, and it was glorious to watch them. It was splendid. The old mob has once again made its name and proved its worth.

Our troops showed them how much grit a Britisher has got. From what I saw of the German infantry I should say they are rotten. Lot of them went on their knees to our chaps and begged for mercy........ Some of the prisoners looked properly fed up. A lot of them were mere boys, but there were also a lot of old men among them. Our battalion showed not the slightest hesitation and fairly carried all before them. They absolutely pulverised the infantry. The prisoners we took thought they were going to be shot. It shows what they do with their prisoners. I might as well tell you that our chaps would have killed the crowd of them if the officers had not stopped them. They remembered what they did to our -------- Battalion. They gassed them and then bayoneted them as they were lying helpless. The Germans used gas shells on us during the bombardment. They smell awful and would soon overcome you, but we put on our smoke helmets and stuck it........ Our commanding officer was hit in the head but refused to be dressed, and stopped with the battalion, but had to go away to hospital when we got back to camp. Our doctor was splendid; he had his coat off and sleeves rolled up and worked very hard...... I obliged by playing the bass in a band the other day.'

[the writer is acting as stretcher bearer at the front for the 3rd time after wounds – A.E.O.]

Driver S.A. Cork. Royal Garrison Artillery. BEF.

'.......... I have not been in the firing line yet, but I am not very far from it. Our battery is doing very well. The Chiswick Times arrives here every week and generally goes all round..... There is plenty to occupy one's mind here, if it is only watching the aeroplanes. In England one pays 3d and 6d to see the pictures of fighting and shells bursting; let them come here and they can see them in reality for nothing.'

Private A Gardner. BEF.

'I hope Chiswick is not nervous over the airship raids.... Our troops are doing very well at the front and I need not ask if Chiswick is ready to turn out. Dear sir, I think when the firms go on strike they should send them out here and send all the old soldiers in their place; that would soon put paid to their extra money. Then probably they would see where they were well off.'

Private C. Wrathell. 11th Hussars.

'I have passed my examination as first class machine gunner and that is the best you can get, and I have been placed on the role of trained machine gunners for the next draft. I got 85 points out of 100 for mechanism, 85 out of 100 for stoppages, 54 out of 60 for mounting and dismounting guns – that is 224 out of 260 – not so bad.

They have made me No.1 in the section and I have to see everything is done all right and get the gun into action and fire it. It is rather surprising that it takes three years to train a German machine gunner and we only get three weeks, so you see we have to make ourselves smart, as we know that when we get to the front we have not got learners to deal with. I am glad to hear Tich Smith is coming over and hope he will stop so that we can have some of our old times over again. I will let you know when I go to the front and hope it won't be long. I am glad the band has won the staff and pace stick again. I should have liked to have been there myself. Good luck to Ralph and the band.'

2 July 1915. *Chiswick Gazette*
Letter from a Dispatch Rider.

He is attached to the India contingent on the Western front with a Triumph motor cycle with 2¾" Dunlop tyres which have withstood the roads wonderfully. He reports that motor lorries supplied 125 tons of shell and 1,000,000 rounds of small arm ammunition in one afternoon. London buses shift troops around.

2 July 1915. *Chiswick Times*
Letters to Mr. Thomas A. King, Hon. Sec. of the Chiswick Working Men's Club.

Mr. King has received news of William Barton (2nd Middlesex) who is in a hospital in Lancashire, suffering from gas poisoning – he had previously been wounded – and of William Baynes (Post Office Rifles) who is now in a London hospital, having been shot through the lung.

Gunner C.A. Faulkner, writing from France to Mr. & Mrs. Gomm, thanking them for a box of cakes.

'The contents were eaten while German shells were flying about from all directions. The country is looking fine just now with growing crops. I quite expect to have to spend the summer out here at least. You would laugh to see our bivouac – two uprights and a crosspiece, with two blankets stretching across the top to the ground. It is all right while the weather is fine, but quite the reverse when wet, you can bet. Me and my mate have named it the 'Abode of Love'.

2 July 1915. *Chiswick Times*
Letters to Rev. Oldfield.

Gordon Barnes. Convalescent Camp, France.

'I was glad to receive your letter, and my wound is getting on lovely. I was hit with shrapnel just in front of the crown of the head, but it is not serious. I am glad your band won this year and I am beginning to think we cannot be beaten. I am sorry to hear Jack Jennings is in hospital, and I wonder how he likes the doctor searching for shrapnel; also I am sorry to hear of the deaths of some of our old boys. I heard our chaps had some rough fighting after they had turned the Germans out of their trenches.'

Trumpeter Squair. BEF.

'Thanks very much for the parcel you sent me. I hear that it was rumoured in Chiswick I was killed, and am glad to say it is not true. Although we have had some near escapes. We had one of our guns riddled with high explosive shrapnel last week, and the bits of shell went through our limber and four shells had a piece sticking in them; and the best of it was they did not explode, and I cannot realise how we got away without losing anyone. We have been a very lucky battery up till now, thank God. Did I tell you one of our men got the D.C.M. for mending wires under shell fire?'

9 July 1915. *Chiswick Gazette*
'Diehards' Diversions.

The diversions of some of the 1/7th Middlesex at the front are described in a letter dated June 24th from Lance-corporal

E.G. Brophy of 'B' Company of that regiment to his sister at Lower Edmonton:

'The other night some of our chaps had some fun. They went out in front of our lines and captured two German flags and 300 yards of their barbed wire. A party also went out with a bell tied round with bushes and this was stuck in the ground quite near the German trench. Attached to the bell was a wire from our trench, and at frequent intervals we would ring the bell and shout 'Waiter.' The Germans opposite us have evidently one or two who know some English for the other night we could hear them calling out "Englishmen no goot."'

All that remains of the 1/8ᵗʰ Battalion is now incorporated with the 1/7ᵗʰ.'

9 July 1915. *Chiswick Times*
Letters received by Rev. Oldfield.

Private Walter Brown. BEF.

'We are at a bit of a warm place now. They tried to blow up the trench we were in, but, thank God, they missed, they went too far and blew up the ground yards behind the trench. The Germans are a cunning lot; you can never see them but they go very near you if you happen to put your head too much above the trench; and another rotten job is getting the food up to the trenches. You have to go across an open space of ground and the bullets come whizzing over your head.......... I thought we were in for a bout. Our guns started firing away, and we were all ordered to stand to. They kept it up about an hour and then we had it a bit quiet.'

Private Arthur Neave. BEF.

'My brother came out of the trenches last Sunday after 25 days. He wrote a very cheerful letter as usual. There are several more Chiswick chaps about this quarter, and all look rather fit. My friends in Chiswick have lately had a shock, as I was reported killed. I have written to them and assured them of my safety.'

Private Fred Bailey. BEF.

'We were on the move all last Sunday, and the division has taken over a new position of the line so it has been a busy week, being at it night and day until everything was settled down. The Middlesex Territorials were stationed in the same village as us, and they had their fife and drum band, which used to play every afternoon and didn't it remind me of home! They played 'Oswald the Second', 'Imperial Eagle', and other tunes we used to play in the band. All that was lacking in ours was the bursting shells, while the Germans used to send over while they were playing. They are now doing their turn in the trenches, so we have lost our music. What is troubling us a lot now is mosquitoes. Plenty of us are walking about with eyes, arms, neck etc swollen through their bites.'

Private E. Cole.

'I am getting along famous. My wrist wound is pretty nearly healed but my toes are still painful. I should like to tell you how I got hit. On the night of the --- the fun started. Our artillery simply tore the ground up and their trenches with it, till --- -o'clock. Then the order came, 'Charge!' and over went the boys like one man. Flags went up, second line captured. Then came the worst: our artillery had not finished shelling the second line when we got caught like rats in a trap between two fires, but all went well in the finish. About 3 o'clock. Crash! My left wrist had been hit by shrapnel, so I had to retire to the dressing station with shell flying all ways, but I put my trust in God and got back quite safely but for a bullet in my toes.'

Sapper Harper Smith. BEF.

'We are having a pretty lively time of it now. We are just three miles behind the lines and the cannonading of our own and the enemy's artillery makes a beautiful although pathetic sight at night. It is also interesting to watch our aeroplanes fly over the German lines in the early morning. I should imagine that the enemy use tons of ammunition on our aircraft but rarely succeed in bringing them down. Give my kind regards to all the boys.'

Private W.A. Alexander. BEF.

'We have been on the move again, and everything seems safe in our new position. We have had two respirators issued to us, so will be well prepared for the next lot of gas they send over our lines We are again warming the Germans up, as we came into action a few days ago.'

16 July 1915. *Acton Gazette*
Private Edward Hewett killed.

Deep sympathy will be felt with Cllr R.J. Hewett and Mrs. Hewett of 87 Beaumont Rd, Acton Green, in the loss they have sustained by the news received a few days ago that their son Edward was recently killed in action in Flanders. Cllr & Mrs. Hewett have resided in Acton for over 15 years and are well known and respected in the neighbourhood.

Edward John Vincent Hewett, 19 years old, was educated at Beaumont Park & Acton Central Schools, & afterwards was in the employ of Messrs. Gosling, the well-known London butchers, later being employed in different parts of the country. Early in September, while he was in Acton, he enlisted in the London Irish Rifles and went into training at St Albans. He was sent to the front on 3rd March, and after a strenuous time, was expecting to be sent home very shortly on leave. The last letter from him was received on the morning of the day on which he was killed, 11th July. The first intimation of his death was received through the letters of the chaplain and a comrade, the latter of whom, on the 11th wrote:

'Dear Mr. Hewett, I am very sorry to say your son was killed today. Ted was with the cooks and their wagon. A shell burst just by the side of them. Six of our fellows were wounded. Ted was hit badly in the back and arm. He died about half an hour afterwards. Poor fellow! He was conscious up to the end. He died painlessly in my arms. I am a stretcher-bearer. We did all we possibly could for him. If it is any consolation to you, he died in the execution of his

duty. Ted was a chum of mine and a favourite of all our company...
His last words were 'Tell my mother and dad I was thinking of
them up to the end. God bless them both'. We all unite with our
deepest sympathy in the loss of your beloved son, who I am sure
was always a credit to you both. I hope in God's good time that
you will be consoled in the thought that he died for his King and
country. I expect we shall bury him tomorrow. I will ask a pal of
mine to make a sketch of the grave and forward it on to you. Ted
will be buried with full military honours. Our officer and sergeant-
major are going to write to you. I will give you particulars of the
funeral after it is over. Again expressing my deepest sympathy to
you both. Your beloved son's pal,

Bert Hardie.

Private Hewett's own last letter home on 3rd July was as follows:

'My dear Mother – I received your paper today. I am getting on
quite well. We are having very nice weather but a bit cold at night. I
am sending you some postcards, five in number, and write back soon
and let me know if you received them. We are cooking in the reserve
trenches and we have had plenty of shells over in the course of the
day. I hope dad is quite well and give my love to all the children.
We are coming back for a rest when we come out of the trenches
and it will be a great rest. Three of the chaps in our regiment have
won the D.C.M. for bravery when under shell fire. Today one of
them was wounded near me, and he came and picked a piece of
shrapnel out of his shoulder. Of course the wound was only slight.
I hope you are quite well and that Grandma and Grandpa are all
right. I must now bring to a close, I remain your loving son, Ted.

As he promised, Stretcher-bearer Hardie again wrote describing
the funeral, letter dated 10 July:

'I was pleased to receive your letter. I can fully realise your great
loss and sorrow, as my father was killed in the South African war,
and I can still remember the loss and sorrow it was to my mother.
I hope you will derive some slight consolation in the fact that Ted

died a glorious death in the execution of his duty to his King and country. Ted was buried with military honours on Monday morning at 11.45am at Bully Grenay, opposite our medical dressing station, within five minutes' walk from where he fell. The grave was dug by our own chaps. The regimental chaplain read the full burial service over the grave in the presence of the medical officer and all the stretcher-bearers and some of his company comrades. After the sad ceremony, we filled in the grave and placed flowers and a little rose tree on it. We made the grave look very pretty and neat. I am enclosing a roughly made sketch. Of course, you understand it was done with an ordinary pencil, and with lack of proper materials, it being impossible to get proper things. You see, nobody is allowed to have a camera out here, so we cannot have a photo of the grave taken. The grave is only about a thousand yards from the German firing line so I think it would be best to postpone your visit for a while. We have left this line of trenches now but you may rest assured that the grave will always be kept in good order by the different regiments that relieve us. Expressing my deepest sympathy ....'

The sad news was confirmed by the War Office in an intimation to Cllr & Mrs. Hewett on Wednesday this week. The late Private Hewett, when a boy, was a member of the St Alban's Church Boys' Guild and of the Bible class at St Albans.

18 July 1915. *Chiswick Times*
News from the Front – letters from Chiswick Working Men's Club members

Received by Mr. T.A. King, Secretary to the Chiswick Working Men's Club:

Private Frank A. Baynes. Writing on 6th July.

Will has made such good progress and I wish I could get home to see him. Everybody seems to think that we shall all get leave before the summer has passed. It is nearly six months ago since we came out here. On rest we always run a sick hospital for the brigade so you can guess we are seldom idle, which is a good thing, as it gives one less time to think about the good people and things we have left behind us. This would be a capital life in some ways especially from the health point of view. Our soldiers all look bronzed and well, and the general health is excellent. Since I last wrote to you we have shifted our camp about a quarter of a mile. The field where we were was considered somewhat unhealthy, and to make matters worse we were surprised one day to see a captive observation balloon rising a few yards away from us. These balloons are sometimes shelled so it was thought wise to shift further away in case the Germans took it into their heads to try to bring the thing down.

We have an excellent site now, and it is simply glorious on a fine morning on top of our hill. Unfortunately, the water supply is a source of trouble out here, but our major has made a dam in a stream close by, which provides us with washing water. For drinking water, our carts have to travel sometimes 10 miles, and sometimes in the 10 miles gets overdosed with chloride of lime, which is not at all pleasant, but we drink it for all that, and then long for a cup of home-made tea. The people out here seldom drink tea, but the English soldiers have taught them the art of making it and if you are lucky enough to be near a town then there is not much difficulty in obtaining it.

When we were in --- we had a piano which provided us with many a pleasant evening. This one got in the way of a German shell, and is now beyond repair. When we went out stretcher-bearing at --- we found one in a dressing station not half a mile from the firing line and this also helped us to pass away a few hours between our two journeys to fetch the wounded in. That building is now in the hands of the Germans and I hope they will appreciate their find as much as we did.

The Chiswick Times of last week, 2nd July, contained some interesting news and I am glad to hear from Reg Wilkie that the 10th Middlesex in India are having a good time. It must be glorious out there, but I expect most of them are anxious to get to Flanders to have a smack at the Germans. Perhaps you would like to know that three of our officers and the two senior NCOs were mentioned in dispatches a week or so ago'

16 July 1915. *Chiswick Times*
Letters from Private L.C. Struggles. Cambridgeshire Regiment.

Written to Mr. Procter, of Messrs. Rankin & Co, by whom he was employed before the war. The letters cover about two months. In the first, Private Struggles, after thanking Mr. Procter for a parcel, says his duties are to guard an ammunition column:

'We are quite near to four batteries and the Germans have been very busy trying to find the range of these. They have been using 'Jack Johnsons', high explosive shells and shrapnel. This last bombardment has been the worst of the war and I can tell you I did have my 'wind up'. A Jack Johnson makes a hole big enough to bury a horse and cart and weighs three quarters of a ton. The Germans are using great siege guns on trains and I have seen half a street with not a single house standing. There is a saying 'It is better to be born lucky than rich.' I am not getting very rich in the army but I hope I shall be lucky. I am very happy and feel in the best of health.'

[In a second letter] 'I am sitting outside my dug-out and the sun is shining beautifully. There has been some hard fighting here and some of my school pals have 'gone west'. Still I shall be able to think of them as comrades who did their duty to their King and country. A grand city, we have left, famous before the war for its beautiful buildings is absolutely shelled to the ground and is beyond repair. I see in the papers that the 'Mad Dog' was going to be Kaiser of Europe by August. I do not think this is possible by the progress he is making. Do you believe a man (shall I so call him) can win who treats women and children as he does? Please thank your staff for their kindness. You cannot imagine how a letter cheers one out here.'

In a 3rd letter he says that in the battle of Ypres their losses were very small compared to those of the Germans. 'The Germans fight well when they are 4 to 1 but soon quieten down when they are outclassed. A 17" shell hit two houses and next moment only a heap of bricks remained. I could not believe my eyes. Last night I was in a listening post, which is a trench 30 yards from the firing line. We have to watch if the Germans may pay a surprise visit or may sap our trench. On such occasions there is no doubt where you would be going. As far as I can say, it would be about 20 ft in the air.'

16 July 1915. *Chiswick Times*
Letters to Rev. Oldfield.

Private W. Lawrence. Army Service Corps.

Am having an easy time of it just now; plenty of good grub, and decent chaps to work with. We are having glorious weather, and I feel quite a different chap now than I did when I was in England and I am getting more colour in my face. Hope everything is quite all right with the brigade. I wish to be remembered to the boys, if there are any left.'

Private W. Brown. BEF.

'We are having a few days' rest. I ran across one fellow from Chiswick, young Whitehorn. What is worth seeing about the ruins here is that the shrine never seems to get hit. There was one behind our trench with plenty of shells flying over it but they never knocked the shrine over although all the other parts of the place were in ruins.'

Driver S.A. Cork. BEF.

'I am keeping quite well as regards my health but tormented all day long with flies. There are millions. They are like German soldiers – knock down 6 and 12 come in their place! I have stings all over my hands and arms but as it is all in the war, we cannot grumble. They bombarded last Sunday but did little damage. The churches here are smashed to atoms. There is one church by our battery; the roof and the walls are all blown in, but the cross on the altar is still standing without a scratch.

I am going to send to the 'News of the World' this week and ask if they could manage it, to get me an old cornet, as we have some very good singers in our battery, but we have no music, otherwise we could have some good times. We are billeted at a farm. Sometimes I help to milk the cows – sometimes I am chasing the cows off the horses' corn – they eat more than the horses. I shall soon be quite a farmer.'

Private Frank Sheppard. BEF.

'I am still in the very best of health. The weather here is not up to much just now, as it rains off and on for the best part of the day; but last week it was simply grand; in fact a little too hot. We are still resting. I shall be very glad when we are on the move again as the time now drags terribly. We are fairly well off now for almost everything except fags. We get 20 cigarettes on Sunday, which have to last a week; not many to waste.'

Private H.W. Earl. BEF.

'I am very pleased to hear that so many of the old boys have responded to the call. I had no idea that so many had gone – 400 – to do their little bit. Sorry to say I have been in hospital again for a fortnight with the same old trouble. Do you know anybody that would send me a few cigarettes while I am in hospital as I cannot get any from inside and we are too far from barracks for our chums to come and see us.'

Private Walter Burch.

'I am sorry to hear of the death of several Chiswick chaps out here, especially Liew Davies and Micky Grifffin as they were old chums of mine. The weather is simply boiling but it is better than rain for the work we have to do. Am glad brigade have again won band competitions. Well done St Mary's!'

Cigarettes can be sent, free of duty, 2s 6d for 200, 4s for 400 including postage. The Rev. A.E. Oldfield can supply addresses if desired. Smaller quantities go cheaper by letter post, 1d per ounce.

23 July 1915. *Chiswick Times*
Victoria Working Men's Club members with the Colours.

At the half-yearly meeting of the club, on Tuesday, letters were read by Mr. Copland the secretary, from members now on active service, who 'regretted inability to be present.'

Private A.A. Williams, 'A' Company, 7th East Surreys, 37the Brigade, 12th Div.

'We are having a fine time out here – plenty of work, mostly trench digging. Ask me if there is anything I should like. Well, I should like a cigarette lighter, a box of Woodbines, and the local paper.'

23 July 1915. *Chiswick Times*
Letters to Rev. Oldfield.

Gunner R.S Hamilton. France.

'Well Sir, there are not many fellows in the battery now who have been through the campaign. We have been in the firing line the whole time. Last week, when we came out of action, we thought we were going back for a rest, but no luck. We came further down the line and went straight in the firing line again.'

Trooper Frank Sheppard. France.

'I can't find words good enough to thank you for that box of cigarettes. I gave my mate one of the boxes as he was as bad off as myself. We are still resting. I cannot understand what on earth the miners had to strike over, but I hope it will soon be settled as, I can tell you, it does not give our chaps much of a heart when they hear of such things out here.'

Private A. Hill. France.

'It seems as if I had been away for years, though I've only been away nine months. We are at present on a short rest. I don't think there is much hope of the Germans running short of ammunition. The last position we were at, they blotched them over in dozens. We were shelled along the road and they also shelled the town in which we were staying. We were in a shell hole, just to remind you that there is a war on. It will please you to know that I am in the Guards choir. We are 30 strong, and with the help of the chaplain and a good piano we are passable. We have some very good concerts out here. I am forwarding you a programme. We are allowed in the swimming baths here and it is grand after a route march.'

The Rev. A.E. Oldfield sincerely thanks 'A.P.' for 5s for prisoners of war, also those to whom he has written for money sent for prisoners and for cigarettes. He is still like Oliver Twist – wanting more.

6 August 1915. *Chiswick Times*
Letters to Rev. Oldfield.

Corporal Dick Inskip. Somewhere in France.

'I am at present in a small village yards from the German trenches. The village is completely ruined. I am in charge of a guard. We are well protected in the event of the Germans shelling. We have a dug-out and a large trench in which we take cover. I was in the dug-out when three high explosives came together. I could not see anywhere for dust and bricks. I think the Germans are very unjust; after being up all night we like to get a nap in the morning so our friends usually send a few souvenirs over. Our boys scored a good haul one day. After firing at a German Taube [an aircraft] the machine burst into flames and fell....

Sergeant F.W.J. Smith. France.

'We left England and went into the trenches right up into the firing line. Luckily we had only two casualties but it was enough for a start. We expect to go in for five days. It puts some pluck into you when you see the regulars walking about as if there was nothing going on. It's a bit exciting to watch the duels with our airmen.'

Bombardier F.C. Baker. France.

'My age is now approaching 26. I enlisted if you remember in 1907 and went to India in 1909. I left the army in 1912 and took up an appointment at Madras as art schoolmaster. I rejoined the army when war broke out and came to France as a driver. We are all anxious of course to get the war over and return victorious. Rumours are as plentiful as flies. Feeling runs high on such subjects as 'strikers', 'slackers' and 'somebody's neglect.'

13 August 1915. *Chiswick Times*
Letter to Mr. Thomas A. King, Hon. Sec. of the Chiswick Working Men's Club.

Private Frank A. Baynes, Belgium.

'We get a little excitement now and again in the way of shell fire, which came rather too close for my liking a day or two ago. Parties of eight men and an NCO are sent up every three days to an estaminet [a small café/bistro] near the line to fetch in the sick and wounded of our brigade. We go out each night to the dressing station and during the day must be ready to be called at a moment's notice One day the Germans sent some big shells over, and some cavalry men, working in a field got hit, so we made a trip to fetch them in. Fortunately, none of them were seriously wounded. When our big guns started going that night, the noise was terrific. One grows accustomed to noise out here. At the end of the three days we are relieved.......

The other night about an hour after 'lights out', at 9.30pm, we were rudely awakened from our slumber by different NCOs yelling for every man to dress and be on parade in five minutes. We marched off in squads to the estaminet I spoke of previously. The whole thing turned out to be a test to see how quickly we could be on the spot to start working. Unfortunately leave has not been granted to us.'

13 August 1915. *Chiswick Times*
Letters to Rev. Oldfield.

Sapper P. Read. France.

'I have just received a letter from Fred Bailey this morning, I am pleased to say he is still alright sir, but I wish I could get somewhere close to him like the old days. There is a band come close to us this morning. I could hear some of the old tunes being played. It seems like old times come back again, sir. Remember me to the old band boys and Ralph.'

Lance Corporal C. Wrathell. Aldershot.

'I am getting tired of it now after nearly 12 months but I hope to go away shortly. I have passed another machine gun course and got made corporal gunner. If I don't get there soon I shall transfer to the Motor Machine Gun Section and get out there that way.'

They sent a trench torpedo over, which makes an awful explosion and after they have sent two or three of these over you hear the snipers start firing, and they carry on like that all day and night. Young Pia has had the experience of being under gas, but I think we have got that whacked now that we have got those smoke helmets. In another part of the line they are trying to burn our chaps out of their trench. I shall divide the cigarettes between Dick Vine, Pickles and myself.'

20 August 1915. *Chiswick Times*
Letters to Rev. Oldfield.

Bombardier R.S.J. Hamilton. France.

'Well, there is nothing to talk about just now, but I daresay there will be later on. One bit of news. I have been promoted bombardier and hoping I shall get higher still.'

Private G. Hawkes. France.

'Every time we go into the trenches we do 14 days at a time, then we come out for a few days.'

Private W. Neave. France.

'The trenches we are in are splendid ones, and are about 10 feet high nearly all along the line, and the Germans in front of us are pretty quiet. They are supposed to have said that if our men did not fire they wouldn't. I think myself they are Saxons. In fact, at 'Trench Mortar Square' you can speak to them from our fire trench, so you can see that they are pretty close'

<u>Lance Corporal C.A. Brand.</u> France.

'I received your parcel with great pleasure today, and as you may be sure received lots of offers from different chaps to tea with them. Most of our chaps are of a Socialistic turn of mind, inasmuch as they think that everything should be equally divided. But I am sorry to say that, with a few exceptions, their belief is liable to a sudden change should they themselves receive a parcel. You remember Sgt. Riches, one of the old boys? Well I met him in the train, he is a private in the London Scottish and he too is on his way to the trenches.'

<u>Corporal R.J. Vine.</u> France.

'Pte. Smith is in my gun section and we are always together, while Fred is a platoon sergeant. Three old St Mary's choir boys. There are also two old Glenthorpe Cricket Club men in this battalion, so we have some Chiswick lads here.'

20 August 1915. *Chiswick Times*

Our boys under fire – more cheerful letters from Richmond soldiers.

<u>Fred Culver.</u> Son of Mr. Culver of King Street.

He is a well-known player for Richmond Town Cricket Club, and has accepted a lance-corporal stripe in the 'A' Company of 7th Battalion, East Surrey Regiment. 'At present we are what the powers that be call 'resting' and are staying in a disused factory. We have a machine gun played on us nearly every evening. When we are in the trenches, we get a good number of whiz-bangs and things about nine inches long charged with very high explosive. I am on the listening post with two others. We go on at 8.30 in the evening till daylight, and we are out in front of our trenches listening for working parties or in case of attack. If we get discovered we lie still and wait till they have finished with their machine gun. Of course we do not do much in the daytime; generally sleep in our dug-out which is called the 'listener's repose'. I could tell you heaps but the Censor would cross it out.'

<u>Private F. Havis.</u> Royal Army Medical Corps. Somewhere in France.

Writing to a friend in Manor Grove: 'Star shells are thrown up each night and illuminate the surrounding country. These indeed are a sight worth seeing for the country is made as light as day – midnight is most picturesque. Horrors are mingled with scenery here. Another event happened on the 18th of this month. The German shells were falling quite close to us. We were forbidden to approach our billets as they were in range of being hit, so we had to conceal ourselves under the ground – in dug-outs. The bursting of shells was like an earthquake. Try and imagine the noise of one, and then remember that there were about eighty which exploded near us.

I have been out to another town which is in absolute ruins. Can you imagine Richmond in ruins; not a wall standing, and holes in the roadway large enough to put a brewer's dray in and then have room for a smaller cart? Such is this town. The church is ruined, and in the font is a crucifix, quite intact. Some of the graves have been ripped open, exposing the coffins. This town is as large as Richmond and every house is in ruins. Whilst I am writing this, our guns are speaking in tones of anger to the Huns and the presents are buzzing over my head.'

Letters to Mr. R. Copland, Hon. Sec. of Victoria Working Men's Club.

<u>F. Clarke</u>, 46th Ammunition Park.

'We are still hanging on out here and waiting very patiently for something to happen. There seems to be a tendency for things to warm up our end. There has been some very heavy firing going around about this last day or two and it sounds as if that big effort is about to commence. I had my baptism of shell fire yesterday. I had to go with some lorries to a place you have heard a lot about lately and take material from a railhead for the Royal Engineers, to what is known as our dumping ground. I had to make three trips backwards & forwards, and it was a case of running the gauntlet, as the shells were whistling and bursting all round and the damage done was awful. I saw the cathedral of this particular town, and it was nothing but a wreck – all very dreadful to behold.

Private A. Williams, 'A' Company, 7th East Surrey Regiment, 37th Brigade, 12th Division.

'We are now in the trenches and at a place where the Germans are only 50 yards away. We call out to them in the morning and some of them look up and speak to us; but it doesn't do to keep up too long, because their snipers are always at work. We gave them a bit of a bombardment the other night, and I think it did a bit of damage, because they gave us such a lively half-hour but did not do much mischief.'

Driver W. Hard. Headquarters staff of the Royal Field Artillery, Divisional Ammunition Column.

'I arrived safely. We are stationed in a lonely spot not far from the firing line. I do not know how long it will be before we start, but I shall be glad when we do, as it is a lonely place – no shops to buy anything – so we have to go without. Still I suppose we must not grumble. It might be worse before it gets better.'

Sergeant W. Sweet. Military Mounted Police.

'The Huns poured burning liquid on our fellows the other morning. Our men ask why don't we do the same, but there, that one word stands firm 'Why?' If our contemptible little army were let loose we should want no burning fluid. Our men have got it, but it is in their hearts.'

H. Barr. 1st Battalion Royal Fusiliers.

'We had a great downfall of rain, which makes the trenches in an awful state and takes such a long time to get them dry again. At night we have an enormous amount of digging to do; the sand and earth stick to the shovel and make it quite hard work. Two days' downfall of rain causes three weeks' hard work to rectify the trenches again. Of course, that's independent of being wrecked by huge shells, which cause an enormous amount of labour. The Germans' gas is a great trouble, but now we have been issued with smoke helmets. We have hardly any fear, considering we can get them on quick enough. Ypres Cathedral and the Cloth Hall are absolute ruins. In fact it would make strangers coming from London weep, I'm sure.'

H.G. Dilloway. 9th Cavalry Brigade.

'We are on a new firing line now. I don't know how long we are going to keep in the trenches; but there, I am just as happy there as anywhere. We are well looked after in clothes and food, so we must still keep on doing our bit. I shall not be sorry when it is all over. I expect everybody is the same. I am longing to get back to dear old Richmond again. I think I am one of those lucky ones or like a cat – have nine lives. I have had some very near ones. Let's hope I won't get any nearer.'

20 August 1915. *Chiswick Times.*
Choirmen in the Trenches. Letters to Mr. Burrell, choirmaster, St Elizabeth's (R.C.) Church

Private G.Eiffes. 'C' Company, 8th Battalion, Royal Fusiliers.

'There have been luckily few casualties amongst the battalion so far. There isn't much chance of picking up the language here as there is scarcely anybody living in this town. Besides the inhabitants do not talk proper French, only a patois. It is a hard job to go to church as all those near us are smashed up by the Germans.'

Driver Edgar Barfoot. Motor Transport. Army Service Corps. Siege Ammunition Column, 15th Brigade Royal Garrison Artillery.

'I've been out here three months and am beginning to feel quite an old soldier, and think that by the time this struggle is finished I shall have had enough excitement to last me for the rest of my days. The longest time we have stayed at one place was about three weeks and during that time our convoy was posted round the church at the small village of ----- which a fortnight before had been bombarded by the Germans.

The church, of course, had suffered most, as best part of the roof had been blown off. The roof of the church had been repaired with thatched straw, and the services continue every Sunday. The second Sunday we were there our chaps heavily bombarded the village of ----- which was seen to be full of German reinforcements. The bigger guns are seldom fired at night, as the flash reveals the position of the gun, which of course is always well concealed. While this was doing I had the privilege of assisting a mass at 10 o'clock on the Sunday, and I do not think it impossible to hear mass under stranger conditions.

The shells which our convoy supply are about 3ft high so you can guess that the howitzer guns are a decent size. A 3-ton lorry can only carry about 20 shells.

I had some knowledge of the French language before I joined up, but since I have been out here, I have been learning it hand over fist, and have now been made interpreter to the convoy.'

27 August 1915. *Acton Gazette*
Verses from the Front.

To the Editor. Sir, A fighting friend at the front sends me a letter. Louis Hanks. 32 Gunnersbury Lane, Acton.

'Like you, I am sorry to see so many casualties. I'm so glad you have the papers as, believe me, I cannot tell you much. Each letter is censored. I cannot tell you even the names of places. There is some talk of us going to where you mentioned in your letter. Then, most probably, we shall be getting leave to come home. But just now we are thinking of going into the trenches again for perhaps ----- days. Last time in the trenches I, with three including a corporal, was put on listening post for two days. It's only five hours lying listening between the two firing lines. If seen, we should have to make a fight, being quite a hundred yards away from our trench. We are billeted in our old school again, but this time the shells are coming over, doing a bit of damage too.

But wait! Revenge is sweet. The Germans will get paid back in their own coin. Our boys here are happy. We would just as well be in the trenches as out, although when out, we do trench-digging by night and a little physical drill to keep us fit. We are having hot weather, and tormented by flies, but, believe me, I do not make trouble of that. I admit at present we have not had very heavy fighting. Our boys have yet to make their name. If it's to be a charge, I'm there, so long as I get a few 'Fritz's' over. I can then say I've done my bit. True, I've left wife and children. Bless them all. I hope they never want, should I fail. I don't want to get knocked over by a sniper while fetching rations or such like. I don't care a bit so long as I'm in the thick of it, and the sooner we get to business the better. I haven't heard from my brother yet. I hope he will get on all right. Also I wish your son good luck whilst doing his duty. God only knows why so many young chaps hold back. What's the matter? We're not on holiday. It's to protect ourselves. If they only knew. Good luck and goodbye for a while. Yours truly. Charles Taylor, 9th Royal Fusiliers. '

The following verses are from his pen, and I call them 'A Ballad of Kitchener's Army'

A Ballad of Kitchener's Army
We are the Royal Fusiliers,
We're waiting for the chance
To have a go at Germany,
And drive them out of France.
For months we have been training,
And now, they say, we're fit
So they've sent us over here,
To do our little bit.
I'm sure we won't disgrace them,
For we know our duty well,
And now we are upon the scene,

We'll make our bullets tell.
Our country called; we answered,
We left our homes and wives,
To fight against the common foe,
Who's taking the children's lives.
To them we'll show no mercy
Their backbones we break,
Then send them back to Germany
As fast as they can make.
So here's luck to the Bonny Boys,
The boys who know no fear,
From one who's proud that he became
A 9th Royal Fusilier.

Charles Taylor.

27 August 1915. *Chiswick Times.*
Letter to Rev. Oldfield

<u>Gunner A. Neave.</u> France.

'My brother Will took part in a big charge, but came through safely and after taking 150 yards of trenches they were shelled with every conceivable kind of shell and bomb that the Germans kept handy. This lasted 24 hours till they were eventually relieved. For my part, things have been rather busy. Our chaps have been continually on the go, some of the drivers doing sometimes 12 hours in the saddle. While going up the other night one of our wagons nearly came to grief. A star shell suddenly went up, and away went the horses, at the same time throwing the two gunners clear of the seat. However after a lot of excitement, they were eventually pulled up with no damage done. It seems wonderful how many altars, also wayside worshipping places, seem to escape damage. It is very interesting to read the other chaps' letters in the Chiswick Times, it is the first part I want to see. A friend sends the paper every week.'

3 September 1915. *Chiswick Times*
Chiswick Working Men's Church club – members at the front.

Letter to Mr. T.A. King, Hon. Secretary of the club.

<u>Private Frank A. Baynes.</u>

[26 Aug] 'Our section has taken over hospital duty since last I wrote, so for a time I am on day work only. We start at 6.30am and work till 6.30pm. My job is as a nursing orderly in a very nice little ward, into which we receive the serious medical and surgical cases. Unfortunately they don't stop long enough for us to do much for them, as the sick patients are transferred to the base hospitals if their illness is severe, whilst the wounded are generally kept 24 hours, or if badly wounded, put on the road to recovery and then sent down to the lines. Just lately, cases have been fewer than what we have been accustomed to, so we are having a fairly slack time. The other boys of the sections still continue to do their bit of stretcher-bearing but at times up our part of the line it is so quiet one would hardly think there was a war on.

I hear from friends at home that you are still having some excellent concerts in Homefields. But even if we don't get concerts, we sometimes get a band playing near or in our camp. The Belgian population of this village turned up in large numbers on each of these evenings and seemed to enjoy the selections every bit as much as our soldiers. My kindest regards to all at Chiswick.'

He enclosed a programme of the band concert that included some Harry Lauder's songs, the waltz ''Nights of Gladness', a selection from 'the Passing Show', a two-step 'Get out and get under' and 'The chocolate Soldier', and the national anthems of the seven allies played at end.

3 September 1915. *Chiswick Times*
Letters to Rev. Oldfield.

Private A. Hill. France.

'Just about harvest time here. The women are doing the work of men. Nothing to see a woman driving a wagon loaded with hay. Boys, aged about 7 to 10 years, drove about a dozen pigs into the fields this morning and have just returned back. So you see even the children have to do their bit. I often wonder what the children at home would say if they had to do all this. And how would the 'flappers' go on if they had to rise about 4.30am and run about in clogs all day?'

Private G. Antiss. France.

'Thank you for the cigarettes. Being on the move we did not get our cigarette issue. So as soon as the boys saw my parcel I was surrounded for about ten minutes, and afterwards there were clouds of smoke around the place. This last three weeks we have been on the march. We are in the same trench that Sergeant O'Leary got his V.C. in. We lost nine in the first two hours through shell fire so we are very eager to get at them.'

Bandsman W. Burch. France.

'May 24th is the date our brigade was gassed, and only about 200 came out of it alive. I shan't be sorry when we see the last of these trenches. We have just got the news of the big naval victory. Poor old Von 'Tit-bits' (Tirpitz). The news has properly cheered up the boys, for it makes up for their Zep raids, only in this last affair we killed soldiers, not females.

I suppose you remember how the Germans gassed our battalion, and then came over and bayoneted them while they were helpless. I would have given some Germans a drink, like I did in the last attack the battalion took part in! I would have given them something else instead. No soft hearts round this quarter now. I would give them gas, liquid flame, and anything else I could get hold of.'

3 September 1915. *Chiswick Times*
Richmond Men's letters to Mr. R. Copland, secretary of the Victoria Working Men's Club.

Driver Richardson. Royal Engineers who served in the Boer War and writes from Ireland.

'I bet they finds it a bit different in France transporting heavy guns that take a tremendous shell. As one lad said 'every time it's like a train rushing through the air.....I think I will be over next month'.

Private H. Hopkins.

Writes on August 14th. 'Our division has just made a successful attack against the Germans, and a very severe cold they caught too. We were in reserve and three previous attacks had failed so our division had to go and do it, and our fellows just showed them what they were made of. On August Bank Holiday morning 200 allied guns shelled the enemy trenches and our reserve line took the first trench without casualties. As our fellows advanced under shell fire the Germans were crouching down in their trenches shouting for mercy. The prisoners that were taken were boys and elderly men. They must be the last resource. Yesterday morning a young chap about sixteen gave himself up, and he said he had a lot of friends who would be willing to come out but cannot get away at present. I will not give an account in writing of the terrible sights witnessed, but may tell of them when I get home.'

3 September 1915. *Chiswick Times*
Private Harold Tompkins with the Cameron Highlanders.

Writes from 'Somewhere in France' – which the Tommies have christened Cats Point Fort. He has returned to the firing line after a few days back at home on furlough.

'The battalion left the trenches whilst I was home, and had to march the same night to ----- in expectation of a long rest, and as the distance was some 20 miles you can see that we were in quite a civilised district. The next day, we were marched to a little town about five miles away and were lined up. After some three hours rest we were inspected by Lord Kitchener, who drove through town slowly in a car accompanied by the Price of Wales. We heard we were going right back to the trenches on the following day, and, as is usual on such occasions, we made a late night of it in the billet with mouth organs, songs etc. It is not because we are happy at the idea of going back – far from it – it is because of the feeling of being for the last time in a billet far from the shots and shells, and we want to make the most of it for the time being.

We had expected, as we had gone so far back, to have a rest for quite a month, especially as one of Kitchener's new army divisions had filled our places in the trenches; but no. After less than a week's rest, 20 miles back, we must go over all the ground into it again. Oh, that weary march that seemed never ending.

At 8.30pm, we set off again loaded up to the teeth. We had to do all the fatigues for the firing line, and in addition, sentry work, and in the event of a retirement our men retire to this fort. The fort is of circular shape, and is exactly like a round trench, the chief disadvantage being that when the Germans start shelling we run more risk of catching a shell, as we are so near the road, the only line of communication, and they cannot shell our firing line too much for fear of hitting their own men. Stray shots from snipers from their fire trench are constantly whistling around us, but luckily so far, there have been no casualties.

The fort is hidden to a certain extent amongst semi-demolished trees, shrubs and houses, and the wind, with stray shells behind the trees, play with one's imagination when on lonely duty. The fort is called 'Cats' Point' because there are two cats who wander about, probably left by the previous occupiers of these demolished houses. Last night one scuttled by me in the darkness, and I could not imagine what it was; it is a shock to one's nerves, which have been gradually undermined by the horrors of this campaign. The day turned out hot and myriads of flies came to pester us

On Thursday afternoon, the Germans treated us to a few hymns of hate, including coal boxes and the high velocity explosive shrapnel.

The next day we had some more shelling, and probably owing to the wet state of the ground, quite a few shells simply buried themselves without exploding. At 8am every man had to go up to the firing line with huge balls of barbed wire for use during an advance, and bring back from the reserve trenches heaps of surplus picks and shovels. Whilst waiting in the reserve lines for these implements an attack made by the Germans on the lines to our right started and for three quarters of an hour we had quite a Brock's benefit. Lights were all along the line, maxims were chugging, bombs thrown and then the artillery opened fire. Of course we did not find out until the following day exactly what happened, but it appears that under the cover of the dirty night they tried to surprise our first line. We were ready, however, and they were repulsed with a loss of some 400 men. I hear authentically that we are going back on Thursday for another short spell – why we don't get a rest I don't know, but I think we certainly have earned more than four days out. I wonder how the miners who have struck would care to do this past week's work for 7s. I think they would prefer their own work.

There is one little incident of an amusing character that happened this afternoon, on parade – the farmer's wife came rushing out – the farm was on fire. We were sent in to quench it.

When the lines are as quiet as they ever are during the day, our telephone operator in the fort sometimes gives a mouth organ concert into the receiver, and by the connection of instruments the concert is heard in every trench throughout the whole division, covering an area of nearly 15 miles. It is quite interesting, and sounds just like a gramophone and these evening performances are quite looked forward to. Despite the severe shelling, the battalion throughout the whole seven days only had 12 casualties, of which 3 are fatal – quite a record for us.'

10 September 1915. *Chiswick Times*
Letters to Rev. Oldfield.

Private A.T. Riches. France.

'I have been in the trenches twice. I left Saffron Walden 1st July. I met one of the old brigade boys on the boat. His name I cannot remember, and I think he said he had been at Malta so you may be able to trace who he was by this information.'

Private E.D. Reed. France.

'I think that there cannot be many of the old boys who haven't enlisted. We get plenty of football in our spare time, and have had several cricket matches which have helped pass the time.'

Bombardier R.S.J. Hamilton. BEF.

'This last two weeks I have not up with the guns. I am going to read the paper and see how the lads are going on.'

10 September 1915. *Chiswick Times*
News from the 'Old Vic' – Victoria Working Men's club

Letters from the Club's members.

Private H Barr. 1st Royal Fusiliers.

'We have had it rather rough this last couple of weeks. Rather nerve-trying. The Division, captured two lines of trenches and a huge mine crater. Our artillery had bombarded their trenches for three days continually. The enemy gave themselves up in great numbers and the bombardment had driven them nearly mad. Our job at night now is to dig them out of the trenches and bury them. The stench is something awful, and I believe if it was not for a smoke we should not be able to stick it. Remember me to all the old boys. Haven't had any cigarettes.'

Private L. Hewitt. Motor Transport. Army Service Corps.

He thanks Mr. Copland for the *Richmond and Twickenham Times* and mentions he had not received the tobacco from Mr. Copland but some has been received from 'The People' and Mrs. Riley. 'Could I have a copy of 'Gunga Din' or 'The Tale of the

Indian Water Carrier' by Rudyard Kipling? 'We have a concert now and again, I should like to recite, only I have forgotten some of them.'

Private G. Sutcliffe. Motor Transport. Army Service Corps.

He thanks Mr. Copland for the 'very bright and cheery letter. Things have been quiet in his quarter and we have been having cricket matches and concerts. Our concert room is generally the local school room. The songs, though not the latest, go down very well. Cigarettes have not arrived yet. Being in the workshop we hardly have any exciting times now as we did when carrying ammunition.'

24 September 1915. *Chiswick Times*
Our boys at the Front – letters from local men with the colours.

Sergeant Mitchell. Royal Field Artillery. To Mr. Newman of Winchester Rd, St Margaret's.

'We have just got into action now 'somewhere' where I may not tell you. This is a very nice country, but as regards men, we only see very old ones. The women are wonderful for pluck; they are actually living in their houses right up near the firing line. This is a fine place for fruit, even along the roads are all fruit trees, the same as our ornamental trees grow at home.'

Private A. Warner. A postcard to Mr. Fred C. Pring, Secretary of Richmond Town Football Club.

'We have a grand gun trench here, with absolutely beautiful bunks to sleep in. We've got plenty of mice, and a cat comes in to catch them. It's a proper little 'grey home in the west.'

Mr. Pring writes that Private A. Warner is a well-known half-back belonging to the club and also of the Richmond Gas Works Football Club. He has also heard from Private F. Hermon who, he regrets to state, was badly wounded at the battle of Hooge. Hermon is well known in the locality as a splendid footballer. On several occasions he was one of the Town's selected players in the first divisional match of the Kingston Wednesday league.

His previous employment was with the Richmond Gas Works, for whom he always played with great success.

Private F. Hermon. Writing from the Red Cross Hospital, Torquay.

He has had eight shrapnel wounds and a badly-bruised arm through being buried in a trench and he is unable to use the limb yet. 'By the way, I had the pleasure of speaking to the King and Queen on Friday. Their majesties visited the hospitals in Torquay. I think my football career is finished, five of the wounds being above the left knee. I think myself very lucky.'

1 October 1915. *Chiswick Times*
Rifleman V. Edge. Writes from the Rifle Brigade. Formerly worked for Chiswick District Council

'We captured some Germans. One old chap; over fifty, and a boy of fifteen. Covered in mud from our artillery bombardment...'

8 October 1915. *Chiswick Times*
St Mary's Old Boys. Stories of the Great Battle (Loos). Letters to Rev. Oldfield.

Bandsman C.A. Brand. BEF.

'We have just come out of a big battle. I thought dozens of times that I was booked. You cannot imagine how terrible it was. The fighting lasted two days. At night time we were moved up close to our trenches and the next morning into the second line of trenches. We were going to attack the Germans. Allied artillery began a bombardment and then mines planted by our engineers went up. It was hell on earth. We charged and captured three lines of German trenches and 300 prisoners in the 300 yards of trench we held. The French captured 18,000 prisoners and some guns. The war will be over by Christmas. We are advancing every day.'

Sapper P.E. Read. France.

Tells of the great advance. A severe bombardment started from both sides. 'Jack Johnsons and Coal Boxes.and shrapnel flying about. Then I heard our officer's voice shouting "Now for it boys!" Then we jumped, all eager to get at the bloodsuckers, inhuman devils. Then we had orders to drop down, very much against the grain, for we wanted to get at them. If one bullet passed over our heads, there were millions of them; I wondered how I was going to get up without getting hit. Two mates got hit on both sides of me, and I was just giving one a drop of water, when one bullet went right through my pack, but doing no damage. Well then we had the order to jump up and at them again. Off we went across the first German trench. We lost our officer, but still went on trench after trench. "Camerade, no shoot." And they put their hands up. If I had my way the bayonets would have gone through them; but we made them prisoners instead. Then we went under the storm of bullets and shell, and captured the village. We cleared out the village and drove the Germans over a hill. I found myself in the front line. It was hellish and I got just what I liked to get – my finger round a trigger with plenty of ammunition by my side, then let go at the Germans. My finger is stiff with pulling the trigger. We stopped until next morning when to my disgust, as I was just getting used to it' the Royal Engineers were ordered back to their billets. My division was relieved. One or two of the 'old boys' were with me.

Their Corp Commander inspected us and said we were worthy of the name of soldiers and highly honoured. My word, St Mary's won't half be able to tell a tale after this, provided we are lucky. I've just received a letter from Drummer W. Bailey in India.'

<u>Bombardier H. Hamilton.</u> BEF.

'Just got over our big bombardment. In the morning our fellows came out of their trenches to give coffee to our wounded, and try to bring them in. We can see everything going on in the Huns' line. One day we saw two Germans cutting grass in front of their trench. We fired at them to scare them and saw them run for their lives. We had a good laugh over it.' He asks for socks and shirts.

Trumpeter J. Burgess. Royal Field Artillery.

'I haven't heard when we are going to the front but hope it will be soon. I have now been made first trumpeter, and am riding out with the commanding officer every day, which is a very easy job.'

8 October 1915. *Acton Gazette*
Mass at the Front – letter from Fr. Donlevy.

The Rev. Father W. Donlevy writes from the front to the Hanwell Catholic Parochial Magazine,

'Yesterday, Sunday 19 September, was an interesting day. I remembered how eventful it had been for us in days gone by – the day of our outdoor procession. All the beauty and splendour of those grand occasions was lacking yesterday. But that Sunday has always brought fine weather – our processions at Hanwell never had their baptism of rain – so too this year. A clear blue sky, a bracing breeze – with these I was cheered as I mounted my bike. My little auto-wheel seemed to get the spirit of the day, and hurried me in record time to my first Mass-station. You have to picture various country lanes meeting at this spot, just a few houses, hedges bordering the fields, horse lines, ammunition wagons in great numbers, and then near a gap in the hedge, a newly-built shed open at the sides, half filled with all manner of boxes of shells and cartridges.

This shed is my church. On my arrival, a sergeant and my altar server were busy building up the altar and hanging tarpaulins at the end of the shed to keep out the rather strong wind. Boxes of live shells were set up in two piles – these were the altar pillars, then a door – probably brought down from some ruined village – was laid across several blankets on top to make an even surface, another for the altar frontal, yet another for the sanctuary carpet, and all was ready. Then from my valise came the altar requisites for Mass.

Meanwhile my congregation was gathering, small parties coming from various ammunition columns, transport and veterinary sections, and a few peasants from around. Punctually at 9.30am, the Asperges was given and Mass commenced. There was a sermon – parts of which were probably heard. I could not always hear my own voice on account of the incessant rumbling of motor-lorries and supply wagons passing just outside. As usual, I gave General Absolution, and most present received Holy Communion. Mass ended and valise packed, I hurried back for a quick breakfast and to be ready to preach at 11 o'clock Mass, which was to be said in one of the large churches of the town. It was a grand sight to see this large church filled with Catholic soldiers. It was grander still to see the great number still who approached the altar rails.'

15 October 1915. *Chiswick Times*
Letter from Rifleman J.F. Bryant of Isleworth – about the Great Fight.

Son of Mr. J. Bryant, 72 South St Isleworth. Writing on 2ⁿᵈ October to his sister at Teddington.

'We moved up late on the Friday night after a sort of council of war, at which some idea was given by our officer of the general scheme, and exact details as regarded our own particular part in the operations. It was a pleasant feature of that gathering that while underlying it all was the feeling that within 24 hours a good proportion of those present would surely be killed and wounded, yet everyone seemed very cheery and confident as to the result and the laughter was in no way forced.

If truth must be told, we were not quite in such high spirits when we eventually reached our allotted station in the trenches, for it was raining and it was going to make it harder. As dawn gradually broke and nothing happened a rumour that had been current earlier, that the attack was postponed, came quietly down the ranks and one hardly knew whether to feel relieved that the tension was over for the time or disappointed at the thought of going back with nothing accomplished.

Still, we waited however, and soon we were crouching low in the trench to get the best possible cover from the deadly artillery fire from the Huns, which broke right upon our trench, fetching down sandbags and parapets, covering us all with dirt and wounding two of our little party within two minutes. Personally I felt that this must entail delay, while our artillery tried to get their guns and put them out. But to my surprise at that moment came the order, "the machine gun section forward!" Somebody murmured that it was murder to go out in face of that fire, but I realised the advantage of the move, and pointed out that it was murder to stay where we were if they kept that shelling going, whereas 50 yards in front, we should be out of that particular zone. Anyway we were over by now, going as hard as we could to clear the neighbourhood of that shell-stricken trench. Soon however, in accordance with instructions, we dropped to the regulation marching pace – so as to arrive fresh and vigorous at our destination, a line of trenches one and a half kilometres distant.

Our view was greatly restricted by the smoke and gas, but presently I made out two platoons marching boldly along in front, keeping as good a line as I've ever seen them do on manoeuvres, and away to the right another regiment and what amazed me for a moment was that I saw nobody drop. With shells bursting in the air all round it seemed, and bullets whistling everywhere, I could scarcely believe my eyes when I saw those lines of men just marching on apparently untouched.

Before we had gone far I stopped a moment to take the tripod from one of our men, he having got a whiff of gas, and being unable to continue with this rather heavy load – 48lb, on top of pack and usual equipment. Stopping to adjust my new load I lost touch with the others, and when I came up with the tail of our battalion, just by the first enemy trench, I found they were dropping fast, and the lines sadly thinning. Our bombers however got into the trench, and were making it secure. The rest of the battalion had passed on, so on I went in their wake, and presently much to my relief, espied the pylon towers of Loos, an excellent landmark for us, since our left was to rest on that village stretching across to the Lens road – so now I had no difficulty in locating our new trench, and was delighted to find our boys already installed in their new quarters and highly elated, you may be sure, at their success.

So you will see from this that Loos was taken, although you might have thought otherwise by the papers. It is true, however, that as soon as we got here, where our orders were very definitely to stop, other troops came over our heads and pushed on further. But we certainly had the honour of leading the attack on Loos and of getting there, and we were still in the same trenches on Monday when that bit of shrapnel hit my arm. Although the wound was so slight I thought I ought not to go back with it, I was not entirely sorry when I was definitely ordered to do so, for I had not had a wink of sleep since the Thursday night, had lost my mac-cape, was wet through, smothered from head to foot in mud to such an extent as I have never before been, in spite of the wet time we had in April and May, and altogether felt quite ready for the bath and bed, which was found me next day at hospital, after 20 hours in a hospital train – itself a luxurious affair.

Our losses in this affair seemed to me as being surprisingly light – although of course many a poor fellow we shall miss went down, including poor old Harry Turner, who was billeted with me at Laurel Road.'

15 October 1915. *Chiswick Times*
Letters to Rev. Oldfield.

Private W. Fowler. BEF.

'Just a line to let you know that I am still going strong. Things are beginning to look up a bit, as now doubt you have read in the papers, we had a smash at them ourselves a short time back, and although I went over with the grenade party I managed to get back safely. I was talking to our chaplain the other day he says he knows St Mary's well, his name is Rev. W.T. Conran. He came straight from India out here.'

Gunner A. Neave. BEF.

'We still get plenty of excitement, what with bomb dropping etc. Some of our boys got into a hot corner with their wagons, but got out with whole skins, although several wagons will be in 'dry dock' as the saying goes. It is a marvel how some chaps got out of it without a scratch, even although some of the poor horses were killed. It was a rare sight on the day of our advance about a week ago to see the wounded come back smiling and so pleased to have got them on the run. A few more wallops like this and we shall soon be back in England, and I give you my word, sir, there's no place like it.'

Private W. Neave. France.

'Well you can see by my address that I am in hospital, suffering from some sickness. As I lay in bed I can hear the waves washing up and down on the beach. My officer was killed in the last trenches we were in.'

Gunner W. Alexander. BEF.

'I am awfully sorry I could not write before but I have been awfully busy just lately moving from one place to another, and now I have settled. It is not a bad job but there are only three of us to work ten telephone stations, night as well as day, which is why I have not been able to write home often. We are having rather bad weather, cold in the day, and raining a lot.'

Gunner A. Clark. BEF.

'The other night we were having tea and having a quiet talk about old times, when the Germans put over 10 shells in quick time. Well, it was very laughable to see the boys go down their dug-outs like a lot of rabbits.'

Driver Sam Cooper. BEF.

'In regard to the fighting I think the troops round here are doing very well. We went into the village church last week, a very old one and beautiful inside. The Germans have made a mess of some of the towns round here. France is a very nice place, but I think I like England best. I saw 13 French aeroplanes up the other day at the same time.'

Driver F.W. Bailey. France.

'I daresay you have heard of the British attack all along the line and of course it was taken up by our lines. P. Read sent me a letter this week. He was in the taking of Hill 70 and didn't enjoy it much. I don't suppose he did, it being his first charge, that has about broken him in. Well, sir, I fancy we are settling down for the winter now.'

15 October 1915. *Chiswick Times*
Chiswick Working Men's Club members in the Great Advance.

One member, a hospital orderly, writing from France on 7th October to Mr. T.A. King speaks of his experience during the previous night.

'We were roused from our slumbers at 4am, to pack up and be ready to move off at 7am to some unknown destination. We did about 12 miles that day, halted in a field and spent the night in the open. Next morning they packed us into motor buses – the first time since we came here we got a lift and drove us up to about eight miles from the firing line. My word, it was a treat to ride in a London bus again, and we longed to ride on for ever. On reaching the town, the conductor yelled 'All change!!'. Then we marched four or five miles nearer the line, spending the night in a field. It rained the best part of the night. The only cover was under our wagons but despite this most of us slept well, being so tired after our march.

Next day some of our boys were sent out to find out the roads that we were to use when out stretcher-bearing and when they returned we received the news that two of our boys had been killed by a shell, and another seriously wounded (he has since died.) One of these boys was a close friend of mine, captain of our section's football team. We all felt extremely sorry for his brother, who is also in my section, and our commanding officer was good enough to grant him leave, so he will be able to give his people full details of how his poor brother met his death.

In the afternoon, stretcher bearers were marched off and the hospital sections (to which I belong) took over two buildings for receiving the sick and wounded. Band 'C' sections had a large hospital for lying cases only, while my section received the walking cases, who were dressed, fed, and then packed into motor lorries or ambulances and sent down the line. We did this for a few days, when the hospital sections were relieved by another field ambulance, and we marched to our present billets. Next day, all the available hospital section men were sent up to relieve some of our stretcher bearers, who had had a very busy time. We soon got to work and for the rest of the time up there worked fairly hard, whether on indoor duty in the dressing station or out stretcher-bearing. The dressing station where the bearers brought the cases to and spent their few hours when off duty, was at ----- but those cellars were to a certain extent shell-proof.

The part of the line in which we have been working is where all the terrific fighting has taken place and very close to where my brother was wounded. Our troops have been very successful round there, and this of course means plenty of work for the stretcher bearers, whose work was very difficult at times. The weather did not improve matters and the trenches down which we had to carry were sometimes inches deep in mud, in which dead men were lying. We are now back again enjoying a short rest. Anyhow we feel all the better for it and are once again back to our normal state after removing days old beards and trench mud etc.'

15 October 1915. *Chiswick Times*
Trials and humour of a soldier's life – About the Great Advance.
Private G. Penfold. Royal Fusiliers, of 8 Caroline Place, Church Court, Richmond. Writes from 'somewhere in France' where he has been nearly two months. For three days he was in the firing line,

but after a time the force to which he was attached was moved to a place nearly a week's distant.

'It was march, march, march, day after day, until we were put in cattle trucks to finish our journey, which took about nine hours. About a thousand British Tommies riding in these cattle trucks. Where we are at present we have taken over trenches recently occupied by the French and African troops. Being in such a deserted place, they have been living in dug-outs made under the ground, and they could not have been very clean. While trying to go to sleep, you may have several rats running over you - not very nice. But we brush them aside and make more fun over it than anything else. You would be surprised to see how we take all the hardships with a good spirit. We do six days in the firing line or front row of trenches and then six days in reserve trench and then out for a week's rest or so.

I expect you have read in the papers by now of the big advance we have made along the line and here as well, which place of course I must not mention – although the place was named on the front page of a paper on Sunday 12th Sept. Near here we had a terrific bombardment and I must say our artillery is doing splendid work thanks to munition workers in England.

We have had some very near shaves. While I and two more were out on a listening patrol one night, the Germans sent up an illuminating rocket, which lit up the ground for some distance around. They must have seen us crawling on the ground, for they sent a whiz bang over us. It burst just above us and we could feel the little pieces of hot shell fall on our backs, but they were too small to do any harm. We treated it as a joke although it nearly caught my mate's coat alight. Luckily we got back to our trenches alright.'

He asks any reader with an old concertina, to send it to him addressed 5822 Private C. Penfold, 16 Platoon, 4th Company, 13th Battalion Royal Fusiliers, B.E.F. France. It would pass away the weary hours in the dug-outs.

Expressing the hope that young men are rallying round and joining the colours in Twickenham & Richmond, he adds 'While on my travels I have come across our old Twickenham comedian, Billy Myers, who used to have the concerts at the Town Hall every year, and we had an enjoyable evening before we moved from the district.'

'I read with regret that you have had the Zeppelins near London; but I might tell you, we have made up for all that, as we have had read out to us by our colonel, the successes all along the line. Very good isn't it? Just a bit of our own back. But you have no idea what the Tommies have to go through just now, it has been pouring with rain for a week, and we have to wade through trenches up to our knees in mud and water. What we would give for a nice bath, but we are lucky to get even a wash in three or four days.

I much regret to read of the discontent in South Wales of the miners there. I should very much like to have them out here only just for a couple days for 6d a day, which is what us married men get. I am sure they would soon alter their tale. On my travels we passed close to where my dear brother was killed, who I hope to avenge. I may have done before now, as we do not know what effects our shots have, for as soon as we fire we have to bob down again. I am pleased to read the 'Richmond & Twickenham Times' every week, which my wife sends out, also the letters from Tommies here in France.'

A young Scotch laddie serving in the Highland Field Company in France, writing to his aunt in Richmond – he says a friend asked if he can speak French yet. The Highland lad replies 'Well, not exactly, but I know how to ask a girl for a kiss.'

15 October 1915. *Chiswick Times*
Letters to Rev. Oldfield.

<u>Lance Corporal Larner</u>. King's Royal Rifles.

'I was taking a message from Brigade HQ to battalion commanders when I came across a man buried by a shell. I ought not to have stopped, but could not see the poor chap stop there, so I helped him get out, and twice nearly got buried by shells myself. I have felt done up since then and have been in a rest camp. Hoping to rejoin my battalion shortly. I have met a lot of Chiswick men out here.'

Private John Swan. 2ⁿᵈ Company, 12ᵗʰ battalion, 5ᵗʰ Platoon Royal Fusiliers also writes.

'I have just come out of the firing line and we have lost 140 men. We were three days without food and water. The enemy were 20 yards away and we were shooting them as fast as we could but they closed in on both sides and continued shelling us for an hour and a half I thought my time had come. They put two machine guns on us.

I was a day and a night in 2ft of water. I have got a bad cold. We saw the wounded crying for water which we could not give them as we had none ourselves. Sometimes they lay there for two days before they were picked up. Some of the sights I saw I shall not forget as long as I live; it was absolute slaughter.'

Private Ted Selmes.

'All I can see is two huge lumps of mud at the end of my legs.' His brother has been killed. 'Although I am feeling upset at Cyril's death, I feel proud he died for the old country. I don't think you can have a finer death.'

22 October 1915. *Chiswick Times.*
Letters to Rev. Oldfield.

The letter writers frequently write how they are in touch with each other and express thanks for parcels, cigarettes and copies of the *Chiswick Times.*

Driver Arthur Smith. BEF. France.

'After being out here nearly twelve months am inclined to think we shall be here for another twelve. The fighting is terrible here now. I believe the harvest festival is at the old church now and I am going to one at the Soldiers' Club.'

<u>Rifleman Albert Wilkinson.</u> BEF. France.

'Mich Locke started a minstrel group which was not very successful. The result was rice and various missiles being thrown.'

22 October 1915. *Chiswick Times*
The Charge in the Great Battle.

<u>Private P. Davis</u>. London Regiment, writing to his parents at St Margaret's:

'Just a line to say I have just come back here after five days' heavy and hard fighting, to get re-fitted, as most of us have only got the clothes which we stand up in. The old regiment did not want asking twice when, at 4.30 on Saturday morning, our fine young colonel stood on a parapet and shouted: "London, the boys are calling you!" We were all over the top with a leap and a shout. The colonel told us a day or two before to 'take it game' and if we got a small wound to push on, and he acted up to it. We had not gone many yards before he got one, but he pluckily went on until another one was his end.

This was happening on all sides, first one officer, then another; your best pal would go down, and another beside him. Poor old 'Gus' Private A Brooks of Isleworth was killed, Bert Evans of St Margaret's wounded, Charlie was wounded – everybody seemed to be stopping something or other, but the colonel's last words stuck in my ears. 'Push on and on, boys.' I ran on. It seemed like a nightmare. The harder I pushed on the further away the Germans' first line seemed to become and the more the bullets.

At last what was left of us arrived at the German parapet, after me tearing half the seat of my trousers away on their rotten barbed wire. After sticking a few and shooting others, we cleared the trench, and went on to their second line. After getting this we rushed on for the village. On our left, the Jocks (London Scottish) were getting through, and our battalion and the kilties rushed the village with a shout. The place was full of Germans. They were just like vermin coming out of every door and hole you could see. It was a proper free fight as we pushed through every street. We had to boom them out of cellars and rooms; in the square it was proper slaughter as we mowed them down. I think I settled a German that Saturday for everybody I knew. I found myself shouting at the top of my voice 'That's for so-and-so'. At last we got through the village and got who was left of them out in the open. We got them right back to the top of a hill and there we held them for four days, when a division arrived and relieved us, what was left of us feeling more dead than alive. We were only just hanging on when they arrived.

It is now that I realise what marvellous luck I have had when I sit down quiet and think it all over to myself. I killed more Germans last Saturday than I should ever have expected to kill in 20 years. Yet we captured some hundreds of prisoners, I could not stick a man in cold blood when he was already badly wounded and asked so pitifully for mercy, for after all we are human, and I can always remember dad's words when we were kids that we are all born but not buried.'

22 October 1915. *Chiswick Times*
Letters to Rev. Oldfield.

Private A. Hill, BEF. France.

'I think the Huns knew it was my birthday. They shelled something awful. I am quite used to them by now. Will you please ask Ern to send me out some of that very fine emery cloth - that blue-backed sort? The damp affects my rifle, and a fellow must always look after his rifle, it is your best friend out here.'

R.S.J. Hamilton. Somewhere in France.

'The weather is not very grand and it don't suit our work at all. We are gently pressing them back, but of course we have a long way to push them yet. They dropped four shells on us again today, but did not do any damage to the troops, though it knocked a big hole in an estaminet. We find it very cold out here. What do you think of the Zepp raid? They seem to like old London don't they? I am very sorry to hear so many of our lads have been wounded, but still that is no disgrace, is it? We have been very lucky since we started firing. We have fired a few hundred rounds of them at different times. We have taken up a new position, we have been all over the place dodging about like mice. We are still in the open and find it a bit 'parky' at nights, so we make tea and cocoa to warm us up. Will you ask some of the boys if they have got a mouth organ they don't want, as one of our men can play one very well? We did have a nice one sent out, but the old thing has been blown to pieces.

I would like to tell you a lot, but of course I must not say anything, just the ordinary. I went to ----- when the place fell into our hands, and I tell you I would rather have stayed away. I expect you have heard all about the scrap we had by now. We had to go up as a burial party, but had to come back owing to the heavy shell fire. I got one or two souvenirs, and hopped off under cover. As I write this on my cap, our guns are firing at a very quick rate, shaking the ground, and our aeroplanes are being fired at not far from me by the German anti-air guns. We do see some sights.'

Private A.A. Gardner. BEF.

'I still receive the Chiswick Times. I am always pleased to read the recruiting successes, but still there are many more wanted yet. There cannot be too many in the field. King George paid us a visit; it cheers one up a bit to see the home folk out here. We are having leave here – a few at a time – but it is very slow. Things are very favourable for us; at least in my opinion, the Zepps are about the most dangerous. They are about the Huns only hope. The way for the young men at home to dodge them is to come out here; they are much safer. I expect they will all have to come before the finish. There is room for every one of them. I must close now, hoping for the safety of the women and children.'

Private J. Bewley. BEF.

'I have been looking to see if I can find any of the old boys. I expect they are hiding away in the trenches. Well I might say they are improving a great deal out here now and I should think if it continues the war ought to soon be over. The sooner the better, as it is not very nice having shells coming over and likewise bursting near you all day and night. It does make you wish you were in England again, to get somewhere quiet, because I might say all you can see here is houses being blown down, and hear the screeching of shells coming over our heads. So you can guess sir, how it is out here.'

29 October 1915. *Acton Gazette*
Letter from Corporal E. Brum – a Beaumont Park 'Old Boy'.

Writing from France to his former schoolmaster, Mr. D. Upton, Headmaster of the Beaumont Park School, Acton on Sunday. Corporal E. Brum of the 1st King's Rifle Corps.

'Please accept my apologies for not writing to you before, as of late we have been busy with the Huns. I expect you have read of our big advance. My word, we did give them the biggest thrashing of the war. When we had finished with them, the Prussian Guard counter-attacked us on three different occasions during the day. Each time we repulsed them. Next morning nothing could be seen but heaps of dead, so they paid very dearly for trying to gain back their lost ground. The British were a bit too tough for them that day, and what's more, we intend to give them plenty more. At the moment of writing, the French guns are speaking for themselves so, what with the noise of their '75s' etc, and ours against the Huns, it is as you may imagine, a trifle noisy, but, of course, most of us are quite used to it. I read in the papers of the 'Zepps" raid on England. What a scare some people must have had! It is very cold; in fact cold enough for snow. Now I will close, with kindest regards to all the boys at the school.'

29 October 1915. *Chiswick Times*
Stalking a sniper – letters from 2nd Lieutenant W. Hine.

Writing to his brother, Mr. Walter H. Hine, 23, The Broadway. He tells in three letters of the efforts made during a five week period to shoot a sniper, who aided by a periscope, had caused not a little anxiety:

'There is plenty of work here, though we get a few days' rest in between times. Have had one or two narrow squeaks, but still, a miss is as good as a mile. Only about three hours ago a private and myself were taking pot shots at a sniper I had discovered with the aid of glasses, when he retaliated with a rifle grenade. It kicked up a lot of earth near by, but did no damage. We promptly retaliated with five rounds rapid each. The blighter had got himself dug in. He has been sniping the last five days and nights from the same place.

In the next letter 'That sniper is still up to slight tricks, but we have quietened him greatly. I can assure you I haven't done with him yet. I have found out that one can never get rid of a sniper by just blazing over the parapet at him time after time from the same position. So this last week I have found three different spots where one could see him and have had them properly fixed up with steel loopholes and screened. I have pinched a rifle, and am waiting for a telescopic sight to come from the BSA people which I sent for. Now this cussed fellow is dug in, so my idea, when I have all things fixed up, is to draw his fire on to the old spot by some hastily fired shots in his direction, then as he bobs up, to reply. I shall have him dated with two good shots, and myself, from the other three positions. From no place is he more than 500 yards, so I think if we do not manage to hit him, we shall at least make him dry up. I am only waiting for the sight for myself, so as to make sure of him. He has kept very quiet the last week, so quiet that I think the beast has bobbed a little, but we have let the place alone, so he will be bound to try his luck again. I will give you the final results next time.'

In the 3rd letter. 'Many thanks for your letter received a few moments ago, just after I had finished a lobster. I guessed that all would be rather anxious over the last do, but we proved lucky and got off light; only got the backwash. Still it was warm, but I am still in one piece. An aeroplane of ours brought one of the Albatross type of Germans' down. It had two machine guns on it and its engine was a 200hp Bens. Some engine. The two men in it were smashed to pulp. It fell from about 4,000 ft. I was speaking to the fellow that brought it down, and he said they absolutely came on him unawares out of a cloud. The Germans tried to get above him but failed. Our chap then turned a machine gun on it and in about two minutes down came the German – very slowly at first, as the plane still had some resistance left. Then all of a sudden as the air drifted in, she dived with a sheet of flame and smoke behind. It is the sixth the chap has brought down. There was a rush for souvenirs, but he had himself landed and allowed no one near.

Now about Fritz. Well the elaborate arrangements I made all came to nought, and we came to the conclusion that the blighter is using a periscopic rifle so that he can fire without putting his head above his sniping pit. Still it was imperative he should be put a stop to, especially as he plugged a corporal of the ----- Regiment. So it was decided to oust him by night with bombs. The bombing officer, myself, and six men, went over the top at 10pm on Monday night last, after carefully studying the ground by day. A ravine runs between the two lines, so that in the bottom one is comparatively safe, unless you put your foot on a German patrol. We got in the ravine, and crawled up the other side to within about 15 yards of their first line wire. Now his position was just inside that. There we lay and waited, eight of us, each with an egg bomb. Well, we waited until 11.10pm knowing that it was his habit to snipe during the night at our patrols out in front just to pass the time away. It had been arranged that the moment his rifle flashed we threw – quite an easy throw – and then slid back in to dead ground at the bottom of the ravine, until the certain retaliation was over. Well, as we expected, at 11.10pm bang and a flash. We all rose as one man and lobbed these eggs at the flash. We heard a hell of a yell as we scuttled back, and then about three machine guns opened harmlessly over our heads. In the morning after we got back, and daylight broke, we saw that where his place was the wire and stakes were messed up and the pit had been badly bent. Since, I am glad to say, he has been exceptionally quiet. Now, our scouts reported last night that they came across the body of a German in the ravine. It took us just five weeks to get rid of him.'

5 November 1915. *Chiswick Times*
Letters to Rev. Oldfield.

Bombardier R. Hamilton. Somewhere in France.

'I am in the wagon line with the horses now, and we have moved to a new place and it is very bad indeed, but still we have to put up with it. The weather is very wet out here and also is very cold. Well I see the lads are going on splendid, and I wish them luck. We have left our good place in which we could get two or three enjoyments at nights, but we have to get on at nights as best we can. We have big fires at night to keep ourselves warm. I am going strong and hope to get my leave about January.'

Driver F. Mockler. BEF.

'On 25th September, when the charge was made, we had orders to stand to and nearly the whole time it was raining. France is not a nice place, for they don't have good roads.'

2nd letter. 'I am glad to say our battery came from the fighting very successful. I have not met any of the lads yet. I shall be jolly glad when this is all over. I receive the Chiswick Times each week, and it is quite a treat to see some news of the lads and what they do on active service. I think a good few of them were in the great advance. Only a few more of them, and then I think the Germans will be properly fed up.'

Private W. Stanley. BEF.

'Thank you very much for the parcel. The underclothing was just the very thing I have been waiting for. I don't know how we miss the falling pieces of shell. The weather is getting very cold. I receive the Chiswick Times each week from a kind lady, Miss A.T. It is a treat to read a little of what is going on at home.'

<u>Sergeant F.W.J. Smith</u>. BEF.

'Vic, Johnny, and Dick Vine are also in the pink. Well sir, we are in the trenches again. It's a bit hot just here from bombing attacks every day, either startling us or by the other things – excuse me calling them things, but I feel I should be lying if I called them men. As big as they are, I don't think there is an atom of manhood in them. I went through Ypres the other day. What a sight it is to be sure. To tell the truth, I don't think it could have been more wrecked if there had been an eruption here. You will have heard of the Cloth Hall, if you have not seen it. It is absolutely a mass of ruins, and they are still shelling what is left of it. I have heard people say the Germans are running short of ammunition; true, they don't shell so much as they did two months ago, but they seem to exchange shell for shell with us just here. Last night they shelled us about 100 of the biggest, not doing much damage. We had six chaps hit, not seriously. I think this is all I can stop to write this time as things are getting a bit noisy and it is pouring with rain.'

<u>Sapper C.A. Cossins</u>. BEF.

'I am sorry to say I have not seen any of the old boys that I know, but must have been with several of them in that big advance that was made on 25th, 26th and 27th. Thank God, our company only had one casualty, and that was only a slight wound. He has since returned to duty. We have been moving from one place to another, but think we have settled down for a time in present quarters in dug outs, and I can assure you that they can be made quite comfortable. I should be very grateful if you would send me a pair of socks as the ones that are issued out to us are like children's after wearing them for two or three days, they shrink so much. We are in one of the old health resorts, but I can assure you it does not look very healthy at present. Nothing but ruins for miles. The Germans have even broken open the coffins in the tombs. I expect it was to take the jewellery, even the rosaries from the necks and leave the body exposed. You must excuse writing as the butt of my rifle is not the best of writing desks and my candle is at its last gasp.'

5 November 1915. *Acton Gazette*
St Mary's and St Andrew's (Acton). Lads at the Front.

Miss Jessie Graham has compiled a list of those in the forces connected with St Mary's Lads' Club, the Sunday School and the Bible classes at St Andrew's – 258 names, from 190 different families. Those on the list who have fallen in their country's cause are:

H. Ellams, W. Golding, A. Groves, A. Hewitt, F. Honhold, W. Jessett, E. Missey, A. Warman & J. Wilson.

'We should like,' writes the Rector, Rev. G.S. de Sausmarez, 'to express, on behalf of all the parish, our deep sympathy and regret with their friends and relatives. But we and they must all feel that, though cut off in such early manhood, they have really done their work and won their rest.'

Letters had been received from several on the list:

<u>Private H. Ellams.</u> 3rd Middlesex. A former Sunday school teacher:

'I received your letter in the firing line, but did not mention my wound, as it is a soldier's duty not to make a fuss of a trifle. I am proud to belong to the class which showed such a fine spirit as to forego the annual outing while their comrades are facing death. I have been to several services in the trenches and it makes one think of home. I shall be glad when it is all over.'

<u>Sapper Reed.</u> Royal Engineers. Signal Depot.

'Thank you for the letter and the most welcome parcel of tobacco. A Taube (German aeroplane) was over us on Friday, but he was a bad marksman. He dropped one bomb in a field about 50 yards from the camp and off he went.'

The list of names will be retained for future reference and when the war is over it is proposed that the roll of honour be prepared and hung in the club for a perpetual memorial of those who volunteered to serve their King and Country.

In addition to the late H.J. Ellams, the following teachers in St Mary's Sunday schools have joined the forces: W.H. Burch, E.G. Humprey, J.A. Lawrence, G.E. Loxton, H. White.

12 November 1915. *Chiswick Times*
Letters to Rev. Oldfield.

<u>Sapper C. Cossins.</u> Somewhere in France.

'We are away from the trenches for a short time. The weather is cold and wet. Things are very quiet at present; our chaps and the Saxons are even waving their hands to one another on the front. You will hardly credit it but it is perfectly true. You would hardly know there was a war on if it weren't for the artillery.'

<u>Private W. Oliver.</u> BEF.

He writes that he is one of the oldest old boys who captained the football team on its trip to Jersey. They are on rest now but not out of range of shell fire.

'I know our boys are eager. We know they hate us, for they shout to us sometimes, "How are you --- Kitchener's dogs?" When we catch a working party we make them shout. They are very bad hearted men all of them. We enjoy ourselves as much as possible. When in the trenches we do guards at night and most of us work in the daytime, digging or repairing trenches, for we have got a lot to do now the winter is coming on. We want more dugouts to sleep in, for it is very cold out here and damp now, so I am in charge now of a lot of men doing these. I have done one and the captain said it was very well done, or if anything is wrong they send for me. I was never a shirker, and it would do a few of the younger ones to have a turn. I am getting on now for 37 years of age, and got two children. Most of our battalion are married men, but they do not care so long as our wives and dear little children are being looked after. I should like to be going along on that fire engine now; anything for life.'

19 November 1915. *Chiswick Times*
Letters to Rev. Oldfield.

Private C. Brand. BEF.

'We are in 'stand to' billets after being in the trenches in knee deep mud for four days and nights. We have been doing four days in and four days out for six weeks and hope for a rest soon. I had a narrow escape last week. Three of us were out on night patrol between the lines when we met a ten man German patrol. Neither side is allowed to shoot when on patrol and must either tackle with bayonets or 'hop it'. We were outnumbered and escaped while the Germans wondered what to do. They are cowards or they would have come at us with the bayonet.'

Driver Fred Bailey. BEF.

'With the help of working parties the division is fixing drying huts in every divisional company's billet for drying clothes when out of the trenches. The huts are grand affairs with windows, concrete floors and two stoves; the work is on hand to prepare for the winter. It is a good thing there is not much harness cleaning; only plenty of dubbin to keep it soft.'

Driver J.M. Clarke. BEF. France.

'The weather is cold and water and mud is everywhere. Last winter was similar but now we have wooden huts with stoves to sleep in and are quite comfortable at night. Remember me to Joe Sparks and I'm sorry to hear about Sonny Mount Stephens illness.

Trooper R. Squair. BEF. France.

'I think I am safe in telling you that I shall very shortly be home on leave. I don't think the war will last more than six months. I have the replacement mouth organ the Rev Oldfield sent after the old one had been blown to death. We are in tents and I hope the wind will not blow them down like it did in our good old camp days.'

19 November 1915. *Chiswick Times*
The battle of Loos

<u>Private Topping.</u> 9th East Surreys. Military hospital at Edinburgh.

A member of Thames Valley Harriers and a shop worker employed at Slaters, George Street, Richmond. He writes to a member of staff at Slaters.

'We got put into the trenches on September 25th ready to make the attack on Sunday the 26th. We got mixed up with West Kents and I never saw any of my pals, only our sergeant, who is a good sort. Our guns had been firing at them for about a week without a break, day and night. When it got light the Germans bombarded us, but all shells dropped behind the trenches. Suddenly they stopped firing. Then our guns started again and pounded them.

The attack started Saturday morning early; we were under the command of the First Army. About 11.30 we got the order to stand to for fifteen minutes and then we got the word "Go." Out of the trench and over the parapet we got, and away we went. The Huns were about 1,100 yards ahead, so we could not double all the way. About halfway our boys started falling; what with shells, gas, machine gun fire, it was hot.

I got to the firing line all right; barbed wire in front; our guns had not touched it, and it was thick. I had fired off about ten rounds when I got such a kick in the side; I thought it was a kick from one of the boys as they crawled up to the firing line. I loaded up again and fired off another five rounds, and then I felt the blood running.

One of my mates behind me had to take off all my kit and cut off my coat to bind me up. While he was doing it I got a bullet through the shoulder, which fractured the scapula.

I then had a lay down and rest; our line had to retire, so I got up and went with them, as my legs were all right. I never expected to get back as they had the machine guns on us and were mowing us down. I had a sporting chance to lay down and wait until dark or make a run for it, so I decided to run, and I did run too. Talk about luck. I at last got back to the trenches and the dressing station. I did hop it back to the dressing station and then had to go about two miles before I got to the Red Cross Hospital. There we waited till next morning for the motors to take us to the base hospital.

My shoulder is getting on fine, and so is my side, and a wound in my foot has healed all right. The thing that upsets me most is that I cannot sleep much. I have had only one good night since September 24th; the nerves of the shoulder and arm are the cause of it.

I have written to Frank Ive to ask about several of my mates from Richmond, who I think are wounded and prisoners of war. I had a narrow escape of being taken. I expect I shall be home a week or two before Christmas.'

Private T.C. Ratcliffe. D Company. 7th East Surreys. A former Richmond Postman writes to his home in Richmond from a hospital in England.

'We had a very heavy bombardment, and expected an attack, which did not come off. That was when I got wounded with shrapnel. I deeply regret to hear the news of the death of Lance-corporal F. Culver, with whom I was chatting before he was knocked over. He was in the best of sprits and was well liked by all who knew him.

I was also with Private Murton, and asked him how he was getting on and he said, 'The same as you. Waiting to have a go at them.' But, poor chap, he has given his life for his King and Country.'

A man attached to a machine gun section. Writes to his uncle in Richmond.

'We have had plenty of rain, and trenches and dug outs are falling in. With a few punts and boats we should think we were on the river. Our trenches are only 75 yards from the enemy, but our chaps are always merry and bright, though they have a grumble now and again. I should like to think all the slackers at home could see us, and they would sign on I bet. You cannot think what it is like until you see it for yourself. I hope they are all helping now.'

Sapper H. Mason. Royal Engineers.

'We are at present in the mining district of France, and wherever you look you are sure to see a coal pit shaft. We had the King round here last week, but his accident prevented him from reviewing the guards, who, by the way, got wet through waiting for him."

26 November 1915. *Chiswick Times*
Letters to Rev. Oldfield.

Sapper P.E. Read. BEF France.

'Thank you for the cigarettes and the Chiswick Times. Bob Hamilton is on leave in England, C.Wrathel is out in France, and W. Woodhead who has written to me is only 100 yards away in the trenches but I've not been able to find him yet. What sort of weather are you having in the land of peace? We have had it hard here up to our knees in mud and water but long jack boots and a long waterproof cloak keep a little wet out.'

Private F.J. Pearce. BEF France.

'Towards night the Germans started with their Maxims going for a good time, so we began to wonder what was up. This carried on for two more nights so during the third day we set our guns aimed at the top of the German parapet. As the daylight began to go they started again, but this time we were ready for them and opened fire. Whatever the result was we cannot say, but they never started again. We also know that their trenches are in a worse state than ours for the other day we caught them emptying palefuls of water over their parapets, so we had a few shots at them that stopped them.'

Driver W. Heath. BEF. France.

'The cocoa and sugar are thankfully received, for we can easy get hot water off the women here, but it is a bit of a job to make them understand what you want. It is a good job if you can understand French, for the people are very good and give us anything.'

3 December 1915. *Chiswick Times*
Letter to Rev. Oldfield.

Private A. Riches. BEF. France.

'I have both legs bandaged up for swollen veins but is still marked fit. We are well looked after for the cold and wet, as we have been issued with rainproof capes and goat skin coats for cold and gum boots, which come up to one's thighs for the wet trenches. Not seen any of the boys and expect to be in the trenches for Christmas.'

17 December 1915. *Chiswick Times*
Letter to Rev. Oldfield.

Sapper P.E. Read. BEF.

'I expect to be home on leave after Christmas and I read in the Chiswick Times that Fred Bailey will be as well. I had a pleasant discovery the other day. While out watching shells bursting I heard the voice of command 'form fours'. I looked across to see which regiment it was and was surprised to see Dick Riches in the London Scottish. I cannot explain my feelings when I saw him. The first old boy I have seen out here. Then there was a little chatter on old times. Dick's billet was opposite mine, and he had been there three days, and I did not know it. We had only five minutes because he marched off to the trenches. I tried to find him when he had done his three days but was too far away.'

17 December 1915. *Acton Gazette*
A Gunner in France.

Gunner A.E. Hawkins. Royal Field Artillery, a nephew of Mr. & Mrs. Hemmings, Church Rd, Acton, who left England for France in April.

'The embarkation from England was very smartly done, and the manner in which our motor cars and cycles with sidecars and guns were handled into the ship holds was splendid. We rode our machines right across France and saw a good deal of the country en route. One was struck by the absence of young men and the number of women engaged on the land. It was not long before we received firing orders, and away we went through the city of Ypres while the enemy was paying it marked attention. It was a sudden breaking-in. The place is a mass of broken brick now and one could not help casting a glance at the awful destruction of some of the world's finest Gothic architecture. The most novel thing to me was the 'star-shells' which are fired by very pistols from both front lines, in order to observe night working parties putting up barbed wire and repairing broken parapets. The light given out by one of these shells is dazzling and shows up the land clearly for miles. One has to be quite still and hide the face (the best thing to do to conceal movement). It makes one feel proud to be a Britisher to witness the fine spirit which dominates everything our boys do here. The sense of comradeship is predominant everywhere. Though naturally the toll has been very heavy, the ascendancy is being attained and held by the Allies on the Western Front. Germans including Prussian Guardsmen gave themselves up a fortnight ago. There is no doubt that the enemy is sickened to death by repeated promises, weary waiting and falsehoods deliberately circulated to hoodwink them.'

31 December 1915. *Acton Gazette*
Tramways Employee's Narrow Escape. Lieut. A.H. Capper of the 1st Butts.

Lieut. Capper was shot in the head when leading a platoon out of the trenches near Ypres on 17th October. He was unconscious for three days and was left without a sense of sight after an operation. On 17th November, he embarked from the Boulogne hospital on the hospital ship Anglia which struck a mine two miles from Dover. He was brought up to the deck. A nurse fitted a life-belt, and he was told to jump into life-boat that of course he could not see. He fell into the water and after 10 minutes was hauled on board a gunboat. The sailors wrapped him in blankets and dosed him with hot milk and rum. For a 'flash of time' he reports he saw Dover harbour clearly. Now in the Empire Hospital, hoping for a full recovery.

8. Gallipoli

A Navy and Army Mediterranean Expeditionary Force (MEF) attempt to secure the Dardanelles at Gallipoli ended in disastrous failure.

26 March 1915. *Chiswick Times*
Letter to Rev. Oldfield.

Private Alfred R. Cox. Royal Army Medical Corps, Malta.

'Getting tired of inactivity and have doubts about ever going to France on account of developments in the Dardanelles. Looking forward to playing the organ at St Mary's church again. Had arranged to play at a barracks church but was shifted to another place.'

30 April 1915. *Chiswick Times*
Letter to Rev. A.E. Oldfield.

C. Humphries. Boy. Late HMS Ocean. Malta Hospital.

'Our ship sank while firing on Turkish forts in the Dardanelles. We did not lose many lives, but your box is gone. When we got hit, three destroyers came alongside and I jumped and slightly sprained an ankle. Don't think I am down-hearted because I am as happy as a sandboy.'

15 May 1915. *Chiswick Times*
Letter to Rev. Oldfield.

Gunner Albert A. Golding. Mediterranean Expeditionary Force.

'You will have read in the papers how we effected a landing at Gallipoli, and at what cost.... It is very hot here during the day, but very cold at night. We have to dig a trench to sleep in, and are continually under shell fire, and of course, when in action, rifle bullets also. My battery has been very lucky, for during a week's hard fighting, we have lost only one man and three wounded and three horses. The infantry have lost very heavily. It is almost impossible to wash and shave here, for we cannot get water, except what is carried from the shore. We are getting good food. Tea and sugar (no milk), bully beef, and biscuits and dried vegetables, jam and cheese. However, there is one article very scarce – matches. They are worth their weight in gold, and you see men drinking water for tea because it is impossible to obtain matches. The sale of matches was prohibited in the troop ships.......... Arriving at the Dardanelles......... Since then things have been very lively. The beach was covered with barbed wire, and the cliffs behind honeycombed with trenches containing maxims, and though a lot of our poor fellows were shot in the boats, I pay this tribute to those who landed and had a very lively time.

I don't think it will take long to subdue Turkey, but can foresee further trouble.'

25 June 1915. *Chiswick Times*
Letter to Rev. Oldfield.

C.G. Osborne. On H.M.S -----.

'What a time I've had since I saw you. Now, to proceed. We proceeded east, reaching the Dardanelles. Then the fun commenced, the first action of the bombardment taking place, the outer forts, Seddul Bahr and Kum Kalessi, having a warm time. The firing ceased for the day about 5pm. We started early the following morning and you may bet the little pills woke them up. My word, it was a sight. We finished firing about 5pm, after a very successful day. We commenced operations again in conjunction with the French fleet, and the 'Lizzie' firing her 15 inch guns at long range. After we had silenced the forts our other ships went in and smashed them....'

2 July 1915. *Chiswick Times*
Letter to Rev. Oldfield.

C.G. Osborne. H.M.S. -------- in the Dardanelles.

'We went to --------- and remained there (the weather being too bad for operations.) The Queen Elizabeth must have had a charmed life, shells bursting and dropping all around, yet not one striking her. Nothing startling happened after this till when Admiral V.A. de Robuck hoisted his flag on the Queen Elizabeth and decided to enter the Narrows and silence the forts. We entered the Straits at 10am and steaming at 7 knots, on the European side, the Turks firing at us the whole time with field guns, we replying with our 6m guns. As soon as ------- was sighted, we opened fire on the forts at a range of about 14,000 yards with our 15 in. guns blowing up a magazine soon after commencing. At 2pm the French closed in to short range and opened fire on all the forts and after half an hour retired to allow Ocean, Irresistible, Triumph and Prince George, supported by Queen Elizabeth and Lord Nelson, to take their places.

It was while this was being done that the Bouvet was seen to list heavily to starboard and disappear in a minute, having struck a mine, which exploded her magazine, only about 50 men being saved. Soon after this, news reached us that the Irresistible and Ocean had struck mines and sunk. We went as near to the former as possible and took on board her men who had been rescued. It was a pitiful sight to see the poor chaps, who had lost everything but what they stood up in, yet through it all, they were cheerful. Several lost their lives owing to the Turks firing on them. All this put a damper on what as otherwise a successful day.'

23 July 1915. *Chiswick Times*
Letter to Rev. Oldfield.
<u>Gunner A.A. Golding</u>. Dardanelles.

'We are progressing slowly by reason of the trench warfare, and are still up against the Achi Baba fortified hill. We are expecting to gain some ground this week. Fresh troops of Kitchener's army are arriving daily, and some of the infantry have been relieved. We are wondering if we shall have the same luck after three months fighting in the heat of the day with no opportunity of a good bath. We are sadly in need of common necessities of man, and one feels the strain. I should esteem it a great favour if you would send me some tobacco.'

13 August 1915. *Chiswick Gazette*
Lieutenant Scammell in the Dardanelles. A narrow escape.

Lieut. Digby Scammell, of the 1st Field Ambulance, R.N. Division, formerly a member of the Acton District Council, writing from Imbros, an island near the mouth of the Dardanelles, where he had gone for a short rest:

'It is a much more difficult job than we anticipated, but we are getting on slowly but surely, and we hope to get it over in a month or two. I came out of camp at about 9 o'clock this morning for a lazy day, and have wandered over the hills to a valley between three hills and am now lying under a fig tree with the homely bracken for a couch. All around me are blackberries, just ripening, pear trees, olive trees, grape vines and apples all to be had for the picking as everything growing appears to be common property. In the distance I see the oxen treading out the corn, as they did in the time of our Lord, the same old wooden tools, forks and ploughs. You would almost think, lying here, that you were living in those olden days, until you turn your head and see the ships in the harbour.

It is now nearly 5pm and the only people that have been near me were a couple of youngsters gathering fruit, and a couple of shepherds with their flocks. It is beautifully warm, and one requires very little clothing. The sun is very hot so the shade of the trees is pleasant, and makes one feel lazy. We dine, however, at 7.30, so as I am one and a half hours from camp, I must soon be moving. I have had a fortnight here and return to duty tomorrow or next day. I met one of my Boy Scouts at Gazba Tepi – Leslie Shaw. The boy joined the New Zealand contingent and I found him carrying ammunition to the trenches. He is only 15½ years old. Mr. Savigear's son is also here, driving a motor ambulance. He recognised me and made himself known.

I had one of many narrow escapes the day I came over here. I was riding to the beach on a motor ambulance, and a shell pitched on the opposite front wheel, and exploded, breaking the driver's arm, and knocking him off his seat on to the top of me, pinning my head to the wheel. The car was just descending the incline towards the beach, and there were eight wounded men in it, so you can imagine our position. The driver, however, showed great presence of mind and faithfulness to duty. Although badly wounded, and suffering from shock, he climbed back to his seat and stopped the car, thereby saving what might have been a terrible smash. After stopping the car, he again fell off his seat, but by this time I had released myself and caught him as he fell off. No-one else was hurt and I got off with a bump on the head, and a sprained wrist. I have recommended the man for the D.C.M. and I think he thoroughly deserves it. There are, no doubt, equally deserving cases occurring every day, but they are not seen by an officer and are therefore unrecorded. The men are really splendid and show a most unselfish spirit. They are all keen to help one another in difficulties, or to give a share of what they have to one more in want.'

27 August 1915. *Chiswick Times*
Letter to Rev. Oldfield.

Gunner A.A. Golding. Mediterranean Expeditionary Force.

'We have established a record for the mountain battery, having fired at 80 yards range and received much attention from the Turkish bomb-throwers while so doing. We are taking part in the final move of the game which should checkmate Mr. Turk. We are very short of water here, but can get a bathe in the sea without shells dropping around us.'

27 August 1915. *Chiswick Times*
Brave and bright – cheerful letters from the danger zone.

<u>Sergeant R.W. Thurlow.</u> Mediterranean Expeditionary Force. Letter to Mr. Copland, Hon. Sec. Victoria Working Men's club.

'Where we are now, we can get nothing, not even a smoke now. Our stock is used that we brought off the ship, so we have not much to do in our spare time. The mails are just beginning to come all right. I've had the 'Thames Valley Times' sent out by mother, and one or two 'Mirrors' and they have livened things up a lot. We are camped just off the beach, and a Turkish gun has been playing all along the beach ever since we've been here. He is known as 'Beechy Bill.' We have been dropping them a few, backed up by a torpedo boat destroyers and monitors, so it doesn't give our position away. We are living, sleeping, and in fact doing everything on the ground. Our beds are not so soft as they are at home. They consist of a blanket and a waterproof sheet on the ground, but we manage pretty well considering. My sub-section has got two dug-outs, but not very large ones, so we all sleep outside in the open. You lay there and hear stray rifle bullets buzzing past. The first night or two we were here, I don't think any of us slept but we don't take any notice of them now.

Young Reg Chamberlain is still with me and is quite fit and well as I am glad to say we are at present. We had an exciting time at the different ports and bays where we stayed coming out here. We could buy what we liked off the small boats which ran up alongside. I must stop now, as they are just starting to come over again, right over our heads and straight on to the beach. I heard yesterday that a gun laid out over two dozen men, and four mules, but its only chance shots, as they have to come over three hills before they pass us.'

September 1915. *Chiswick Times*
With the 10ᵗʰ Middlesex – Private Geoffrey Needham.

In a series of letters written from 28 July to 20 August, the last being from Cairo. Private Geoffrey Needham, 'B' Company, 2-10ᵗʰ Middlesex Regiment, gives his family in High Road Chiswick an idea of the experiences of the voyage in the Mediterranean and the fighting in Gallipoli.

'5ᵗʰ August. 'We have just left Port Said. Isn't it hard to realise that we have been on the water nearly three weeks? Most of us are getting properly fed up with it. Am just off to make up my bed for the night. I say bed – it consists of one blanket on deck – we need nothing over us.'

'20ᵗʰ August. The terrible fighting at the new landing at Salt Lake is described by him while in a Cairo hospital.

'We've been in action and the regiment has lost very heavily. I've escaped so far with nothing worse than a badly twisted ankle. We are now convalescing here. Adams (you remember him) is with me. He has had a little bit chipped off his ankle by shrapnel. He's about the only Middlesex survivor I've seen yet, except a couple of sergeants and three officers. I must now tell you about our three days in action. We landed on the Lala Baba side of Salt Lake. It's a new landing made two days before by the Australians. You're under shell fire from the time you land there. Shrapnel too! All day Monday and Tuesday morning we were doing fatigues on the beach. This fatigue was unloading big guns from the transport tenders. Ammunitions, stores, and all have to be lugged ashore under heavy shrapnel fire.

The British cruisers and monitors, although bombarding the hills all day, have so far been unable to silence these Turkish guns. On the Tuesday afternoon we crossed the Salt Lake and went into the firing line. The Middlesex got right up to the first trench (or rather, dug-out as there are no proper trenches), losing heavily all the while. Then I got separated from the main body. This is how it was – I went out with a small party to try and get in some wounded – Captains Foley and Britten we were trying for. Couldn't find them – managed however to drag in Lance-corporal Ridley (old William Street chap). When I came back the Die Hards had gone, so I went into a trench with the Royal Welsh Fusiliers, fired about 50 rounds at the Turkish devils, ran forward with the Royal Welsh in a charge, fell over and twisted my foot under me, spent the night in an old vineyard. Still under fire (snipers are the worst, they shoot with such uncanny accuracy). At dawn on Wednesday morning I set about crawling the three miles back across the Salt Lake to the beach, reached there in safety and was taken aboard the hospital ship. Went from there to the small island. Sailed then to Alexandria via an old Aberdeen life boat. This morning we came to the military hospital here by the Egyptian State Railway and an R.A.M.C. motor. Except for my foot – pretty painful, though no blood shed, I am fit and well. Hope you are all feeling as well and jolly as I am. Haven't had a mail yet, although I expect you have written. Will write again shortly.'

1 October 1915. *Chiswick Times*
Lieutenant C.H. Pank. 10th Middlesex in Gallipoli. Letter to Lord Cheylesmore, dated 9th September.

'As it is just a month since we landed I thought perhaps you and the members of the County Association might be interested to hear how one of their 'younger children' was getting on. We left England on 17th July, and were three weeks on the voyage out. We called at Malta, Alexandria, and Port Said, and finally landed here about 2am on 9th August. The first day we remained on the beach helping to land stores and whilst there experienced our first shelling..... We had a few casualties that day, but not many.

The following day we went into action, and almost immediately came under severe shrapnel fire. Then, as on the previous day, the men never wavered, and came along absolutely steadily. I am sorry to say our casualties to date are rather heavy. Six officers (four killed) there may be a doubt about one, but I am afraid there is not and two wounded. And about 200 other ranks killed, wounded and missing. So far, although the weather has been hot, it has been beautifully fine; but of course this pleasant state won't last much longer. I must apologise for writing this letter in pencil but here we have no luxuries. My writing table is the top of a biscuit box. I will write again later and let you know how things progress with us.'

1 October 1915. *Chiswick Times*
Letters to Rev. Oldfield.

Corporal A. Richardson. Malta. Australian Territorial Force.

'Just a line from one of your old boys. I have been ill with choleric fever. Getting better but not well enough to walk far and I have got to pull up a few pounds in flesh. I sent you a postcard from Gallipoli.'

Rev. Oldfield writes that Richardson came from Australia and is now in a London hospital.

Driver A.E. Sparkes. MEF. Gallipoli.

'I was never more surprised when who should I meet but young George Allen. The last time I saw him was in Bedford when we had a boat out on the river together. The weather is hot and the rainy season is approaching. I shall not be sorry to hear the last of the war, so that I can get back to my old job at sea again.'

Corporal George Allen. MEF.

'I have met Bill Wells out here. On the 12th the Turks gave us a hot time and we had to lie in our trenches all morning and listen to the shells fly over the top; not nice things to have thrown at you.'

Gunner A.A. Golding. MEF.

In hospital in England having been in the peninsula. 'I was on board the Royal Edward when it was sunk. I had a small loss not worth mentioning as I assume the parcel Miss A. was sending was on the Royal Edward.'

15 October 1915. *Chiswick Times*
Life in the Dardanelles. The Girl Sniper.

Private Percy Hawkins, "A" Squadron, Westminster Dragoons, of Upton House, Gloucester Road, Teddington writes.

'Shells are passing both ways. Bullets constantly fluttering against the sandbags. The enemy were only 500 yards away and our sentry was constantly on the look out for an attack. Cold steel they do not like and they sneak up and throw a bomb or snipe us. They leave all the advance work to us. Snipers are the cause of all the trouble. Eight men have been lost in one section. Another was shot through the hand when he held it up to call someone. Two were shot after dark when they went back for provisions and as a result we went without food the next day.

A sixteen year old girl, painted green with a green rifle hid in a tree top and killed numbers of our men before she was found out. Then she fought tooth and nail until a bullet ended her career.

I have seen awful sights. Heaps of dead and dying with wounded crawling to our trenches after having been without food or water for three days. Some had limbs missing and were caricatures of their former selves. Another point against the Turks is their explosive bullets, which, on striking a bone, make a hole as large as a saucer.'

For three weeks I have worn the same clothes and have only washed twice, water being in short supply. The days are hot and the nights cold and we have no blankets or covering.

A battle has just started up in the air between a Taube and our airship ..... Soon our batteries will commence, and then it will be stand to arms, and with loaded rifles, await eventualities.

To capture a Turkish trench we had to cross three miles of open country to a hill nicknamed 'Chocolate Hill'. We were under a hail of shrapnel and bullets. How anyone escaped alive I do not know. Men were falling in heaps. Gorse and bushes caught alight, and numbers of wounded were roasted alive. When we gained the Turkish trench we were without food and water for sixteen hours. We set about improving the trench with sandbags. There are still many dead around us, but directly one attempts to bury them sniping starts.'

5 November 1915. *Chiswick Times*
Letter to Rev. Oldfield.

Private Joe Brown. MEF. 2-10th Middlesex.

'We only arrived at this rest camp a few days ago. Bert Chandler told me Bert Golding was out here, but don't know what side of the Peninsular he is on. We often run across chaps we know. My pal has just been down to bathe, and he has been round the Indians' cookhouses, and we are going to have a feed of 'patties' that is the name we give them, but we don't know what the real name for them is'.

5 November 1915. *Chiswick Times*
Chiswick Working Men's Club. Letters from Gallipoli.

At end of September they were in the first line of trenches 600yds to 900yds away from the Turks.

Private Kilbey. 'I am living in a dug-out with George Grubb and two others, also plenty of flies and am quite used to living in little holes in the ground. Our cooking and washing arrangements would no doubt amuse people at home. We make biscuit porridge by grinding biscuit and adding a little Nestles. Pancakes are made with biscuit flour and water boiled in bacon fat, and alleged rissoles out of ground biscuit, bully beef and perhaps a bit of onion. These are delicacies compared with the usual fare of biscuit, jam and stew. Some days we get bread, and it works out about six men to a loaf.

We wash out of cut down biscuit tins. Water is scarce and five or six use the same water and sometimes we miss a day. We also wash clothes in cold water. They won't get white, of course, but assume a nice sandy tint.

The flies here are most aggressive. Thousands surround our jam tins. I am writing this letter with a fly net over my head, kindly supplied by H.M.Government. I still have to wave a hand to keep them off. They seem to have a lot more right to our food than we have.

At nights we sleep in our overcoats and boots to keep the cold out. Heavy dew falls. The daytime temperature is just about right. Not too hot, but it is practically dark at 6.30pm.

We are still optimistic and expect to have our duff at Christmas in England. Please send anything in tins but they should be well wrapped in strong cardboard boxes. Some boxes get smashed and the contents lost. A good many chaps only get the wrappers instead of the complete package."

In a footnote, Private Grubb says that Hillier and Dexter are both well.

Private G. Grubb.

'At present we are in huge uncovered dug-outs on the top of cliffs with a sheer drop to the sea. There are cold north winds with rain and how we manage to live through it I don't know. Many fall sick and are sent away to hospital. We are much worse off than cave dwellers – they did have a cover when it rained. The only cover we have is a waterproof groundsheet around our shoulders and we sleep on the ground and wake to find the blankets wet through.

Food is not so bad with the aid of parcels from home. Cakes should be in air-tight tins otherwise they arrive mouldy.

Bert Chandler is progressing as well as can be expected. Hillyer is all right. His name being mixed up with Hilliard when the latter was injured by a shell. Artillery duels seem to be the only things going on at present. You hear the bang, and look towards the hills to see the result – an immense cloud of dust. Ships' guns and land batteries firing away and causing the Turks to duck. We have had some shells over, but not so many as we used to get, thank goodness.

Needham has turned up again and except for weakness of the ankle is quite fit. Several men and officers have rejoined us during the last few days.'

12 November 1915. *Chiswick Times*

A wounded man's appeal.

Corporal F. Dear. 1-10th Middlesex, writing from North Ward, County of London War Hospital, Epsom.

'Having the Chiswick Times sent to me every week since I have been in hospital, I have noticed you are asking for letters from the Chiswick boys now on active service or wounded in hospital. I am glad to inform you I myself am an old Chiswick lad, and was wounded with the 2-10th Middlesex Regiment at the Dardanelles while in charge of a party of 48 men who had been cut off the night before. I got the order from a staff officer to take the men and reinforce the firing line. I got them out, and advancing across Salt Lake, we came under a heavy shell fire. I dropped my men down under a ridge for cover, where we were only troubled with some snipers. One man was hit in the right arm. He was also a Chiswick lad. I got along to him, bound his arm up, and coming back, I was hit through the left wrist and hand.

My brother, Sergeant W. Dear, of the Duke of Wellington's Regiment, was wounded in France last year, and is now on active service in the Dardanelles. My brother-in-law Private H. Wheatley, of the 1st Devons, was killed in action on 30th October of last year. He was the son of the late Mr. Henry Wheatley, of Chiswick. And I have also a nephew, Trooper C. Wrathell, of the 11th Hussars, now on active service in France. I should think by the Chiswick Times that the lads of Chiswick have answered the call fairly well, but I hope those who have not yet joined will roll up and do so at once.'

12 November 1915. *Chiswick Times*

Life in the Dardanelles.

Letter received by a Town Hall official.

'We have landed safely and are well. I don't like this place at all. It's hot in the daytime and very cold at night. It's a bit rough living in dug-outs – not much room – six of us in an 8-foot square hole, with plenty of shells banging about where we live. Shan't be sorry to get back to England again. Must say we get plenty of food out here. The worst of it is we have to have stew every day, get no butter. If we want to buy cheese, it is 4lbs for 6s. Cigarettes are 1½d a packet of five, and we have to order them a week before we get them.'

19 November 1915. *Chiswick Times*
Letter to Rev. Oldfield.
W.P. Braley. 2/10th Middlesex. MEF.

'I was wounded on 10th August and was in the 3rd Australian Hospital on an island before being sent to the Convalescent Camp. Getting on well but things are monotonous.' He complains about the flies.

26 November 1915. *Chiswick Times*
Letter to Rev. Oldfield.
Private G. Quelch. MEF.

'I have been in hospital for a fortnight suffering from dysentery, a complaint which is very bad here. I am feeling weak and will not feel much like using a pick and shovel when I rejoin the boys. We attended an open air service on Sunday and the Welsh R.A.M.C. fellows improved the singing. Three shells came down during the service but no one was injured and the service was completed. Pleased to hear that Bert Chandler is back home.'

Corporal G. Allan. MEF.

'Not met many Chiswick lads although there are plenty here. Weather is wet and cold. I hope and trust the war won't last much longer. Must close now as it is dinner time, and we are going digging.'

Gunner A.A. Golding. MEF.

'Thank you for the parcel. Now on the island of Lemnos, 47 miles south of the Dardanelles working as brigade quartermaster storeman so I find myself to a certain extent linked up again with civilian life. The news from Flanders and France is great. Of course, the action of Bulgaria has complicated matters, but makes it more necessary to finish the job.'

26 November 1915. *Acton Gazette*
Fireman at the front – letter from Arthur Mitchell.

Mr. J. Mitchell, the resident engineer at the Acton Fire Station, received a letter from his son Arthur, with the Mediterranean Expeditionary Force. Members of the Fire Brigade had sent him a watch.

'I am very pleased with the watch, as I shall be able to see the time at night when I am on guard. Wal is still in hospital and will be for a couple of days. Young Johnny Woollard I know was wounded in the trenches, just behind me, but it was only a slight wound in the feet. Now he is on base duty. Gudgin was a bit dicky the other day, but is well again.

We are still in the dugouts by the sea, and on digging and other fatigues, but there is one thing about it – we do get a decent night's rest, which we did not a little while ago. The weather here is very changeable, first it is very cold and now it is just like English weather only a little more wind here. I am in the bomb-throwers now and attending a class of instruction. They go off with a bang, but there is not much in it – just like cricket. I never felt better than I am now. Just remember me to them all at the station and Holfords and everybody else.'

3 December 1915. *Chiswick Times*
Letter to Rev. Oldfield.

<u>Corporal H. Chandler.</u> 2/10th Middlesex. In hospital in the Dardanelles.

'I don't think my regiment has disgraced Chiswick out there, as they were a battalion formed since the war, and very young, but the way they advanced across Salt Lake under shrapnel and rifle fire would have done credit to any regulars. We went across in half companies in line at six pace intervals and three hundred yard distance, making eight lines following each other. This was our baptism of fire, and although chaps kept dropping the lines never wavered; and we had to keep stopping to avoid getting too close to the line in front. There was no hurry; it was a steady walk, and the dressing of the lines was nearly perfect, but I think everyone breathed a sigh of relief when we found cover in the reserve trenches. We then advanced to the front line of trenches, which we were in for three days. We were then relieved and taken to the reserve trenches where we were for another three days. We were then relieved for rest.

We came back to the beach and were working night and day carrying water and bully beef from the boats. It was while on the beach that I got hit, as during the day you are always under shell fire, although at night the Turks do not fire, as they would show our chaps their gun position.

Well sir, I think the 2/10th Middlesex, which contains so many of your boys, will do all that is asked of it wherever they are sent and will be a credit to Chiswick. Wishing to be remembered to all St. Mary's old boys who know me, not forgetting Bert Golding.'

17 December 1915. *Chiswick Gazette*
Corporal Wilson in Gallipoli.

'We have been through some terrible ordeals. As the boys say, it is hell itself, and I must say that that is the nearest description one can give. We received our baptism of fire on the first day of the landing. We landed minus opposition at about 2am on Sunday 9th August, by lighters which charged at the beach and fixed themselves firmly in the sand. The boats of the lighters were then lowered and we jumped off. We unloaded our stores, and dropped down to sleep for a few hours.

About 5.30, we heard a terrific explosion, and I jumped up. The Q.M.S. looked at me and I at him. Then he said 'That's one of us, Roy, boy'. Then it went again and we discovered that it was one of our land batteries. Needless to say, there was no more sleep. We prepared a hurried breakfast of tea and a biscuit (we carried three days' food).

The Turks had got our range perfectly, and they kept popping away, but their shells were evidently of poor quality as a large percentage failed to explode, probably owing to sand. I got up to go over to some rocks to take cover, when I heard another one coming. I dropped down and the thing screamed over my back, and buried itself in the sand, only a yard or two behind. I had one more narrow escape that day, of a similar nature. They shelled us on and off all day, and their bag amounted to one killed and one wounded. It was our first loss. When our fellows were burying the poor chap, they absolutely shelled the party, one dropping almost on the edge of the grave.

The next day, our boys were ordered up to the line and away they went, cheerful and quite happy. To get to the line, they were obliged to go over land absolutely barren and flat for about two miles. They opened out in extended order, and went up in perfect order, just for all the world as though they were on a parade ground, despite the hail of shells. I remained behind to get their food up to them, so I cannot describe their experiences to any extent. I only know that they were commended on the splendid way they advanced, and that they lost rather heavily.

My orders were to get off with a party and the Q.M.S. to draw rations, a distance of three miles through heavy sand, and minus water. It was getting very hot, and the omission of this precious fluid was very hard to bear. We arrived at the A.S.C camp and after drawing rations, we sat down to get some dinner – bully beef and biscuits. After that, we had quite a pantomime loading the boxes of food on to the Indian pack mules. As fast as they were loaded, they bolted, throwing off the boxes, thereby undoing all our work, and compelling us to start all over again. The heat was terrific, but our boys laughed and thoroughly enjoyed the fun, especially when the blacks started shouting at them.

Eventually the time came to start off with the convoy. We were told that the battalion was in 'such and such a direction' and that's where you will make for. Easier said than done. Away we went, and so did the snipers; we were sniped from all directions, but what shots! They all pinged wide and we arrived, minus casualties. Returning we were not so lucky, losing some mules and one Indian. This job lasted for several days and our experiences were very varied and much too numerous to mention here.

7 January 1916. *Chiswick Times*
Letters to Rev. Oldfield.

Gunner A.A. Golding. MEF Mudros.

'Many thanks for unexpected parcel. As time is drawing on, and there are no signs of my spending Christmas at home, I must take this opportunity of wishing you a Happy Christmas and a brighter New Year. Lord Kitchener visited these parts last week, and I am optimistic enough to consider that coming events cast their shadows before them. History shows that when a Britisher is apparently beaten, he astonishes everyone by winning. The weather is now very severe.'

Gunner A. A. Golding. MEF. Mudros.

'As you will see I am not in Serbia. I did not know Fred Bain is shifting (moves are made without reason). Christmas will be very dull. Mails can only get ashore on calm days. Winter has set in. We feel the cold more after the intense summer heat.'

16 January 1916. *Chiswick Times*
Letters to Rev. Oldfield.

Gunner Matthew Bain. In hospital in Egypt.

'I have been wounded in the legs. It was by a nasty shell. I am well looked after sir. I wrote to you whilst I was at the Dardanelles. My brother Fred is at Salonica. I think I am a very lucky man by being at the Dardanelles since the landing, which is now eight months ago, and have only just been hit.'

Private W. Braley. Convalescent Clearing Station, Mediterranean Expeditionary Force.

'In answer to your letter, which came as a pleasant surprise, I am pleased to say I am in A1 health, I think I am rather lucky to being able to say so, for the climate has played havoc with some of our fellows. You can quite understand what a change it is for us boys out here, and at times things get monotonous. Still this is only one of the many troubles one meets on active service and we manage to get over it. I may re-join my battalion any day now. I received the Chiswick Times last night, it was like old times to get a glimpse at the local paper once again.'

21 January 1916. *Acton Gazette*
Ghastly story of Gallipoli – Acton man's experience.

Letter received from Private Turney – of 47 Churchfield Rd, Acton, known to his Acton friends as 'Simmy'. He is an old Priory School boy, for some years a keen member of the 2nd Acton Company Boys Life Brigade & the Acton Congregational cricket & football teams. He joined the 7th Royal Fusiliers soon after the outbreak of war, was wounded and sent home from France early 1915, and went out to the Dardanelles last September. Now in St David's hospital, Malta with frostbite & yellow jaundice.

'You will be surprised to hear that I am at Malta in hospital with frostbite. On November 26, I was in the trenches when a monsoon came on about 8 o'clock at night. It started with lightning and thunder, much worse than we get in England. Then it started to rain, but after about half an hour it began to rise in the trenches. It got higher and higher, and it came down the hill at such a rate that it filled the trenches in no time. We managed to scramble out on the top, but there were hundreds who got drowned. The Turks were the same. It left off about two hours after. We were standing in the open, the water being up to our knees. We stood in this for about six hours till it went down. It went down to our feet, then we started to dig ourselves in behind the trenches, which were still full. I lost everything. Well, by the time we finished digging, it was morning. It was only a cover for our heads, as we had no tools to dig trenches. The next morning over came the shells, shrapnel bursting all round us and bullets whizzing all around.

We got no rations that day, as no one could walk, for as you put your foot down so you sank down to your waist. All next day it was raining, we had to stand still in it. At last night came. It began to snow and then to freeze. It was terrible. There were fellows dying with the cold and others groaning. It was a terrible night which I shall never forget. Another fellow and myself were leaning against each other, breathing in one another's face and neck to get a bit of warmth. It was just like slow murder – fellows as stiff as pokers, killed by the cold. About 3am, we had the order to get back if we could. It took me a long time to bend my legs and my feet – well, I did not know I had any.

The sight was awful. There were fellows stuck in the mud like dummies, frozen to death. They had sunk in the mud, and could not get out, and so froze to death. I went in several times past my knees, but being a bit strong I managed to get out. It took us a long time to get back to brigade headquarters, as at every foot we put down, we would sink down to our knees. There were about 60 got back there out of 700. There were other regiments who were the same, but our lot seemed to have got the worst of it. When we got back we had a new change, which we all badly wanted. We were smothered up to our faces with mud. We then had some hot tea and something to eat. Each day after there were fellows going sick with their feet so that they all slowly went into hospital.

There were two new drafts came to take over the trenches. After a week's rest we joined the new draft – the rest that were left of us, which were not many. I got a job as stretcher bearer. I had no sooner been told off for the job than we were sent to fetch a chap in. There were only two of us. We went off, both of us being weak on

253

our feet. We followed the trench along and at last we came across the fellow. He had been hit with shrapnel in the head, and had half his head blown off. My mate and I looked at one another and then at the poor fellow for about five minutes. We both thought we were put on a fine job for the first case. He was down in the trench and as we tried to lift him, we sank into the mud, so we had to go back and tell the sergeant that we could not lift him out so he sent three more men and at last we managed to get him back all right. The next day I went sick with my feet, which were very painful and could hardly walk.

I got admitted to hospital in Turkey, but I was only in there three days and I got sent back to my regiment. I went back to the firing line and got my feet wet again. I had the job of digging dead men out of the mud, and at night-time I was in charge of a party to bury them, as I was the only one who knew the way about. After we came back from the trenches, I went sick again, and got admitted to hospital. I went straight on to the hospital boat and then to Malta. I am now getting on very good and hope to be out fighting again soon.'

'But now, after three months, things are considerably altered. Everything is a treat now – food excellent, conditions better, dug-outs like palaces; in fact we could not be more comfortable at home. We have done the rough work and prepared the way, and just give some of the slackers the hint that there is plenty of room for them to come and give the old Die-Hards a rest.'

28 January 1916. *Chiswick Times*
Letter to Rev. Oldfield.

First Class Stoker. R.M. Osborne. Haslar.

'I am still improving, but will not be out of here for a few weeks yet. I saw Alf Punter last week. My brother Charlie and his wife came to see him Sunday. He is still doing very well and expecting promotion to wardroom rank very shortly. Please thank Mrs. W.J.H. for sending the Chiswick Times.'

25 February 1916. *Chiswick Times*

Letters to Mr. Copland, Victoria Working Men's Club.

Bombardier Thurlow. Royal Field Artillery.

'I was in Gallipoli and managed to get a parcel to my brother in Egypt. Naturally our life is a busy one. No doubt we shall be in action again soon. None of us are satisfied with this place and it is agreed that the sooner we are 'in it' again the better we shall like soldiering'.

Private S.P. Langston. Middlesex Regiment Convalescent Hospital in Cairo.

'We were suffering from exposure about the middle of December, and after a time in a field hospital were taken in small boats, which had to dodge the Turks' shrapnel and high explosives, which luckily fell wide. It feels good to be safe in the hospital ship, with its nice beds and white sheets. The nurses are very good to us, doing all they can to make us comfortable. It seems strange to see a woman. Those on the hospital ship were the first ladies we had seen for nearly six months. Being on the Peninsula reminded me of the old song 'Put me on an island where the girls are few!'

17 March 1916. *Chiswick Times*

Letter to Rev. Oldfield.

Acting Bombardier A.A.Golding. Egypt.

'Apart from the distance in miles between us, we are nearer as regards the receipt of letters. I am very glad of course to be away from the Dardanelles, but feel at times that our sacrifices were in vain, especially when I think of the hundreds, even thousands, of graves of chums. It was not to our discredit that we could not do things which men could not accomplish, and I think that all who knew Gallipoli will agree that we all rendered a good account of ourselves. Pleased to hear Bert Chandler is going on so well, and Ralph and Ted Allen. There is an Allen from Chiswick on board on the lake and if possible I will pay him a visit. Now I may acquaint you with the change of rank since last writing – I am an acting bombardier now, sir.'

24 March 1916. *Acton Gazette*

Private W. West, formerly of Oaklands Road, Hanwell school teacher, writes from Alexandria, Egypt.

"We reached Sulva Bay 11pm on August 21st. We soon had our baptism of shell fire from the Turks shelling us regularly at meal times for half-an-hour. Without any breakfast we started on fatigue work, unloading the ship and including pumping water out of the pontoons. I staggered up the beaches with boxes of jam, milk, bacon etc, now and again dashing for cover when the Turks staffed us with their shells. Luckily many did not explode, but we had casualties every day.

We carried on for a fortnight – four hours on and four hours off. In the period of four hours off we had to do our washing, sleep, cook our breakfasts and deepen our dug-outs and got precious little sleep.

After a fortnight we moved up to the reserve trenches at Hill 10 and got our first experience of sniping. We had to move forward towards the Turkish trenches and from 8pm till midnight dig a communication trench. Bullets whistled about us the whole time, but in two nights we sustained only one casualty.

After a quiet spell we moved round to reserve trenches in Salt Lake and finally to uncovered dug-outs on the Lala Baba cliff side. Here we slept by platoons thirty or forty yards up the cliff.

Towards the end of November we experienced the worst thunder storm of my life. The noise of the 6in and 9.2in guns on the warships were a whisper compared with the thunder which was awful, terrific and quite awe-inspiring. The darkness could be felt and the torrential rain washed us out of our dug-outs. Packs, equipment and great-coats were soon buried in mud, and afterwards had to be literally dug out.

Following that came intense cold, snow, frost and gales. We had no protection, several had lost great-coats and blankets and few had underclothing. In this state we had to man some trenches near Lala Baba. That night finished off hundreds of us. We were carried in large numbers next morning to the clearing station and on December 1st left the peninsular, and soon found ourselves in hospital in Cairo.'

20 October 1916. *Chiswick Times*
Letter to Rev. Oldfield.

Herbert Rose. Somewhere abroad.

Safe and sound. He would like to know how Harry is getting on. 'We were lucky. We came out of the boat that I suppose you heard was sunk ..... I would have written more often, but cannot get any paper. I had to cadge this.'

9. Egypt and Palestine

The British had a garrison in Egypt to protect the Suez Canal. The garrison was strengthened against the Turks and by the end of 1918 the British had occupied Palestine and Syria.

3 December 1915. *Chiswick Times*
Letter to Rev. Oldfield.

Corporal W.A. Reed. He had been in the trenches at Loos.

'Now in Egypt under canvass with my shirt off, as it is very hot. I read in the papers that the navy has got the Germans in an iron grip. I think the war will last till the middle of next year. It is quite a treat to be miles away from the trenches and not to hear the shells passing over your heads.'

16 January 1916. *Chiswick Times*
Letters to Rev. Oldfield.

Gunner Matthew Bain. In hospital in Egypt.

'I have been wounded in the legs. It was by a nasty shell. I am well looked after sir. I wrote to you whilst I was at the Dardanelles. My brother Fred is at Salonica. I think I am a very lucky man by being at the Dardanelles since the landing, which is now eight months ago, and have only just been hit.'

Private W. Braley. Convalescent Clearing Station, Mediterranean Expeditionary Force (MEF).

'In answer to your letter, which came as a pleasant surprise, I am pleased to say I am in A1 health, I think I am rather lucky to being able to say so, for the climate has played havoc with some of our fellows. You can quite understand what a change it is for us boys out here, and at times things get monotonous. Still this is only one of the many troubles one meets on active service and we manage to get over it. I may re-join my battalion any day now.

I received the Chiswick Times last night, it was like old times to get a glimpse at the local paper once again.'

4 February 1916. *Chiswick Times*
Letter to Rev. Oldfield.

Corporal G. Allen. MEF base, Egypt.

'So sorry I have not written sooner, as we were not allowed to, as the officers could not censor the letters; the reason for that was that we were leaving shortly. How are the boys getting on? I do hope they are all sticking together and keeping the band going. I am just longing for the time when we all get home and have a good march with our band, which we all were and are so proud of. Well, we enjoyed ourselves on Christmas morning. We had a church service; then in the afternoon we played another regiment at football and defeated them 4 goals to 2. I captained the Middlesex team and scored two goals.'

4 February 1916. *Chiswick Times*
Letters to Rev. Oldfield.

Private G. Quelch. MEF. Somewhere in Egypt.

'We left the Peninsular five weeks ago. The nearest town is about 35 miles away. When we first arrived there was nothing but sand to welcome us, but now it is all tents, and any amount of canteens have sprung up. We have a YMCA here too. With the different kinds of food we buy, we are able to considerably improve the army rations. We have plenty of drills and although it is supposed to be winter, we find it pretty warm at times. I am glad to hear A. Reffold & B. Chandler are doing well, but am sorry about A. Cox and C.T. Cook. Have just finished three and a half hours route march on the sand and it is hard work plodding through sand.'

Gunner A.A. Golding. Somewhere in Egypt.

'I was very pleased to get your Christmas card and letter. As you will observe by the address, I am now in the land of the Pharaoh. I may not speak of matters previous to the curtain dropping on the 'play at the

Dardanelles' but this much I may say. I think that 'home', the magic place to which our minds are ever turned, is still a thing to dream about. I think the Division will find work to do here for a few months to come. Every man who was in action at Gallipoli will welcome the new position. It will mean the enemy dashing to destruction against hopeless odds instead of vice versa. I felt highly honoured passing through famous Egyptian battlefields and I am now in the desert.'

11 February 1916. *Chiswick Times*
Letters to Rev. Oldfield.

Corporal G. Allen. MEF. Somewhere in Egypt.

'We have not got any of those shells flying around us now, so we can walk about in peace and comfort. How are all the boys getting on? Wait till we all come home, we shall have a band to march round to church with, and what a day that will be. We will let the people of Chiswick know that St Mary's can still turn out one of the finest bands in London......

Trumpeter G. Keywood. MEF.

'Just a line to let you know we have arrived out here. All the boys wish to be remembered to you, and they say it is somewhat different to Margate. We had a pleasant voyage. It is very warm but we are close to the sea.'

18 February 1916. *Chiswick Times*
'A couple of Scraps' Twickenham man with the 'Die-hards'.

Sergeant R. Seymour, 2-8th Middlesex Regiment, in Alexandria – writing to Mr. W. Howell of the Twickenham Club.

'We have moved into a more useful sphere of work. Our camp is right beside the sea, in which we have some jolly fine bathing. On the other side is the desert. We are miles from civilisation, and that is about all I am allowed to tell you, although if you have read in the papers of our doings on this front you will have a pretty good idea of where we are. We have been out to a couple of scraps, but in neither did we get anything very exciting. We spent all Christmas day at a fight, and had a lovely view of the whole affair without being able to get right into it ourselves. We have a bit of excitement now and then, but now are quite used to it, and settled down. It is a strange life after the long time we spent in barracks, but we are absolutely fit and as happy as we can be as far away from all.

I expect you have heard how we travelled on this 'tour' of ours. I enjoyed myself well at Gibraltar, and was able to go into Spain and see a bull fight among other things. When we left there we called at Malta but did not land. Then we went to Lemnos, the Dardanelles base, and saw all the fleet and various ships in the fine natural harbour. After 24 hours there we were taken to Alexandria and thence to Cairo. After a few weeks in barracks there, we went under canvas for training. The sights of Egypt are well worth seeing... In this way we are much better off than our pals in France because they had not had much variety of scene and we have been able to see things which would have cost us a tidy bit at any other time.'

18 February 1916. *Chiswick Times*
Letter to Rev. Oldfield

Gunner Matthew Bain. Hospital in Egypt.

'I have good news for you. My wounds are almost better, but I am still in bed. I got up the other afternoon for a couple of hours to a sofa, and I think I shall be coming to England when I am well enough, which won't be long. I am very pleased to tell you that I have heard from my brother Fred and he tells me that he is going on all right. But he has the same opinion as myself – he wishes the war was all over and he was back in England. Your letter gave me another surprise, when I read that Tom was in the 2nd Life Guards. He must be getting a fine big fellow to get in that regiment. Well, Sir, I wrote and told him to carry on. Tom is my fifth brother to join the army. This is a very nice hospital and the doctors are so clever and nice to the men, likewise the sisters, and I have a few visitors to come and see me. Several of my old comrades and the major of the battery often come and bring me cigarettes and sweets. He is a very nice officer and cares for me very much.'

3 March 1916. *Chiswick Times*
Letter to Rev. Oldfield.

Corporal G. Allen. Somewhere in Egypt.

'Enjoying ourselves very much. We are camping out in a desert and it seems like the old times again when we used to camp out at Margate. We have a YMCA tent where we do all our writing and have our sing-songs, and an afternoon off each week to play football, and have an open-air service on Sundays. We also have a day's leave and four of us had a donkey Derby and I tell you it caused a bit of excitement, seeing us bumping up and down. I met Bert Sparks out here. He is in the signal service.'

17 March 1916. *Chiswick Times*
Letter to Rev. Oldfield.

Private T.D. Rose. Somewhere in Egypt.

'I saw Bill Wells the other day. I was walking in the street when heard someone shout out 'Tom Rose!' and I was very glad to see him, as he is the first of the boys I have run across. Then yesterday, I met one of his regiment and asked him what battalion Tom was in. So I went about six miles and when I got there not one of the boys was there, only some of the newer ones and I was disappointed. I don't suppose I shall see Bill Wells again as we are moving soon. We find it very different to France'.

24 March 1916. *Chiswick Times*
Letters to Rev. Oldfield.

Private Joe Brown. Somewhere in Egypt.

'You will notice I am at a rest camp. The battalion is a few miles down the line. I was sent to the hospital 6th February and then on to here and am now doing very well. I am pleased to hear Alf Evans is in England but did not think his feet were so bad. I must say Egypt is a very nice place; the weather is lovely. I am going to the pyramids in a few days, they are only a few miles away and I hope to have my photograph taken with the Sphinx as the background.'

Private F.W. Barnes. Somewhere in Egypt.

'As you see, they have sent me out here again for the third time after being invalided from France & Sulva Bay. We are out in the desert amongst the Arabs and it is very warm, you have to go about with almost nothing on. It is about 110 degrees in the sun, and 90 in the shade. We don't have much time for ourselves; when we do you can bet we make good use of it and we have to keep a good look out for the natives, as some of them are like cannibals – go mad – but never mind, it won't last much longer and I shall be home for good.'

28 April 1916. *Chiswick Times*
Letters to Rev. Oldfield.

Corporal T.D. Rose. Egypt.

'Some fine work has been done, not only capturing the Senussi's towns, but also rescuing sailors that were made prisoners last November, their ship having been sunk by a German submarine. They were in a shocking condition; no clothes and had been living on snails. An officer had escaped from the Arabs, but after walking 20 miles had to give in through exhaustion, and was recaptured, stoned and spat on. The Senussi guns were fired by Turks. I had a letter from Wally Woodhead and Frank Cooper. They are in good health.

I went out last Sunday in a car about 25 miles and found a cave. The first thing I saw was a hole one yard in diameter. We dropped down about 12ft, and there were three passages in it about 15 yards long and 5 wide. The walls were marked with Egyptian figures.'

5 May 1916. *Acton Gazette*
'Die Hards' in Egypt.

Private Alfred Fysh. Middlesex Territorial Regiment writes to his parents at 5, Elm Place, Ealing Green from convalescent hospital at Alexandria, Egypt.

'I think I deserve this rest after 14 months without a day's leave after hardships and privations at Matruh. The only work I have to do here is make my bed each evening. The niggers do the rest. The fighting at Saloom, Sidi Barani and in the Matruh district is entirely finished. We annihilated the Senussi.'

He enclosed an account, written by a reporter who is also in the hospital, of the rescue of 92 British sailors who were torpedoed in the Mediterranean and taken ashore as captives. For five months they were starved and their clothes were in tatters when rescued by a British armoured car convoy. The report had been considerably censored.

19 May 2016. *Chiswick Times*
Letter to Rev. Oldfield.

Private George Quelch. Somewhere in Egypt.

'Have recovered from the Peninsular complaints. Quite a number of Chiswick lads have joined us, one being young Goddard. We have had new uniforms issued and no longer walk about looking like tramps. It is very hot and the flies are nearly driving us dotty .... Time we had fly nets issued. ... We had a nasty sand storm a few days ago, blowing marquees and canteens down, and it was a hard job to get about, being difficult to breathe and see. We have just been inoculated and are having 48 hours rest, the unfortunate part being we are miles from nowhere and have to be content with lying in the tent and being pestered by flies.'

2 June 1916. *Chiswick Times*
Letter to Rev. Oldfield.

<u>Corporal G. Allen</u>. Somewhere in Egypt

'I have not written before as I have been busy studying a new gun. I have been sent to the Imperial Instructional School for three weeks, when I hope to become an instructor in my battalion. So far I have done very well, getting three firsts in an examination. I have got four more examinations to go through. The weather out here is terrible. I am sure we shall all be grease spots soon.'

9 June 1916. *Chiswick Times*
Letter to Rev. Oldfield.

<u>Bombardier A.A. Golding</u>. Somewhere in Egypt.

'We are many miles from any civilisation in the desert, not a great distance from the Holy Land. But not on a picnic. Imagine walking in marching order 25 miles in one day on sand which under the heat of an African sun burns our feet. Or better still, imagine a walk of 25 miles along a stretch of seashore on the deep sand unwashed by the sea, and you will arrive at the condition of things here. We are rounding up an enemy or tools of an enemy cut off from civilisation. We even depend upon a tobacco tin of water for shaving and for use of our daily ablution. However we are old campaigners and know the value of water. I have not run across any of the boys yet, and I don't suppose I shall now. It was a hard blow after fighting a campaign to a finish with the ----- Division, to find they went home and left the only territorial ----- of the division to be attached to others, and have our second summer under conditions far from pleasant. I think the enclosed cutting from 'the News of the World' will interest you. I hope you are getting less attention from the Zepps. The last news I heard was the capture of Treziboud and the fall of Kut. In regard to the latter I hope the Russians can push on towards Bagdad. I am fairly well.'

16 June 1916. *Chiswick Times*
Letter to Rev. Oldfield.

Bombardier A.A. Golding. Somewhere in Egypt.

'The boys are indeed scattered about the globe, in fact I think you have a representative in nearly all the fields of operation, even Germany. At present we are attached to the Anzacs – or what is left of them – in Egypt. A fortnight ago we reached the shade temperature of 125 degrees with 135 degrees in the sun. We are continually on the move. Like our neighbours in Mesopotamia we are not over-blessed with water. Tom Rose is the other side of Egypt.'

21 July 1916. *Chiswick Times*
Letter to Rev. Oldfield.

Acting Bombardier A.A. Golding. Somewhere in Egypt.

'A great blow to lose Lord Kitchener but must be a stimulant to all to carry on. Tramping around the desert is monotonous especially as we never get a brush with the enemy. We are provided with shorts of the football pattern. On the Peninsular we used to cut down our trousers but this is now forbidden.'

4 August 1916. *Chiswick Times*
Letters to Rev. Oldfield.

Bombardier A.A. Golding. Egypt.

'Thank you for the parcel that I shared with others. A parcel of Gold Flake came from Mr. O'R in New York. Also though the Peninsular was bad I preferred it to this hard campaigning without results.'

Private Joe Brown. Egypt.

'We have had a week's holiday. A jolly time in the sea and a pass to the town. Now back in the desert as hot as ever in the tents. Hope to go back in a few days if only for a regular supply of water.'

1 September 1916. *Acton Gazette*
Voices from the Desert. St Mary's Acton Lads' Club letters.

'We are somewhere in Egypt at a very lonely outpost fifteen miles from the nearest town. Things are very quiet apart from a few big guns practicing. Our chaplain is very good. The battalion is spread out over such a long distance that it is impossible to arrange for all companies to have a service on a Sunday. We had ours this morning (Wednesday). In Gallipoli services were held under shell fire so you can imagine the great difference here.'

Another reports that the nearest town five miles away is out of bounds. 'The first two days I was here there was a fearful sandstorm, much worse than any London fog. We have a few canteens on the camp, but have to pay very high as there is no competition. I am 'hors de combat' after a typhoid injection and cannot take part in the sports – football and boxing. Because of the heat drills marches take place at 4am and another hour in the evening. Everyone remarked how fat and well I am looking, but I expect the fat will be gone in a few weeks' time. The flies are a perfect nuisance.'

A third says he would like to get away for a swim in the Suez Canal. 'This is the place where the Israelites had their forty years; no wonder they grumbled. The chaplain delivers interesting sermons usually about the Israelites in Egypt. I wonder if we will be home by Christmas.

20 October 1916. *Chiswick Times*
Chiswick Working Men's Club. Letters received by Mr. Thomas A. King, secretary of the club.

George Grubb. In Egypt.

'I am with Needham, both fit and well. I don't know where Kilbey is. After a series of moves we are near a pretty town and undergoing inspections by various generals. We may be booked for the other side soon. We had a couple of swimming galas when we were by the canal for a short time. We did not participate in the fighting, although we were in reserve and would have welcomed a chance of a go at our enemy.'

27 October 1916. *Chiswick Times*
Letters to Rev. Oldfield.

Corporal S. Allen. Egypt.

'We have moved to a good place at last since we left Suvla. I have now been put in the band, which I think will turn out very good. Could you send me a fife and a few matches. I'm sorry to hear that Fred Smith was killed and that others have been wounded. I honestly think they have done their bit. We have been inspected by a Major-General who complimented us on the smart turn out. We are now nick-named the Bluebell Battalion. Had a surprise visit from Bert Sparks.'

Private E. Ward. Egypt.

'My pals and I have been on short rations for fags and are grateful for those you sent us. I have run across G. Allen. We have plenty of water now, but the flies are rotten. I look forward to the end when some of us will be able to compare notes and tell a few tales.'

24 November 1918. *Chiswick Times*
Letter to Rev. Oldfield.

Private E. Ward. Egyptian Expeditionary Force.

'Still quite well and attached to a Railway Company of the Royal Engineers but I'm not allowed to tell of the work we are doing. There is a better aspect for Christmas than last year.'

29 December 1916. *Chiswick Times*
Letter to Rev. Oldfield.

Private W.G. Warren. Egyptian Expeditionary Force.

'Pleased to hear the boys in France and Greece are doing well although it must be cold, rough and a bit miserable for them. The weather in Egypt is glorious by day, but bitterly cold at night. Egypt is a very interesting place except for the monotonous desert. The lower class of Egyptians are rather simple in their ways and rather amusing. Our brigade has been trekking across the desert for a week and are not far from the Turks who are retiring mile after mile and hardly striking a blow. Our boys are anxious to get within striking distance.'

2 February 1917. *Chiswick Times*
Letter to Rev. Oldfield.

Private W. Goddard. Egypt.

'Thank you for your letter. I was laid up in a convalescent camp with rheumatic fever but expect to be joining the battalion in a day or two. There are a good number of old St Mary's boys in the regiment. Had a letter from Walter Smith.'

2 March 1917. *Chiswick Times*
Letter to Rev. Oldfield.

Corporal Tom Rose. Egypt.

'We are having fine weather but very cold at night. We are miles from civilisation. Still we keep smiling, that's the way to win the war. I see by the last telegrams that we had had another victory at sea; they can't get over the boys in blue, and everything seems to be right with the Tommies so we must look forward to a speedy victory and I hope an everlasting peace. Not seen George Allen or the other boys but hope to soon.'

23 March 1917. *Chiswick Times*
Letter to Rev. Oldfield.

Private E. Ward. Egypt.

'I'm glad that you have heard from Charlie. I thought he was in France. I have not seen Keywood since last writing. It is just the opposite out here – hot and cold – but plenty of sand storms, and then we have to work, because it plays old Harry with the track and derails the trains. Must leave off as I am going on duty.'

11 May 1917. *Chiswick Times*
Letter to Rev. Oldfield.

Private W.F.G. Quelch. Egypt.

'No doubt you have read by now how we spent the day after Lady Day. It was warm work but I think we gave the Turks and Co. his money's worth. We are spending Holy Week just outside a very famous city and we were reminded by our padre it was here where Samson stole the city gates and where St Paul converted a very rich man. The land here is practically all cultivated and after the desert it is a good change.'

25 May 1917. *Chiswick Times*
Letter to Rev. Oldfield.

Corporal G .Allen. Egypt.

'I am now in convalescent camp in ----- getting over a wound I received at Gaza on the 19th. This makes the second time we have been in action there. Young Goddard was wounded the same day. I daresay that you have heard about the Middlesex being mentioned, and I can tell you that they have got a good name. We were told of what we had to do and the boys advanced and captured the position. I had a letter from Will Smith and he says he is stationed in ----- in the Army Ordnance Corps, not a bad company to belong to, but they have plenty to do. Please remember me to all the boys.'

29 June 1917. *Chiswick Times*
Letter to Rev. Oldfield.

Private G. Quelch. Somewhere in Egypt.

'We are resting after two engagements with John Turk. Having had many moves recently I have been unable to write as often as I could wish. Several local lads were wounded in the engagements, the names you no doubt know by now – G. Allen and J. Dexter. The history of the Biblical places here is very interesting, but owing to the absence of our padre, we are missing his lectures very much.

He was wounded in the last engagement, but despite his wounds, he hung on to us for several days. The news from the different fronts is magnificent, and if it continues 'the day' should not be long. Reffold and Hillier wish to be remembered to you and all the old boys. As it is dark and lights are not allowed owing to night raids by Turks, I must conclude.'

13 July 1917. *Chiswick Times*
Letters to Rev. Oldfield.
Corporal Tom D. Rose. Egypt.

'We wouldn't notice the heat were it not for the flies, and most of them want to sample the jam on the bread, and they don't go down very nice with the jam. If it were cake it would be different; we could fancy they were currants. Still we keep smiling and long for the finish, which I don't think is far off.'

Private W. Goddard. Egypt.

'I was only slightly wounded in the right arm. I was hit on 19th April and re-joined the battalion within five weeks and went to ----- and ----- and had a good time; it was a nice rest. I like ----- the better, it is several degrees cooler and some grand bathing can be had. It reminded me of those dear old times we had at Margate. George Allen and Johnnie Dexter are back again. Both are in the pink. Could you send me Walter Smith's address?'

12 October 1917. *Chiswick Times*
Letter to Rev. Oldfield.
Private George Quelch. Egyptian Expeditionary Forces.

'Back now about a fortnight from ----- and found it a good change from Palestine. Please excuse the short letter to give you an idea of the small amount of time we have to ourselves. We leave our training area about 5am, having breakfast en route, are practising and arrive back to our area between one and two in the afternoon. This is followed by midday meals, and then a two miles march to the sea, where we enjoy a good swim. By the time we get back and have our evening meal it is dark, and we feel more like sleep than writing by one candle-power light. So please excuse this note.'

19 October 1917. *Chiswick Times*
Letter to Rev. Oldfield.

<u>Corporal G. Allen</u>. Egyptian Expeditionary Force.

'Well, sir, everything about here is much the same. We came out of the trenches about three weeks ago after a spell of nearly a month in, but I find it better in than out. We are doing plenty of training now in full packs, and I might mention we are going through 'some'. We do not see much football here. We saw quite a lot before we went up to ----- but now those times have finished. In fact we have to turn up our legs to make new feet. I see that some of the lads are getting leave from France, and I think them very lucky. We have been out here since 19th July 1915 and all the leave we get is a week to -----.'

26 October 1917. *Chiswick Times*
Letter to Rev. Oldfield.

<u>Trooper W.H. Bryant</u>. Palestine.

'At present we are on a beach, having a rest. I might add the rest was needed. After being up the line living in dust clouds from morn till night and drinking no nice well water, one began to get fed up. We have been here a fortnight and it is surprising at the change in the fellows, all merry and bright and ready for some more fun (chasing Johnny). The regiment spent last winter in -----. Since being back here I have spent six weeks at a school in ----- and had a ripping time. I visited the Pyramids, various mosques and other places of interest. Owing to some religious objections, we were not allowed to take photographs of the interiors. A party of Australians made a wonderful discovery whilst digging in a Wadi. They struck a shrine which had been buried 1,300 years and some of the inscriptions are still legible.

It took a party of ten men 14 days to get it away. Unfortunately we arrived when it was too late to see it. The Australians have packed and covered it with oil ready to send to Australia.

I have been in Divisional HQ for a few days, and whilst there attended an evening service held in a very crude place – a dug out with a bank left around to sit upon, the altar and cross carved in the sand wall, with an ordinary blanket lying in front. We thoroughly enjoyed the service.'

9 November 1917. *Chiswick Times*
George Holden.

He trained in London till October 1915 and then went to Newbridge, 26 miles from Dublin, for further training. He arrived in Salonica in December 1915 and then Egypt in June 1916. Salonica was cold and Egypt very hot. They are at a rest camp due to 'go up' on 18th October.

21 December 1917. *Chiswick Times*
Letter to Rev. Oldfield.

Private Will Davies. Palestine.

'Doing our best to give Johnny Turk orders to quit. We moved into position two days ago before the stunt in a raging thunder storm – the worst I have experienced. Old campaigners say storms in this country rarely last more than half an hour. This one out stayed his leave and lasted four hours. How it rained! While the lightning was awful, yet wonderful.

We were on the road to the land of milk and honey – a cold, wet but cheerful crowd – and we pitched our camp and waited for orders. The next night we were under canvass – a huge hospital of canvass that would easily cover the whole of Homefields and no easy job for 'Johnny' used to come to look at us by air. But give him his due; he never showered his blessings on us, though some of his shells made us think seriously now and again.'

28 December 1917. *Chiswick Times*
Letter to Rev. Oldfield.

<u>Private Will Davies</u>. Somewhere in Palestine (cont.).

'Well, the night following this event, the great 'stunt' followed. I shall never forget it as long as I live, what with our bombardment and Johnny's reply, it was pandemonium let loose, but with the dawn, it seemed to be dying fainter, and with the dawn came the news that Johnny was going homewards as fast as he conveniently could. For the fortnight following, we worked as I have never worked before, night and day, with hardly a respite. Now, at last, we have been taken out of position for a rest, and you can bet it is appreciated. I had several Chiswick boys through my hands, but with all the business of those days, I have forgotten their names. I can tell you they were well to the front, as usual, and from all accounts made a great show. As for this country where we are, it is just a dry chalky dust, which the slightest wind blows up into a cloud which nearly suffocates a chap and makes him look like a jolly old miller, and incidentally, spoils all his grub. The water has the persistent taste of chloride of lime, and unless heavily disguised with cocoa, wants a bit of forcing down, and as you know thirst here is a thing to remember. And the flies – proper army corps – settle on you and make the day unbearable. Thank goodness they only keep the day for revelry. The day is still mighty hot and the nights just as chilly.

News of the war outside comes only in spasms. People at home know much more of the position of affairs than we do; all I know is we have done well. Gaza fell with fewer casualties than was expected. Beersheba fell to a clever master stroke. In short the days have gone well for England, and the fighting forces have done magnificently... We shall be on the move shortly and I hope to get to the land of lemon groves etc. I would prefer anywhere west of London, but that is a joy to come.'

<u>8 March 1918.</u> *Chiswick Times*
Letters to Rev. Oldfield.

<u>Private Ted Ward</u>. EEF. (Egyptian Expeditionary Force)

'I have met up with some of the Chiswick boys and been the guard on a train that transported General Allenby.'

<u>Signaller Harry Greenham</u>. EEF. Egypt.

'My ship was torpedoed on the way to Egypt and the men sang hymns while the nurses were safely got off. "Abandon Ship" came two minutes before she went down. I owe my life to the lifebelt I had on at the time because I can't swim a yard and was picked up after two hours.'

<u>9 April 1918.</u> *Chiswick Times*
Letter to Rev. Oldfield.

<u>Signaller Harry Greenham</u>. Egypt.

'In good health again. Sorry to hear the rotten news about Ted Loche who had not been in France for very long. Haven't seen any of the Old Boys yet. The heat is as much as we can stand. Pleased to hear the band has got going again. None of the military bands I have heard beat the old band yet.'

<u>2 August 1918.</u> *Chiswick Times*
Letter to Rev. Oldfield.

<u>Private T.D. Rose</u>. Egypt.

'Have been having a very busy time but now at rest waiting to be sent to another front. Saw George Allen in Palestine. He called out my name as I boarded a train on which he was the guard. We went through the Holy City and I saw David's Tomb, Temple of the Rock, Golden Gates, St Stephen's Gate, Pools of Betheada, Church of St Anne where the Virgin Mary was born, Church of the Holy Sepulchre and the Garden of Gathsemane. Also went to Bethlehem.'

25 October 1918. *Chiswick Times*
Letter to Rev. Oldfield.

Signaller G. Quelch. Egypt.

'The old local battalion has been split up after four years. The signallers were transferred to the Royal Field Artillery – a good change as we do route marches and treks on horseback and do not have to carry that old pack. Five of us reported to a battery in the valley. I was admitted to hospital with malaria and am progressing most favourably. Life here is most glorious after Palestine. Splendid victories in Palestine reflect great credit on General Allenby, "Johnnie" Turk is in a terrible state. I should not like to be in his boots. I am now cut off from all the Chiswick lads that were in our old battalion and have no idea when I shall see them again.'

10. Singapore Mutiny

14 May 1915. *Chiswick Times* **Singapore Mutiny – Capt. Grenville Smith**

On 15ᵗʰ February 1915 up to half of the 850 Sepoys (Indian soldiers) of the 5ᵗʰ Native Light Infantry at Singapore mutinied. Four of the regiment's eight companies were involved and the remaining four companies did not join the mutiny but scattered in confusion. The regiment was an entirely Muslim unit. The mutineers had been subjected to propaganda from the Indian Ghadar Party that was campaigning for Indian independence from British rule. Other factors were the unpopularity of the commanding officer, Colonel Martin, amongst the men as well as British and Indian officers, slack discipline and weak leadership. Also Britain had declared war on Turkey and the Sultan of Turkey was widely regarded as a leader of the Muslim world. The Regiment was due to be transferred to Hong Kong but rumours were circulating that their destination was Europe or Turkey to fight against their fellow Muslims.

100 mutineers went to obtain ammunition from the Tanglin Barracks where 309 Germans, including crew members from a captured German light cruiser, had been interred. The German prisoners were invited to join the mutineers but very few did so.

Capt. Grenville Smith of the 8ᵗʰ Middlesex Territorial Forces Reserves wrote to his parents at Brooklands in Hounslow describing his experience of the mutiny.

'The mutineers shot down the guard at Tanglin POW camp, the commandant, an officer, 5

five men and a German prisoner. Three men under Corporal Todd, who used to live with me, got away and gave the alarm.'

Capt. Grenville Smith was off duty, dressing to go out. Civilians were being shot down in the streets. He set out with a guard and linked up with men from HMS Cadmus who had killed eight of the mutineers. They came under fire and bivouacked in the road for the night 400 yards from Tanglin camp. His group was in civilian clothes and he sent a requisitioned car back to get khaki clothes and helmets.

'Every man's blood was up, and most of them had seen the bodies of murdered civilians.'

At 4.30 they attacked the mutineers under fire and rescued the colonel, three officers, Mrs. Cotton and 80 Malay State Volunteer Rifles who were down for training. He lost one of HMS Cadmus killed and six wounded.

Similar fights were going on in other parts of the island against 600 scattered mutineers. His party took 200 prisoners, some saying they were loyal, but their rifles had been fired through. 'Our only troops were 70 Cadmas men, 100 Royal Garrison Artillery ,250 volunteers and some armed civilians.'

By the time French, Japanese and a Russian cruiser arrived the affair was well in hand and scattered parties were being rounded up.

'The mutiny has hit me badly'. He had to buy four uniforms and equipment costing 600 dollars. These were at his quarters outside the POW camp and all were gone or spoilt 'on my boy going up to get them.'

'We are now very busy furnishing firing squads for the execution of the mutineers. Last week we furnished a firing party of 110 men for the execution of 22 mutineers. So far 32 have been shot, and there are many more to come.'

'It was touch and go for two days, and then, thank goodness, we got the upper hand. Fancy five days without a shave, bath, wash or clean up. You can guess what I looked like. I was in command of the advanced guard in the above fight. I was first in Colonel Martin's bungalow, and now have a very nice souvenir in the shape of a silver cigarette case from some of the members of the Malay Straits Volunteer Rifles.'

Colonel Martin and a detachment of the Malay States Volunteers held out throughout the night. Loyal Sepoys who volunteered to join them were ordered to a safe place to prevent them being confused in the dark with mutineers.

'On Saturday afternoon we are having a burial service with military honours of the people who were murdered and fell in action during the mutiny – 42 or more. The Singapore Volunteer Rifles to which I am attached (exclusive, of course, of the civilians who were killed) suffered the most, having eight killed and three wounded.'

Over 200 sepoys were court-martialed and 47 were executed. 64 were transported for life and 73 imprisoned from 7 to 20 years. The remnants of the regiment left Singapore to see active service in the Cameroons and German East Africa. A Court of Enquiry heavily criticised Colonel Martin who was retired from the army.

11. Africa

In Africa the British and South African armies were in action against the German colonies.

19 March 1915. *Chiswick Times*
Letter from a rifleman – 'Somewhere in South Africa'

'We have finished with the rebellion – an unhappy business. Took many rebel prisoners – a sorry, ignorant, unkempt lot who, when asked, said they did not know until it was too late that they were rebels because Beyers, the Defence Corps Commandant, had called them out. We have been in German South West Africa for six weeks – it is simply sand, sand, and sand. We all wear veils over our helmets. We are pushing slowly ahead and the day is not far distant when another bit of red will be added to our empire.

The Germans counted on the Boers rising on their side, but thank goodness we had Botha – 'Louis' as our men affectionately call him. He is splendid and our fellows will go anywhere he leads. I often look through a little book uncle gave me – called Guide to Chiswick – it recalls happy days. A German patrol ventured too near. Good shooting and it won't worry anyone any more. Our nights are spent in trenches – sleeping in full kit. I wish our little war was over so we could have a chip in Europe.'

When the war began there was a rebellion in South Africa, whose leaders included General Beyers, seeking re-establishment of the Boer republics that were defeated in the South African war (the Boer war) 1899 – 1902. The South African government quickly put down the rebellion and joined with the British Army in capturing the German colonies in South West and East Africa. Louis Botha was prime minister of South Africa.

10 September 1915. *Chiswick Times*
Richmond men in East Africa.

Mr. Burgess, a master at the Vineyard Boy's School, has received a letter from Private A.F. Claydon who is with the Royal Fusiliers in East Africa. Claydon tells how in 'this small world' he has met in an outpost Mr. Cornell, a former master at the school.

'Out of a dozen Richmond boys out here, four have been connected with the school. The voyage out was very fine. We all laughed at the roughness, but landed with good hearts amid the palm-clothed bays of Mombassa. At night on sentry go we can hear lions and jackals. The country teems with game – deer, zebras, giraffes, ostriches, and buffalo living on the plains by the thousand while lions and wild pigs appear to inhabit the dongas.

The coastal plain is a table land six to seven thousand feet high and highlands rise to eleven thousand feet. We camped on the high plateau covered with luxuriant grass, waist high and broken by ranges of hills covered with thick scrubby bushes. It is very hot during the day, yet at night so cold we require our thick overcoats when on duty. From my tent we can see Kilamayaro some seventy miles away.

We have had the luck to have been in one fight. We captured Bukoba, the wireless station, and German guns on the shore of Lake Victoria, and waded under fire through deep swamps up to our armpits. In the fight I lost all sensation of hunger and other personal feelings, but learned the real value of water. A chum was killed by a sniper while going on an errand of mercy.

The Germans are the same race out here, using explosive and soft-nosed bullets, marking their guns with the Red Cross flag, banking them close to the hospital and using the latter as a temporary arsenal.'

Another letter has been received by Mr. Bickford whose son Frank is also serving in East Africa in the Royal Fusiliers. He describes the same battle as Claydon. 'We had to take a hill and the enemy were well hidden.' He waded four foot deep streams and had to sleep in wet clothes. Mr. Bickford is serving in the Volunteer Munitions Brigade and has two sons in the army.

12 May 1916. *Chiswick Times*
In German East Africa – letter from Private E. Oxlade.

Letter dated 20th February, to his mother at 4, the Vineyard. He says the force he is attached to trekked for a week, covering an average 12 miles a day, the greater part of the marching in the early morning owing to the heat. 'I rather enjoyed passing through the new country and fresh scenery, and I kept wonderfully fit and did not even feel stiff or get sore feet, like the majority of the fellows. So I was rather sorry when we came to the end of our journey for the time being. Water was again very short, but we managed to get sufficient, thanks to the heavy rain that fell the first few nights. This enabled us to start off fresh in the morning with a full water bottle instead of an empty one, and you need it, too, when one has to live chiefly on bull beef and biscuits, which is not very appetising and requires plenty of drink to help it down.

We have been here eight days and have had a busy time, practising different attacks from 6.30 to 10.30 and in the afternoon, the usual trench digging. Apparently we are the only troops in British East Africa who understand that work, for they leave that to us wherever we go and needless to say we are sick of it. This seems a very healthy spot. It is only a mile from German territory, and quite close to Kilimanjaro, the snow covered mountain. We are still at a good altitude, so the heat is not so intense, but the nights are very cold, and we notice it with just one blanket. Sometime next week we are pushing forward to the next advance camp, some 20 miles away, where we will be joined by the rest of our division. Our forces in different parts of the country are pushing forward, and when we all get going I think the Huns will have a hot time. They have been driven out of the Cameroons, and this will be next.'

In an article in the *Doncaster Gazette*, he describes his life at a lonely outpost.

'Life on one these outposts, situated in country never before visited by white men, is one long thrill. Extra precautions have to be taken guarding the precious water hole (a few feet of green slimy liquid, the nearest water for 20 miles) always keeping a sharp lookout for the sly cattle raiders and an ever open eye and ear for the prowling beasts – lions, leopard, hyenas and rhinos, which come seeking the precious water.

One outpost stands out in our memory. The report came in that one of our most valuable and successful scouts had been ambushed and volunteers were called for a search party. Early in the morning, the patrol moved across the rocky wilderness and we made for a certain water hole, which we knew he would visit if still alive. After several days of anxious waiting, when we had almost given up hope, one of our own native scouts came in bringing with him a mule, from which dangled some of our equipment.

Reassured by this find, we decided to remain in our position until supplies gave out....on the last day one of our picquets spotted a small party away in the distance which proved to be our long lost scout. Without a boot on his blistered feet, minus all clothes except a stained tattered shirt, tanned and dirty almost beyond recognition, parched with thirst and as hungry as a wolf, he struggled into our camp. He could hardly speak. We gave him some tea and a little boiled rice, and he revived. The first thing he managed to whisper was 'For God's sake, give me some salt'. He had lived on fresh-killed meat for nearly a fortnight, and he kept us thrilled for hours as we sat round the camp fire. His transport mules carrying his supplies had broken away, alarmed by the roar of a lion, and though starvation was impossible, the constant feed of meat surfeited and sickened him. Early next morning, according to orders, we had to start back, and once again we experienced all the terrible pangs of thirst, for we were obliged to cross six miles of blistering caustic soda lakes, carrying blankets, cooking pots, ammunition etc, that should have been carried by coolies, who failed to put in an appearance. For 18 miles, over rocky game tracks, through thick elephant grass, in 120 degrees, we sweated and swore from early morning to late at night, when we finally staggered into the wayside station.'

16 June 1916. *Chiswick Times*
The Campaign in East Africa – a Richmond man's experience.

Letter dated 31ˢᵗ March, from Private A.P. Clayden, Royal Fusiliers (Frontiersmen), son of Mr. A. Clayden, Red Lion St. He has been in East Africa over a year. Several Richmond men are serving with General Smuts' force in German East Africa.

'By a stroke of luck, I can let you have a letter, and this time I have a tale to tell but he who rules over our correspondence will make that tale the poorer, and much must be left till all is over. It is a great pity one cannot retain impressions and events in precisely the same condition as one received them. You cannot describe scenes that occurred while you are tired out, after you have rested. The impressions are blurred and altered, but nevertheless interesting.

I wish I could give you details of forced marches across the desert, covered with a clayey black dust which smothered us and made us look like niggers and the joy when we came to a water hole or river in which, when we had made camp, we bathed and felt happy. One river had soda in it, which made us thirsty and as we had a long march the next day, over a dried up barren country to the next river during the intense heat, this made us feel it badly. But the joy when we discerned the belt of green trees, showing the presence of water, can scarcely be imagined, but every part of one's being cried out to be taken out of the glaring sun and heat that enclosed one in the air, and came up shimmering from the ground.

But it was on, always forward. Never as the crow flies, but twice staying for a day's rest in a camp, made always by a river and with a view to its defence. The country varied as we progressed, and we gradually drew into the rainy region where the hand of man was visible, producing things which help life to appear pleasant. I could tell of plucking lemons, limes and oranges from their trees and bushes; of digging up and cooking sweet potatoes; of roasting and grinding and drinking local grown coffee; and of scores of other novel interesting things.

About a week ago, we were attacked as the moon rose one night and they kept it up for some four hours. But, by Jove, the Germans got it hot, and it was distinctly warm while it lasted. Their bugles sounded the 'Charge' and then the noise started and the bullets flew but we came out all right. They didn't. The following day, we did the attacking and again they caught it badly, we capturing one of the Konigsberg's big guns and forced the enemy to retire. The fight was a very stiff one for they had a fine position. Fortunately the sand was very easy in which to dig, and as our general's name is Shepheard, you can imagine the wags soon got to work about our digging – in at nightfall, amidst the palms. During a scrap one's emotions are very varied, but I think the noise of the big guns worries one most.

So here we are for a short rest, if one can rest in the heat by day and the stuffiness by night. Every night it rains and often in the day, and each time now I hear it I feel pleased, for I am under a roof, and have recently experienced the doubtful pleasure of being in the bush, clothed only in a cotton shirt and shorts, all night and the rain coming down in torrents the whole time. I did not know so much misery could be crowded into a night, but an hour after sunrise we were quite dry and warm. This has happened several nights and now I am none the worse for it.

We have crossed many rivers since we started, some difficult, others easy, and all very pretty, where Nature has been profuse in her handiwork. One of the most interesting sights was to watch a pioneer corps make a ford for the transport. In two hours they had levelled two banks, cut down trees, filled up holes in the riverbed, put logs down to make it easier for the wagons to pass over the soft earth, and allow the whole column to pass with comparative ease, though with wet feet and legs. It was a fine sight to see them though they destroyed a beautiful part of the river; one could not but admire majors and other officers as they stood knee-deep in water helping to saw trees, crow-barring up their roots, and giving orders as to carrying out other parts of the work.

I wondered how long Nature would take to make it real again. Nevermore would that spot bear the appearance it had before we came, but she would probably soon take the wand and create another scene, beautiful as before in a very short time. Now I have been right round Kilimanjaro, and seen this world's wonder from all sides, and the more one sees of it the finer it appears to be. Never before have I been so close to the mountain, nor have I seen it under such varying conditions. No artist could translate its very transient shades and colours. The sun catches it, or the clouds drifting round its peaks break and divide, showing the snow-cap above and curling round its neck, like a soft woollen comforter. One can truly say the gods have been good to us showing us this wonder in such varying circumstances.

Of course you will want to know how we fare regards food on this Safari. Well, jolly good. Better than when in a standing camp. Of course there is the inevitable bully and biscuits, but we always get tea and sugar or coffee, and either dried fruit or jam. One day, when we were right in the wilds, we were served out fresh butter. It was great, one could taste the cream. The next day bread and fresh meat were served out, in fact on several days. So you see we are scoring.

I hope things are all well and going on as usual. We know nothing of what is happening. All this is a wonderful experience and I am jolly glad I had the opportunity to see these things.'

5 April 1917. *Chiswick Times*
With General Smuts in East Africa.

<u>Private A.F. Clayden</u>, Royal Fusiliers, writes on 1st February to his father, Mr. A. Clayden:

'Once again we are in the big rainy season, when it rains for weeks. This time we have not the big mountain to look to as we had at Moschi last year, but a range of smaller mountains clothed with trees and from which several rivers seem to start.

It would interest you to know perhaps that we are back in a sort of civilisation now, where guns do not fire and all is at peace, but for how long I do not know. You have probably learned from the papers that we have been on the go again. It was fairly hot while it lasted, but the usual thing happened – they went, and quickly too. It can't last much longer, although the rains must have a great effect on the time.

I wish the authorities would let me write to you of our movements and give names of places. It could do no harm now that the tide of war has rolled past them, for we have just finished another stage in our marching through Africa. This time it was an easy trek, fine weather all the time, good food, but through a district noted for all the fevers in the country. But we are out of it and I took no harm.

The heat was terrible. At one place near a huge lake, the water of which contained too much soda for it to be drinkable, you could almost make tea without a fire. I was never so thirsty in my life. Still we saw a school of hippopotami playing in the lake, a unique sight. Later we reached the great river and saw crocodiles in it and heard them all night, and felt sorry for a wounded Indian who had to stay on an island all night. However he survived. We were able to get a number of wild pig, very fine eating, but not equal to the kind at home.

The fighting on this trip was stiff at times. Captain Selous was killed. We are all extremely sorry he has gone, for he was such a fine type of man, and one that when you saluted, you could willingly salute the uniform and the man. I have never known him during the two years out here to ever do anything except that which was inspired by high ideals, and he died in that particular part of the country he knew so well, and where he had made some of his greatest triumphs in the hunting world. We are much grieved at his loss.'

4 May 1917. *Chiswick Times*
Letter to Rev. Oldfield.
 Private R. Jennings. South Africa.
 'We had a nice time coming across. I hear we are here for a little time and then going up the line. The people here are very kind to us all while we are here and invite us to concerts now and again. I hope all the boys are in the best of health and going strong.'

12. Western Front 1916

The Battle of the Somme started on 1st July and continued until November. Seven miles were gained by the Allies. 128,000 British and Empire troops died.

<u>7 January 1916.</u> *Chiswick Times*
An Old Eton Street Boy's letter.

<u>Driver II 61st Howitzer Brigade.</u> Writes from France.

'I don't mind the cold, but the rain and mud beats us, having no stables for the horses, they tred it like a ploughed field. Mud halfway up my legs. We sleep in our clothes in a barn. We got shelled out of our wagon line but we were laughing every time a shell came over. You can hear them coming. I was sorry to hear about poor Fred Culver's death. All the old boys are falling one by one; there won't be many left by the time this terrible war is over, but we must cheer up and bear it. If Mr. Bashford sees this I hope he will remember me to the boys of my old school in Eton Street.

Glad to see single men are being made to join up. We can then get some relief and leave. Women, children and dogs do all the work here that men do in England. The war will last months yet but we will win in the end. Houses burnt down by the Germans are being rebuilt so we are not afraid of them advancing. I would like a pair of jack or rubber boots because I hasn't got a spare pair.'

<u>7 January 1916.</u> *Chiswick Times*
Letters to Rev. Oldfield.

<u>Trumpeter R. Squair.</u> Somewhere in France.

'I have joined my battery quite safe, just in time to go into action with them. Sorry to leave the old home after short leave but still it had to be done. I had rather a rough passage across this time. Well I have to settle down to the old ways again now, and the first thing

I have to do is any amount of letter writing just to let them know I have got back safe. We are nearly up to our knees in mud, so you can guess what it is like.'

14 January 1916. *Chiswick Times*

A.R. Wilkie has been gazetted 2nd Lieutenant with 3-9th Middlesex Regiment.

'Wilkie' is a Chiswick lad and lives at 69 Paxton Road. When Rev Sandberg was curate at the Parish Church, he was in the Sunday schools and a very active member of the Chiswick Church Lads' Brigade, gymnasium, football and cricket club, after which he became a very useful member of the Working Men's Church Club. Joined the 10th Middlesex in 1909. Two years later he went to the machine gun section. Sailed for India on 29 October 1914 and returned to Chiswick on 7 Nov. 1915. On 16 Nov. 1915 he applied for a commission, granted as stated above.

14 January 1916. *Chiswick Times*
Letters to the Chiswick Working Men's Club
Gunner C.A. Faulkner.

'I am just about getting used to walking in slosh. The country on this front is very flat and a lot of the fields are continually under water. Our chaps in the trenches have all got wading boots now and they need them, poor fellows.'

14 January 1916. *Chiswick Times*
More letters from the Front.

Lance Corporal C. Larner. Attached to the King's Royal Rifles in France, writing to his brother.

'We have just come out of the trenches near Ypres, and we are in huts. We have had some awful times here, and we get wet to the skin. We have to wear thigh boots for the mud and water is plentiful. They shelled us terribly yesterday but we had no one wounded. We have a patrol out every night to see if there are any working parties out, and I had to go out and then they gave me the job on 'listening post'. That is in front of our barbed wire 'No Man's Land', and you have to stop out all night to see that they do not cut our barbed wire; and it is a rotten job I can tell you. It was raining when I was out, and I had to lay in water. We have fried chips out here – civilians sell them; but there is one thing missing – they do not sell fish, so we have fried eggs instead. Well, no more this time. Love to all – I am your loving brother, Charles.'

An 'Advertisement' ' comes with his letter, addressed from a base hospital, the writer is 'apparently a patient, and retains his sense of humour'.

To Be Let

Three minutes from German trenches.

This attractive and well-built dug-out, containing one reception-kitchen-bedroom, and up-to-date funk hole, 4ft by 3ft. All modern inconveniences, including gas and water.

This desirable residence stands 1ft above water level, commanding excellent view of the enemy's trenches. Excellent shooting (snipe and duck).

Sergeant Curtis was prior to war in charge of one of Messrs. A. Sanderson & Sons Departments, and a member of the Bleak House Club Committee.

'12pm, Christmas Eve. A few impressions whilst they are with me. In the first place, I must tell you we are in a reserve billet some three miles behind the firing line. Our artillery keeps up an occasional fire, and from the wooden hut in which we sleep the flare lights from the trenches are plainly seen. An hour since I went to another company for definite news of our Christmas dinner – the field in which I found them, a morass of mud. My business with the Sgt. Major concluded, I inquire my best way back and am informed, 'right incline to the dip (represented by a ditch), left incline to the road.' I follow the instructions. The left incline taken, I biff the mud. I curse, picking myself up and proceed to take the right incline. Again a false move and I measure my length a second time in the mire. The thick mixture covers me, runs up my sleeve. Never mind, tonight is Christmas Eve; so I forget the falls and seek out the hut in which Acomb, Smith, Harris etc lodge. There are the lads; bottles galore on the upturned boxes – chiefly stout. Piper (the tenor) in full song. I enter and join in. Well received. Why had I not been in earlier in the evening? I find myself involved in heart-to-heart talk with Harris, a kindly fellow, chiefly about patrol work between lines, in which talk his wife and youngsters frequently find a place. Gist of confab is that, although married, he must take his risks. Of course I agree, but I would it could be otherwise.

Then follow much manoeuvring for the remaining bottles, more shaking and retaining of hands, the passing of compliments, plans for the future revelry in peace times, if the fates decree, and away I slither to find my own doss house. Oh snakes! From stout etc to champagne. Of course, I take up (and empty) the goblet. Many parcels have arrived – cake and sweets, cough tablets and toffee, nuts and muscatels. We swallow the lot. Much pleasant banter. I'm tired, not so the others; they settle down to a few hours of pontoon card game. Well let them do it. As for me, I will get down and maybe I shall forget just how awful that chap's voice sounded this evening when he sang 'Mona' in that little estaminet.

Christmas Day – A late breakfast. It rains like the very devil. Smith is skating towards the ditch, but not the same Smith as last night. Oh me. His face is adorned with numerous evidences of a tumble. He confesses complete ignorance of the affair...... but derives much satisfaction telling me how the Sgt. Major journey forth in the night, got stuck in the mud, left his boot therein, and landed back in the hut with one boot and one sock. A search party this morning brought in the other items. Some of the lads in sore plight. You can't realise how slippery is this mud.

From the officer of D company we N.C.Os have received a cigarette case and cigars, and each man a box of chocolates etc. Christmas puddings for all from Army & Navy (regimental issue I think), and cigarettes and tobacco from the Oversees Fund. Our little lot seems to have been subscribed for in Bucharest, as cards of acknowledgement to that address are enclosed.

4.30pm – Well the Christmas dinner is over, and I am truly glad it is. Think of a long canvas hut, with a shaky table running its length. At one end a large tin containing roast beef, and another peas, carrots, and beans. On either side of the table a board supported by trestles, and seated thereon sergeants in varying stages of happiness. They feed from plates, tins and for implements use knife and fork (rarely), spoons, pocket knives and (keep it dark please) fingers. An officers' fund has ensured beer in plenty. Christmas pudding follows and good it tastes. But I wish they had extracted the stones from the raisons forthcoming, our friends, the sergeants are replaced thereon. Dinner over, cigars etc.

Sunday morning – Last evening, Acomb, Smith etc and self, armed with sandbags, called in at a little estaminet, and spent a cheery couple of hours. Just on turning out time (8 o'clock) we filled our sandbags and toddled back. Piper (the tenor) extremely blithe. But events proved too much for him, and he retired early with tears in his eyes, the tears due to an overfull feeling in the tummy. Smith a complete failure. His last night's gruelling has left him poorly, and like Piper he retired early. So, Acomb, Randall, Harris and self held the fort alone and at 11pm I went home to my bed.

And that finished the first Christmas Day I have ever spent away from England, and taking into consideration just where we are, and what we are here for, I really cannot say I have not had a fairly good time – fun in plenty, right good fellowship, and pleasant reminders from home. Of course, comfort we cannot expect. But I'll not regret a second of it, if and when I have the good fortune to finish with this game for good.'

<u>Mr. Harold Avens</u>. In France, writing to his father at 19 Oxford Road.

'6th January 1916. I spent four days or rather nights in a baker's oven in a ruined house within 500 yards from where I got wounded in July. We had to take refuge in the oven on several occasions when the Germans started shelling. Five of us were inside once, when a shell burst within five yards. The place was in a shocking state – trees chopped about all over the place, and thousands of rats and mice seem to delight themselves in running over you while you are sleeping. The Germans seem to have about twice as many shells as when I was here last. I suppose it must be imagination, but they do chuck their stuff about in a terrible manner. We are now spending four days in a stable. It is not much of a place, compared with home, though it is just like heaven to us. I had a good wash this morning, first time in 12 days, so I am feeling quite funny. Have they got conscription yet? As far as I can see it is not any nearer.'

<u>14 January 1916.</u> *Chiswick Times*
The Kaiser's Tears.

<u>Lance Corporal E.C. Williams</u>. 8th East Surreys, writing on New Year's Day.

'We took over a trench and in the afternoon we sent up a huge mine, and then our artillery gave it to Fritz hot for a bit. Soon after this, Fritz began to bombard. I was off duty in a dug-out and big shells began bursting uncomfortably near the roof. We thought nothing of it for a bit, but we soon began to see that things might get warm. Some of the shells went into the ground and then blew up. They were like small mines and threw up the earth just in front of our front door.

After about another hour of it, I smelt an irritating smell, and my eyes smarted. The stuff tasted like strong horse-radish. One of our mining rescue men came round with oxygen and told me to fix my smoke helmet as gas was on. I thought at first it was the real poison gas, although I had not heard the hiss or seen the cloud. It turned out to be merely stuff from 'Weeping Willy' shells, or as the villagers call them, the 'Kaiser's Tears'. Our officer has since told us that we had some of the asphyxiating gas.

At one spot our trench was blown up, and we had to climb over the top of it. Coming back later, I stepped into the darkness and fell off the top, rifle and all. My word I was in a pickle. Some saucy German had the sauce to fire his rifle, so I went down our trench and fired a shot from two or three different fire steps to make him think that we were all waiting for him, but Fritz did not come. I felt awfully wild having to go through all that rather nerve-racking business. I almost wish that Fritz had looked in. When we get the order to go and see Fritz, I hope to have my own back for a most uncomfortable afternoon. Nobody in our trench was hurt.'

14 January 1916. *Chiswick Times*
Letters to Rev. Oldfield.

Driver Jack M. Clarke. Somewhere in France.

'I don't know how long we shall remain here but I shall be very glad to go up the line again. They have a nice recreation hut and concerts here and they do all they can for our comfort and their kindness is fully appreciated by all, no matter when one enters the huts, there is always a rush for refreshments. I hope all at St Mary Magdalene's are well. I was on guard on Christmas Day, but enjoyed a good dinner and on dismounting at 4pm spent Christmas evening in the soldiers' club just outside camp and enjoyed a musical evening. Since then we have been very busy.'

Gunner E. Triggs. France.

'Things are about the same here, though the Bosches tried to smarten the parade up just before Christmas. On that day however it was very quiet, owing no doubt to the Huns getting an extra ration of sausage. I spent a quiet Christmas in a little French village but I am now up again midst shot and shell, as the song has it. When

I first got back to the battery, there was plenty of mud and we have made about three shifts since then, and cut a grass field up in next to no time. We are better off up here, the rain can drain away. Harold is still with the horses, he informs me, so I guess he is having a happy time.'

Sapper R.H. Spratt. France.

'We have moved further up the line now, but it is just as bad as the last place, most deserted. Still about five miles from the firing line. We can hear the guns rattling away at times. I am quite comfortable. I and three others have a bed which we have made up in a stable, and we use the stable as a workshop. We have electric light fitted up in it, so you can guess how comfy we are. I have been on the lookout for some of the boys, no luck yet.'

Trooper R. Squair. France.

'The Germans got very brave the other day upsetting our Christmas. Well, we had what we call a mad half-hour with them. They got one leg over the parapet and I doubt very much if they had the other leg left to get over. At any rate, we let them have about 2,000 rounds of H.E and all that was left was a second-hand shop hanging on to the parapet. I expect they thought we had gone home for our Christmas dinner. All the same, we were there, and they were not. The French also gave them some Christmas greetings. You can guess there was no football going on this time, in fact there was some business done this Christmas.'

21 January 1916. *Chiswick Times*
Christmas at the Front.

E.J.Hogan writes to one of his club mates at Twickenham from somewhere in France:

'At present I am having a bit of a rest from the battle's roar and staying at the wagon lines, about three miles behind our guns, messing around with horses, ammunitions, supplies and Mud. The capital 'M' is because hereabouts it runs to three feet deep on average, and is the thickness of Irish stew. Christmas Eve night and Christmas morning I was on guard wading around after the horses that had broken loose, and started for Blighty. About 1am, the Allemands started strafing the country around. Our guns awoke, and went at them, and between them woke up the 'heavies', who nestle round about our wagon lines, so there was soon a deuce of a din. Even by 'Alice's' people (Alice slings many hundredweight at a time) – even they turned in their sleep. This quieted them down a bit and restored peace on earth. Then I took a squad and buried a dead horse. When we went for tea there was none for me. I promptly got orders to saddle up and take two wagons of shell to the battery. Coming back some howitzers let drive altogether. The horses ran away and there was a deuce of a tangle of legs and traces. Altogether, a merry Christmas.'

16 January 1916. *Chiswick Times*
Letters to Rev. Oldfield.

Tom Owen. Flight Squadron. Somewhere in England.

'I am quite an old soldier now, it being about three months since I first joined the colours. The squad drill soon found the weak spots. After you have been in the corps some time, you get a machine placed in your charge and are responsible that everything is in proper working order. I have been 'up' as they term flying here. The sensation is rather fine. Air mechanics like myself are all taken up by the pilot in the observer's seat. I expect to go overseas shortly.'

Privates A. Long & H. Broadley. BEF. France.

Just a few lines to let you know we had the luck to be in billets this Christmas and we enjoyed ourselves very much. We went to church on Christmas Day; our church is a wooden building, but the service was all right, which we enjoyed. Then we had our first roast dinner of roast beef etc and then a concert. So you see we had a merry time. Weather is very wet and the road and fields flooded. It makes it very difficult to get about.'

<u>Gunner Alfred Evans (Robin)</u>. Royal Horse Artillery.

'All friends will be delighted to know that the bullet which went through one lung and grazed the other, after above had brought down a Taube, has been successfully extracted after a very difficult operation, and that Robin is going on splendidly. My great grief being that this bullet stopped me bring down more Taubes.'

21 January 1916. *Chiswick Times*
Après la guerre. A letter from France.

'What a world of meaning lies in those few words, and what a meaning to the world. From every nation will go up a long-drawn sigh of relief to think that this awful wastage of human life will cease when the above heading has become an accomplished fact. What tension will be released. What a feeling of thankfulness and joy tinged, it is true, with a feeling of apprehension on the part of those who have relatives and friends fighting in distant parts of the Empire, until they are assured of the safely of their loved ones. I wonder how many times a day that phrase is used in the country I am in at present. What a re-union of loved ones, what floods of emotion will be released when this devastating war is over. Many homes are broken up for ever. Widows will miss the loved face of the father of their bairns; old wounds will be re-opened when Henri, Jules, and Jacques return to their villages and their families. Then indeed will the poor widow's lot be hard to bear.

Here in this country, with the war at their very back door, the people live right in the very turmoil of it all and at night, when the estaminets open to Tommy, the villages ring with laughter and song, punctuated at intervals with the roar of the guns. No one takes the slightest notice of them, for all – soldier and civilian alike – work, eat, sleep to that accompaniment on the Western Front. Enter any of these estaminets between 6 – 8pm and what a babel greets one's ears. Here in one corner of the café are seated the few old Frenchmen who use this particular resort, and strange though it may seem, they look right out of place, for the rest of the place is crowded with Tommies. Here is one batch of A.S.C.M.T. drivers discussing the relative merits of the Austin lorry. We turn from them to the next table, and here we find a group of riflemen having a heated discussion with a couple of burly Guardsmen as to the number of honours their respective regiments possess. These are completely extinguished by a 5ft 2in Artillery driver, who claims for the Royal Regiment more honours than any other corps in the army and he is probably correct. Behind the bar, with a beaming face, is madame, busy supplying the wants of the boys (and incidentally making a small fortune) with a Pathephone rattling out marches and songs galore, making with the mixed dialects, an indescribable din.

Yes, I am inclined to think that the people of those places in the war zone will regard the war with somewhat mixed feeling when it is over, for I make bold to assert that never in the history of the country has so much money changed hands in the villages as now. Well, the boys know what they want, and what they want they get, if it is possible, and small blame to the French people for supplying the Tommies' needs. They themselves are often put to great inconvenience, owing to the military exigencies of the situation, but have long adapted to all sorts of conditions and show their native common sense.

Tommy has won his way into a great many family circles, and a great number of marriages will undoubtedly take place when they have finished their little job out here. Many buxom lassies are learning English for the time when they will join their soldier bridegrooms in England après la guerre. When one realises what those words mean, it seems almost an impossible task to put on paper one fraction of their potent. Yet great as the task appears I have tackled it in the hope that not one of the readers of this letter who has it in his power, in whatever capacity, will hesitate to apply that power and so bring to a consummation all the hopes, joys and reunions that will take place all over the globe après la guerre.'

21 January 1916. *Chiswick Times*
Letter from the Firing Line.

Corporal A. Stroud. 7th East Surrey Regiment. To a Richmond friend.

'Christmas is not a happy one out here and I hope all the boys will be home for next Christmas. I don't think I'll grumble about the mud on the Dysart fields towpath to Ham again after what we have been through. There is something special about the mud out here. We laugh afterwards at the fine pictures we make when we get stuck and have to pull each other out, though there is not much laughing at the time for there is generally enemy snipers and sometimes shells trying to catch us on the hop.

I am at present billeted in a farmhouse or rather the pigsty or hen roost ..... It's got a roof with just a few tiles missing. The front has been disposed of by a shell, but we have managed to make a new one with an old blanket. An old tin with a few holes makes a fireplace and as other parts of the farm are in ruins we can pinch a bit of wood for a fire. We do not have to dress for dinner as our hosts are either in the farmyard or else gone to some other part of the country. Our pals, the Huns, just remind us now and again that they are keeping a watchful eye on us for a whiz-bang will play with the tiles or a heavier shell knock a hole through a wall every now and then.

Read the D.M. (Daily Mail) you sent me, and I guess there is a lot of truth in it, but things are not quite so black, I am thinking though they might have been better a bit earlier. Still, it's no use crying over spilt milk and we have got to peg away and make the best of it. It is easy for men to sit at home by a big fire and write leaders for the daily paper, but if they only had to do the same out here in a mud-sodden trench they might have a different account to give.

I am sorry to hear about Harvey recently reported wounded and missing for he may have been picked up and in some hospital, possibly taken prisoner by the Germans. I understand from the

D.M. that the slackers have got to come up at last. I only hope it's true. My brother in the R.E. P.O.S. is in Egypt and soon to go to the Balkans. He says it is a bit rough, but has settled down and is enjoying himself with warm weather and plenty of rain. The weather here is not very cold but rotten wet and blowing a gale, and in these ruined hovels gives one the creeps.

I walked round one the big towns the other day, but did not think much of it. The places look dirty and nothing like old England, and they know how to charge. A candle costs 2d or 3d, a small loaf 7d or 8d, a tin of milk 10½d. Beer is a penny a glass, but the public bar at the Hope would fling it back at the landlord, and tell him they did not want the water he washed his glasses in.

I would like to put the T.Ts (Teetotallers) in advanced trenches on a cold night and then see if they would refuse a tot of rum about two o'clock in the morning.'

22 January 1916. *Chiswick Times*

Private F. Baynes. Chiswick Working Men's Church Club.

Delayed letters have now reached him. He is working at an advanced dressing station. They send the worst cases to their hospital four or five miles away. "A Fairly good time at Christmas. Hope next year we shall enjoy Christmas at home. A pantomime, 'Dick Whittington', was organised and played by the 85th Field Ambulance and is going to tour the camps.'

28 January 1916. *Chiswick Times*
Letters to Rev. Oldfield.

Private F.J. Pearce. BEF.

'The weather here is a lot better now. Most signs of recent floods have gone, we get a glimpse of the sun for an hour or so during the day. We had a bit of a do with the Alimons on New Year's morning. Our lads went over and cut their wire then the trouble started. Our lads with a load of bombs, went at them, throwing all the time and drove them out of their first line, making short work of those that remained. The Germans were all in their supports and reserve lines now, so our bombers came back. Then our artillery had a word to say, and played the mischief with them, sending shells like hailstones dropping among them, and we were firing rapid at them for over an hour. It was only about a couple of nights before they were yelling out, 'When are you coming over?' but we have not heard from them since, except the day they brought one of our airmen down. They were then yelling like maniacs. But a few hours afterwards they saw one of their own fall – not a word.'

Privates A. Long & H. Broadley. BEF. France.

'I received your letter safely. My chum Broadley was anxious to read it. I must tell you he is one of the cooks for the battalion and he is the handyman. We are both well and happy, and the weather now being fine, it is quite a treat to be able to get about in the trenches. We are doing plenty of fatigues, repairing trenches which have been knocked down by those wiz-bangs, which are not very nice to come in contact with.'

Sapper P.E. Read. BEF. Somewhere in France.

'I have arrived here safely, but it was a very tiring journey, for when we got to ----- we had to march up to the rest camp on the top of a large hill. We had to sleep up there for the night, which was very windy and wet, not saying anything about the rough passage across the Channel. Men being up from rest camp for a night, they put us into a train the next morning and landed at our destination at half past eight on Friday night. Then had to walk eight miles. Never found my billet in the dark so we put up in a barn in a field, and found our billet next morning, and the Germans must have known that I was back, for as soon as I got into the billet, they let four big shells over, which exploded just at the back of our billet. Just received a letter from Fred Bailey, he expects to be home in four or five weeks' time.'

Sergeant F.W.J. Smith. BEF.

'Been out here six months now, and I am afraid it would be silly to try and predict the end of the war. The Germans made a gas attack on us about four days ago, but they met with a great disappointment, I can tell you, for about 40 machine guns opened fire on them, and they were not long before they decided that the attack was a failure. We had about ----- fellows gassed, but not badly, as our gas helmets are splendid things for fighting it. Well, sir, I am pleased to tell you we are back from a well-earned rest and I expect to be getting leave.'

4 February 1916. *Chiswick Times*
Letters to Rev. Oldfield.

Bandsman A. Collard. Somewhere in France.

'I have been awarded the D.C.M for good work attending to the wounded under shell fire in a battle my regiment was engaged in. I receive the Chiswick Times each week, so I am not lost for news of what goes on in Chiswick; also it is good to know by the old boys' letters that they are well and still keeping the old flag flying. I enclose a photograph of our stretcher bearers, taken during a battle in which we were engaged and you will see that I have fallen asleep over the box. The fellow marked with a cross was the first to have the D.C.M.'

Private A. Long. In the trenches, France.

'Received your parcel this morning and immediately shared it with Broadley, for which we both thank you very much. We also had the pleasure of another one of our lads to join us, named William Baverstock who joined our battalion just recently. We are finding plenty of work, going on fatigue for timber and footboards to help repair the trenches. Weather being fine it is quite a treat to move about.'

Sapper P.E. Rea. BEF. France.

'I am still going strong. I have just received a letter from Joe Punter. He is going on all right. They have a band and he is the big drummer – keeping up his old job so that he won't be out of practice when the band is complete again. Will you please let me have some cigarettes as the others I had with me got buried by the explosion of a shell; it left me without any at all. That flash lamp has come in very useful now for I can see along in the dark now without falling down any holes.'

Trooper R. Squair. BEF. France.

'We are still in action... plenty of 'bag' just now. Saw some prisoners that came past us last week. I expect they had left school but it is very doubtful. They looked as if they wanted some of our Christmas pudding that was sent to us from London. There was a stone as big as Chiswick in my piece, but none the more for that they were very nice.'

11 February 1916. *Chiswick Times*
Trench Warfare and Christmas Day in France. Sergeant W Bowgen of the Victoria Working Men's Club writes to Mr. Copland.

'Just out of the trenches. One or two very narrow squeaks. Once while going the round of sentries I was only a couple of yards away when a bomb dropped killing one man and wounding another. It is the shells and bombs that do all the damage in the trenches. There is little or no danger in rifle fire unless a man is fool enough to stick his head up like an Aunt Sally for the German snipers to have a pop at, and they rarely miss.

Our transport has had a very rough time bringing up supplies to the trenches. The road is under close German observation, and they very often drop a few 'coal boxes' to wish them good evening, blowing a few of them and our grub to glory. I was in the first trench all the time; only 70 yards from the German front line and in one place only 30 yards, and a merry time we had at night sniffing at each other.

Our communication trench, by which we left, leads out to a very big town that is now a heap of ruins. On leaving the trench we come under German artillery fire; but got clear with one casualty –

one poor fellow struck in the head by a piece of shell while passing through this heap of ruins.

A party of engineers was coming up and one shouted 'Good Old Richmond'; it was a Sandycombe Road man who knows you well, but we couldn't stop as we were in range of the Hun's guns. A few yards further on I saw a lancer blown out of his saddle without injuring his horse.

I was rather amused at what I saw in the English papers – Tommy enjoying himself at Christmas! No doubt some did, but our boys must have been in the background as regards the good things. Our Christmas Day Menu. Breakfast, boiled bacon. Dinner, stew (whether French or Irish I don't know, but I should say Irish for the enormous amount of meat in it.) Tea was three courses – cheese, jam and a joint of beef (extracted from a tin). None the less we enjoyed ourselves, and many of us, if we live, will remember the splendid blow out we had in France on Christmas Day 1915.'

11 February 1916. *Chiswick Times*
Letters to Rev. Oldfield.

Private Harry S. Smith. BEF.

'I am getting on nicely. Still a bit weak, after being in hospital, but I shall be all right in a few days. I have been out here now nine months. I have very nearly forgotten what Chiswick looks like. I hope to come on leave in a few weeks' time. I have been having a very warm time since I have been out here. Three weeks ago a Taube came over and dropped seven bombs on the place I was operated in. I have not run across any of the lads I knew in Chiswick. I should very much like to see some of the old boys. Getting very cold weather out here now, and raining every day.'

Signaller W.G. Howe. BEF.

'At the place where we are there is a church which has been shelled to the ground, but the crucifix is still standing upright and intact. We are just in reserve billets but we go up to the trenches tomorrow night and our guns at the present are wishing the Kaiser many happy returns of the day, it is deafening.'

Bandsman Walter Burch. BEF.

'Thank you very much for Dick Vine's address. I suppose you know young Cole is in my battalion again. Well Sir, we are having very rough weather, the mud is plentiful. We had a bit of excitement our last time in the trenches. We blew a mine up under the German trenches and about an hour previous they attempted a bombing attack upon us, but after they had thrown about 6 or 8 bombs they ran back to their own trench. Our artillery are certainly the masters round here now.....'

11 February 1916. *Chiswick Times*
Hints for Army Recruits – what to take with you, what to leave behind.

A correspondent sends us the following useful hints – he has, he says, consulted several old soldiers and they advise:

Razor – army razor is useless

Strop - none issued in the army

Shaving brush – army brush falls to pieces in hot water

A waistcoat

A pair of easy shoes of any kind – tennis plimsolls do well, but should be quite large to put on after marching or to wear in camp or barracks

Handkerchiefs – none supplied in the army

Undervests – if you wear them

Shirts – a couple

Pants – your own may be more comfortable than the army issue

Writing materials

A pocket knife is useful, and if your watch is not valuable, retain it and have a shield fitted to it.

Leave bad temper and 'back-chat' at home. They do not pay in the service.

18 February 1916. *Chiswick Times*
Letters to Rev. Oldfield.

Private A. Brand. Somewhere in France.

'It is very cold in France now, and we have had a snowstorm lasting some hours. The weather in fact is very bad, and the trenches are in an awful state, despite all efforts to keep the water out. Some little time ago our neighbours opposite (the Germans) played us a dirty trick. Our trenches being lower than theirs, they amused themselves by pumping the water out of their trench into ours. Our shouts to them to desist proved futile, as you may expect, so we had a nice job pumping night and day until we got rid of the Allemand's presents. I would be very much obliged if you would send me a pocket flash lamp, as without its aid there is a pronounced tendency to tread on ground which is not there, and it is not the pleasantest feeling in the world to hoist oneself out of sundry shell holes filled with water.'

Sapper Harpa Smith. BEF. France.

'I have received the cord from Edinburgh today and am trying it. I find it very perfect and effective. *(note: chemical cord for protection from trench plague – vermin.)* Just at the time of writing they are shelling us and it has become a daily occurrence. It is a sight to watch the civilian population rush for the cellars.'

Sapper P.E. Read. BEF. France.

'I was out for a stroll yesterday and who do you think I saw coming towards me between the horses? Well it was Bobbie Squair. You can guess what sort of a meeting it was to see one of the old boys. He is only billeted about three quarters of an hour from me. He said that W. Woodhead is with him as well. I should like to go and see him but I cannot go until after tea, when it is too late to go that distance for we all have to be in our billets by 8 o'clock, but I might slip over on a cycle. I was talking to Bobbie so long that I was very nigh late for patrol. He said I am the only old boy that he has seen since he was out here. I am a little more fortunate for this is the second man I have seen. He is not altered much, just as lively as ever. I asked him if he had sung that song that he sang at the concerts once – that was in the good old times – 'Always Looking Forward'.

Bandsman A. Collard. BEF. France.

'Well, I earned the D.C.M for good work in attending to the wounded under shell and rifle fire. I shall never forget that day, because I had a very narrow escape myself. You must not think I have done anything marvelous. I have only done my duty to the best of my ability and I sincerely hope to carry on to do so.'

25 February 1916. *Chiswick Times*
Letters to Rev. Oldfield.

Private A. Long. B.E.F. France.

'I am still in the pink of condition and am busy doing fatigues in the trenches. A bit of excitement, Fritz bombing us with a kind of aerial torpedo, which our Tommies have named 'Minnies'. They glide through the air and drop nearly in the trench causing a big explosion, which blows the trench to pieces. Well, one of these fell near this trench, and blew the parapet in, and burying one of our chaps, and Broadley and I and a few others were soon getting him out, and he was not injured only badly shaken up, and while at this job they were still falling near, and we thought every minute one was going to catch us, but we had the luck to get through all right. The weather here is fine, being extraordinary for this time of the year, it being a pleasure to be able to move about. Hoping the brigade and band are still up to the mark.'

Private G. Elsley. Somewhere in France.

'Weather still very miserable. I dropped across Corporal Hagget again the other day. He is back here again with his regiment, all fit and well. We are having a bit of a rest now from the trenches, after a strenuous time in them, including the winter, making my second, but it was not so bad as last winter. We have plenty to do back here – flag drill, telephone work and route marching so you see they keep us fit.'

<u>Trumpeter R. Squair</u>. Somewhere in France.

'Everything is about the same only that I ran across P. Read as I was coming back from the line the day before yesterday. I thought it was about time I ran into somebody from Chiswick. There are some others from the old place not very far from me, but I cannot run into them somehow or other. It is funny that we are so near and yet so far.'

<u>Gunner W. Woodhead</u>. BEF.

'You will be surprised to know I have left the battery, but I do not know how long for, so I am having my letters addressed to the battery. I am now attached to the Ammunition Park, which is a nice change, after being in action two months right off the reel, especially as the Germans have been busy just lately. They have taken a fancy to using what we call 'tear shells.' If one of these bursts anywhere near it makes our eyes water, and nearly chokes us, which is not at all pleasant. I am certainly looking forward to some leave, but there is a certain amount of luck attached to getting it. Our battery has been out here now 12 months and only 40 have been on leave. I heard from Perce Read just after he came back from leave, also Tom Rose. Frank Cooper was getting on all right last time I heard. I was congratulated by an officer for very good gun-laying, hitting a German sniper's house six times with six shells, so you can guess it did a bit of damage to it.'

25 February 1916. *Chiswick Times*
Letters to Mr. Copland, Victoria Working Men's Club.

<u>Sergeant G. Shefford</u>. Royal Engineers.

'behind the lines we are resting in a small French village, the natives, chiefly women and young lads, are busy on the land, ploughing and sowing, utilising cattle for the work. The land is extremely flat but heavy, owing I expect to the bad drainage system and numerous artesian springs. When in the firing line last, we came across one of these springs in a communication trench and it was most difficult to keep the trench drained for use. We are quartered in a fairly decent house, furnished but empty when we took over, the owner, I think, having gone to war. We make good use of his cooking utensils and I sleep like a top on a spring mattress except when the rats get too bold. The last night or two has seen a great increase of these pests.'

Lance Corporal J. Sutcliffe.

'We are very close to the line but have not been up yet. I must not talk too soon as I think we shall be going up some time this month. Not seen much excitement yet, only aeroplanes being bombarded. Walking outside my billet a week ago and saw a chap whom I thought I knew. Who do you think it was? Young Chamberlain in the R.F.A. from Victoria cottages. I guess we were some surprised to see each other. I will rest now, so that the rats can have a marathon over me.'

Sergeant. Hansell. Rifle Brigade.

'Merry and bright in spite of the company of rats. The weather has been much better since I returned, quite spring weather, the sun shining lovely and helping to cheer us up. Returning from leave I arrived here about 8pm Monday evening and into the trenches the next day and we had a hot time. We lost our captain, a fine man he; but it's all in war.

Thank you sincerely for all the good things forwarded to me as I know that there is a lot of hard work and worry in getting all these good things together, in addition to the expense attached. It is very nice for me to know that the people's thoughts at home are always with us.'

Bombardier Thurlow. Royal Field Artillery.

'I was in Gallipoli and managed to get a parcel to my brother in Egypt. Naturally our life is a busy one. No doubt we shall be in action again soon. None of us are satisfied with this place and it is agreed that the sooner we are 'in it' again the better shall like soldiering.'

3 March 1916. *Chiswick Times*
Letters to Rev. Oldfield.

Driver J.M. Clarke. Royal Garrison Artillery. Meath Hospital, Dublin.

'I expect you will be surprised to hear I am sent home. I am still in bed (rheumatism etc) but am very comfortable and am getting along nicely. Hope it will not be long before I am home for a few days' rest. It was very bad luck to get into action again and only last a few days. I got drenched several days running and finally got rheumatic fever. Before I left Southampton I met Jennings, who used to be in the band, and he was going to France touring I should think it would be a great idea to arrange a reunion at the conclusion of hostilities.'

Corporal C.A. Brand. BEF. France.

'Received your very welcome parcel today. Just the kind of necessaries one needs out here. We chaps out here have all more or less the happy (or ought I to say unhappy) knack of exploring the depths of sundry shell holes, ditches etc and of course the merits of these same shell holes are fully commented upon by the luckless ones, and I am afraid 'Mrs. Grundy' would hardly approve of the rather lurid language employed. So, sir, you see, the lamp you sent me will be a boon.'

[(Note: anyone desiring to further reduce the amount of the said lurid language can do so by forwarding a lamp or its price to Rev. A.E. Oldfield for consignment to France.)

10 March 1916. *Chiswick Times*
Letter to Rev. Oldfield.

Sapper P. Read. France.

'Thank you for the parcel. The weather being very cold, the cocoa is doing a world of good; and the pudding, you can, guess, went down lovely. It came just right for dinner and my chum and I set to boiling some water to put it in. The salmon we made sandwiches of, to have while at work. So you can guess, sir, how a parcel like that is welcomed, and the socks, and the body cord is perfect I think for it acted so with me. I have not seen Bobbie Squair since. Isn't it funny seeing an old boy once, then you might not see him again for months? Has Fred Bailey been home on leave yet, as I have not heard from him for some time? I hope he is all right.'

17 March 1916. *Chiswick Times*
Letters to Rev. Oldfield.

Signaller W.G. Howe. France.

'I came out of the trenches last night and we had a rough time of it – plenty of snow and also plenty of rifle grenades. The first night we spent in the trenches the enemy blew up a mine. I can assure you the shirt and pair of socks were most useful and I am sure that body cord will be effective as one of my platoon mates has one, and he says his clothes don't go for a moonlight trip now without orders.'

Corporal F. Inskip. BEF.

'My battalion has been away from the trenches nearly a month. We were informed that we were not out for a rest, but for training, and well we know it. Have a parade before breakfast, then 9 to 1; there is a N.C.O's parade from 2 to 3.30, then every fortnight a night march. It may interest you to know that today is my birthday, (19).'

Gunner Matthew Bain. Royal Garrison Artillery. 'B' Central Ward, Western Hospital, Manchester.

'I had a letter from my mother and she told me my brother Tom was up on leave and that he looks quite smart, and the last time I heard from Fred he said he was in good health. Most cases in this hospital are frost bites, and several poor fellows have lost their toes. I know you will be pleased to hear that my wounds are healed and I can walk nicely with the help of a walking stick, and hope to be leaving hospital shortly.'

<u>Driver Jack Clarke</u>. Royal Garrison Artillery. Meath Hospital Dublin.

'As you say it is rather Irish to take me to Dublin. However we are on the way home. I am up today and feeling much better. We are treated splendidly here. The doctor, Sir John Moore, tells me none of the organs are affected in any way and it's due to being constantly wet through and exposure which caused the rheumatic fever; but apart from being run down and weak, I am well and should be home in a fortnight. I arrived here only in blankets and lost every bit of my kit. There is nothing I am wanting, thank you very much indeed, as we are issued with fags, paper and envelops and plenty of good food.'

Friends will be glad to know Driver Clarke has put on nearly two stone in weight in Dublin.

24 March 1916. *Chiswick Times*
Letters to Rev. Oldfield.

<u>Lance-corporal E.Cole</u>. France.

'Well sir, I am getting along lovely since I have been back with the regiment and have got promotion on a new machine gun we are using. We have been for a rest for a month, but for the first time back since the rest we held some trenches which we captured off the Huns, which were in a terrible condition compared with our own, with heaps of dead about, so we had a lively time for another 'kick-off'. Dear Sir, I shall be pleased if you can send me a local paper as it is quite a treat to read some of the old boys' letters and see how they are getting on, as I haven't had much luck running across many of them in this part of the line. Though I saw Harry Mitchell one day as I was passing in a motor, but could only shout 'How do, Harry!' and wave the old cap.'

<u>Lance-corporal C. Wrathell</u>. Somewhere in France.

'I am pleased to tell you we are encouraged at sport out here, and our section has entered for the brigade cup, but am sorry to say we have no rig-out so if you have any of old St Mary Magdalene's left, we should be glad of them and we will keep the old colours flying. We are in the semi-final. I have only met two Chiswick boys – Baldwin and Abbott.'

Trumpeter J. Burgess. Somewhere in France.

'We are doing very well here at present and pleased to say we are having some lovely weather now, because we had quite three weeks of nothing but rain and snow. I saw Reg Eydmann this morning and he is looking well. Tell the lads I wish to be remembered to them and hope to be home very shortly to play the big drum again, which I think is a lot better than being out here, but never mind, roll on peace. – Your little big drummer, John.'

24 March. *Chiswick Times*
Letters to Rev. Oldfield.

Gunner Fred Bain.

'I am glad to hear my brother Matthew is on his way home and that Tom is getting on well in the Life Guards. So Fred Bailey has just been home on leave. Well I am glad to hear that. I hope to meet Bert Golding in my travels.'

Sapper J. Jennings. Somewhere in France.

'We have been on the move and just settled down in a new sector of the firing line. Just as we got into the village everything was quiet until yesterday when they started strafing us with 'coal boxes' and 'wizz bangs'. We had only dug-outs and some were full up with water. Well, we had to make the best of it.

I had a narrow escape, walking down the road with my dinner in the Dixie, and one burst over my head. I ran up against an old wall for cover, and the pieces were falling on my shoulders. I waited till it was a bit quiet, then made my way to a dug-out and just got to the bottom of the stairs when one burst just outside and took the wall away, where I took cover a minute or two before, and landed in the officers' cook-house. As luck would have it, nobody was in at the time; then I ran back to our hut. Had been there about a quarter of an hour when one landed outside the hut. Well, sir, after that it became much hotter, and I think all the company did the only thing that could be done and that was to sit still and hold tight –that was the nearest we have had of the 'coal boxes' and I was glad when they stopped. They were trying to find the gents who were strafing them, but were unlucky.'

Sapper P.E. Read. Somewhere in France.

'I see by your letter that Fred Bailey's letter and mine still come by the same post, but it was a pity we were not home on leave at the same time. I have just received a letter from Fred Bailey whilst I am writing this and am pleased to say he is still in the pink. According to George Allen's letter in the CT, he seems to be having a jolly good time of it. I have not come across Bobbie Squair or Dick Riches lately. Mother tells me she showed you those photos that were destroyed by a shell. I should have told you before but being an everyday occurrence I never gave it a thought. I was sitting about half a dozen yards from the shed in which I sleep, when we heard a 'Black Maria' as they call them, which pitched right into my bed, sending everything sky high and me flat on my face on the ground. Thankful to say, I was not hurt, but much shaken up, but sorry to say some of my chums perished. It set fire to the barn and all my clothes and equipment. That was the only one that was so close but they come every Sunday, for the Germans make it a speciality to do their strafing on Sundays, but I think they are no class.

31 March 1916. *Chiswick Times*

Gunner C.A. Faulkner.

'It is fine to hear the birds singing and to see the trees in full blossom and about to break into leaf, as we know the time is coming when those other birds of the air – the aeroplanes – will be singing merrily. It is a busy job for our aeroplane scouts. I must say this is a very lucky battery. We have had only three slight casualties since we came out last July. A great deal depends on the battery's position, which is a very good one indeed. The artillery on this point have been very quiet this last week or more, doing very little firing. This must be very galling to the poor infantry lads on our front, seeing that the Germans are doing a lot of shelling and we not retaliating. We gunners are anxiously waiting for the day when we can let them have our little lot.'

14 April 1916. *Chiswick Times*
Letters to Rev. Oldfield.

Lance-corporal E. Cole. Somewhere in France.

'Many thanks for your welcome parcel and cuttings from the Chiswick Times, which were very interesting. Well, sir, I am sorry I have not written before as we have been pretty busy lately as Fritz has got rather excited because we have taken an important position from him and sent one of his death traps for a trip to the sky; in fact he got that excited that he tried to paste us with the artillery, but our boys proved best men and gave them some iron rations which defied the best men in their trench, if they had one left, which I am doubtful, to put his head over the top.

We are off to church parade, conducted by one of the bravest men I have met, who attended to our wounded under the most heavy of bombardments, and one word from him seemed to make a new man of you, never mind how browned off you are, as you soon get browned off sitting in mud and slime all day, the shells flying over your head like small trains. It cheers us up thinking Fritz is worse off than us yonder, stopping a few of Lloyd George munitions.'

Gunner H. Triggs. France.

'I must admit I am just a trifle fed up after 20 months out here. I very much hope to be coming home on leave again shortly, so I shall be trotting around to give you a call. We are at present in camp, been here about a fortnight, but we shall soon be back in the firing line again.'

Lance-corporal C.Wrathall. France.

'I don't know how long this war is going to last, but I shall be glad when it is finished. I am now in the same section of the line in which A.Booth was killed. I have been reading of the conscientious objectors, and I do not think much of their excuses; if they could only see the villages out here – not a house standing – I think they would alter then. Well, I must draw this letter to a close, as I have a gun rod to dry.'

Sapper P.E. Read. France.

'Just a few lines to thank you for the parcel which I received three days ago and the contents of the parcel put new life into a man. They say the rum that they issue to the troops puts life and warmth into the body, but a cup of cocoa beats all their tots of rum. There is nothing that beats a good blow out of cocoa. Please congratulate Bert Golding when you write on being made an acting bombardier and please say I hope he will still climb the ladder and be bombardier without the acting attached to it. I have heard from Fred Bailey, Tom Rose and Wal Woodhead and am pleased to say they are all safe and well.'

21 April 1916. *Chiswick Times*
Letters to Rev. Oldfield.

Sapper P.E. Read. Somewhere in France.

'I am pleased to hear that Jack Clarke is better and at home. I have seen Tich Wrathell. We had all last night together, talking of the old days, which you can guess is nice, for to see old faces puts fresh life into a fellow. We shall see one another for three days, for he is in no.15 hut and I am in no.2 in the same road. We used to call him 'Tich' but he is not much of a Tich now, nigh a head and shoulder taller than I. I am very glad that you have sent me those addresses, sir, for now I can write to more of the old boys in spare time, which is very scarce.'

Signaller W.G. Howe. France.

'I am on a new job now, it is as miners' fatigue. It is not a bad job at all, plenty of excitement. The Germans strafe us often; they give us a dose of shrapnel, rifle grenades and rum jars, which is their latest in grenades. The other night when our fatigue party was coming out of the trenches on the way to the motor buses which take us back a good way behind the lines, the Germans turned a machine gun on the road on which we were walking. Consequently we had to lie flat on our faces. A mine was blown up last night and it shook us up like anything.'

Driver R. Hutton. Somewhere in France.

'Thank Mrs. T for us for sending the CT which Hudson and I greatly enjoy reading. We were glad to see Perce Read was all right. One cannot imagine the sight of the houses and tombstones smashed to atoms, and even the bones of people blown out of the earth. I have only come across Reg Eydmann and J. Burgess at present, but I hope to see some more before long.'

20 April 1916. *Chiswick Times*
Letters from Captain Ansell.

Mr. Ansell, of Old Palace Place, the Green, well-known etcher and architect, was gazetted captain last month. Earlier he had served with national registration work in Richmond, then took a commission and went to France. Mrs. Ansell, who has left Richmond temporarily, now writes to say that in response to her appeal through our columns, she was able to send to her husband 250 pairs of mittens for his company. The men were very grateful for the gift.

From one of Captain Ansell's letters – account of a day's work:

'At 5.30, I wake and listen to the rain beating on the roof and strafe the Kaiser. It is the worst moment of the day; everything is beastly. I wonder why I ever joined the army. D—-- grunts and swears. I grunt and swear, and P—-- then appears with the shaving water, in an old Nestle's tin. Then I get up, dive into my Bedford cords, and endeavour to lace them up in the dark. I miss the lace holes, and then light the candle. D—- is meanwhile in bed, having shaved overnight. Then I get into boots, either ankle boots and leggings or field boots that are too small in the leg. I proceed to shave without a mirror. I complete my dressing and go out into a muddy camp that resembles most other muddy camps.

There is a row of officers' huts near the cook houses, to ensure that officers, having got to bed very late owing to censoring men's letters and writing company rolls, shall be awakened at unearthly hours by the cooks making up fires, preparing breakfast and so on. The tents run down the slope, so to speak, and are coated over with mud and green paint to make them invisible to Bosch aeroplanes which might come over. Down one side are the horse lines and the wagons. There is one way into the camp, a way that is deep in mud churned up by motor lorries.

The men line up by the fires and receive their breakfasts – tea, bacon, bread. We go into a wooden hut used temporarily as an officers' mess, and have tea, bacon, bread and jam. At 7.15 our first working parade is held. The men line up in sections, each under the lance corporal, and we move off with a space of 50 yards between our sections to allow traffic to get past us. Our work is principally at one point. The men are apportioned to their jobs and set to. I visit everybody in turn. We dig and repair and sandbag and rivet and make gun emplacements and all sorts of interesting things. The men are keen, and enjoy the work when it is fine, which it is today.

We seem to be as safe as Richmond Green where we are. At 4pm we dismiss the men, and they march back to camp. At 4.30 they have their hot meat meal. We have tea and then do clerical work till dinner, which is a boring meal, owing to the lack of imagination of the cooks. After dinner, we hold audience of the C.S.M and the sergeants. We arrange the work for the morrow. Misdemeanours are brought before us. One man was hauled before me for laughing loudly on parade. It struck me that a man who could laugh on an early morning parade, in heavy rain and deep mud, really deserved a medal, but I only gave him the prize giving. I regret though that I did not inquire what could have made him laugh. It must have been amazingly funny. I don't think anything on earth could make me laugh at that time in the morning.

When the business is completed, we censor the men's letters. There is an enormous lot of 'as it leaves me at present' and that kind of thing, and one gets bored stiff after reading some 50 or 60. I wrote the last paragraph in a room in a farm after having had lunch. Close by us was a so-called chateau, with a shell hole in the roof and a gun emplacement in the cellar, and now I am in bed finishing the letter. I have not seen anyone I know yet out here. I expect I shall meet a friend one of these days going along a filthy muddy road.

This morning, we had an accident. A lot of 'A' company men were sheltering from the deluge in an old cart shed, an open thatched affair, when the gale blew down the whole affair on the men. I was not there but D----- was not far off, and started getting the men out. I heard of the accident and commandeered a motor ambulance and a car, and ran along to the place. Our chaps were being got out on stretchers; 13 of them were injured – broken legs and shoulders and collar bones. We got them all into ambulances and off to the hospital before our doctor arrived. We then weighed in to move all the timbers and thatch to see if any other men were under. When it was clear that all the men were out we set out for home. It was lucky that no more were hurt considering the circumstances.'

20 April 1916. *Chiswick Times*
Duties of a 'linesman' – letter from Gunner J. Lucas.

Son of late Councillor A. Lucas, writes from a convalescent camp at Boulogne. He has been in hospital from influenza and serious breakdown after service in the firing line. He is recovering and expects to re-join his battery.

'I have had a few exciting moment during the course of my duty, which consists of telephone work. When not on duty, I take my turn as a 'linesman' and patrol the battery wires, which run to the observing stations and the trenches etc. At times the linesman can be seen and is sniped at by the enemy, at other times shells come unpleasantly close and give us more work by cutting the wires. I have the somewhat doubtful pleasure of one of Krupp's inventions explode within three yards of me. I was covered with dirt and mud, but the pieces of shrapnel flew over my head, probably due to the fact that I had thrown myself down flat, and that being close to the shell it had exploded upwards.

As a rule, the noise made by an approaching shell gives pretty good warning to get down, but there is one small shell which is very nasty. It is known as the 'whiz-bang' and arrives in such a hurry that all you hear is a 'whizz' followed by a 'bang' as the brute bursts, generally just above your head, hence its name.'

28 April 1916. *Chiswick Times*
Letters to Rev. Oldfield.

Private E.C. Smith. Somewhere in France.

'Well sir, I have been having a hot time of it the little while I have been here. I have had the pleasure of seeing a mine exploding, also being in the bombardment, but I assure you it is as much as I want to see for a time anyway. I had a letter from Harper; he says he is OK and there is not much doing where he is so I guess he will get it warm later on. There has been some fine work executed by the boys, and I believe they won't let the Germans rest until they get a good hold on them, which I know won't be very long. I came across Tom Garside, who used to live in Rickets Road, in the trenches one morning. I had previously met him in Canada, but did not know he had joined the army; he was taking a look over the parapet when I noticed him. He seemed surprised when I called him Tom. We had a talk of old times and he is in the same battalion as myself. Glad to hear that Arthur Smith and Dick Powell are on leave. I hope they will have a good time, as when they come back I guess it will be pretty hot. It interests me very much to read the Old Boy's letters. One says he was present when our boys sent up one of the German death traps up in the sky. I was a little way up the line when that scene occurred so I guess we are not far apart. We are not allowed to mention names of places; it is very awkward to find one another. We may be only 100 yards from each other. I am in a fix as to who sent me the Chiswick Times but I thank them very much. I must close as the candle is burning pretty low. How many Tich's are there going to be on the St Mary Magdalene's roll, as I understand there is another in France?'

Driver R. Hutton. France.

'I am pleased to hear all the lads are going on well. It quite reminds us of the old chaps when we read their letters in the Chiswick Times, received every week from Mr. T. I expect everyone is in khaki now. The conscientious objectors should be put in the front line trenches; they would not object for long. Wishing you a happy Easter and thank you for the palm.'

5 May 1916. *Chiswick Times*
Letters to Rev. Oldfield.

Driver R. Eydmann. Somewhere in France.

'We often have our wagon line shelled, but up to the present, we have only lost one shoeing smith and one horse, also having one horse wounded. I am sorry I cannot stop to say any more.'

Private C.A. Brand. France.

'I arrived back here on the 12th. The weather here was awful but I am pleased to say it has changed lately, but we are all fed up with this and shall be very glad when it is all over. One of the old boys is here in the person of Len Webb, with the R.A.M.C. Fred Harvey, one of the old choir boys, also is with the same corps.'

Driver F.A. Bailey. France.

'Well today would have been an outing, I suppose if all had been well, but sir with a bit of luck – this war over – the lads will be able to mobilise once again and have an outing next Easter. The Allemand airmen as usual are taking advantage of the good weather, paying us many visits today. One of them became a victim to one of our airmen as early as 6 o'clock this morning and, spiteful like, he dropped his bombs as he came down. Then he had the luck to drop in their lines. I have heard from Tich Wrathall this week. He is in the same region as Perce Read…I wish I could get their way a bit and be with them. Enclose photograph which I think is best to be expected.'

Driver C. Owen. France.

'Thank you for your most welcome parcel, it's quite a change out here to get a nice tin of salmon, which I am very proud of. We are having the best of weather here now and I hope it will last, as it is so much better for getting about with our horses and wagons, as we are going over some funny ground just now. May God spare you and yours from getting hurt by Zepps.'

Driver F. Mockler. France.

'I am sending you a copy of our battery's gallant dash round 'Shrapnel Corner' composed by one of our drivers. It is a true story which happened on December 19th when the Germans made a gas attack. I hear often from C.Owen and he is also A1. I have been out here nearly 12 months now; the time passes so quick.'

5 May 1916. *Chiswick Times*
Life in the trenches.

A Richmond soldier home on leave from France told one of our representatives that one very soon gets used to trench work, which is not at all bad. Whilst on duty in the trenches, the only thing a soldier thinks about is how to dodge the shells and the snipers. On some days one experienced some narrow escapes, but on the whole it was not very dangerous if a good look-out was kept. A man must, however, be continually on the alert, as in some cases the enemy trenches were only a few yards away.

Sapper P.E. Read. France.

'We are up the line again and having a lively time of it. The Germans tried to gas us two days in succession and you ought to see the clouds of gas come rolling along. Of course we had to put on our gas helmets. Then they are sending over plenty 'tear' shells as well, for one came close to our billet. I ran out thinking some of our section was hurt – right into the smoke. It could not have been more painful than if they had stuck a lot of pins into my eyes. It doesn't seem to affect the eyes afterwards, only makes them ache when we have got over the pain when it first catches our eyes.

I have heard from Fred Bailey. He is going on alright but the censor cut out a lot of his letter. I am close to where I saw Tich Wrathell and expect to see him again before long.'

19 May 1916. *Chiswick Times*
Letters to Rev. Oldfield.

Driver F. Mockler. Somewhere in France.

'I saw William Carpenter last week. It was a surprise for me, but I was sorry we could not speak as we were out on the march. I have now been transferred to the column, so will you please write address— (Address can be supplied to friends – Rev Oldfield.)

Driver Jack Clarke. France.

'I am on gymnasium work here, and at present have been appointed acting bombardier. I came across Will Crisp and Maidlow, late brigade boys, and was so pleased to come across them, and enjoyed a chat about old times. Both send their best respects. I expect to remain here for a while and if all goes well I shall get on alright and perhaps get a higher rank. Anyway I can only do my best and see what happens.'

Bandsman W. Burke. France.

'I suppose you read of the 'scrap' we took part in. I must tell you our chaplain, Rev E.N. Melish won his VC on this occasion. He is attached to our battalion and is always in the firing line, cheering us up. He is the idol of the boys here. Well, sir, can you tell me how Corporal F. Inskip is getting on? He received a nasty wound in our charge. I hope he is getting over it. It is very hot out here at present, both sides doing a lot of shelling, and the enemy is rather free with his gas again, but we have good helmets to fight against that. By the way I left the stretcher bearers a month ago and have gone in for bombing – rather a funny change, but I had been on that job rather too long. Ted Cole who is a lance-corporal on our machine gun, is only a few yards from me at present.'

26 May 1916. *Chiswick Times*
Letters to Rev. Oldfield.

Corporal R.J. Vine. Somewhere in Flanders.

'We had a nasty turn the last time in the trenches, and caught it hot several times; got a lot of our old friends, the 'sausages'. Puts the wind up for some, to see one come sailing over like a cricket ball, in shape like a huge German sausage. Case of 'get out or go under.' Ah well, we are now enjoying a so-called 'rest' which consists of a lot of hard work. Arthur Martin is still in India as is Orchard.'

Bandsman A. Collard D.C.M. Somewhere in France.

'It is a great pleasure to know the grand St Mary's boys are doing well and still helping to keep the old flag a-flying. Jack Clarke must have had some hard times, so glad to know that he is quite well again. It will be a grand thing when compulsion is passed so as to get some of the lazy ones out here to do a bit. If we are to believe what is going on in Germany, I do not think that this great 'football match' will last long. I call it this because we are all trying to win the great goal which we are confident to win.'

2 June 1916. *Chiswick Times*
Letters to Rev. Oldfield.

Private W.J. Powell. Somewhere in France.

'Life is rather dull unless we are in action. The same thing every day, drill in the morning and a general clean up in the afternoon. I have lost my horse while I was home. He went lame and nothing could be done for him, so they cast him; so now I am riding a sick chum's horse till my remount comes up. I had rather an enjoyable afternoon yesterday watching sports given by our division in honour of the general and troops that have been holding out so gallantly at Verdun, and I think I can honestly say they enjoyed it, especially the native trick riding. We had very hot weather last week, but now are having rain again. We sleep in the fields now – more healthy and cleaner. My chum and I have built a spanking booby hut out of sheep hurdles and waterproof sheets, so are very comfortable. As the saying goes: 'We don't care if it snows.'

Private F.C. Smith. Somewhere in Belgium.

'Many thanks for you nice parcel and letter. Those herrings and pudding went down fine. We haven't had any 'spotted dog' for quite a long time now and it came as a gentle surprise to us. I received the piccolo in good shape. The weather is fine, makes one feel he would like to dump all his kit. As it is we have been relieved of our blankets, which makes the pack a great deal lighter. I had a letter from my brother Harper, and he is getting along fine. I might also say that the vermin cord acts wonderfully. You will shortly see Tom Garside as he is coming home on leave in three weeks.'

Bandsman W. Burch. Somewhere in France.

'I am still in the best of health - thank you for the cigarettes. I gave a box to Ted Cole, a box each to my two chums and kept a box myself. We all thank you very much for them. Our last position was a very warm one. The enemy used plenty of trench mortars and seemed to rely on them nearly as much as on their artillery for knocking our trenches about. Of course we did not take it lying down and gave them as much as they sent, especially our artillery. I see they have passed the Compulsion Act. I think it will help to finish the war quicker.'

2 June 1916. *Chiswick Times*

Concert at the Front.

A young officer, at the front, writing to his parents in Chiswick.

'I am quite OK and very busy. I am at present camped in a pretty little wood at the back of the firing line, on the one side of which I hear the roar of the guns in the trenches and on the other, a band is giving a concert of lively music. The effect is very weird to say the least. I enclose a type-written programme of the concert, which you will see contains some good music, but the success of the evening was the music hall song 'Are we all here?' – and when three or four thousand Tommies shouted 'Yes' at the top of their voices the effect was great, and must have given all the Germans in the neighbourhood a big scare.'

9 June 1916. *Chiswick Times*

Letters to Rev. Oldfield.

Private G. Elsley. Somewhere in France.

'We are hard at work now with pick and shovel, getting ready for the event. We had a fortnight's hard training. I received your parcel safe and was glad of the clean change of clothing as I had been doing some rather dirty work. Fritz is the same as usual with his strafing but it is a lot different to August 1914, for we are superior to him now in men and guns. I reckon I am one of the lucky ones, 22 months constant warfare without a scratch. Sgt Haggett is still going strong. Well sir, I must 'ring off' now as I can hear the sergeant calling in gentle and persuading words 'Fall in with shovels' – sounds like work.'

Driver R. Hutton. France.

'I expect you have read in the papers about the gallant 16th Irish Division. I met Johnny Burgess, the other day, and we were talking about the good times we had with you at camp. We are getting a bit tanned by the sun now.'

16 June 1916. *Chiswick Times*
St Mary's Old Boys. Letters to Rev. Oldfield.

Private Charlie Brand. Somewhere in France.

'What do you think of the Russians sir, quite back on form again, don't you think? I saw Len Webb a few weeks ago. I see that our navy has had its wish gratified, much to the German navy's undoing. I fancy the German navy's losses were heavier than they admit.'

Private W.J. Powell. France.

'We have been near to the shore and nearly every morning we took our horses on the sands. We are now back in our old billets. We have been issued with shrapnel proof helmets, like the French have got. I cannot say we like them as they are so heavy. Life in the billets is rather the same day after day, drill or exercise for the horses in the morning, fatigues in the afternoon till tea time, and then clean saddle, have a wash and brush up and bed, or rather sleep.'

Sapper J. Jennings. France.

'We have been on the move once more. While we were resting by the roadside a motor came along and I just glanced at the driver, and to my astonishment I saw it was Frank Sheppard, corporal in the ---. He has been out here from the start in August 1914 and it's about four years since I saw him. You can guess how pleased we both were. He has been looking out for Perce Read and Bob Squair. I like this place but I expect they won't keep us here long as it's too good to stop at.'

Sapper P. Read. In hospital. France.

'I came through my operation all right. I went out yesterday for the first time on the cliff overlooking the sea, just like Beachy Head, only not quite so high. I expect I shall be going up the line shortly after I have been to convalescent camp.'

30 June 1916. *Chiswick Times*
Letter to Rev. Oldfield.

Lance-corporal J. Caygill. Somewhere in France.

'Have been busy twice coming in the trenches and the week we had out we had to go in every day as working parties. Fritz gave us a bit of gas last Friday, but it did not affect any of our boys. We put up a notice board "Achtung Czernovitz Evobert" – (Czernovitz captured). The Germans did not fire at it as expected. Have not come across any Chiswick boys yet. Things are very quiet here.'

7 July. *Chiswick Times*
Letters to Rev. Oldfield.

Private F. Charles Smith. Somewhere in Belgium.

He thanks the lady who sends him the *Chiswick Times* and has been reading letters from the old boys especially the one from Charlie Reffold who is patrolling the North Sea. 'Not a very nice job as Fritz seems to be getting quite bold with his big ships. I think he is getting more than he bargained for with us, and now the big Russian advance seems to have shattered all his hopes of gaining any more ground. Our boys are confident of victory, although we are getting hit pretty hard here. We have taken up daylight saving as you have in England.'

Driver C. Owen ("Chicken"). Somewhere in France.

'Alive and well. Been very busy and in another part of France now. The church is a terrible wreck. It seems a pity they should play so much havoc with the places of worship, as most churches out here seem to be built in a better style than at home; but there is a good reason for knocking these lovely places down, as they are in the way of direction of fire. The church here was a splendid place before in was wrecked. At the top, outside, is a bronze figure of a priest holding a little child in his hands, and how it keeps there is a marvel. Our engineers say it weighs 5½ tons. It's solid brass but I am afraid it won't stand much longer.'

21 July 1916. *Chiswick Times*
Letters to Rev. Oldfield.

Corporal F. Sheppard. Somewhere in France.

'You will have heard of the big smash we had and the sight I shall never forget or the sound of the guns. I saw a good deal of the fighting because I was at the first dressing station. The spirit of the wounded lads was marvellous. The main problem was finding enough fags for them. I lost my cigarettes, razor and soap when a shell hit our billet while I was away on the road. I was left with what I stood up in. Young Jennings and I met and were surprised to see each other. He was waiting on the side of a road to go into action.'

Sapper P.E. Read. Convalescent camp, France.

'I am playing in the hospital band and have come across Bewley who has an arm wound, and he said it sounded like me when he heard the F flute. He has heard from Fred Bailey and he wishes he was there instead of a chap who can't read music in the band and only hangs the band back. Everybody else can read music. But it does not beat the old band.'

28 July 1916. *Chiswick Times*
Letters to Rev. Oldfield.

Private E. Kirkham. France.

'I witnessed the great advance from a distance. First about six mines went up and then the air was filled with gun bombardment like a continuing rumble of thunder. The aeroplanes have been doing good work but it is rotten when one of them comes down. They risk their lives every time they go up.'

Bandsman A. Collard. In a hospital in England.

'I was in the big push for seven days and the enemy shelled trenches we had captured. I was in a trench bandaging the wounded when a shell came over and killed six and buried a few others. I thought it was all up with me. I was unconscious for four hours and speechless for three days. I hope to be out soon but not with a bandage and stretcher but with something I can get my own back with. The Germans are shooting the wounded and stretcher bearers. A German prisoner at the hospital said they had given up all hope of winning. If the munition workers can send plenty of shells it will lead to great victories, and, please God, towards the end.'

Signaller George Elsley. 1st Hants Regiment. In hospital in England.

'We got over the top at 7.30am July 1st.. I managed to keep going until a 5.9 shell burst pretty close putting me out for ten minutes. I found I was only slightly wounded with a smashed finger and suffering from shock. Passing through various dressing stations I ended up in Boulogne and then England. Hope to be on furlough before long. My first wound was slight after 23 months without a scratch, so I am still lucky.'

Driver A.S. Smith. France.

'I hear that St Marys' Old Boys are suffering very heavily lately. And I too have had some narrow escapes.'

8 August 1916. *Chiswick Times*.
Letters to Rev. Oldfield.

Bandsman Walter Burch. France.

'Alive and kicking. We have been having a warm time and so has Fitz. Since the offensive started you would marvel at the ground we have taken. Their dug-outs are splendid. Some of them are 20ft underground with steps leading down to them. I reckon Fritz thought he was stuck round here for the duration. I am worried that I have lost touch with Ted Cole and sorry to hear that Dick Vine and Johnny Goddard have been wounded. I was slightly wounded in the left leg by shrapnel, and another piece smashed my water bottle, so once again I had a lucky escape. The boys are certainly doing their bit. If a lot of us get over this we should all get together and celebrate the occasion.'

<u>Lance-corporal E. Cole</u>. No 3 Infantry Base, France.

'Sorry not to have written before. I have been wounded again, this time in the face. I happened to spot him coming. So I expect he thought he would exchange compliments through his artillery, but I don't expect the poor chap meant any harm; he only thought he'd try to tickle my machine gun up, that's all. Never mind, near shaves are getting common things in a lifetime now.'

<u>Lance-corporal W. Oliver</u>. France.

'We took part in the big advance; our battalion did exceedingly well. We are out of the trenches now for a little time to get fit and made up. Expect we will be back in the trenches again in a day or so. I do not think they will stop going ahead now till they have driven them right out of France and Belgium. I shall never forget that morning of the 7th when we first went over the top with the coolest of courage, a thing the Germans cannot understand, for German prisoners told us we were all good fighters and stickers. They told us they had had no food or water for three days for our big guns did give them beans. We went over three times and captured a battery of guns, which we are having presented to our battalion, and they are going to be sent to Hounslow Barracks. All I hope is that I pull through so I can have a good look at them. The Germans do not leave much behind but they had no chance with these. Private H Macdonald was wounded. He got it in the shoulder the second time we went over; there was only one man between me and him when he got hit. He said "Jumbo, I have copped it in the shoulder." So I said "Is it much?" He took it well and said, "No, not much." So we kept in the trench some time after that with all the big shells dropping on all sides, but we still kept our heads till the order came to retire, and we could not make it out, for no English soldier likes to retire. We found in the morning that we had gone too far, but not much, only that we had no proper cover.'

11 August 1916. *Chiswick Times*
Letter from Private H.J. Firman. 1-8th Battalion.

1-8th Battalion Middlesex regiment. Formerly a clerk in surveyor's department at Teddington. Now lying wounded in the 2nd Birmingham War Hospital.

'I have had the misfortune to get in the way of a Hun shell. I had a marvellous escape and am really lucky to be here at all. I was buried in a dug out and was struck in the elbow and knee and had one or two other minor wounds. The hospital organisation in France is excellent. The fighting in our sector has been very heavy, and although our losses have been enormous, we still remain masters of the situation. The Germans are always ready to surrender, and it is only their officers and NCOs that keep them together. Our bombardments are awful and if it was not for the very deep enemy dug-outs I do not think a man could live anywhere near the shelled area. Send us more shells – it is the only way to win. Our losses have been rather heavy, but I am glad to say we have upheld the glorious name of the Die Hards. After convalescence I shall be granted a short sick leave.'

18 August 1916. *Chiswick Times*
Letters to Rev. Oldfield.

Private F.C. Smith ("Tid"). France.

'Thank you for the cigarettes. A good supply and the boys wanted to know if I was going to open a shop. The usual issue every Sunday missed out last week. I have heard from Harper and have met Carpenter in the trenches.'

Sapper R. Spratt. France.

'The weather is grand. I am stationed in a fairly large town where there is a swimming bath I use, and also a YMCA hut where enjoyable concerts are held. I am proud of the plucky action of Tiddler and I am very sorry to hear of the death of Fred Smith. About 1,500 attend Sunday church parades in a theatre. The last sermon was 'Son, be of good cheer.' – appropriate to the times.'

<u>Gunner Harold Triggs</u>. France.

'We have been taking part in the big push and there has been little time to write. I find that I am not becoming obese, and also that the parasite insects still cling a little too tenaciously to me. Although we get a so called clean change from the laundry the dirt is so eaten into the linen that it would take caustic soda to fetch them clean. We have been on bad rations lately owing to the transport demand for munitions. Bully beef and biscuits and Machonochie rations in tins. One is not going to get fat on that. I have met my brother Bert who has returned after two months' convalescence.'

15 September 1916. *Chiswick Times*
Letter to Rev. Oldfield.

<u>Lance-corporal Walter Burch</u>. France.

'In the best of health. Everything going great for us just now. Our troops and the French are doing marvels. I was pleased with the news that a Zeppelin had been brought down. We all went mad with joy. An aeroplane dropped four bombs near us but no one was hit. I am still in the Grenade Club. All right if you give your mind to it, and no more dangerous than any other job.'

22 September 1916. *Chiswick Times*
Letters to Rev. Oldfield.

<u>Sapper R Spratt</u>. France.

'Many thanks for your parcel. It came at a favourable time when I and my chums were short. I am stationed at the same place and we still have Sunday services in the local theatre. The swimming bath is now closed owing to shelling. Very large shells are coming over and people have cleared off out of the danger zone. Remember me to the boys that are left; I don't suppose there are many now. I still play the flute but have forgotten some of the tunes.. Send the music of some of the marches please..'

Sapper J. Jennings. France.

'I'm very sorry to hear the sad news of some of the boys and am keeping a lookout for their graves but have not found any yet. We are suffering bombardments and it is hard to hear one another speak at times. We advance little by little every day. About 100 prisoners came through yesterday.'

Staff Sergeant C. Evans. Lord Derby's War Hospital.

'I played in a cricket match and we lost by an innings and seven runs. The hospital chaplain played for the other side, scored 69 and took nearly all our wickets. This is a nice place with a fine sports ground the only trouble being it is a long way from Chiswick.'

29 September 1916. *Chiswick Times*
Letters to Rev. Oldfield.

Corporal J. Cayhill. France.

'I have been slightly wounded in the right hand. I must think myself lucky to be alive after sticking the great British advance for six hours. I was the only N.C.O left in my platoon. I was carrying on after I got hit until an officer made me go back. The ground we advance over was so churned up by our shells that the edges of the holes were touching each other. It was quite a common sight to see the dead Germans and parts of their limbs sticking out of the ground where they had been buried by our shells. I accounted for a few Germans before they had me. We took the first line of trenches, caught some prisoners and left some men to take them back, and as soon as we passed them they started throwing bombs at us. Well, they will throw no more.

I have got a watch, a coin and a button as souvenirs. Also had a helmet which I gave to a fellow who was lucky enough to get to England.

No doubt people are wondering what the new type of engine is like in His Majesty's Service. Tank or caterpillar; they did their work splendidly. We heard them going over during the early hours of the morning while waiting in the shell holes to make our start. We were just as anxious to see what they were like, just like the folks at home are. Old Fritz was absolutely scared when he saw them; they ran back for their lives which didn't last long.

Sir, I must thank you very much for the cigarettes. I shared one box with the boys of my section, who were very pleased with the favourite cigarette.'

Lance-corporal D. Davies. France.

'Thank you for the parcel. The weather has broken up, cold, wet and miserable and mud is fearful – up to the ankles. The boys out here may be optimists; be that as it may, they all tell you it will be over by Christmas. We have given the Huns the proper kybosh lately and that new invention has been doing valuable work. Once it gets going it is absolutely irresistible. I have two of the old boys with me here – Peters and Archer.'

6 October 1916. *Acton Gazette*
Gunnersbury Nurse in France.

The Rev. C.N. Whitfield prints in the St James Gunnersbury Parish magazine a letter from Miss V.M. Palmer, a Red Cross Nurse on an ambulance train in France. The train collects casualties and patients from casualty clearing stations and conveys them to base hospitals. It carries about 600 patients and is staffed by three sisters and three medical officers.

'When we are up the line we can hear the guns distinctly, but it is wonderful how soon you get used to them. You would be surprised if you could see what a cosy little bedroom a first-class carriage makes, and you get used to sleeping with the train in motion, in fact it is not an uncommon experience to go to sleep at the base and wake up to the sound of the guns.'

6 October 1916. *Chiswick Times*
Letter to Rev. Oldfield.

Private W. Hales. France.

'Just a line to let you know I am still in the best of health. We have been very busy moving and have not had time even for a wash. What do you think of the Big Push? We shall push them a little more presently. Water is scarce so when you get it has to be looked after. We have had it pretty rough this last month or two, but never mind, we always get over it. When you go to bed you can hear the guns going off, and it is just like lighting in the sky. I shall be glad when it is all over so we can get back to dear old Blighty.

20 October 1916. *Chiswick Times*
Chiswick Working Men's Club. Letter received by Mr. Thomas A. King, secretary of the club.

Private C.F. Watkins. Honourable Artillery Company.

'I crossed the channel – reached then other side – and am stationed about 3½ miles from the firing line. Just after we arrived we saw five English planes flying over the German lines. They were frequently potted at but not hit. Half the battalion is in tents the others in huts, I have been lucky enough to get in a hut. Last night there was a fairly heavy bombardment.'

20 October 1916. *Chiswick Times*
Letters to Rev. Oldfield.

Private F.C. Smith. Canadian Expeditionary Force.

'Quite safe and well. I guess you will have heard of the Canadians success..... in which our battalion took part..... We were the first to jump the parapet .... Took the objective .... And held it and that's the main thing in this line of business. The tanks – those peculiar shaped instruments of war made Huny move quick. He thought it better to run towards our trench and give himself up ..... They would throw up their hands and shout 'Mercy, Kamerade!' .....They would give us all kinds of little useful articles ..... watches and chains, rings ..... Some of the boys came out with ..... revolvers, binoculars, spiked helmets and a few instruments ..... please thank Mrs. T.W. for the Chiswick Times.'

Driver R. Hutton. Near Portsmouth. Has been sent back to England because he is under age.

'I was sorry to leave the boys. I had been through a bombardment and had transported rounds for a gun battery. I came across Wrathell but had no time to talk to him as he was just going up to the line.'

27 October 1916. *Chiswick Times*
Letter to Rev. Oldfield.
Gunner H. Triggs. France.

'It's a hard job to get sugar here for love or money, not that I'm blessed with much of either. I think the war has knocked all the love out – worst luck. Shall not know what home or love is shortly if it keeps on much longer. We had better settle down for another six months or more, though I'm afraid the offensive is rather feeble at the moment. The bad weather prevailing has stopped the strafing a bit. I still get the Chiswick Times but it is only war news, criticising and surmising on the duration and what should be done and not done after it is finished. I am very grieved to hear that such a lot of Chiswick chaps have gone on the long journey beyond; still it's for a good cause, and the odds are we shall have a reward in the near future.'

3 November 1916. *Chiswick Times*
Letter to Rev. Oldfield.
Driver F.A. Bailey. In the Field.

'Thanks for the parcel. Contents came in very handy. I am now back at the place where Fred Smith was killed; and what a nice mess we are in. Mud and holes are plentiful – We can put up with it all in good part. I have seen a tank – a very good invention. I have heard from Walter Smith and from my brother in India. There does not seem to be any Zepp raids in London lately. I suppose our defences at home about knocked them right out. Anxiously awaiting the end of the war.'

10 November 1916. *Chiswick Times*
Letter to Rev. Oldfield.

Private C.F. Smith. France.

'Bad weather. Rain and mud. I am playing in the band with the instrument you sent out. I notice other old boys are in bands and we will have a good one when we return to England. We are billeted in houses – six to a house. Would be grateful for a pack of cards. I have had a letter from Harper who is among the imperial troops.'

17 November 1916. *Chiswick Times*
Letters to Thomas King, secretary of Chiswick Working Men's Club.

Private C.F. Watkins. Lewis Gun Section in France.

'Three days after leaving England was in the front line for 16 days. A heavy bombardment caused some casualties on the second day. Last Sunday we severely staffed Fritz but his reply was very feeble. When our section was moving back to the support shells fell close by, shrapnel flying in all directions, but we all got through safely. Back in the rest camp we all had a good hot bath and a change of clothes. It has rained daily and we are just about up to our necks in mud.'

17 November 1916. *Chiswick Times*
Letter to Rev. Oldfield.

Company Sergeant Major E. Allen. France.

'Have returned from the trenches where we were up to our necks in mud and water. They started sending over tear shells that made our eyes water. After that we had some very big shells which broke our trenches in and, of course, we had to repair them. Was glad when we were relieved so that I could have a wash; it seems to liven one up a bit. While writing this they are shelling us, so I am writing it down in the cellar. Remember me to all the boys. Excuse the paper, it is so scarce out here.'

24 November 1916. *Chiswick Times*
Letters to Rev. Oldfield.

Gunner H. Triggs. France.

'I am at present in rather low spirits and health. I am walking like a mechanical toy that wants winding up. I have been out here 27 months. We have had plenty of work transporting ammunition. Rations are rather bad. It can't be helped but you want something more nourishing than bully beef and biscuits. I've seen a tank – rather a queer object. No wonder Bosche got scared when he saw an army of them coming towards him. The authorities are getting very charitable lately. They have issued us with a pair of field boots; last year we had nixy apart from a pair of rubber gum boots at half price.'

C.M.S. E. Allen. France.

'We went over the top on Monday morning, and how well the boys went. You would have been surprised to see them standing along the top of the trench waiting for the signal to go forward and when it came they all went forward like one man, and gained our object. We came out of the trenches on Thursday morning at about 2am. The C.O. said he was very pleased with the boys. Thank you very much for the Woodbines, they came in handy, and I hadn't got a fag on me when we got back.'

1 December 1916. *Chiswick Times*
Letters to Rev. Oldfield.

Private E. Archer. France.

'Just finished ten days in the trenches and now able to write a letter. The Old Brigade has done its share and I hope that when it is over it will be remade again. I had a marvellous escape going into the trenches. Two shells dropped just in front of me, and as luck would have it, they were duds, (hard luck Fritz!). We were lucky not to have a drop of rain but the last two days were bitterly cold. Hoping to see some of the old boys any day. I have joined the Bombers Platoon; it is not so bad.'

Driver A. Colegate. France.

'Getting on alright. We are up to our necks in mud, but still merry and bright. We have not had a wash for a fortnight, and are not in a very safe place, but if you were to hear the guns you wouldn't think the war would last another five minutes. Fred Mockler's battery is not very far away.'

Driver Fred Brown. France.

'I have been on the march for twelve days and am in a very quiet place after a warm time in action.'

Trooper Tom Bain. France.

'The weather is bad and we have had snow. Could you answer this sum in simple proportion: If a man can walk eighteen miles a day with full pack on bully beef and biscuits, what could he do on eggs and bacon?'

8 December 1916. *Chiswick Times*
Letters to Rev. Oldfield.

Lance-corporal D. Davies. France.

'We, Peters, Archer and myself are still going strong. We are back in the reserve trenches but expect to move up again any day now. This is a very quiet place in comparison to a certain quarter, but it was famous about a year ago for some very stiff fighting and conjures up unpleasant memories for me and poor Liew. Our chaplain has won the Military Cross for good work in one engagement. He is the most cheerful man I have ever seen under fire and he cheers up the boys remarkably. If 'Pic' and 'Babs' have come to this division I haven't had the luck to strike them yet.'

Driver A. Colegate. France.

'Still in the land of the living, which I think myself lucky as it isn't very nice with 'Jack Johnsons' dropping round us all day, but we are so thickly covered with mud that if they hit us I don't think they could do us much harm. I'm in hospital at present with trench feet but will be back with my battery by the time you get this letter. I hope to see Fred Mockler. How Fred Stanley is getting on?'

Trooper Tom Bain. France.

'I am grateful for the parcel particularly the socks as we cannot look after our feet sufficiently with so much walking in a day. I and my chums are going to have a rare feast tonight. We are getting some real bad weather.'

Sapper P.E. Read. France.

'Thanks for the parcel especially the cocoa this cold weather. We warm it up in our 'dixies' over a small fire with one lump of coal in the trenches. Glad to hear that Bob Alexander got home with his wound. It's a wonder anybody gets along without getting hit. I haven't come across any of the boys in this fresh part of the line. The trenches are up to the eyes in mud, but goodness knows how old Fitz gets along, for the shells continually keep pouring into his trenches but serves him right.'

Private Sid Tillcock. France.

'Still in the land of the living. I like to hear the news of the old boys and expect that there are not many young men left in Chiswick now. Best of luck to all of them and a safe return.'

8 December 1916. *Chiswick Times*

Chiswick Working Men's Club members at the front. Letters to Thomas King.

Sidney Loader. France.

'I hope Chiswick people will be able to bear the terrible prices at home. I am in a North Country division now with a very gallant reputation. All the men, apart from three London Territorials, are pitmen.'

22 December 1916. *Chiswick Times*
Letters to Rev. Oldfield.

Driver Arthur S. Smith. France.

'I am weary of this terrible war and am living in hopes of another leave shortly. I have been here for 25 months and have had eight days' leave in all. I have heard from Walter once or twice and he is cheerful. Mother tells me Pickles is expecting to come out again shortly. I have heard from Ted Allen who has had rather a rough time of it. They shall have Christmas there again and he wishes all the boys as happy a Christmas as possible.'

Sergeant H. Hencher. France.

'I arrived over the duck pond quite safe, and not at all sea sick like I was when we went to Margate. It is a surprise to find me out here after two years instructing recruits. I expect to be in the line shortly and see some of the lads. I don't think there are many left at home, and I think dear old Chiswick has answered the call very well. We are having concert parties and there is a picture palace here. The rain is terrible. We can't grumble, it is those poor fellows that are out in it all day. Never mind, it is the old saying 'Keep a stout heart me lads.' Remember me to all I know.'

Corporal F. Sheppard. Ward 22a, Bed 1,272, 1st Eastern General Hospital, Cambridge.

'I was sent home for a complete rest on account of my health breaking down. I arrived here yesterday after a good journey across the water. It is not to be wondered at my health giving way, after being out there from the very start, only 168 hours leave in 28 months, so I think I have done my bit. This is a very nice hospital but I shall be glad to get out, but the doctors tell me it will some time before I am allowed out. Will you be good enough to tell the lady that sends me the Chiswick Times that I am home as I have not got her address.'

Sapper Harper Smith. France.

'We have been so busy this last month that it has been practically impossible to write. I think very often that I have been very fortunate indeed, as I have been out here for twenty months, and have not yet stopped anything. Charlie is going on very nicely.'

The Rev. A.E. Oldfield wishes all his old boys a happy Christmas, and that the New Year may bring them victory and a safe return. He regrets influenza has prevented him writing to them all.

13. Mesopotamia

Early in the war the British had troops in the Persian Gulf to protect the oil refinery at Abadan Island. Subsequently, after setbacks, the whole of Mesopotamia (present day Iraq) was captured from the Turks.

<u>21 January 1916.</u> *Chiswick Times*
Fighting against thirst – how a British force endured and won victory.

<u>Gunner B.Gunning</u>. Royal Field Artillery. Writing to his parents Mr. & Mrs. Gunning, Ferry Rd, Twickenham.

He describes his experience of hard fighting, whereabouts not given, but presumed to be on the Tigris in Mesopotamia.

'We moved out of camp about 4pm on 27th Sept. and crossed the river. Then started on a five mile march, and were told to go easy with our water as we should get none the next day. We arrived in our new camp about 6.30pm and lay down on the sand for a couple of hours rest. At midnight we moved out of camp and took up a position a few miles away, about 5am on 28th opening fire at 5.30am. At 6 o'clock we got the order to advance, which we did for about two miles, when we dropped into action again and opened fire on some trenches. Our major properly cleared the Turks out of them, for after he had got the range he sent in a hellish fire that no man could possibly live in. Again we got the order to advance and now the sun was making itself felt, it was getting extremely hot.

We started to advance, and here a lot of ticklish work faced us, for we had to go through a bog, into which the horses sank up to their hocks. After we had got clear of the bog, we travelled about a mile and dropped into action again. The major got the range to some trenches and, my word! Didn't he pump some shell into them! The Turks flew the white flag, but we had been bitten too often with their white flag tricks. As they kept firing on our men, the major continued firing on them until they stopped and surrendered.

By now our water bottles were empty, and we were feeling dry. We advanced another few miles, and dropped into action. This time they opened fire on us, their shrapnel spluttering over our shields and wounding one man. But although we found it so dry and found it hard to speak the men stuck to the work like heroes, and at length we silenced their guns. By now, we were gasping for water, and any man would have given his month's pay for a drink. We advanced again and formed up a few miles from our last position. I was lying under one of the vehicles, and I didn't care a hang if I got killed or wounded, I was so thirsty. A chap lay next to me and there was another man on the other side of him. All of a sudden, there was a whizz and a bang, and a chap in the centre got one in the leg. Some more shells came over, and there were men and horses falling in all directions. The drivers got mounted and we retired about 100 yards and came into action.

Our force then started retiring in a very orderly manner and about a mile back we all formed up. It was here that I took some water bottles to get some water from the marshes. When I got there I was told that it had been poisoned but I said I didn't care if it was poisoned or dosed – I meant to have a drink. I then filled the bottles and took them back. What a taste that water had! It was salty and tasted like salts, quinine, and sulphur mixed. After two hours halt at this place, we advanced again, and the whole of the artillery came into action in one long line and then we let hell loose. We opened fire on a four gun battery and completely smashed it. The enemy made several attempts to fetch their teams up to take the guns away, but we made it so hot for them, they had to retire, leaving the guns behind. By this time we were absolutely gasping, and the salt water in our bottles made us worse. There was no sign of water, for the river was about four miles away, and was held by the enemy in force.

About 8.30pm on the 28th, we got the order to advance and were told we would reach the river that night. After trekking about two miles we halted and camped. We made inquiries as to the position of the river, and were told it was a mile and a half away, and if we wanted water to go and fetch it. But this was impossible as the Turks held the river and it would have been death to attempt it. So thirsty and weary and our throats and lips cracking, we lay down and tried to forget our troubles by sleeping, but we got no sleep that night and men were to be seen walking restlessly about. The only noise to be heard was the groaning of dying horses and mules and a strong glow of language from men who could manage to speak.

Morning dawned at last, and what sights were to be seen, I shall never forget them. In our lines, were horses dead and dying from thirst, and dead mules everywhere. To our rear were the four guns we had shelled the evening before. On three of the guns the detachments were stretched out dead and on the other a Turk lay dead with the breech block in his hand. At 5.30am on 29th we harnessed up and waited for an hour, and during this time I helped to attend to a wounded Turk. He had been shot through the thigh, and he used his water bottle for a pillow. I took it from under his head and gave him a drink. As I poured it into his mouth it ran over my hand. It was ice cold and I don't know how I resisted drinking it up for him, but I knew that I should reach water before him, so I put the bottle back under his head. I am sure that if I had met him on the desert alone I would have shot him for that water.

We moved off about 6.30am and passed through a Turkish camp which they had left in disorder. We kept pushing on, and I felt that I must sink to the ground to sleep or die, I didn't know which, but I kept going. All of a sudden, there was a cheer and a rush for there was the river 500 yards ahead. Horses and men went mad, and I shall never forget the sight of horses and men dashing for water, and when we reached it, we went in up to our necks and let the water run into our mouths. How nice and cold it was. Never till that moment did I know the value of water, and no one can know until they have suffered what we suffered for 42 hours with one bottle of water and a heat of 120 degrees in the shade, and the lord knows what in the sun.

We won the day and were complimented by all the generals and the viceroy, but it was nothing more than determined British bulldog pluck that carried us through to victory.'

19 May 2016. *Chiswick Times*
Letter to Rev. Oldfield.

Bombardier R. Hamilton. Somewhere in Mesopotamia.

'You will be surprised to hear I have been out of France for about three months. You could get water everywhere in France but here you have to get near a river. We have just tried to relieve General Townsend, but the Turks were a little too strong for us, but still we shall get through next time. We could see the Turks fire their guns and hundreds of their infantry. Our advance started at 5.30pm.and kept marching till 12, and opened fire at 6am. I have been reading the Chiswick Times and find that some of the lads are out here. I am keeping a good look out for them.'

19 May 1916. *Chiswick Times*
Letter to Rev. Oldfield.

Bombardier F.C. Baker. Somewhere in Mesopotamia.

'I am sorry I have not answered your letter before. I am not feeling in the writing mood. We have been on the move East. We left France at the latter end of December, were in the Mediterranean when the Persia and Ancona were torpedoed. We had a couple of real submarine scares – one by day and one by night – and but for the vigilance of our naval escort no doubt our ship would have been sunk. We had to tranship at ----- as our vessel was too big to get up the ---- to -----. We were not long in ----- before more embarking on river steamers and barges to proceed up the Tigris.

A very historical country this is, no doubt, but nothing interesting from the pictorial point of view for it is as flat as a billiard table, and just here not a tree can be seen for miles. At our back, some 50 miles distant can be seen the Persian Hills. We of course form part of the relief force to Kut-el-Amara. We have attacked twice – the first on the Turks' camp from the right bank of the Tigris. We bombarded the camp but they had become too strong. The attack on the 8th was on their main positions at Essin Canal – again they were too strong or else expected the attacks.

We were seven miles from the Tigris, and the enemy held the only water supply, so after the first attack failed we just hung on and then fell back here, a retirement of 20 miles. The artillery had to retire battery by battery, one covering the other the whole time. Quite different to France, but what we are trained to in India. We lost a few, but I think the Turks lost more. The trouble here is the water – the river is practically the only source for cooking water, for the wells are all tainted with saltpetre. If good water is to be had anywhere near us we get it for our allowance when on the march.

One does not wash nor shave then, unless the water is too bad for cooking with. Two others and myself arranged to go to the Tigris on the night of 22nd February for water so that we could have a good drink of tea and fill our water bottles in the morning. We set out. The moon had not arisen so the only thing was to avoid noise. The most ticklish thing was the actual getting the water. The Turks just over the way were digging, talking, and cooking their food. However, not a shot was fired, and we even managed the luxury of a wash. We repeated the operation only 200 yards from the ----- Redoubt. This time the water was from a marsh and a hole had to be dug before sufficient water could be collected. The moon was nearly full and we had to creep down about a mile or so. Imagine us giving each other instructions not to let the bucket rattle. We got safely back with six buckets full but two were lost as one of us fell over when our sentry challenged him. So far my health is good.'

9 June 1916. *Chiswick Times*
Letters to Rev. Oldfield.

Bombardier R.S.J. Hamilton. 'Somewhere in Mesopotamia.'

'We are now in Mesopotamia and it is very hot, but still I would sooner be in France as the weather is better. The flies out here are troubling you all the time and I am hoping for the war to end. We are slowly advancing. The fighting out here is different to France, but still we shall get over it all right. I received a postcard from Johnnie Goddard, he is getting on famous. I believe there are some of the lads out here and I am looking out for them.'

30 June 1916. *Chiswick Times*
Letter to Rev. Oldfield.

Corporal F.C. Baker. Mesopotamia.

'Quite well although tired consequent of the heat which is terrific and is not yet at its full height. Bitterly disappointed that Kut has surrendered at the time when we all would see its relief because we were only a few miles off. It seems the fiercest fighting of the whole campaign was in vain. We are entrenched and the Turks do not give much trouble except dropping bombs on us from the air that do not do much damage. A little excitement is welcome. I believe my brother Gordon is still in Egypt and may be sent to France. I hear my brother Laurie has enlisted.'

29 December 1916. *Chiswick Times*
Letter to Rev. Oldfield.

Sergeant F.C. Baker. Mesopotamia.

'Back from leave in India but haven't yet received the parcel you sent me. Conditions are better now. The weather is cooler and the rations are better. On leave I was weak from fever and jaundice. The life nearly taken out of me. Now I am old self.'

2 March 1917. *Chiswick Times*
Letter to Rev. Oldfield.

Driver Fred Peters. Mesopotamia.

'I am glad to hear that nearly all the old boys have joined up. Remember me to those that are at home. Our boys out here give Johnny Turk a warm time. I saw Bill Higgins when I was in Egypt and he is lucky to get to India for leave. The heat in the summer is stifling out here.'

9 March 1917. *Chiswick Times*
Lieutenant Wyatt's last letter from Mesopotamia.

Lt H.E. Wyatt, an officer of Bedford Park Cadets, death in action was reported last week – this letter was received one day this week by Lt. Vincent Clarke, one of the cadets and is probably Lt Wyatt's last letter.

The first part is dated 29th December last.

'I am writing this to you in a front line redoubt, where I have been for the past week, but thank goodness we are shifting tomorrow, as the rains have arrived, which means the transport mules with rations find it too difficult to get up to us. We have to live in large holes as dug-outs, as you cannot burrow under the earth, otherwise the roof would fall in and bury you, so we have to be content with the sky as roof. Last night the rain came down in torrents and I was fairly soaked. I tried to sleep but my feet were so cold and wet I had to get up at about 4.30 and walk about until breakfast time. Until the rain came, I thoroughly enjoyed myself. When we move from here, we are going back to tents. I fell in with my company after seven weeks touring, and within two days was in action with them. It was not a very terrible affair, but one of my gun team got wounded.

Days here have been beautifully warm, but nights are very cold. The great luxury is water – and one seems to go about in a constant state of filth. I am covered from head to toe in mud – I hope when it dries some of it, at any rate, will break off.

I hope you all spent a very happy Christmas. We did not have a bad time under the circumstances. Great excitement when the ration carts arrived – to see what they had sent us. There were some magnificent plum puddings from the Daily News & Daily Telegraph, and good rich fruity cakes from the ladies of Bombay. Lord Curzon sent 70 dozen bottles of champagne for the officers of my division. So you see we did not do badly. I stayed one night on my way up with an officer in charge of the mule transport and came along the next day with the carts as far as the dumping ground, where the various brigades collect their rations. There were about 200 carts for our division alone and there are ---- divisions to be supplied. I rode on to my company on the top of the rations in one of the carts, and had a fair joy ride. The cart had no springs on it, and when it went in and out of the ruts you had to hold on both sides to prevent being pitched off on to the desert. I had eight miles of that. I have not drawn a horse yet, but expect to shortly. There is one in our section and one away ill, so that I shall probably have the one we have at present eventually. I rode it about 13 miles the other day, taking the mules down to be watered. The enemy we fear chiefly here is the Arab as he is very ruthless. They have got some very find horsemen, and are very daring. The Turks' chief delight seems to be to send over a few shells, we don't worry very much about them and give him a few back in return, just to show there is no ill feeling.

I wonder if you have got your machine gun yet. I fired my gun in the scrap the other day for a few rounds, just for a bit of fun, but with what results I don't know as Johnny kept pretty well to his trenches. At one place where I stopped, I just missed Japper Robinson – his battalion had left two days previously. I should have liked to have knocked across him out here.'

1st January 1917.

'A very happy New Year to you all and all my friends in Bedford Park. We have been resting since Saturday, and expect to move up to the firing line again in about two days' time, and probably shall be there about a fortnight, before being relieved by another brigade. At present we have the luxury of tents. Although supposed to be resting, we have a fair amount of work to do, keeping the men up to scratch, watering and exercising the mules and horses. We have nearly 100 mules to a company, and about 12 horses, so that the transport is no small matter.'

9th January 1917.

'I don't know when, if ever, this letter will be posted. I am out of envelopes, but have sent to a pal at the nearest spot where there is a bazaar, to send me on some, in the hope they will come someday, but very few parcels seem to reach us. There are at least two somewhere en route for me. On Sunday we had a brigade ceremonial parade in the afternoon when the commander-in-chief pinned MC and DCM ribbons on the breasts of those who had earned them. It was like all military parades, a case of waiting well over an hour for a job that lasted about ten minutes.

Yesterday I spent the day examining men for proficiency pay. There were seven of us on the job on different subjects. I took 'care and cleaning', and points before, during and after firing. I have got a nice quiet day today, as the company have been out on a strafing expedition. One officer had to be left behind to look after the camp, and the lot fell to me. If I lose the chance of distinction, I at least save my skin, which is some consolation. Have had to start writing on the other side of the paper, as paper is beginning to run short. This is an awful place for supplies; not like France, you cannot get things posted to you. If you write home, it takes six weeks for the letter to get there, and then it's very problematic if a parcel ever gets to you. I had quite a shock – found I had only a fortnight's shaving soap and wondered what would happen, when I discovered some very small samples of Williams' soap amongst the stores, so bagging half a dozen saved myself for a month or two.

This is a terrible place to find your way about. I got lost the other night, and almost gave up in despair, thinking I should have to stay where I was till the morning, when my foot stippled on a telephone wire, which I caught hold of, knowing it must lead to some depot, and as luck would have it, it led straight to my own redoubt. The land is very flat with practically no landmarks and the maps are all inaccurate. The rains are holding off so far. We have only had a shower or two, but it has turned very damp, cold and misty. The other morning we had such a thick fog, I might have imagined I was back again at Odemit.

We had a strange contrast here on Sunday. The RC padre was celebrating Mass in the open, while about two miles away, our artillery was pouring its 'hymn of hate' as hard as ever it could do. Most of the men here will be overjoyed to get home again. I censor some of their letters, and they are all frightfully fed up with the country. Personally I don't mind it, but do seem to be at the end of the earth and miles and miles from everyone.

I see in 'Punch's Almanac' there is a picture of a padre and a tommy riding in Mesopotamia in the drenching rain, and the Padre has been telling the tommy all about this being the site of the Garden of Eden. The only reply he gets is 'Well, if this is the Garden of Eden, it wouldn't take any flaming sword to keep me out of it.'

The other night, the wind sprang up suddenly, and I heard some noise going on in my tent, and a minute or two afterwards, the tent collapsed, passing right over me, without touching me, leaving me lying in the open with the moonlight sky as my canopy. I stood it as long as I could, but the wind was very cold, and I saw rain clouds gathering, so rolled up my valise and stay for an hour or two in the mess tent. Luckily the tent fell over my belongings and prevented them from being blown away. One of the worst ordeals here is having a bath in the open with cold water, and in the cold weather it takes some contemplating, but it has to be gone through pretty frequently out here if you want to keep your health.'

17th January 1917.

'Must close tonight as I believe letters are being collected. Have been up in the front firing line for the past week, and goodness knows when we shall get out of it again. It is pretty warm up here with the bullets flying about – the snipers are the worst – they get on our working parties at night. I have been out for the past two nights in charge of a working party. At first I did not at all relish it, especially when I heard the machine gun firing in my direction, but I have got more or less used to it now, especially as so far, by luck, we have escaped casualties.

Was awfully pleased to get your letter and all the news. Was sorry to hear you were unable to attend the prize-giving, but hope next time we shall all be there. Was also sorry to hear that Reg has been suffering again from his old wound, but perhaps under present conditions it is just as well to be way from actual fighting – it is no picnic. It is a gloriously fine day here today, quite warm, and the Turk has not yet started his evening hymn. Well, goodbye and the best of luck.'

27 July 1917. *Chiswick Times*
Letter to Rev. Oldfield.

Sergeant Fred Baker. Mesopotamia.

'I regret I have not been able to answer your letter before on account of the recent big advance. The papers have given fuller accounts of the fighting than any news I could write, but I really must say that the success is greater than any of the men expected. The Turk is thoroughly beaten, for even in his fight to retain Samara and Kifri, he may have fought stubbornly, but at the same time he had ideal positions for defence, which he abandoned without making full use of it. This battery in particular has had some hard times, forced marches etc, but on the whole we have had little cause for complaint as to supplies. The health of the troops is far better than at this time last year, although the hot weather has come sooner.

We are stationed at a post on ---- forming a small mobile column for punitive expeditions against the tribes of the desert Arabs, who are in the habit of raiding the railway occasionally. They are true savages, and practise great cruelty on any who fall into their hands – torture, mutilation, robbery and death. They have vast hordes of sheep and cultivate small areas occasionally. Their camels, donkeys, and ponies are splendid animals, especially the latter, and so, for that matter, are the men and women themselves; they are all muscle and seem to live on nothing. The country from and about Samarra is of a different character to that in the south. There are ridges of small pebbles and the soil is more sandy. We have dust storms in plenty down below, but up here they are murderous and cover the whole countryside.

Baghdad, when we passed through, was an interesting place no doubt, but there was nothing marvellous about it. A fine sight from a distance, but on close inspection, filthy and overcrowded. I hear however that since our occupation much improvement has been made and much sanitary work put in hand. I have kept well in health all through and the only thing I miss is good and plentiful water, as we are some miles from the Tigris, and our water is limited to bare necessities. Reading matter of any kind would be very acceptable, please.'

2 November 1917. *Chiswick Times*
Letter to Rev. Oldfield.

Private J. Sutch. Mesopotamia.

'We are very happy out here and have a concert every Saturday just to make us happy. I heard about some of the Old Boys when I was home on my final leave, but not heard since. I hope we shall all see each other when all is over and settled.'

14. Salonica

In October 1915 an Anglo-French force landed in Salonika in North East Greece. The purposes were to prevent a Bulgarian invasion of Serbia and to open up a diversionary front against the Central Powers. Both failed and stalemate ensued until Bulgaria crumbled in 1918. British troops were also in Serbia fighting against Austrian invading forces.

7 January 1916. *Chiswick Times*
Letter to Rev. Oldfield.

Rifleman Albert Wilkinson. British Army in the Field.

'I have had a trip on the water and had a very good voyage and landed safely at Salonica. I have now been here nine days. I have not heard much news lately as I have not had a mail the past few days.'

14 January 1916. *Chiswick Times*

Gunner F. Bain. Salonica Force.

'I received your parcel, which you thought I might not get, being on the move. Well, Sir, seeing that you have sent another, I have promised to distribute same amongst my working mates, and they also thank you in anticipation. I am glad to hear the boys are still stepping up to the colours. I am sorry some of the boys have gone under Sir; still we must take it all, it's for a good cause.'

16 January 1916. *Chiswick Times*
With the forces at Salonica.

Frank Baynes of the Chiswick Working Men's Club writes to Mr. Thomas King, the Club's secretary.

'We are now in camp about four miles from Salonica harbour, awaiting orders. We get daily news of a sort as regards the fighting out here, and expect to move up soon, but I do hope we remain here until after Christmas as we are looking forward to some sort of a good time amongst ourselves, but our one great hope is to receive some of our very much overdue parcels. By the way our address now reads: '85th Field Ambulance, 3rd London T. 28th Division, Salonica Force.

I wonder how many annual dinners will pass before we shall meet again in such numbers as we did in 1913. Every good wish to you and all for the New Year. Ernest Stockwell asks me to send his best wishes to you.'

4 February 1916. *Chiswick Times*
News from the Front – Chiswick Working Man's Church Club.
Private Frank Baynes, Salonica.

'We are in a camp about 1,500ft above sea level, hills and mountains all around us, and the only troops we come into contact with belong to our own brigade or division. We are now busily engaged in digging dug-outs for billets and the dressing station. At times it is hard work, but it has been so frightfully cold that the exercise keeps us warm. This morning we found everything covered with about six inches of snow and there is still plenty of it coming down. The transport of our stores will be a difficult question in this weather. The only roads around have been made by our troops and to get to the main roads to Salonica one has to cross many hills and ravines so you can guess what the country is like that we are in.

You will be pleased to know that all the papers you have so kindly sent have all arrived. Some letters arrived yesterday marked 'Damaged by fire and water on the ship'. Some of the letters were badly damaged and I expect there are a lot we shall never get. We have received a number of parcels, but there are still a large number to come. Fred Brett, captain of the 'Old Boys' has got a commission from the Artists' Rifles.'

4 February 1916. *Chiswick Times*
Richmond Royal Army Medical Corps man's journey from Alexandria to Salonica.

'We passed several picturesque islands, one with the top of mountains peeping through the clouds, and also a wonderful sight of snow topped mountains on the mainland. Our boat was very comfortable like all hospital boats. We had cots for beds with feather pillows and mattresses, and our food was of good quality and cooked in very good style – the best we have had since leaving home.

After arriving in port we had to help unload the ship from 1am to 4am. The work proved very exciting. A very heavy load nearly fell on us from a good height into the hold where we were at work.

We are encamped in a very pleasant position outside the town at the foot of some mountains; surrounded on two sides by mountains and the sea is a short distance on another side. The weather is good on the whole, with cold mornings and nights, but we have had several severe days of cold and damp and a biting north-east wind direct from the mountains, with rain sleet and snow. It was a great trial to us after the hot weather in Egypt. Such weather is quite enough under canvass with nowhere to go to get warm, and the tent and ground are wet through as well as the blankets when you wake up.

Our work is partly in the town, and as we go down by lorry at times there is plenty of excitement as the roads are awful with great holes here and there.

The town is out of bounds for all troops, except those that go direct to their work, but we do not mind as the town is a dirty and insanitary sort of place. Also it is unsafe to roam about at night outside the camp except when you go in a body.'

11 February 1916. *Chiswick Times*
Letters to Rev. Oldfield.

Sapper H. Jales.

'I am still A1. Now serving with the Salonica forces. Since landing we have had to cross a range of snow-clad mountains, the passage of which occupied us days, and as we had to carry full packs, we did not get such an enjoyable time. The country being so rough, and the roads as bad, it is difficult marching from place to place. At present we are under canvas, and as the snow is on the ground, it is very cold; but we are hoping for the summer to come. Owing to the lack of good roads we have very often to rely on bully and biscuits, and bread is a luxury here. Not much excitement here at present, but may be very soon.'

Private J.W. Moss. Salonica Forces.

'I have just got a few minutes to spare, so I am writing to thank you for the parcel. It is quite nice to get some news of Chiswick. I am sorry I could not write before, as we are always on the move. When we were in the trenches in France we only had one casualty and that was one of the signallers, so we have been very lucky. But I pity the poor fellows who are in the trenches right through the winter.'

3 March 1916. *Chiswick Times*
Chiswick man at Salonica.

Private Frank Baynes. Letter to Thomas King of Chiswick Working Men's Church Club.

'We have finished digging dug-outs and the mules are claiming our attention. These animals are to help us getting about with the wounded when fighting comes off. On each side of each mule is an armchair seat for carrying sitting cases. All that is required is a man to lead the mule. Seems to work all right when the path can be seen or when the mule is in good humour. What the results will be under fire I leave you to guess. Still, the Bulgars do not seem very anxious to do fighting at present.

I see the Zepps have visited England and one visited here about a week ago and Salonica suffered pretty badly. It wakened us from our slumbers and we wondered whether the Bulgars had arrived. The military authorities have agreed to compensate the Greek families who had suffered. I am told Salonica is an interesting place. We are forbidden to enter except on duty.'

3 March 1916. *Chiswick Times*
Letters to Rev. Oldfield.

Sergeant A.H. Tompkins. Salonica.

'I am in the best of health after a voyage on water dodging submarines. It is very cold here, especially at nights, and we are under canvass. We have had the Zeppelins here. We don't do so badly for food considering the miles it has to come, thanks to our navy. I haven't come across more St Mary's boys since I met Dick Siggers in Flanders. There is plenty of work here for us engineers, especially roadmaking. Received the Chiswick Times from Miss G. It is a treat to get a bit of news from the old town as papers are very scarce and we hardly get any news. We had a pretty service on Sunday night on the bow of the boat in harbour by twilight.'

Sapper H. Jales. Salonica.

'I am still engaged in the great game. I should be very pleased if you let some of the old boys know my address and it might happen that some of them will have to come here. We are issued with a sheepskin but it is only an inducement to vermin. The snow is just melting on the ground and as we are under canvas you can realise how we feel. It is very miserable at nights owing to lack of lights. Candles are the only means of lighting our 'hotels' but as money is nearly non-existent, and a candle of three inches costs you 2½d, you can quite understand that we are often without light. At nights when I lie on my ground sheet, I often think of the old camp at Romfields, under the most ideal conditions. I have not seen your company of the Church Lads' Brigade since some time before the war but I expect you have given a good number to the services since the call first started. Before I left Southampton I met Jennings, who used to be in the band, and he was going to France touring. I should think it would be a great idea to arrange a reunion at the conclusion of hostilities.'

Sergeant A.H. Tompkins. Somewhere in Greece.

'Just a line to let you know that I am going on all right here; it is getting a bit warmer now, though we have had three days rain, which has made the place somewhat like Flanders for mud. We are very busy making roads and I have got a ticklish job – for I have 600 Greeks and Serbians working under me, and it's a job to make them understand what I want, but I am learning a bit of Greek now. Haven't come across any St Mary's boys yet. I see they are having some sort of conscription now, which is rather a pity; I think Chiswick has responded well. We are not near the firing line. Should be glad of a few books or magazines as we have nothing to read here. I have the Chiswick Times sent regularly by Miss G.'

31 March 1916. *Chiswick Times*

Mr. Frank Baynes, Salonica.

'Everything goes on just the same out here; we have plenty of work and fairly good weather. I understand that some of our mails have been lost, thanks to German submarines. We expect to go on trek next week for four or five days, carrying as little as we possibly can. Should we take the offensive out here, we should have to discard many things, as it will be impossible to march very far over these hills and mountains unless one travels light. Our pantomime was reproduced last night and we had a number of nurses up from the hospitals about and in Salonica to witness the performance.'

In another letter, Frank Baynes sends a cutting from a Salonica paper – an impression of the town as seen by a Britisher.

'Narrow cobbled streets seething with all manner and condition of humanity, uniforms gaudy and quiet, jostle through the throng;

crowded cafes overflowing on to the footpaths, and streets alive with the clatter of a score of tongues; the shouts of the vendors or weird-looking sweetmeats, the clank of swords, the clink of glasses, the multi-coloured mingling of East and West, and everything bathed in blazing sunshine make a unique & never-to-be-forgotten picture. This – and much more – is Salonica.

Venerable priests in black gowns and flowing beards; Greek officers resplendent in glittering medals and orders; swaggering French clad in the familiar blue; deformed beggars; howling street merchants; ladies of fashion decked in the latest from Paris, all are component parts of a dazzling ever shifting kaleidoscopic scene. The sight of a couple of British tars with short clay pipes and rolling gait leaps to the eye gladly. They stroll the narrow streets with easy familiarity. Three officers of the Senior Service stand chatting at a corner. They seem equally at home here as anywhere else on the globe. Calm, cool and slightly bored, they appear to display just as much polite interest in things as they do when on shore at the Fiji Islands or strolling down the Strand on a sunny spring morning. They are the true cosmopolitans, equally at home and at ease, patrolling Macedonian lakes in swift motor boats, blowing the Hun off the face of the waters in the South Pacific, or sipping their coffee and listening to the band in Salonica.

A swarthy nondescript individual with a dressed goat, fresh from the butcher's shop, slung carelessly over his shoulder, boards an electric tram which comes jangling noisily up the street. His fellow passengers include an immaculately portly son of France, two priests, a Greek officer, a bevy of laughing Jewesses, and a nut-brown French colonial. The bell clangs under the motorman's foot and the modern Juggernaut with its miscellaneous freight rolls swiftly up the narrow street. And overlooking all, are the grim grey ships of war, studded in the lazily swelling blue of the Mediterranean, contemptuously indifferent of the myriads of miscellaneous fishing smacks that crowd the harbour.

Rudyard Kipling once stated: 'East is East & West is West, And ne'er the twain shall meet.' He was wrong. They meet at Salonica.'

28 April 1916. *Chiswick Times*
Letter to Rev. Oldfield.

<u>Sapper H. Jales</u>. Somewhere in Greece.

'I take great pleasure in thanking you for the parcel. I could not write when it arrived as I had no paper. The paper and envelope I am using are a gift sent by the Queen Alexandra's Fund to the Mediterranean Expeditionary Force. The gifts, though scarce, come in useful, I being fortunate to receive a writing pad and a cake of chocolate.

To return to the parcel you sent. Cutting the duff cake into eight portions put your grand efforts at Rumfield camp into the shade. Seeing the delicate operation would have made you roar with laughter. My comrades in the tent thank you for your kindness – a change from the usual diet. I wrote to Jennings the day after I received his address from you.

I hear there have been several Zeppelin raids over the homeland recently, but I sincerely hope they haven't done much damage or caused any loss of life, especially to non-combatants. I enclose a few flowers which I picked on the mountain sides around here.'

19 May 1916. *Chiswick Times*
Letter to Rev. Oldfield.

<u>Rifleman Albert E. Wilkinson</u>. Salonica Forces.

'Weather for the last few days has been beautiful and just like an English summer, and we are able to bathe in the sea occasionally as it is close by. Just completed a manoeuvre lasting 36 hours. I was pleased to get a letter from Alf with photograph of himself and Bill Bowley. I get the Chiswick Times and read of Alf Evans. I hope he will soon get well, he must have suffered terribly. I am pleased Bert Locke has joined the Sherwood Foresters – better known as Notts and Jocks.'

2 June 1916. *Chiswick Times*
Chiswick man at Salonica.
Mr. Thomas A. King, of the Chiswick Workmen's Club, sends in a letter he has received.

'Just finished an eight days trek across country. Good weather and all are fit and well. An exercise took place with another regiment acting as an enemy. Ernie Stockwell and Mac are quite well. The Rev. Farmfield is attached to one of the units and I wonder if he is one of the two famous brothers, one of whom has been living in Brentford.'

2 June 1916. *Chiswick Times*
Letter to Rev. Oldfield

Private F.W. Barnes. Somewhere in Greece.

'They have shifted me from Elferdan to Salonica and I am attached for water duty. I have to test the water to see if it is fit for the men to drink, so you can see we must not drink any water. Two days after we landed one of our battleships fetched a Zeppelin down. They are very hot on them out here.'

7 July 1916. *Chiswick Times*
Chiswick Working Men's Club letter to Mr. King.

Letter from Salonica.

'I would like to have seen the Empire Day celebrations at the Chiswick Empire that I read about in the Chiswick Times. Letters and papers reach us but there is a hold up with parcels. Perhaps they are storing them up as a pleasant surprise. We have been marching beyond Salonica and if we go much further will be near the frontier. The country is glorious. A good place to spend a short holiday. Cherries are abundant but we are too tired to pick them and at 2d or half a drachma for a hatful. Whilst on the move reveille has been at 1.30am and we move off at 4am. A bit like daylight saving and the worst part of a march is done in the cool hours. There are absurd rumours of embarkation for France, Egypt and even England.

Daylight saving is in full swing. But not like at home because the time remains the same. Whilst on the move reveille has been at 1.30am Breakfast at 2.30am And move off at 4 a.m. to get the worst part of the march done in the cool hours, and in most cases a rest in the afternoon.'

21 July 1916. *Chiswick Times*
Letter to Rev. Oldfield.

Rifleman Albert Wilkinson. Salonica Force.

'In best of health and grateful for the parcel especially the shirts which are much cooler than the regimentals. I've heard from several of the St Marys' boys.'

The Rev. Oldfield adds that Wilkinson has five brothers serving – India, Greece, Mesopotamia and North Sea.

15 September 1916. *Chiswick Times*
Letter to Rev. Oldfield.

Gunner F. Bain. Greece.

'Our heavy guns have been in action day and night and we get 'some pills' in return. I think about the St Mary's Boys' tour to Margate and how our band paced to the beach, and the gymnastics on Monday nights. We will have winter again in four weeks and I hope it won't be as cold as last year. This seems a peculiar country – at times like India and the next day cold and rain like Scotland.'

6 October 1916. *Chiswick Times*
Letter to Rev. Oldfield.

Sapper H. Jales. Salonica.

'I have received your letter after rather a long time, having left Malta before it arrived. Now back at base and expect to re-join my company in a few days. We are near the sea but are not allowed to bathe and I miss the dip in the briny since leaving

Malta. Rumania's declaration for the allies has put more heart into the lads and they think it is a big step in the direction for peace. There are soldiers of all the allied nations on the front wearing their different uniforms.'

20 October 1916. *Chiswick Times*
Chiswick Working Men's Club. Letter received by Mr. Thomas A. King, secretary of the club.

'It is monotonous with doing nothing and the sudden alternations of heat and cold. We are pleased to hear of the fall of Combles in France. I was extremely sorry to hear of the death of my old Hogarth schoolmaster, Mr. Matthews. He did wonders at the school and was the ideal school master.'

10 November 1916. *Chiswick Times*
Letter to Rev. Oldfield.

Gunner F. Bain. Greece.

'Our captain has been killed. Terrible thing. Shells were dropping close but we never got a scratch. We believe it was a splinter that caused his death. I am writing now under 6ft of rock and 12ft long into a large-sized hill, so am under a bit of cover.'

17 November 1916. *Chiswick Times*
Letter to Rev. Oldfield.

Sapper H. Jales. Salonica.

'We have made a bit of a forward move – crossed the river and attacked the Bulgars, driving them from three villages. It was rather a hard job bridging the river owing to the swiftness of the current, and the attention paid to us by the enemy, but we did it without accident. The enemy counter attacked as we were putting up plain wire with prickles and lost a couple of good pals.'

24 November 1916. *Chiswick Times*
Letter to Rev. Oldfield.

Sapper H. Jales. Salonica.

'We have been doing well and have taken several villages. I am in one of the cottages which are rough affairs but better than a bivouac during wet weather. We are on a very large plain and in front are mountains already covered in snow and I expect it will soon be on us. Christmas is coming and I expect lots of parcels will arrive, and I hope to get a Christmas pudding. We hear rumours about moving to France and leave, but it all vanishes – like it comes – in thin air.'

1 December 1916. *Chiswick Times*
Chiswick Working Men's Club letter to Thomas King.

Frank Burgess. Salonica.

'After tramping about Macedonia a few hundred miles, climbing up most of its hills, besides being pestered with innumerable flies, mosquitoes, etc, the powers that be decided it was about time we started strafing the Bulgars. This we have been doing for some weeks now, and with some success. Villages have been captured and we are at present occupying one of these badly battered places, close to the line, and at the same time we are running an advanced dressing station. Very much to our surprise the Bulgars took it into their heads to sling over some off their much needed shells yesterday afternoon, but beyond creating a little excitement that's about all they accomplished.'

8 December 1916. *Chiswick Times*
Letter to Rev. Oldfield.

Sapper H. Jales. Salonica.

'A sudden change of weather and the place is like a quagmire. Fortunately we are no longer under canvas and although far from luxurious, and a bit draughty it affords cover from the rain. With the aid of a few logs for firewood we have rather decent evenings, although sitting round a fire makes one long for home rather too much. I will try to meet Bert Golding but there are small hopes of doing so because he is in a different division and, unlike France, all movements are done on foot. I read with pleasure the splendid work done by the French and the British Expeditionary Force.

What kind of machine is a tank? We imagine all kinds of shapes but as we have not seen a photo or sketch we are still in the dark as to their real shape.

Awaiting the arrival of a parcel because we rarely get the chance of anything except the army issue of food.

The only thing that gives us trouble is the safety of our folks at home from the air raiders. It pleases us very much to hear that our airmen had succeeded in fetching three of their 'baby killers' down.'

8 December 1916. *Chiswick Times*
Chiswick Working Men's Club members at the front. Letter to Thomas King.

Frank Baynes. Salonica. Royal Army Medical Corps. (RAMC)

'We are still in the old village and the troops continue to do good work and we have to go further forward to collect the sick and wounded. Some tracks are under three or four feet of water but we manage to get the litter and mules through. Old Bulgarian trenches are another obstacle, particularly at night. Some leave had been granted but not to all troops and there is little chance of getting home. Letters take a long time to get here.'

5 January 1917. *Chiswick Times*
Letter to Rev. Oldfield.

Bombardier A. A. Golding. Greece.

'Many thanks for very nice parcel received today. We were in rather a bad way for rations, and for over a week have been like canaries, whilst officers and men alike are absolutely without a smoke. There has been no issue for three weeks of either tobacco or matches.

The conditions here are indescribable and in my own movements I have gone from bad to worse. In Gallipoli we got a fair share of fighting and other privations. In Egypt we had very little fighting and terrible heat. But here it is a matter of living in the clouds by day and marching miles over continuous mountains. And with a famous man's words in mind that a soldier marches on his stomach, I am surprised that we are able to march at all. Thanks, however, to you, this is all changed for a few days, and, at any rate, this Christmas dinner will be a great improvement on that never-to-be-forgotten fare at Yuletide 1915. Now sir, I will conclude, hoping that we shall soon be in a position to dictate the terms of peace and all the boys return.'

26 January 1917. *Chiswick Times*
Letter to Rev. Oldfield.

Sapper H. Jales. Salonica.

'Pleased to see your old company of the Church Lad's Brigade has given the highest number of lads to the colours. You have just cause to be proud. Things are quiet at the present but there is always plenty to do. Very cold now but we have warm clothes, but wet weather would put the roads in a bad state. We had a good time at Christmas interrupted by a visit from a Taube, which very soon returned home.'

26 January 1917. *Chiswick Times*
A Sanderson's employee on the Eastern life. Lance Corporal T. Eades, with the Army Service Corps in Salonica.

'The characters in our camp are extremely varied, it would take a Dickens to describe their life histories. Their ages run from 40 to 60, and we have gingers, meaty fruges, baldies and frosty faces, humpbacks, 'K' legs and wonky eyes. Our nickname on parade is 'Ally Sloper's Cavalry'. The excessive heat 'knackered' the fat one, and the icy wind of the mountains is cutting down the thin ones, whilst the malaria reaps from all grades.

I don't remember if I answered your letter, for I burn all letters to boil up mess tins of cocoa and oxo. In this country there are no trees, consequently firing is scarce.

The Greek native (a brigand of the mountains) was taking the birds (ducks) out to a patch of grass where other companies also feed their birds. When he brought them back the orderly sergeant counted them in one short. After calling him a thief (true alas) he was told the value would be docked off his pay. Next day he again took them out, then when they came back they were three over. 'Never mind' he said, 'I may be short tomorrow. The natives are a dirty thieving lot of unshaven, unwashed scoundrels, they drink mustik (aniseed & mentholated spirit.)

I am not anxious to go to France for after all there is a sort of charm about the East, its weird costumes, mixed dialects and garish colours bring the Arabian Nights vividly to one's memory.

Temporary field huts are built of milk boxes filled with earth. Christmas was a great time with turkey, geese, ducks, beef, mutton and a whole host of other good things, with plenty to smoke and drink.'

26 January 1917. *Chiswick Times*
Christmas at Salonica.

Private Frank Baynes, serving with a field ambulance, writes to Thomas A. King, Secretary of the Chiswick Working Men's Church Club.

'Christmas dinner was tremendous. In the evening the pantomime club performed 'Aladdin' in a large Greek village barn that holds about 800 and is also used for church services, concerts, etc. Although there are no women to take parts some of our boys make charming girls.

One small strafe did not necessitate much ambulance work. Mails have been few and far between probably due to the state of the roads. When it rains in Macedonia, one gets wet some.'

16 March 1917. *Chiswick Times*
Letter to Rev. Oldfield.

Bombardier A. A. Golding. Salonica Forces.

'I am keeping fairly fit. The weather here is very choice, some days fine and cold, but generally snow or rain. I should like to hear from or see 'Apples'. I believe his regiment is not far from me. I was pleased to hear Bert Chandler is making good progress. It must be good to see one at least of the old boys exhibiting past form. Remember me to Ralph and all the boys. It must be strange to have women in such masculine jobs. It is two years since I sailed away from dear old Blighty and even the memory is worth fighting for now.'

20 April 1917. *Chiswick Times*
Letter to Rev. Oldfield.

Rifleman Albert E. Wilkinson. Salonica Forces.

'I am still in the best of health. Have you received two letters sent a short time ago? I am afraid the U-boats had them. I still get the Chiswick Times regularly. I was very sorry indeed to hear that Mr. L had passed away. I was very pleased to know that Sid had met Will and are able to meet each other often. The weather here lately has been fairly good. What a splendid figure the War Loan reached. I think it must have opened the eyes of the world, anyhow it is something for 'Big Willie' to get off his chest. I see things have been greatly in our favour lately especially in the Far East. I think this summer will see the end.'

20 April 1917. *Chiswick Times*
Letter to Rev. Oldfield.

Assistant Bombardier A. A. Golding. Salonica Forces.

'As you say, the position on all fronts is greatly improved and even the changes in Russia are in our favour. I am hopeful of obtaining a leave during the next few months. It is half the battle to keep free from fever etc. The Bagdad success should have a great effect in the East, but with others I look to the Western Front to complete the business. I think that efforts on that front and the enemy's internal conditions will prove the deciding factors. I am not an optimist. I used to be, with visions of Constantinople before me, and although hoping to see great things this year I should not be surprised to see another year dawn before the great day. Please note my regiment number is now 301,507. I have gone in for signalling and find a change almost as good as a rest.'

1 June 1917. *Chiswick Times*
Chiswick Working Men's Club. Old Boys on active service.

Frank Baynes writes from Salonika to Mr. T.A. King (Secretary of Chiswick Working Men's Club).

'My section has won the inter-section football competition. We cheered up a boy who, although talkative, seldom smiles, by crowning him King of the May with tall reeds and a wreath of wild flowers. To everyone's delight he smiled rapturously.'

13 July 1917. *Chiswick Times*
Letter to Rev. Oldfield.

Gunner F.J. Bain. Salonica Force.

'Sorry to hear 'Ginger' Hill is in hospital. Nothing serious I hope. Pleased to hear Ralph is going on all right. My congratulations to Bob Osborne and George Mochler on their marriages, also Fred Buckley. Everything was beautiful on my voyage back in spite of subs.'

10 August 1917. *Chiswick Times*
Word from Salonica.

Frank Baynes writes to Thomas A. King of the Chiswick Working Men's Club.

'Parcels are taking two or three months to get here. I am extremely sorry to hear of the air-raids on London. We have experienced air raids and in a place like London they are bound to do damage and cause loss of life. I don't want to see any more of Macedonia. Give me dear old Chiswick. There are a good number of fruit trees near the camp and we are getting plums, apricots and cherries and expect apples and pears later, a welcome addition to army diet.'

He works in a hospital. 'I have recently been instructed in the art of taking blood smears of malaria patients.'

24 August 1917. *Chiswick Times*
Letters to Rev. Oldfield.

Gunner F. Bain. Salonica Field Forces.

'It seems a long time since I had a letter from you. Of course, we are quite aware that the mails are not so frequent now as they were, as I used to get letters within a fortnight before I went on leave, but now they take about double that time. It is very hot here still and awfully close at night. Things are favourable here up to the present. Hope they are the same at home. Please remember me to the boys. Excuse paper – scarce.'

Gunner J. A. Cooper. Somewhere in the Balkans.

'I heard from Sam a short time ago and he is sticking it well. We are getting some very hot weather here, plenty of flies and mosquitoes. I shan't be sorry when I get a leave, but there don't seem much hope yet. I have been out over two years on active service.'

31 August 1917. *Chiswick Times*
Letters to Rev. Oldfield.

Private W. R. Gibbs. Camp, Salonica Forces.

'As being one of your old brigade boys in the good old days, I am now taking the pleasure of writing a few lines in remembrance. Things out here are fairly well and I keep in fairly good health myself. We have been out here 12 months now, so I am getting used to the conditions of this kind of life and climate. Within about half hour's walk, we have an American YMCA and also Church Army Hut, which are very nice indeed. Dust storms are great in this part of the country.'

Driver R. M. Heighes. Salonica.

'I am in hospital, wounded by bomb explosion in April. You can guess how glad the boys were when King Tino abdicated. But when they heard about the air raid in London they soon changed their tone.'

5 October 1917. *Chiswick Times*
Letter to Rev. Oldfield.

Private Frank Dawes. Salonica.

'Your very welcome letter of 30th June has been a long time in finding me, but I have been in four hospitals, so your letter has been round them also. I have been suffering from dysentery, thankful I am getting better. Sorry to hear of the deaths of George Hall and Harold Triggs. Those air raids in England must be rather trying.'

2 November 1917. *Chiswick Times*
Letter to Rev. Oldfield.

Driver R.M. Heighes. Salonica Forces.

'Many thanks for your letter of 22nd July, just received. I am quite well again, able to resume my duties but not up the line, I am sorry to say, because I am marked P.B. 2x which means permanent base. I suppose you have received Corporal A. Struthers' and my letters. It was a coincidence being both wounded in the same arm and in the same convalescent camp for massage.'

9 November 1917. *Chiswick Times*
Letter to Rev. Oldfield.

Private W. R. Gibbs. Salonica Forces.

'Just two picture postcards. This is one of Salonica's fine churches I have had the pleasure of seeing, although it seems very difficult to make the priest understand you. They seem very backward in the English language. Again we are just the same with Greek, so you may well guess the rest. I am still in the pink.'

23 November 1917. *Chiswick Times*
Letter to Rev. Oldfield.

Gunner J. Cooper. Somewhere in the Balkans.

'Thank you for the Chiswick Times. I have not met any Chiswick chaps here yet. Fred Bain must be on a different front as I have not seen anything of him. It seems like being here another Christmas; this will be my third out here. I had a letter from Sam and from Will, and they are both sticking it well. I see by the paper there has been a few air raids. I daresay it makes the people a bit nervy. Roll on the finish and let us get back to Blighty once again.'

18 January 1918. *Chiswick Times*
Letter to Rev. Oldfield.

Bombardier A. Golding. Salonica Forces. December 12th.

'I have been in hospital with malaria for three months but hope to be back with my battery in time for Christmas. A 'prominent man' in England says that only those who had committed crimes had not had leave. This was a slur. I have been on active service in the Mediterranean for two years and nine months and have not had a crime of any sort.'

15 February 1918. *Chiswick Times*
Letter to Rev. Oldfield.

Gunner F. J. Bain. Salonica Forces.

'Pleased that the new band in Chiswick is going well. I remember the old band – those were real days that I hope will come again. Weather is splendid but bad weather is expected.'

19 July 1918. *Chiswick Times*
Letter to Rev. Oldfield.

Private J. Satch. Mediterranean Expeditionary Force.

'Cannot grumble. Plenty of food, sports and concerts, but the worst part is we cannot get leave to see my dear wife and child. But it cannot be helped. In this country there is nothing but open ground just the same as in France – where it is more serious. I am afraid the war will last longer than we think but we must keep going till the end.'

15. Ireland

The Easter Rising occurred in Dublin in April 1916. Maybe references to the rebellion were suppressed.

26 March 1915. *Chiswick Times*
Mr. T.A. King, secretary of the Chiswick Working Men's Club, ,received a letter from an old member.

Driver A.R. Hoskins. 25th Battery, Training at Athlone Barracks, Ireland.

'Been here ten days, seems like ten weeks. Nothing but pigs, mud and donkeys. The voyage here was rough, but would be thankful to rough it again back to England. But won't get back until we are trained.'

14 January 1916. *Chiswick Times*
Letters from members of Chiswick Working Men's Club.

Corporal Hoskins. Writes from Donegal.

'I am well but whose fault that is, I cannot tell. I put it down that though by rights I ought to be one of the unlucky ones, my fool's luck gets me through. Living in this part of the globe has given me to understand what the meaning of the word 'transport' must be. I have come to the conclusion that it is short for transportation, the penalty they give instead of death. And I can assure you that transport amongst those snow-clad hills spells death at every corner. We have to make the outlying forts every day; it is about four hour's journey, but we think ourselves lucky if we manage it in 14. There is a wagon lying now on its side, halfway down the cliff, that warns the drivers it is dangerous to try to slide your wagon and horses down the slope.'

5 May 1916. *Chiswick Times*
Letters to Rev. Oldfield.

Private A. Gardiner. France.

'As I write I see the paper states that the rebels have captured Dublin Post Office. I would rather have read that they had raided the so-called non-fighters. A conscientious objector should be made to pay for one soldier's keep during the war, or should be made to come up when compulsion is put on the book.'

7 July 1916. *Chiswick Times*
Chiswick Working Men's Club letters to Mr. King.

Trooper S. Barrington in Dublin.

'Sunday is our worst day as we have to stand by for emergencies.' Mr. King writes that judging by the tone of the letter Dublin is not yet a bed of roses. His force is inspected by Sir John Maxwell who commands them as the finest yeomanry regiment he has had pleasure of inspecting. 'We sent a draft to Egypt last week and they had a fine send off.'

Mr. King has news of three brothers. Sydney Ward has been seriously wounded in France. Sgt Charlie Ward is now in France from Salonica. Ernest Ward is still in Dublin, but able to go for motor car drives and hopes to be transferred to England.

16. Western Front 1917

On the Western front the British Passchendale offensive failed. Tanks were used at Cambrai but little ground was gained.

5 January 1917. *Chiswick Times*
Letters to Rev. Oldfield.

'Darkie' Alfred Davis. Canada.

'Wishing you the best of happiness in the future year. All is well. Brother Harry in France and 'Lighty' on board troop-ship, will be over.'

Signaller W.G. Howe. Belgium.

'It was very dull Christmas for us out here, raining all day and it was just like any weekday. We went to work just the same, and Fritz got strafed just the same, and in fact more so. When I read about the Kaiser's attempted peace conference it made me laugh, but our boys out here would very much like peace, but not on his terms. I would be very glad if you could get me a razor, as my one the army issued is worn out and useless.'

Private A.A. Gardner. France.

'We are just looking forward for our Christmas turkey. It is very quiet, and in another hour we shall be in church, praying for that speedy victory, which I hope will come before another Christmas arrives. Dear Sir, surely the silver lining must break through soon. This dreadful calamity must appeal to everyone as they sit at table this Yuletide trying to make the best of their absent ones; those empty chairs must tell the tale of war. I think, sir, if everyone gave his mind and thought to the winding up of this dreadful war, instead of looking forward to the best paid jobs at home, and think of the sacrifices of his manhood out here, and turn out here a good many months, then the Yuletide would be much smoother. I can only wish yourself and Chiswick a happy New Year and close with my new address.'

Private E. Kirkum. Edinburgh.

'I was glad to get away from that Somme; it made me rotten, but I am glad to say I am gradually getting my old self again. It is cold up here now and I don't like the idea of spending Christmas in Scotland, for the Scotch don't keep up Christmas Day, only New Year's Day, but I suppose I shall have to put up with it. I hear the French are making good progress. If they keep on like that the Germans won't last long.'

Private F. Stanley. France.

'I now take the pleasure of writing to you to let you know my address as promised before leaving Blighty. Well Sir, things have been going fine for me since I left, I met some good boys when joining the battalion, and I spent a very happy Christmas. Our battalion is out for a rest, going back to the line sometime next month. There is a few of my chums arguing the point about football and I was well in the game. My brother Will has been promoted to sergeant; also George has had the luck to be placed on the staff at ----- and I am still a full-blown private after nearly two years six months. I cannot account for that sir.'

19 January 1917. *Chiswick Times*
Letters to Rev. Oldfield.

Private A. Gardner. France.

'I hope Chiswick made merry Christmas as we did out here. We had rather a jolly time, considering the object we are out here for; but still sir this is the third Christmas in France and I don't think we shall see the next one out here. Of course, we cannot talk war ideas, or you may not receive the letter. I expect the Chiswick Times got lost this time as one or two letters have gone astray. Christmas time, as you understand, there is practically half the food home cooked and sent out here, besides the mail, and something must go astray. I wish it was those U-boats, it would not matter so much. Well, sir, I hope we are well awake this year to make a bold bid for final peace.

There will be great sacrifice I expect, but I hope it brings victory with it. I don't think the opposition is so strong now. I think they are like the Zepps, proving a failure.'

Drummer Ben Ross. Scots Guards.

'Just a line to wish you the compliments of the season. I am getting my full drummership this week, a slight promotion from boy as junior drummer to drummer, so my pay increases 7d to 1s.9d a day, but I have more work to do down here and the weather is not a bit like Ramsgate. We were getting for the last three days rather a cold welcome for me.'

Sergeant E. Allen. War Hospital Bradford.

'You will be surprised to hear I am in hospital in Bradford suffering from nephritis, and they have been starving me – feeding me on milk when I would sooner have something to eat. I think it won't be much longer now. I know the Germans are getting fed up by the way they give themselves up.'

Sergeant-drummer R. Witcomb. 6th Queen's Regiment.

'Sorry to hear Ted Allen, Bob Alexander and others are in hospital and I wish them a speedy recovery. As you say, I suppose I will be in for the duration, as this is a 'C.1' regiment, home service; and I started a corps of drums three weeks ago, and they are getting on A.1. When I was transferred to this regiment and they saw I was a sergeant drummer, they said 'You are just the man we want' so I am some use, after all, it seems; but I shall be glad when it is all over and I can carry on the L.D.C.L.B. drum again. Give my kind regards to all.'

26 January 1917. *Chiswick Times*
Letters to Rev. Oldfield.

Driver Fred Bailey. France.

'Received your letter safely. Ted Allen did not last long and is lucky to get back to Blighty so quickly. Perce Read and I might get our leave at the same time about the end of March. Christmas was a rather dull affair this year. We kept it up as best as possible on the 24th and on Christmas morning at 4am we were back on the road to the line.'

Corporal Walter Burch. France.

'Thanks for the welcome letter. Surprised to hear Ted Allen is back in England so soon. I hope his illness is not serious. There seems to be quite a lot of Chiswick lads in Hospital. I met George Hall a few weeks ago. He is a corporal in the Machine Gun Section. I expect there will be an end to this war someday, and I do not mind how soon it comes.'

Drummer C. Addlestone. Devon.

'You will be surprised to hear from me after all this time. I have had two of your old boys with me, Witcombe and Hamblen, who has now gone to the front. I have got two years' service and should have been at the front but am unfit marked C3 for the last six months. They keep me here because I am in the drums. Our chaplain is the Rev. C. Digby, well known in the sporting world – boxing mainly.'

2 February 1917. *Chiswick Times*
Letter to Rev. Oldfield.

Trooper Tom Bain. France.

'I have been in hospital for the last month with fever but am better now. Just returned from the trenches and I can tell you it was cold – five or six inches of snow. Please send me another Asiatic cord – the old one is finished.'

9 February 1917. *Acton Gazette*
Rev. Mcleod and his Critics – a reply from the front.

Rev. W.A. Macleod, vicar of All Saints, South Acton, serving with the forces in France as a chaplain, writes to his parishioners:

'Before I do anything else, I must thank you for the beautiful Pyx you have given me. It is most useful for taking the reserved sacrament to the wounded and sick in the wards. The number of communicants varies very much. Though the great majority of those in the clearing station are labelled 'Church of England' hardly any seem to have ever heard of Confirmation or Holy Communion. At other times I find a large number of well-instructed and regular communicants. One morning I had the privilege of taking the sacrament to 14 men in one ward. My work is rather disappointing at times for no-one stays more than a few days here, and I have just time to get to know them when a train takes them all away, and the station is filled up with a new lot of wounded and sick.

I hear some 'patriotic' person has been criticising, in the local press, my action in coming here. Of course everyone has a right to his own opinion, but the value of their opinion naturally depends on the individual who gives it. We could judge better how much importance to attach to this anonymous scribbler if he gave his name and address. All I have experienced here only goes to confirm what I felt for a very long time, that this work is of the highest possible importance, and that no consideration of any kind should keep a man back who has the opportunity given him to do it.

I am perfectly certain that my absence for a few months will not make the slightest difference to anyone who really understands the need to be out here.'

23 February 1917. *Chiswick Times*
Letters to Rev. Oldfield.
Private F.C. Smith ('Titch'). France.

'I am quite well. Have been getting the CT regularly. Bitter cold weather but better than last year when we were up to our waists in water and mud. I read in the French papers that America has declared war on Germany, but I do not see it in our papers, so conclude it is only a rumour. I think Fritz will have an excuse if they come – they cannot fight the world. Most of us think it will finish this year. I hope it does as I am fed up. However we keep smiling.'

2nd <u>A.M. (Air mechanic) E. Lange</u>. Royal Flying Corps.

'I joined up on 1st February and passed a trade test as an air mechanic. Had great trouble leaving my old firm where I was charge-hand over 15 machines. I was on motor work of no national importance, so I can say I am doing my bit.'

<u>Corporal W. Tillcock</u>. France.

The snow still on the ground and very keen frosts. We hear America has declared war on Germany. As to the authenticity of this rumour, we must await our edition of the London papers. I quite agree about the Huns latest submarine warfare threats. It shows the state of things of their Hunnish warfare tactics.'

2 March 1917. *Chiswick Times*
Letters to Rev. Oldfield.

<u>Sergeant H.R. Griffin</u>. In the field.

'Having passed all the required tests, I am now a qualified first class pilot, holding the rank of sergeant in the Royal Flying Corps, but being desirous of obtaining a commission, I have forwarded the necessary papers to England. The previous papers were cancelled at my own request owing to the fact that I preferred the opportunity of being a pilot to a commission in the artillery, as originally intended.'

<u>Sapper Harper Smith</u>. France.

'I am sorry to have kept you waiting so long for a line but have been on the go so much that we very often forget days and dates and let mealtimes slide. You should see the mud we have got to go through now. The change in the weather from the terrible cold damp to a little warmth was welcomed, but everywhere we go now is up to our ankles in mud.

After keeping a sharp look out for some of the boys out here from our native place, I suddenly came across my brother Charlie. You can guess how I felt after all this long time. I may say he looks splendid, in fact I have not seen him look so well before. He was in a small village, not an hour's walk from me, having apparently come out for a rest. Although it poured with rain all day, we managed under the circumstances to spend a very pleasant time. Yes, he still keeps up the reputation of the L.D.C.L.B as he plays the piccolo in the regimental band. His pal is also a very musical fellow in the band with him so there is no doubt he will be an expert flautist when he comes out. Well sir, I have been receiving the Chiswick Times very regularly for which I must thank the sender very much. After I have finished with it, I forward it to my people in Canada so you can see how the paper is welcomed.'

Trooper Tom Bain. B.1 Ward. Third London General Hospital.

'I am getting on well. You will see by my address that I am in dear old Blighty. It is quite a treat after the Somme. I am still in bed, sir, but hope to be up in a few days. I am a bit sick of bed. I have not been on my feet since the 5th February.'

16 March 1917. *Chiswick Times*
Letters to Rev. Oldfield.

Private F. ('Bat') Locke. Urniston Hospital, Blackwater Rd, Eastbourne.

'I am wounded in the thigh and am in England. I got my Blighty on Sunday morning at 6 o'clock, and we took three lines of German trenches from him on the Somme. It was grand going over; nobody was hit till we started digging the trenches deeper. I hope you will not be worried as it is not serious.'

A few lines thanking you for your most welcome parcel. You would not believe how it cheers us up to have anything sent from Blighty, it is all we look for day after day. We have been having rather a stiff time of it out here lately, but still we keep smiling. Please excuse letter being short as we are just getting relieved for a short rest.'

Driver Fred Brown. France.

'I shall be glad when the war is over and I think all the boys are about fed up with it. Would you let me know if you have heard from Ted Maidlow who joined the Royal Marines, as I never seem to get a letter from any of the boys. We are having very good weather for the time of year.'

Private W. Hales. France.

'I was very sorry that I did not see you when I was home on leave. It is very quiet where we are now but we sometimes do a bit of strafing but nothing to speak about.'

Corporal Frank Sheppard. First Eastern General Hospital, Cambridge.

'I am going on as well as possible but this complaint takes a long time to get cured of. I am allowed up for half a day at last. I see by the CT that Fred Allen is in hospital with the same complaint. I hope he has got over, Sir, with his milk diet by now, as I have had enough of it. We had a service for about an hour on Sunday night. I must say we have got some fine chaplains here. All of them have been out to either one of the fronts; in fact one of them has been wounded three times. Will you send me Arthur Smith's address? You know who I mean. 'Ginger.' I must thank Mrs. C for the CT. I pass it on to a sergeant who lives at Acton. It keeps me in touch with the doings at home. I think the town has done very well indeed with men and money too.'

23 March 1917. *Chiswick Times*
Letters to Rev. Oldfield.

Private C.A. Brand. France.

'This is the first opportunity I have had to write since my return to France as we have been so busy. I was very sorry that I was unable to see you before crossing but my departure was quite unexpected. As you see by above address, I am now in the 7th Battalion of the same regiment, Platoon 'C' company. I have not seen any old boys since I came back except Bert Mears of Corney Road who is my chum in the platoon. The weather is rotten and has been for the past month, not so bad now, but continually raining but this is preferable to the terrible severe snowstorms and cold we experienced of late.'

Private G. Chandler. France.

'Many thanks for the parcel. I can assure you the shirt and socks will see service before long, as you know they are things we require most. I had a mixture of cocoa, shirt and socks when I opened the parcel, but that is a mere detail, and the cocoa that was not in the socks etc was still in the box – but I can tell you sir, it is not in the box now. I have had another move since I wrote to you, and expect to shortly more again. I have not had a chance of giving your message to Wally Burdy, as he has been on parade each time.'

30 March 1917. *Chiswick Times*
Letters to Rev. Oldfield.

Private H. Broadley. France.

'In answer to your most welcome letter. It leaves me in the pink just now as we are having fine weather for a change. I should like to know how Ralph Witcomb is going on as he was a sport before the war. I suppose the brigade is going all right, in fact I suppose the best of them have joined up to do their bit. Remember me to Mr. Long, as I cannot forget his boy Artie as we used to call him.'

Pioneer H. Norman. France.

'Very sorry haven't written for such a long time, as we have been rather busy moving about. Pic and I are both in the best of health and so is J. Jennings who is also with us. What do you think of the news of the last day or two? Splendid isn't it?

The weather isn't so cold, although it is anything but warm, but we are in very comfortable billets. We are lucky, being three of us together especially as there are two other Chiswick lads here, so we have many talks of our local experiences. We have got a football team together and are keeping fit for when the 'Bluebirds' turn out again when it's all over. Should be obliged it it's possible for you to send us a pair or two of old football boots as although we have got footballs and shirts we find it impossible to get boots.'

Lance-corporal <u>Walter Brown</u>. France.

'I was very sorry to hear about Joe Brown and Brock, two good fellows, but I think our boys will make up for it this spring and give them what they deserve.'

5 April 1917. *Chiswick Times*

Dug out 90ft deep – pathetic scenes in recaptured French villages.

In a letter to his wife, living in Isleworth, a quartermaster sergeant says:

'The Huns have retreated from our front some miles. We at present are in reserve, so I expect we shall have to repair and make roads.

The Huns nipped out of the way very quickly here, afraid of being cut off. The ---- and myself found time today to go over into the vacated trenches of the Germans. They are on a bigger scale than ours and the dug-outs go down in places to 90ft below the surface, and are made as if they intended to stay.

The poor villages on either side of the trenches have suffered dreadfully. It must have been hell to have lived under our artillery fire. One village that they occupied has been razed to the ground. There are shell holes all over the place, some big enough to put a horse and cart in.

It seems to get on one's nerves this incessant roar – it has been fine here the last day or two to be free from artillery fire. It is sad to see the people now that they know that the bombardment of their villages has ceased, returning to what were once their little homes. One old man had a piece of wood in his hand, and on being interrogated what he was doing, informed us that the piece of wood was a piece of his bedstead – all that was left of his house. In some villages of course, some of the houses have escaped, and along the road now and again you will see an old French cart with people presumably taking their belongings back to their old homes.

I think we English should feel thankful that we are not placed as these people. Some of the people who talk so flippantly of the war because they are alright, should be made to come out here for a while, and then their tone would change. It is no safe place in the villages, roofs half off, walls lopping over and tiles dropping off now and again. I saw a church this morning with its steeple half knocked away and the other half leaning over ready for the wind to blow it over. It is very strange that although crucifixes are very common out here, two or three in each village, always one as you enter the village and one as you leave – they all seem to escape.'

13 April 1917. *Chiswick Times*
Letters to Rev. Oldfield.

Corporal Walter Burch. France.

'George Chandler told me he had received a letter from you. We are having some better weather. I hope the pleasant news is pleasing all at home. You can look for something sensational from this front very shortly. In fact you may get the news by the time you receive this letter. Our guns are hammering them in no half-hearted style. In fact, things look very rosy all round at present.'

Gunner Harold Triggs. France.

'I have just found a few spare moments in which to write letters. What spare time I have had lately was spent in sleep as we have been going it very hard indeed on the push and now we are just waiting. We seem to be quite indispensable. We are in an awkward position to obtain any little luxury. I have not had the luck to run into any Chiswick chaps lately.'

Private Fred Stanley. France.

'I have been waiting anxiously for your letter sir. Yes, it is as you remark, very good news of late and I am of the same opinion as you. I do not think the end is far off. Let us hope we are right for the sake of all. So Bob has married again, I should like a line from him. It is a long time since I saw him last. Could you give him my address and ask him to drop me a couple of lines.

I am fit as a fiddle, I believe I have never been in better health. I get the CT out here every week and I see that the lads are all doing well. We are on a continental tour now at the Government's expense. I am sorry to say it is nothing like our old trip to Margate. Still it is all for the good of the cause and we do not grumble.'

Private Joe Catton. France.

I arrived in France quite safely in the ----- regiment and having any amount of snow here and terribly cold, but we make the best of it as I think what we are doing is for a good cause. I shall be very pleased to hear from you any time convenient as having a line from Chiswick cheers people up for we are like stray sheep out here.'

Private J.W. Creak. France.

'I have received a copy of the CT from a friend and read the old boys' letters to yourself, and thought it was about time I wrote a line or two to you. I have been here since October and have recently been sent down from the line, unfit. Still I can do a little bit for Blighty. Hoping to see you and all friends 'apres la guerre.'

13 April 1917. *Acton Gazette*
Artillery in the open.

Bombardier J. B. Lucas, writing to Mr. Fred Pring of Kew Rd, says:

'There has been a little excitement during the recent advance. The batteries have been entirely in the open, and the taking up of ammunition has been a risky and lengthy job. The procedure was to send it on pack horses, limbers being unable to go right up owing to shell holes and barbed wire. The destruction caused by our heavy batteries to the enemy trenches was wonderful and the holes made by our trench mortars are enormous. The enemy dug outs were strongly built, and divided into any number of compartments, all boarded with matchboard. Most of them however had been set on fire by the enemy before vacating them. I spent a few days in one in the old Bosch 4th line – it had been turned into a telephone exchange by our people.'

20 April 1917. *Chiswick Times*
Letters to Rev. Oldfield.

Driver A. Colegate. France.

'I expect you will be surprised to hear that I have met one of the old boys out here, S.Cork, and he is in my battery, and it is very pleasant to meet someone from the old place. Please excuse short letter as there isn't anything we are allowed to mention.'

4 May 1917. *Chiswick Times*
Letters to Rev. Oldfield.

Driver Fred Brown. France.

'Thank you for sending the boys' addresses. Harry Brown's battery has come out for a rest after doing good work. The weather here is very miserable but the Tommies don't care a bit. They are always happy and I think the way we are going on, it won't last much longer, as I think Fritz is on his last pins.'

Gunner Harold Triggs. France.

'I was extremely pleased to receive your letter and parcel and the latter was most acceptable indeed as we were a bit down in the dumps at the time. We are very busy just now with the Huns, keeping them on the run.'

Pioneer Harold Norman ('Babs'). France.

'We seem to be making very good progress still, don't we? Weather is very treacherous here, and it has rained and snowed practically continually since Saturday. Pic got your letter last week and is keeping like myself in the pink. I think Jack Jennings is all right, although I haven't seen him for over a fortnight. I must dry up as it is bedtime.'

<u>Sergeant E. Allen</u>. Eastbourne.

'Eastbourne, a very nice place too. I went before the doctors yesterday, and they told me I was to take everything very easy as I was very much run down. I don't know what they are going to do with me here so I must wait and see.'

<u>Private J.W. Creak</u>, France

'Have met one or two Chiswick lads here recently – J.Blizzard, who was wounded last October and has just come out again with a draft, and Hannan, of Wood Street.'

<u>Private W. Oliver</u>. Lewes, Sussex.

'In answer to your most welcome letter. Well, I am having a long spell of hospital life and I do not seem to improve much yet. My arm is still very bad; as soon as it improves, it breaks out again. They cannot make it out; they put it down to poison in my blood for I have still the piece of shrapnel in my back with which I got wounded, for when they operated on me they could not get it out, so I always feel it, at times very bad too. I do not know if they are going to try again and get it out, for if it keeps hurting me. I shall ask them to do so.'

11 May 1917. *Chiswick Times*
Letters to Rev. Oldfield.

<u>Trooper Tom Bain</u>. Eastbourne Convalescent Camp.

'We are getting some grand weather, my 'nasal organ' is already skimmed. I was taken out on the sea in a rowing boat yesterday. It made me think of Windsor with the old brigade. I expect I shall be seeing sunny France again if they keep me here many weeks.'

<u>Sergeant Walter Burd</u>. France.

'I am very sorry you had a letter returned, but it was an accident on my part in not telling you I had left the divisional bombing school. You see, the school was broken up and I was sent to re-join the battalion in a hurry. Since then I have been promoted to sergeant. I am very sorry to hear such a lot of the boys were in the casualty lists. I cannot find out anything about G.Chandler and I have not seen him since the battalion came out of the last attack. I expect by this time you will have had a letter from him telling you he is in hospital. I cannot tell you anything about the war, in case the censor objects. I saw Ted Cole with our second battalion a few days ago. He was looking well.'

25 May 1917. *Chiswick Times*
Letters to Rev. Oldfield.
Gunner Harold Triggs. France.

'Here we are again. The 'Contemptibles' are still going strong. We have taken part in all this present offensive movement, with hardly a spell, except when marching from one sector to another – if that can be called a spell. I am afraid our nerves are getting tested this time. This seems to me to be a reaction that takes place just before the death, and a strong reaction too. Well, I can't seem to write any variety in my letters. Some people might think it a very exciting life; no doubt it is, full of incidents, but which to us becomes a dreary monotony. We have to put up with scenes here which we never dreamt would happen during our quiet human existence at home. In fact we did not know we were born before this dreadful turmoil commenced. Still, I am proud to have been able to fight for my country, and perhaps freedom, and I hope to see through to the finish. Bert is back in France again (3ʳᵈ time) and Arthur has been called up, expecting to be sent any day. Bill, who used to be librarian of Chiswick Public Library, went to Canada five years ago. He volunteered but was rejected. So you see, we have all been trying to do our bit. My sister is on the Army Pay Office staff.'

Lance-corporal Albert Collard, D.C.M. Norfolk War Hospital, Norwich.

'I am getting on fine. They are going to let me get up tomorrow. A treat after being in bed three weeks. The wound is healing up a bit. The eye is not open yet, but the doctor says it is quite all right. What lovely weather we are having, and it is such lovely country round here, it will be quite a pity to come away.'

Sapper Walter Smith ('Pic 2nd'). France.

'The weather is grand. I have just had a letter from home and they tell me that Bob Alexander has lost the use of some fingers, which I think is very hard luck for such a young fellow. I heard from 'Pic' last week but not had the luck to meet him. I believe he is in Belgium. Not heard from Arthur for a long while. Has he written to you lately? I have not seen a letter in the Chiswick Times from home. I have it every week because it is very nice to be able to read the letters from the old boys.'

Cyclist J.S. Bewley. France.

'Thank you very much for those useful items which you sent to mother to be forwarded to me. We had just come in from chasing the Boche. It is about the first time we have done our original work which we came out here for and I must say things are rather brisk here just now, with us doing our utmost to push ahead.'

Private Lionel H. Turfrey. France.

'Just a line or two to let you know I am quite well. I have been out here a month now sir, and I think it is quite long enough. Have you heard anything of the Bewleys, as I saw Walter when I was on leave and he said he was coming out, and he said he was going to write to me. My address is -----, somewhere amongst some ruins, but I suppose we must look at the best side of things sir. Cheerio! – PS. Forgot to post this, but we had to go into the trenches; sending it on to you now I have come out.'

1 June 1917. *Chiswick Times*
Letters to Rev. Oldfield.

Private F.C. Smith ('Titch'). France.

'When I receive the CT, the boys here always kid me about it. They say 'Where is this Chiswick? Whereabouts on the map is it?" and several other chippy remarks; but since the open-air bath has been opened and several pictures have appeared of it in the 'Daily Mirror' they have said very little on the subject. They have got wise and found that there is a Chiswick. However it will be 'some' town when the boys come back again. Well sir, I have very little news of importance although naturally I could tell you something real, but it's the censor. I had the luck to run across Billy Heath, the chap who had the bass drum in the old drum and fife band. I was so surprised I could hardly speak, however after several minutes our minds were far away in our old little town. Kindly give my best regards to all the boys.'

Private W.E. Davies. En route.

'Well, I am well on the way, just concluded many hours train ride, jolly glad to finish it though all the way it was gorgeous scenery. So we have now reached a place where the weather is just a foretaste of what is to come. Some call it genial weather, I call it hot. I miss the papers a lot. I did try and translate the 'Petit Journal' but it was a bit of a job. I shall be glad to have information from home. Half-hour before leaving I met a man who was organist at St Mary's and on the boat, met a chap in the Royal Field Artillery from Glebe Street.'

Private F.W.J. Catton. France.

'I received your letter safely, but I have been transferred to the seventh. I have met Bob White, and he told me his brother was killed in the Royal Engineers. I also met another chap called Leonard – I forget his other name – he was in your brigade about the same time I joined. He is a corporal in the Royal Army Medical Corps.'

15 June 1917. *Chiswick Times*
Letter to Rev. Oldfield.
Corporal David Davies. BEF.

'I am down the line now, by that I mean at the base. It was last Sunday and our people were putting up a bombardment of Fritz's lines that is invariably a preliminary to an advance. And the Huns, by way of retaliation, put up a barrage on our support trench, which I was unfortunately holding with some of the boys of our platoon. It was perfectly terrible whilst it lasted, and I congratulate myself on getting through the ordeal, if not scathless, with minor wounds.

I was buried by falling debris, and after the barrage lifted, it took the boys a considerable time to extricate me, with nothing more serious than a wound on my somewhat prominent proboscis and bruises on my chest but no bones broken. The most tragic part of the affair is that my chum, a private in my platoon, and one of the best lads that ever breathed, was killed by the same shell. There was I on the ground pinned by massive baulks of timber, and my pal beside me, and I was powerless to help him. His dying words were 'Corporal, help me' and believe me sir, I did try, but I hadn't the strength. Now I have practically recovered, and I am expecting my discharge from hospital very shortly. By the way, G. Peters is in my platoon, and when I came away was safe and sound. I hope the remainder of the lads are OK and that they continue so.'

22 June 1917. *Chiswick Times*
A study of German prisoners.

An article by Corporal G.B. Ingram-Smith, Middlesex Regiment in *Fall In*, the organ of the Duke of Cambridge's Own.

'When German prisoners are taken to the rear they throw away their shrapnel helmets and assume their hateful trench caps. Some are awful sights in those hideous, round, peakless caps perched upon their heads. German NCOs wear shiny black peaks to their caps and walk along with noses in the air, casting looks of withering contempt at their British escort. But when an escort brings a bayonet under Mr. NCO Fritz's nose the look changes to one of alarm, and he hurriedly murmurs. 'Me prisoner – Kamerad.'

The officer prisoners always bear a haughty manner, and even attempt to show their escort some part of the contempt with which they treat their own men. Our men take little notice and this seems to annoy the Hun officer more than anything. One German officer recently told one of our officers that we would probably win the war, but would need only one boat to take our troops back to England afterwards. This shows the sort of braggards they are.

One can usually discover the difference between one German nationality and another, apart from their distinctive caps, by their demeanour. Prussians are always the most troublesome and haughtiest. Saxons are the finest looking fellows and usually the most ready to surrender. They always profess they are unwilling to fight us but are compelled to do so by the Prussians. Next to the Saxons the Saxe-Coburgers seem the most amenable. The Bavarians do not seem so proud as formerly, and evidently are being taught docility by means of our shells.'

29 June 1917. *Chiswick Times*
Letter to Rev. Oldfield.

Sapper P.E. Read. Somewhere in Belgium.

'I am still in the pink, and more so now I am in the same place as Fred Bentley, as we knocked against one another last night, so you can guess we had a good talk over old times and how we have been getting on since we have been out here. I am sorry to see that there are a lot of casualties amongst the old boys, but I am pleased to see that most of them are slight. Yes, Fred Bailey, Pickles, and Babs have a good job; good luck to them. Thank you very much for the photo of the crucifix in memory of the old lads that have fallen in this war. It is very good, sir. How is Mr. Bond going on now? Fred and I were conversing over it last night, wishing that we were back in it at a church parade. With the best of luck we shall be back before long to make it better than it was, and a little smarter in drill, and step out just like old soldiers. What say you, sir?'

6 July 1917. *Chiswick Times*
Letters to Rev. Oldfield.

Private E. Edwards. France.

'I have been going to write for a long time, but something always crops up – a Dixie wants filling, or rations have to be drawn, and a hundred and one things which we have to do in our spare time.

We have had a great charge since I last wrote, and things look a lot brighter for us, although the end seems a long way off yet. We have had the hardest nuts to crack, except for last big smash up, so you can guess we have had a lively time of it. When the boys go over now, they go over and stop there, and it is more than Fritz can do to shift us. With all his concrete shelters and dugouts, he can't hold his line very long once we have made up our minds to have it. I have not seen any of the old boys yet. We have heard about the air raid on London.'

Private J. Brock. France.

'Sorry I could not write before, but we have been so busy, the result of which you will no doubt have read in the papers – the latest big push I mean. Our battalion was in the affair and did some really good work, capturing several field guns, machine guns, prisoners etc. My sister tells me that the force of the explosions (which were mines) was felt in London. The ridge under which they were placed was held by Germans, but it has now disappeared. The prisoners came rolling in in a state of absolute terror, and when they saw our tanks coming over, they kneeled down before them.

We are now well out in the open country under canvas. It is a treat here, very quiet and glorious weather. I read in the papers about the recent air raid on London; I was glad to see they had not touched the west side of London but I was sorry to see that so many had been killed.'

Corporal E. Cole. Convalescent Depot. France.

'I have quite recovered from my last wound, as no doubt you know this is my fourth one. Thank God we are still going strong in front and I don't know how we stick it at times, for I am sure last winter was the worst one we have had out here, and the only thing that kept us going was the thought of coming home to see the old faces again, which I am anxiously looking forward to as I have been out here since November 1915 this time, but shall not worry just yet, as I have been given a job to look after the boys' letters, so you can guess my feeling when I come across one in your handwriting.'

13 July 1917. *Chiswick Times*
Air raid on London.

A Long report on local experiences. Bombs were dropped some miles from Chiswick although the local alarm was sounded. Shelter was taken – some inside the Catholic Church. Anti-aircraft guns were heard. There was no sign of panic and people watched the aerial display with the keenest of interest. In the Catholic Church, where women were sheltering, a missile came through the back of the church at an acute angle striking the floor of an aisle close to a pram holding a baby and buried itself deeply. 'A crowd of hysterical women' rushed into the presbytery. There is no truth in a rumour that a baby was killed during a baptism.' Later it was reported that the missile was a shell from a British gun.

13 July 1917. *Chiswick Times*
Letter to Rev. Oldfield.

Corporal W.G. Howe, D.C.M. France.

'I need not tell you how grateful I am to you for sending that parcel of cigarettes. I was just dying for a smoke, so they came at the right time too. Also thank you for the photo of the memorial crucifix, it is splendid. But it is very sorrowful to see that so many have made the supreme sacrifice, and yet it is consoling to one to see that they were not skulking from their duty to King and country. In the same camp there is a chap named W.Goodall, a Chiswick man. He said he belonged to the brigade.'

27 July 1917. *Chiswick Times*
Letter to Rev. Oldfield.

Corporal David Davies. Somewhere in (censor deleted).

'We are out of the line at present, but expect to be in it in a day or two. Very sorry to hear about George Hall's death. I well remember the day when he was top boy cantoris and I was No.3 descant and then there was Dick Vine, top boy descant. Poor old

Dick, he is about the worst of all. Do you remember at Dover Sir, when my cap blew over the cliff? I certainly shouldn't have been a soldier now if old Dick hadn't had the presence of mind to grab my ankles as I was disappearing. But what a contrast between those days and now! Surely our lads have done their bit.'

3 August 1917. *Chiswick Times*
Letters to Rev. Oldfield.

Private F.J. Pearce. BEF.

'I am once more in the scrapping area after my leave at home. I never saw Jock Wrathell as I should have liked to have done. Things are very lively here again. Something doing again in Belgium. That belt you gave me, I am pleased to say is champion.'

Private F.C. Smith ('Titch'). France.

'Very sorry to read in the Chiswick Times of death of Harold Triggs. We used to sit next to one another in Hogarth school until the day I sailed to Canada. I got to know him well and I am sure a better chap never lived. We have just finished our rest which we should have had long ago – our first since 9th April. A long time to wait isn't it? However we made 'go' of our holiday. Our football team secured for the battalion the Canadian Corps Championship. We are waiting to play some Imperial Battalion for the 1st Army Championship. We had the misfortune to lose our centre forward. We had our church service on Monday owing to the day previous being wet, and the service over, the chaplain was preparing for Holy Communion in one of the company huts when 'Fritz' sent over a shell which burst in the very hut. Later the C.O came and read the official communiqué of the Russian advance. The reaction practically at once set in, and I guess today there are very few who are thinking how lucky they were to escape a shell that caused casualties.'

Corporal Jack M. Clarke. France.

'I have had a pretty heavy go of fever through getting wet and no change. So long as I am dry I can stick anything. However I am much better and am staying in a convalescent camp. The food is good and there are plenty of recreation huts. I am on the 'gym' staff here, and I fancy that will keep me here for six weeks, after which I go to ----- again, so I shall be content to bring fever and ague on again, although I stuck the first and second winter in the line.'

24 August 1917. *Chiswick Times*
Letters to Rev. Oldfield.

Private Lionel Turfrey. BEF.

'Fairly decent weather, but we have had a good time in the trenches, this time for 12 days – rather a long time, sir. But we are having a blow now for a little time. Mrs. Wrathell wrote and told me Tich had been home on leave. I hope he has had a good time, as there are no good times out here, sir, not like old Chiswick. I have found out, by the way, who that chap was who was always round at St Mary's, his name is Hawkins. We have another chap come out now from Devonshire Road, opposite Mr. Cox the clock maker, he came in a new draft. Frank Kingston is keeping fairly fit, sir. I see him nearly every day. He is in 'B' company and wishes to be remembered to you. I tell you what you could send me sir, if you don't mind, that is, the old 'Chiswick Times' as it's always handy to read. My sister's husband is still in hospital at the base and Bernard is quite well. When we left the line, Jerry was getting rather quiet but took mad fits now and again, and when he did he sent everything over – 'pineapples' and trench mortars, and everything you can't get at Gamage's.'

Pioneer W. Sheppard. Bedford.

'You will no doubt be surprised to hear from me at the above address, but I have been joined up about a month and have been very busy with exams. I never felt better in my life. If I pass, which I hope to, I shall be sent to ----- or ----- and then to German East Africa. I had a line from Frank. He is now at Ballyhinta Co. Down, Ireland. I also had a letter from Dick Vine who is now about settled at Grohurst Green, near Guildford. I saw Mr. Grosvenor at Blackpool after a struggle, as the camp is about three miles from the station. He has a staff job so he has nothing to worry about.'

31 August 1917. *Chiswick Times*
Letters to Rev. Oldfield.

Private Fred Stanley, 'Digger'. France.

'I have taken a great interest in boxing, and should be very much obliged if you could send me out a set of gloves for training. I have entered in the regimental turn-out twice and got away with a second prize each time. This last time, I got away with a thick lip and 10 francs. I only wanted to black my face that night and could have imitated a coon all right. It is a fine sport and I like it. Do you think we shall have peace before long?'

Private Arthur Agar. France.

'I have been in France, having landed on 10th July last. I have not been up the line yet, but am expecting to go practically any time now. I am pleased to say that I am with one of the old boys, Tom Smith. Since I have been here my brother Jim has landed out here, but I haven't any idea where he is. Today has been a proper August day, and we need many of them to dry up the mud caused by so much wet. I heard from E. Archer and understand he has been in hospital and is now at the base.'

7 September 1917. *Chiswick Times*
Letter to Rev. Oldfield.

Corporal D. Davies. Somewhere in Belgium.

'I have bad news. Poor old George Peters has, I deeply regret, been killed in our last action. His company had a German strong point to take which was simply infested with German snipers and machine guns and they lost heavily. As far as I can gather, poor George was killed by a sniper. Kindly convey my deep sympathy to his people and tell them that his loss is keenly felt by the boys in his platoon. I was in his platoon for some months and we went through several engagements together. He was never found wanting at a critical moment. Tell them I shall use my best endeavours to ascertain whether he got a decent burial and if possible I shall erect a cross. George must have died within a few yards of my brother Llew, the only difference being that my brother died two and a half years ago, and that the Germans have occupied the territory meanwhile.

I ran across young Fred Bailey last time we were out, and we had a decent time together. I may run across Perc Read soon, for his division is operating upon our left. Also I may strike Arthur Smith, because they are near us too. I have met Drummer W. Allen another of the Old Boys, so you see Sir, it has been quite a gathering of the clans.'

14 September 1917. *Chiswick Times*
Letters to Rev. Oldfield.

Private H. Greenham. On a signalling course.

'We are on parade nearly every hour of the day. Learning lamp signalling. Fritz seems to know troops are stationed here and last time he came he wasn't just satisfied with dropping bombs on us. Still I am not grumbling or I might as well have stayed in civvies. How is the old brigade getting on? I suppose the old band is getting a bit groggy, but I hope you will keep it together until the old boys come marching home.'

Sergeant F.J. Harris. Australian Expeditionary Force.

'Thanks for letter and photograph. I will take it back to Australia. Keeping safe and in good health. Out of the lines at present. Good news from all fronts and hoping the end is in sight. Fortunate to have as my C.O the officer who brought us over the seas. I hope there is no more names added to the shrine.'

21 September 1917. *Chiswick Times*
Letters to Rev. Oldfield.

Gunner R. Clements. Tank Corps.

'I have been in this corps seven months and am getting on very well with my work. Expecting my A.C.1 leave; I have not had any leave since I joined up, but still I cannot grumble as it is not very hard work in this corps. The place is very picturesque down here, about the prettiest place I have ever been in, the only fault is that it is rather an isolated district. But still a book passes many an hour away on a weekend pass to -----.'

Sapper R.H. Sprett. Norfolk.

'I thoroughly enjoyed my ten days' sick leave and am now looking forward to a few more. What do you think of Tidler the 3rd joining the navy? Quite a surprise when I heard it. I am at present in a large convalescent camp and I am likely to be here a few months, as I am in Group 5, the last being 6, as we have to be down to Group 1 before we are fit to go back to our respective depots, so I think I have done well. Remember me to any of the boys that are left.'

Sergeant Walter Burch. France.

'Thank you for your letter which I was very pleased to receive. I did not see you again when I was on leave as I was very queer and could not get about, I thought I would have to go sick but managed to stick it somehow. My brother is getting on well and is now a full corporal in the Royal Flying Corps. The news is very good just now and if the Russians were only playing the game, this business would be nearly finished. Best wishes to all the boys.'

5 October 1917. *Chiswick Times*
Letters to Rev. Oldfield.

Driver R. Eydmann. BEF.

'Keeping in the best of health. I have just got settled down to this sort of life again after being home for ten days leave, and I can tell you it wants a lot of getting used to. I have met Johnny Burgess.

He has been back from leave about a week. That belt you gave me is a great comfort indeed and I shall always recommend them.'

Corporal W. Tilcock. France.

'Keeping fairly fit. Have been to various parts of France, having moved about a lot. We are fairly comfortable except that 'Jerry' seems to have a great liking for nocturnal escapades and seems to think that we prefer his bombs to having a comfortable snooze at night. Sid is still in hospital - some considerable time now. Am living in the hopes of getting leave shortly. Kind remembrance to all the Old Boys.'

12 October 1917. *Chiswick Times*
Letter to Rev. Oldfield.

Sergeant David Davies. BEF.

'No doubt you will be pleased to hear I have been promoted full sergeant. I received a lot of letters asking for particulars about poor George's death. All I can say is we recovered his body from between the lines and that he had a decent burial in a grave, and his boys erected a little wooden cross with his name, number and regiment. It was a most trying time for the battalion, we lost many good lads but we gained the position. We have had a very rough time lately, but still we hope to have a better time in the near future. I have seen my younger brother. Found him in the line operating on our left. We had a fine time together and a lovely 'tuck in'. I don't hope to see him again very soon for we have shifted. I heard from Fred Bailey since his return from leave and he reports all's well.'

19 October 1917. *Chiswick Times*
Letter to Rev. Oldfield.

Sapper P.E. Read. BEF. Flanders.

'Just a few lines to let you know that I am going on allright at present. I am sorry I have not written before as I have been so busy and now I can only do so with my left hand, as I have poisoned my right hand and cannot use it at present, so I am attempting this with my left hand, but I don't think I am making a bad job of it, wondering what you say, sir? Yes Fred Bailey happened to get his leave not long after me. I thought we should manage it together, but no luck. So the Huns have been visiting London pretty regularly lately, but I think they have checked them now and that the French and our airmen are paying them back in their own coin on some of their big places. I see in the Chiswick Times that Fred Bailey has met Davies and one or two more of the old choirboys. I wish I had been there, for you cannot realise the pleasure of seeing old faces out here, sir, to discuss old times over again about camp, football, not forgetting the band.'

26 October 1917. *Chiswick Times*
Letter to Rev. Oldfield.

Trooper Tom Bain. BEF.

'Pretty decent weather out here now. Thank you very much for the Chiswick Times. It is a treat to read a bit of local news. I have heard from my brother Fred, in Serbia, he seems to be quite well. My brother Matthew has been sent to India. I think he will have a better job out there than when he was at the Dardanelles.'

9 November 1917. *Chiswick Times*
Letter to Rev. Oldfield.

Signaller Sid Maunder. Somewhere in France.

'We are in the line but still we are very comfortable and I don't mind adding we could just about stick this for the duration. We are some distance underground, with electric light which comes on in the morning and goes out at night, and we signallers have some beds – yes, real beds – which have been found in some village nearby. It's just like home from home. My brother is quite well. Each week we have the CT sent out from home and it's quite interesting to read our chums letters that come from east and west. The weather, I suppose, we must not grumble, a bit cold at night when we are on duty.'

16 November 1917. *Chiswick Times*
Letters to Rev. Oldfield.

Sapper P.E. Read. BEF.

'Very thankful to you, sir, for that sweater, for it keeps me nice and warm, otherwise I should feel the cold, but I hardly feel it at all now, as my body keeps as warm as toast. Pleased to hear the band is getting on well. I remember the times when we all first learnt 'Galanthea' but I am sorry you have no 'F' flute or piccolos. What a band we shall have if we all are lucky to get back after this, sir. Thank you for the photograph of the old band boys, it did me good to look at the old faces.'

Private F.C. Smith. (Canadians) France.

'Pleased to see in the CT that Ted Cole had won the Military Medal. I should be glad if you could send me a picture of the band taken at Margate. I only wish we could have those times over again, we sure did have some fun, especially when you used to fly round. The weather has been pretty bad. Glad to hear Pic and Bobs will get their leave soon, although 'soon' sometimes means a long time. A Happy Christmas for yourself and all the boys.'

Gunner Jack M. Clarke. British War Hospital. Bath.

'So sorry I have not written for so long, but since November 4th I have been ill. I was sent across last Saturday. I am still in bed but much better; nervous breakdown. I have been in the hardest fighting since the end of July in Ypres sector, and was in the running at Passchendaele. I collapsed one morning on the gun floor, and had to leave the line. I have been through five different hospitals. We are nice and comfy here and the food is good. I am marked by the medical authorities to be kept at home. Hope to be in our dear old church on Christmas Day. I am glad to hear you have turned out a band; 'well done'. I sincerely hope I shall be able to do my share in the brigade, and I hope this war won't last for ever.'

23 November 1917. *Chiswick Times*
Letters to Rev. Oldfield.

Private J. Ager. France.

'I thought I would let you know that my young brother Arthur is reported missing, and unofficially a prisoner, since the 12th of last month. I know he has written to you since he has been out here, and I thought you would like to know about him. The tuition I received on the flute while in the old band has served me in good stead out here as I am in the band as piccolo player. I read in the CT about the new band which you have started and hope it will be as successful as the old one was.'

The Rev. Oldfield reports that a postcard has been received by Arthur's parents from Limberg confirming that he is a prisoner of war and well.

Gunner W. Crisp. BEF.

'I was very pleased to receive your most cheerful letter. I see you have got old Ted Allen home, and I bet he is not sorry. When you see him ask him to drop me a line. I should think our old friend Polly will have a lot to say after this, how he went over the top in his tank. As luck would have it, I stopped in ----- and your letter arrived just in time, so I thought I would sit down and write straight away.'

Private P. Vine. BEF.

'Your letter to hand, I have noted about its contents. I remember Walter Brown who used to ring the bells quite well. By the way my brother Dick is all right, he is living at Guildford; my other brother Wallie is in Hampshire, training men. Sid is still in China, doing well, and I am at the same place. It is a cruel sight to see the villages and churches that are blown to pieces, nothing only bricks left.'

7 December 1917. *Chiswick Times*
St Michaels Men's Society. YMCA in France.

Rev. J.A. Wilson spoke to the society about the YMCA work in France. Ministers of different denominations co-operate. Food is provided and often men have to queue for 40 minutes. There is only one YMCA hut for every 5,000 men. No profit is made and any surplus goes towards providing more huts. Profits from the cinemas will go to providing homes for disabled soldiers and sailors at Bournemouth.

21 December 1917. *Chiswick Times*
Letters to Rev. Oldfield.

Private C.C .Chivers. BEF.

'Sorry not to have written before. Have been in the big advance of November 20th and have been holding the line ever since. We have been having very stiff fighting. The worst experience of any engagement I have been in. Have come out safe and sound but have lost a great many of my comrades. Shell and machine gun fire was terrific. I have heaps of letters to answer having received them all at once when coming out of the line. Over 70 bags of mail were waiting for the battalion. You can imagine the excitement of our lads when they were given out.'

Sergeant Walter Burch. BEF.

'Still A1 and thanks for the woodbines. We were right out of smokes and they came at an opportune moment. Have not been able to write lately but we have been very busy. And the people on our right even more so as no doubt you have seen in the papers. Fitz was caught napping as it had been very quiet on this part of the front – the last place he thought we would attack. It goes to show we are as smart as him and can successfully attack whenever we want to. Glad to hear Ted Cole has got the M.M. and may he live to wear it. I have not seen him since the Arras push when our two battalions met.'

Private F. Barcham. BEF.

'Still in the pink. We are only allowed to write two letters a week. Haven't come across any of the old boys but see from the Chiswick Times that most are well. I hear you have started a new band and hope it will be a success.'

Rifleman George Nash. France.

'This is the first opportunity I have had of writing a proper letter as we have been moving about a lot since I came out. We have just come out of the line for a few days rest ... we have managed to get a fire in our hut, as we found a stove and made a chimney out of biscuit tins, so we managed to make ourselves fairly comfortable.'

17. Italy

An expeditionary force was sent to Italy to assist the Italian army against Austrian and German divisions.

28 December 1917. *Chiswick Times*
Letter to Rev. Oldfield.

<u>Private P.Vine</u>. Italian Expeditionary Force.

'Many thanks for the two boxes of woodbines I received today.... I gave all the boys a packet in my platoon. They came at the right moment as we can't get fags out here at all. Well sir, since I wrote, I have had a long trip, I have arrived in Italy. A very trying journey and have done a great deal of marching to get here. I have seen some strange sights. I daresay you know there are places along the roads to pray at; it would be a pity for the Germans to overrun the place. We can hear the guns in the distance and see the flashes on the mountains.'

28 December 1917. *Chiswick Times*
Lance-Corporal H. Clutterbuck of Heath Gardens, Twickenham – a letter from Italy.

'As we crossed the frontier we were surprised by a floral reception. At every station we were given flowers, fruit, biscuits, cigarettes and souvenirs. Our train was decorated with palm leaves and every man looked like a flower garden. Flowers were in our caps and button holes – green, white and red ribbons in our coats and small flags stuck all over us. There were posters and greetings hung on the bridges. 'Vive la France.' 'Good health to good old England.' 'To our victorious allies. After the train journey we started on a march of many weary miles and as we passed through the towns the people threw flowers at us.'

18 January 1918. *Chiswick Times*
Letter to Rev. Oldfield.

Private P. Vine. Italian Expeditionary Force.

'Thanks for the woodbines. The Italians are holding the Germans back which is why we have been a good distance from the line but likely to go up at any moment. We had a good Christmas with roast pork and Christmas pudding.'

18. Western Front 1918

The German armies, reinforced by extra troops and equipment after the war with Russia ended, launched offensives on the Western Front. Allied armies fell back by as much as 50 miles. Allied counter advances, strengthened by increasing numbers of American troops, led to the end of the war.

4 January 1918. *Chiswick Times*
Letter to Rev. Oldfield.

Sapper P. Read. BEF.

'Still going on A1. Thank you very much for the parcel which I received on Christmas Day on coming back from church in the YMCA Hut. The shirt and socks were just what I wanted, and I shared the soup and pudding with my chums.'

25 February 1918. *Chiswick Times*
Letter to Rev. Oldfield.

Rifleman George Nash. France.

'I was in the line on Christmas Day but came out safe and made up for it later with a Christmas dinner, cigars, cigarettes, a whist drive and a concert.'

25 January 1918. *Chiswick Times*
Winter at the Front.

Trooper S. Barrington gives an account of his journey from the base to the trenches. 'Our biggest enemy has been the severe weather. 'It took three days to get to the front when the train took the wrong turning and we ended up in a town wrecked by the Bosches before they evacuated leaving every house in ruins.'

1 February 1918. *Chiswick Times*
Letters to Rev. Oldfield.

<u>Sergeant Walter Burch</u>. BEF.

He has no news of Ted Cole (Rev. Oldfield has since learned Cole is a prisoner).

'The weather is better. I hope to get leave but that depends upon the coming German offensive. If he does come over he will get it hot. In the papers is news about the food shortage at home and how people are fed up with the war. We too are fed up but must not give up and will make a big effort this year so long as we get the men and munitions.'

22 February 1918. *Chiswick Times*
Letters to Rev. Oldfield.

<u>Private Arthur Bewley</u>.

'I am in hospital in Bury and my arm wound is healing.'

<u>Sergeant Walter Burch</u>. BEF.

'I'm sorry to hear how Ted Cole has been wounded and taken prisoner. What about the coming German offensive? We are ready for him. Fairly quiet here – mostly trench mortar and long-distance artillery fire.'

8 March 1918. *Chiswick Times*
Trooper Syd Barrington.

'Recent gas shells and bombs have had little effect but we are anxiously waiting for the German offensive. I watched two of our planes scrapping with two of Fritz's that turned tail with some damage.'

28 March 1918. *Chiswick Times*
Letters to Rev. Oldfield.

<u>Air Mechanic Will James</u>.

'Landing aeroplanes at night is not an easy thing. I expect to go overseas soon and we have been trying to start a drum and fife band.'

Sergeant Walter Burch. BEF.

'Very sorry to hear Ted Cole had has a foot amputated after going through everything as a POW. Very lively on both sides especially with aircraft day and night. I'm expecting leave soon.'

Rifleman G. Nash. BEF.

'All A1. We are expecting big things from Fritz but he will catch a packet as we are fully prepared. I see from the Chiswick Times that the tanks are visiting Chiswick and I hope the fundraising goes well and gives Fritz all he wants in the way of 5.9s and 9.2s. I am in a new regiment and it was hard at leaving the old one. Glorious weather.'

29 March 1918. *Chiswick Times*
Letters to Rev. Oldfield.

Sergeant Walter Burch. BEF.

'Still in the land of the living. Snow and wind here. I hope Ted Cole gets over his wound and that Fritz is not starving him. Any news of Billy Kelly who was taken prisoner in August 1914? I have received the Mons Medal Ribbon and expect service badges soon. I may be posted home for six months perhaps as a bombing instructor and I look forward to being home but, and I don't know why, but don't like the idea of leaving my old battalion. We read a lot in the papers about the coming enemy offensive but I think the Germans smell a rat round this district. Things are not quiet here but I have been in many a worst spot. I hope Japan steps in. Best wishes to all the boys.'

Rifleman Will Lawrence. BEF.

'Pleased to hear that the Chiswick air raid was not so bad, as one worries until we hear from our homes. Glad that Jack Clarke and Goodie Barnes are getting on well and I hope they get their discharges. Glad to hear you still have the old church parades and I hope and expect the old boys will go round to the club where I spent many pleasant hours. Out of the line for a while, thank goodness, as it was a bit cold at night. The sweater you gave me came in handy.'

5 April 1918. *Chiswick Times*
Letter to Rev. Oldfield.

Pioneer W Sheppard. France.

'Thanks for letters and palm and safe and well. Our Division was
the first to be attacked. We bore the most of it for five days. A fearful
business. There was terrific gunfire from both sides. I kept a look
out in the London regiments but saw none of our boys. Most in the
division are North Country chaps. We came out of action and are now
resting. The King and General Plumer visited at two hours' notice.'

19 April 1918. *Chiswick Times*
Letter to Rev. Oldfield.

Sergeant Walter Burch. BEF.

'Thousands have had leave cancelled and there is no need to tell
you why. We have had a very hard time but casualties are not heavy
considering the amount of lead thrown at us. Weather favoured the
enemy for the first six days. Since then there has been a lot of rain
and we were pleased to be out of action and able to get some sleep.
We were under terrible bombardment on Good Friday.'

3 May 1918. *Chiswick Times*
Letter to Rev. Oldfield.

Private F.C. Smith. Canadian BEF

'People in Blighty must think we are losing just now but Jerry
will get it in the neck before long. The weather is unsettled. Glad
I took my leave when I did but it was bad luck that my brother's
leave came just as I was going back.'

17 May 1918. *Chiswick Times*
Letters to Rev. Oldfield.

Private Sid Turner. France.

'I think we have got Fritz by the throat. His advance was to put
the peace terms more in his favour but he has lost a terrible lot of

men. Our machine guns are not a very nice weapon. One German we captured was sixteen and had been in the army for only two weeks. I have just been making a hot dinner over a candle fire in the dugout with some bully beef and biscuits. The biscuits make good dumplings when boiled.'

Sapper P.F. Read. France.

'In the pink. Fritz has only one leg to stand on and has lost a lot of men. He is against the steel of the world, which he cannot break through although he bends it a little. Sorry to hear Johnnie Goddard has been killed and hope Harry Smith is not too badly wounded. Glad to hear the band is going strong.'

Driver W. Carpenter. France.

'We have had narrow escapes in the big push, but things are a bit better now. On our front we have held him.'

31 May 1918. *Chiswick Times*
Letter to Rev. Oldfield.

Driver Fred Bailey. France.

'Had a letter from Bill Smith in Egypt. He supposes a few more St Mary's boys are casualties and taken prisoner. The Germans are trying hard to break our army but I think we'll master him in the end. Everyone seems to be in good cheer but naturally everybody is fed up at times. I hear D. Davies is going into the Flying Corps. I hope the band is up to the form of the old one.'

31 May 1918. *Chiswick Times*
Letter to Rev. Oldfield.

Private Sid Turner.

'I was shot in hand by a German officer and taken prisoner but was left unguarded and by following a railway line got back to a French Red Cross station and then to the British lines. At one place I was cared for by Canadian nurses who were very good. An x-ray indicates I may lose two fingers.'

19 July 1918. *Chiswick Times.*
Letters to Rev. Oldfield.

Signaller W Gray. France.

'I believe you like to hear from St Mary's Old Lads. Saw Bob Scanlon last December and he is OK.'

Sapper P. Read. Army Service Corps. France.

'Going on alright. Glad to hear the bands came in second against older lads and are keeping up the old reputation and that that Ralph conducted the bands. I suppose they disbanded all military bands when Fritz started his tricks.'

9 August 1918. *Chiswick Times*
Letter to Rev. Oldfield.

Private Harry Lewis. France.

'I might come across George Mason who is in the same division as me. I was in England and saw Chris Smith. We came over in the same boat. I do not think the war will last much longer, so we shall have to look forward to the times we have had at Margate. Different here as to what it was at Margate. Here we get shells; there we got sixpen'worth of rock.'

20 September 1918. *Chiswick Times*
Letter to Rev. Oldfield.

Private H. Lewis. France.

'Just come out of the line and feel a lot cleaner. If the enemy shells for an hour our artillery shells him for ten hours so it don't pay him to shell much. I wish I was where my younger brother is, at camp, it would suit me best.'

25 October 1918. *Chiswick Times*
Letter to Rev. Oldfield.

Private F.V.C. Smith. Canadians. France.

'The Old Boys seem to be well represented over the fighting area; hope they will all have the luck to get back safely. You will have some fine stories very shortly. The boys here that are convalescing get down to the beach for a little exercise. I am in the band which plays at concert parties and sometimes for the officers who are convalescent in a large house by the beach.'

19. Russia, 1918

British troops were dispatched to Russia to fight on the side of the White Russians in the civil war against the Bolshevik government.

20 September 1918. *Chiswick Times*
Letter to Rev. Oldfield.

Bombardier R. Hutton. Russia.

'Arrived safely after a pleasant voyage thanks to the Navy. Under canvass close to a few wooden huts. Everything here is made of wood. Around us are miles of forest and hills – a very pretty spot had I been in England. The earth is all swamp – barren and difficult to get around. During this part of the year there is no darkness – a beautiful sight at midnight when the sun sets. The weather is treacherous – warm in the day and very cold at night. The Russian people look as though they have suffered a great deal. I hope the two bands are still going strong and keeping up the old reputations.'

20 December 1918. *Chiswick Times*
Letter to Rev. Oldfield.

Robert Hutton. North Europe Expeditionary Force in Russia.

'This is a great adventure. When we arrived there was the midnight sun. Now it is winter here and there are the northern lights – a thousand searchlights of mingled green blue and white. The days are all darkness and there is plenty of snow. One day it was 30 degrees below and the next day a spring day at its best. News of the armistice was read to us a few days ago. Fighting has finished in France but not in Russia to our discomfort. We hope to give the Bolsheviks the same as the Huns received. Very sorry to hear Len Allen and Will Lawrence making the supreme sacrifice.'

21 February 1919. *Chiswick Times*
Letter to Rev. Oldfield.

Corporal Robert Hutton. Northern European Expeditionary Force, Russia.

'Thanks for the parcel and particularly the jersey – the most warm producing garment a Tommy can have for this horrid country. The weather is so cold that railway truck wheels crack like a rifle shot and dogs are used for transport purposes. They can draw surprisingly heavy loads at a good pace. Winter clothing has been issued and it takes about half an hour to dress each morning. – Three pairs of socks, long stockings, Shackleton boots, jersey, cardigan, leather jerkin, a Burbury suit, a fur cap and a fur lined greatcoat. Yet with the thermometer at 30 degrees below we are glad to get back into the hut and warm air. London must be looking like pre-war days with the boys coming home and all the lamps alight which we hope to see before long. Rumours say we are leaving soon but if we travelled by rumours we should by now have travelled round the world.'

5 September 1919. *Chiswick Times*
Letter to a local resident from a Richmond man serving with the navy about a raid on Kronstadt in Russia.

'Something happened on Sunday equal to Zeebrugge in brilliance and glory. While the operation was in preparation the aircraft carrier HMS Vindictive's band was playing and the Bolshies at Petrograd must have thought we were not alert and enjoying ourselves.

We arrived at Kapuri Bay off Kronstadt at about 11.30pm. A beautiful moonlit night suitable for an air raid. The planes reminded me of the raids in the Great War, and the coastal motor boats (CMBs), scooters as we call them, recalled stunts with the Harwich force under Tyrwhitt. I was on middle watch and at 1.20am we witnessed large explosions and many more followed. The harbour must have been in uproar.

At 8am we received a signal – 'Andrei, Jereskain, Petreopadlosk torpedoed. Submarine depot ship and trooper torpedoed. Further details later. All aircraft returned but three CMBs lost.'

Kronstadt, the impregnable fortress, was impregnable no more – at least to the British Navy. This magnificent achievement was only marred by the loss of gallant lives, but how many Bolshies perished is hard to say. We have no grievance and feel proud we belong to the navy and doff our caps to our heroic brothers.'

Another signal. 'The captain and officers and the ship's company of HMS ----- warmly congratulate the officers and crews of the CMBs on their most gallant success and offer sympathy with those who never returned.'

One CMB blew the obstructions to the harbour entrance while aircraft started the camouflage air raid. The CMBs rushed in and cruised around the harbour and some Bolshies were gazing over their ships' sides in astonishment as torpedoes were released and the scooters fled in the twilight. One scooter dropped a depth charge but failed to get clear. We had a few of the wounded who said the gun fire and barrage was awful.

We would like to be at Blighty but there is work to be done and we all want to be in at the fall of Kronstadt.'

Research indicates that one warship and an oil tanker were disabled in the raid.

20. Prisoners of War

9 July 1915. *Chiswick Times*
Released from Germany – prisoner exchange

Private Walter Matthews of the Royal Army Medical Corps, who was made a prisoner at Mons by the Germans and after 10 months has been released through an exchange of prisoners is now at his home, 11 Lancaster Cottages, Richmond. He has had unenviable experiences which, however, are of great interest, but he is so modest that no doubt he would have refused to be drawn by the interviewer but for the fact that he desires to express his sincere gratitude to those who have been so kind to his wife and children during his absence, and to those who have been good enough to send him parcels. Equally he desires to take the opportunity to appeal to everyone who can do so to help the boys who are still prisoners in Germany, by sending them parcels of foodstuffs.

Private Matthews went through a part of the Boer War, then came out on reserve. He returned to Richmond where his mother lives, and was employed as a roundsman by Messrs. Edwards in connection with their dairy in Friars' Stile Road. His term of enlistment was up in 1913 and he re-engaged so on the outbreak of war he was called up and, leaving his wife and two children, he was soon on his way to France. He was at the battle of Mons, and with over 300 others of the Royal Army Medical Corps (R.A.M.C.), was taken prisoner while attending to the wounded and burying the dead. The British wounded were of the Guards. Pte Matthews was actually engaged in burying four Germans when the R.A.M.C. were made prisoners. With a guard over them, the R.A.M.C. men were taken to Mons station and put on a train for a town in Westphalia.

'We had a bad time. In the front of the same train were many German wounded and that seemed to make the German population more angry with us. We were in cattle trucks and our train was continually being stopped, and the German troops, who were on their way to France, spat at us and in some cases climbed up on the trucks and struck at us. They were the worse for drink. The women who came near the train were as bad as the men in their conduct towards us. You can judge the sort of journey we had there by the fact that it took us three and a half days to go, whereas we came back in 24 hours, when we were released. Of course, when our men were hit they daren't hit back. We had no grub except some stale bread. When we arrived at the internment camp, we had no tents or huts to go into and we were exposed to the rain for three or four nights. Then they put up some tents, which were not much better than being in the open. It was a struggle for food. We had to stand in a line in the rain, and sometimes you did not get any. What food there was insufficient. The food was issued as follows:

In the morning, 4am-6am – half a pint of 'coffee' made of burnt barley. No sugar of course. Dinner, between 12 & 1 – three quarters of a pint of soup, in which were black horse beans, and a very small portion of horseflesh, really unfit to eat, but they had to eat it as there was nothing else until the English parcels came. As each line of soldiers had their allowance, more water was shot in to the soup, with the result that the last line that was served got practically all water. In the evening, about 6 o'clock – maize which was crushed up fine and boiled, making a sort of porridge. At 2.30, a piece of bread, called black, but looking brown, was served out with a piece of sausage (far from nice) about four inches long, to each man. It was issued every 24 hours for tea or breakfast.

It was only the parcels from England that kept us alive. But for those parcels I suppose that very few of us would have returned to England. We were in a pitiable condition up to December. Then the parcels came through pretty frequently, and we used to share the contents. We always relied on getting one or two parcels a week, and with the little bit of German food we kept going. The only extras the Germans gave us was five cigars each at Christmas (which would be worth about a penny for the five in England)

Private Matthews, who went to Aldershot on 5 August, was captured on 26 August.

'When we were made prisoners, the Germans took away our razors and knives, and we all grew beards. We used to feed from 3-pint iron bowls, with which they allowed no spoons. It was our high spirits that kept us alive. That was what the Germans could not understand. They can't understand the high spirits of the British soldier. When we first went there we were all British soldiers together, but later they mixed us with French, Belgians and Russians. But the Russians were afterwards moved and put on farms to work. The huts that the prisoners are now in were built by the English and French who also made railway lines. The majority of the prisoners are now working on farms or in mines. Of course, they have to do the work and for it they get the magnificent sum of a ha'penny a day. Those remaining in the camp received no pay at all. I stayed in the camp as I did washing for the sergeant-majors. There was no possible chance of escape from the camp as there was a German guard and three rows of wire, the middle one being electrified. Maxim guns were also trained on the camp. We got on much better with the guards who were English speaking. For the least little thing that went wrong, there was punishment, and that consisted of being tied to a post for two to four hours. When it was raining or snowing, that was very bad, as our overcoats had been taken from us.

'When we were first there, they used to parade the school children around the camp to look at us, and at first when anybody came to look at the prisoners, the commandant would order us first to stand and then to sit. The soldiers used to be jumping up and down a good part of the day. We first heard in October a rumour of the possibility of our being sent back to England, but that fell through, and the same happened in February. When we heard of it again this time we did not believe it was true. We could not believe our good luck until we got into Holland. We thought we were going into the German hospitals to nurse the wounded. We had such a royal reception in Holland that, after having heard no kind words for so long, tears came into our eyes. We had a very good time on the boat, in fact, from the time we got to Holland right up to now, as I speak, and I am so overjoyed that I don't know how to thank the public for their kindness towards my wife while I was imprisoned out there.

'My employers, Messrs. Edwards, have been very good to my wife, and numerous other people have also been kind. A son was born to us while I was in Germany, and when I received information that my employers and other people had been so kind to my wife it took a great load off my mind. I wrote thanking people for their kindness but I have now discovered only one postcard was received. I hope people will not think it is any fault of mine as I used to write frequently. Numerous friends sent me parcels which, I am sorry to say, I did not receive, but still I am grateful to them. The parcels are going through much better now, and prisoners are more likely to get them if they are addressed properly and tied up nicely and securely. The chief thing the men want is tinned foods. Bread should be put in greasy paper to preserve it. Tea is a God-send to them. Also tinned milk, biscuits and cocoa. Those who have friends there should send them parcels and our men will appreciate it exceedingly. It is the only thing keeping the British prisoners alive. I want to continue to help my comrades. The first thing we did when we got back to Aldershot and received our pay was to make a collection and we got 15s to send the boys a parcel.'

When the prisoners were separated, Pte Matthews was put in No.2 camp. The commandant, who came in December – 'his name was something like Dr Vennerman' – was much better than the previous commandant. He had had an English education and used to do the best he could for them. He got a piece of ground for the Englishmen to play football on. His under officers were also better than the previous ones. Incidentally, Pte Matthews mentioned, that it was no good sending writing paper and envelopes to the prisoners as they had to buy the German materials. The trawler men had a very had time. The Germans said they were minelayers, and if they did anything amiss their punishment was more severe than the other men. As punishment they sent them up on the roof without boots or socks. The trawler men particularly deserved to share in parcels sent as many of them had no friends able to send them anything. He mentioned that he had received parcels from Miss Lang of East Molesey, and Mrs. Harris of Harrow-on-the-Hill, who had presumably seen his name published somewhere. A man who had not received many parcels was Pte Coulston, of the cookhouse at Sennelaager II.

A very curious fact was that the censor in Pte Matthew's camp was a young German who had previously lived in Richmond and St Margaret's and he desired Pte Matthews to visit some friends of his in Richmond and St Margaret's when he got back to England. Three Richmond men whom Pte Matthews knew to be prisoners in Germany were Pte H.E. Wheatley, Pte Westlake, and Lance-corporal Mackay. Pte Wheatley was employed at Richmond Post Office until called up. He is in the Middlesex Regiment and his relatives live in Sheen Rd. Lance Corporal Mackay is in the Royal Irish, and his wife lives at Mary Cottage, St John Grove, with her father, Mr. Gay. 'When Private Matthews left, they were all well. He states, as a note for anyone sending parcels, that his came safely addressed as follows: 'Private W Matthews, 14870, R.A.M.C. Sennelaager II via Paderborn, Germany.'

When the R.A.M.C. men were about to be released, they were called together by the under-commandant, who said, 'Men you are going to your homes and your friends. When you get to the other side you will have thousands of reporters around you, and as long as you speak the truth we have nothing to be afraid of.' He then wished them good-bye.

Private Matthews arrived at Richmond a little earlier than expected on Saturday, but by good luck he saw his wife as she was crossing the road near the station to go to his mother's to tell her of her husband's arrival. He is home on a fortnight's leave after which he returns to Aldershot.

3 September 1915. *Chiswick Times*
Chiswick prisoners in Germany – how to get bread to them.

A Mr. Malcolm writes that most of the bread sent to POWs through Holland arrives in an uneatable condition. However the British section of the Prisoners Help Society, in Switzerland, bakes and sends hundreds of loaves to POWs in Germany. He recommends that no more bread be sent from Britain and that money contributions be sent to Mrs. Grant Duff, at the British Legation in Berne. Because of its geographical position, bread from Berne arrives in good condition.

10 September 1915. *Chiswick Times*
Letter to Rev. Oldfield.

<u>10933 Rifleman W. Ward</u>, 1ˢᵗ King's Royal Rifle Corps, Gefangenenlager, Osterterp, Krais, Appenvade, Schleswig, Germany.

'I have received mother's letter and card. Parcels and letters, although they take a long time, always reach us safe and in good condition. The post is very good considering the difficulties.'

1 October 1915. *Chiswick Times*
Letter to Rev. Oldfield.

<u>Private J.H. Jenkinson.</u> POW. Royal Fusiliers, Block 9, Gefangenenlager, Doeberitz.

'A few lines from England greatly cheer us up. I've received a parcel from a lady with no sender's address please thank the sender.

They should be packed in a strong box as the parcel was damaged. I would be grateful something in the way of bread.'

The Rev. Oldfield has arranged for a weekly supply of bread, baked in Berne, to be sent to a number of POWs.

22 October 1915. *Chiswick Times*
Letters to Rev. Oldfield.

Rifleman W. Ward. POW. Germany.

'The bread from Berne reaches me quite safe and in splendid condition. Sir, could you send me some margarine or anything to spread on the bread, and a pair of socks? I have received four parcels from you since 30th June.'

Private George Jewell. POW. Germany. Letter to his mother.

'Very pleased with the parcel. The contents were all right but the bread was bad and mouldy. I am also receiving a parcel from Berne in Switzerland. Please tell Mr. Oldfield that I thank him very much.'

Drummer George Revell. POW. Germany.

'I have received all your parcels up to date, also the first consignment of bread from Berne. Everything going well. Can you manage to send me a batch of comic songs as we are giving concerts every fortnight?'

5 November 1915. *Chiswick Times*
Letters to Rev. Oldfield.

Sergeant W. Burgess. 2nd Border Regiment, Gottingen, Hanover, Germany. POW.

Dated 11 Oct, received 1st Nov. 1915.

'Many thanks for post card, dated 11th September, received 5th October. I am very pleased to say that I have received two weekly issues of the bread from Switzerland up to date, and both were in splendid condition. It is far better than sending it from England. I have also received the parcels and a postcard from the lady to whom you gave my address, Miss W.H. and I am pleased to say they are very nice and greatly appreciated.'

Corporal Charles Brown. Royal Horse Artillery. Kompagnie Nr 2623, Gefangenenlager, Stendal, Deutschland. POW.

'Many thanks for your parcels I received on 6th September. I am sorry to say the loaves are bad. I have received a card from Switzerland to say they are sending me two loaves of bread every week. I thank you for your kindness for loaves will be very acceptable.'

An Appeal: Rev. A.E. Oldfield has now arranged for a weekly supply of bread to be sent to all the Chiswick prisoners of war in Germany whose addresses he has. He will be very grateful for shirts, socks, sweaters, gloves and underclothing, new or old, for men at the front, which are much needed now, also any cardigan jackets.

19 November 1915. *Chiswick Times*
Letter to Rev. Oldfield.

Private J.H. Jenkinson. POW Germany.

Pleased to receive bread from Berne and he asks for a shirt and socks.

7 January 1916. *Chiswick Times*
Letters to Rev. Oldfield.

Lance Corporal J. Delhwary. Paderborn, Germany.

'Pleased to acknowledge receipt on 16th Nov of your welcome parcel. Thanking you for the bread, which was in good condition. Sir, I thank you to stop it as Lady Jerard is also sending bread. I have received five parcels, containing in all ten loaves, from Berne, and postcard to say they are sending two loaves weekly. I thank you sir for embrocation. If you think of sending clothes, a cardigan jacket or underclothing, I will be thankful for your kindness; or shaving outfit'.

Private F.H. Marshall. 1st South Staffordshire Regiment. POW, Germany.

Just a line to say I received the first parcel of bread from Switzerland. I hope I have the pleasure of thanking you personally when I come home.'

16 January 1916. *Chiswick Times*
Letter to Rev. Oldfield.

Drummer George Revell, POW. Germany.

'Christmas week is here now and we have proper Christmas weather. About 9in of snow on the ground, and this morning temperature 21 degrees below freezing. Five minutes in the open air and there are miniature icicles on a man's moustache. Well Sir the compliments of the season to you and Chiswick.'

3 March 1916. *Chiswick Times*
Letter to Rev. Oldfield.

Private E. Collard. POW. Germany.

'I feel I must write and thank you for your kindness to me in this time of trouble and strife. I have already received two nice parcels from the lady you secured to look after my interests, regarding parcels and need not say how much I appreciate it. In this camp there is only one other Chiswick man, Private Kelly, King's Own Scottish Borderers, so you see we are not very well represented here.'

24 March 1916. *Chiswick Times*
Letter to Rev. Oldfield.

Private E. Pollard. POW. Germany.

'Thank you so much for the postcard and parcel. I am very glad to hear my brother has got the D.C.M. I may also say I am receiving parcels from Miss T.'

21 April 1916. *Chiswick Times*
Letter to Rev. Oldfield.

Private J.H. Jenkinson. POW, Germany.

'I thank you very much for the parcel of underclothing so kindly sent from Berne. I have just received a card from Mrs. B. She sent me a parcel a short time ago and I am very grateful to you both for your kindness. Glad to say the bread is still arriving.'

5 May 1916. *Chiswick Times*
Letter to Rev. Oldfield.

Rifleman W. Ward. POW. Germany.

'Thank you very much for the clothing and bread just received from Berne. I cannot help my mother, only having received one card from since November. Please could you send my mate's (Mick Lock's) address? How are all the boys?'

26 May 1916. *Chiswick Times*
Letter to Rev. Oldfield.

Lance Corporal F. Garrett. POW. Germany.

'A few lines to say how grateful I am to you for your kindness in continuing to send two loaves of bread a week from Switzerland. It is a great help as they come quicker and therefore fresher.'

9 June 1916. *Chiswick Times*
Letter to Rev. Oldfield.

Rifleman W. Ward. POW. Germany.

'Please would you find out for me Mich Lock's address and how he is getting on? I have not heard from him for a long time. Please sir, have you an old football you could send us out to pass the time away?'

20 October 1916. *Chiswick Times*

**Chiswick Working Men's Club. Letters received by Mr. Thomas
A. King, secretary of the club.**

Sergeant McQuinn writes from a German prison camp.

'I was in Mauritius in 1911 and when I returned to Chiswick
in 1914 only one man knew me – Fred Whiting. Most of the old
boys had left Chiswick. I was with the first Expeditionary Force in
August 1914 and was in the battle of Mons and the retirement to
St. Quentin. I was wounded in the leg at Le Cateau and in agony
during a 36 hour farm wagon ride to the St. Quentin hospital. Was
captured when the Germans overran the hospital. After some time
a four days' journey to a German hospital in Gottingen, and then
on October 14th to the Gefangenenlager camp.

I'm employed on the camp staff in charge of the British prisoners
in control of the parcel, letter, money order, and inquiry departments
working from 8am to 5pm – office hours, but often working two
or three hours in my quarters in the evening on correspondence
connected with control and distributions, etc.

I'm treated very well and have separate quarters and many other
little privileges and am on good terms with the camp officials
and always treated courteously. Altogether I am a very lucky man,
considering that I am a prisoner. I'm sorry to hear of the death of
Cllr Leith.'

3 November 1916. *Chiswick Times*

Letter to Rev. Oldfield.

Private E. Collard. POW. Doeberitz.

'Thanks for the bread from Berne which still arrives safely. I
have heard from my sister and am grateful to hear my brother
is still well. Winter will soon be on us; suppose it is the same
in England.'

November 1916. *Chiswick Times*
Letter to Rev. Oldfield.

Private E. Collard. POW. Doeberitz.

'Thanks for the bread from Berne which still arrives safely. I have heard from my sister and am grateful to hear my brother is still well. Winter will soon be on us; suppose it is the same in England.'

26 January 1917. *Chiswick Times*
Richmond prisoners in Switzerland.

Mrs. K. Cook writes about her son, Drummer S. Cook of the 2nd Wiltshire Regiment, a POW now interned at Leysin, Switzerland, and she thanks Sir James Szlumper for his kindness in sending parcels to the interned POWs. She has visited her son through the Red Cross. The Swiss think the world of them. The men are in convalescence at Leysin, 14,000ft above sea level.

23 March 1917. *Chiswick Times*
Letter to Rev. Oldfield.

Private E.Collard. Gefangene Egyptlager. Doeberitz.

'Just a line to let you know that now I am getting along here. My health is better than a few weeks ago. I receive the bread every week from Berne. Just heard from my sister that you were asking about me. Weather here very cold.'

4 May 1917. *Chiswick Times*
Letter to Rev. Oldfield.

Private J.H. Jenkinson. POW. Dyrotz, Deutschland.

'I am still receiving my bread from Berne and I have just received a parcel from the same place. Pleased to say I am keeping well.'

18 January 1918. *Chiswick Times*
Letter to Rev. Oldfield.

<u>Private J.H. Jenkinson</u>. POW. Germany
Though exiled by the luck of war,
We send you greetings from afar.
All doubts in Dyrotz we disarm
Before the coming Christmas charm

1 February 1918. *Chiswick Times*
Letter to Rev. Oldfield.

<u>Sergeant E.J. Cole</u>. MM. Sottan Z., Germany.

'I am a prisoner of war with a nasty wound in the foot, which the doctor said he had saved for me. I also hope, sir, you will write for me to the Red Cross and get me some parcels as it's the only way we can get anything. Roll on the finish of the war and let's gather in the old clubroom again. A message for my wife – Don't worry about me; I am alright and I can stick it.'

25 February 1918. *Chiswick Times*
Letter to Rev. Oldfield.

<u>Acting Sergeant J. Cook</u>, MM. POW. Germany.

'I've been wounded and am a prisoner of war. Trying to stick it and shall get along all right.'

31 May 1918. *Chiswick Times*
Letter to Rev. Oldfield.

<u>Private F. Locke</u>. Sherwood Foresters. POW Germany.

'Cigarettes safely received. I have all the clothes from the regiment so is all right now.'

9 August 1918. *Chiswick Times*
Letter to Rev. Oldfield.

Private G. Lewis. Germany.

'Had the misfortune of being taken prisoner of war. Very pleased to hear Polly Clements has joined the tanks. Pleased to hear George Mason has joined up and he should be a sergeant as he was with in the brigade. [*Six lines blacked out by the Germans*].' He mentions 'a smoke' – one of Tommy's favourite things after a day's work.'

20 September 1918. *Chiswick Times*
Letter to Rev. Oldfield.

Private F. Locke (Bert). POW. Germany.

'I received 300 cigarettes on July 30th on my birthday. I had a grand pudding on my birthday – dates made of biscuits. I would like a pair of boots as I am working in my bare feet, and can't wear clogs.'

Corporal Walter Cole. POW. Germany.

'Could you send me a small packet of literature as it is very monotonous here and nobody has any books. It is four years ago that we were at Margate together. Remember me to all I know.'

27 December 1918. *Chiswick Times*
A Prisoner's Story.

Private Percival V. Wagstaff of the *Chiswick Times* printing staff has returned after a stay of nine months as an unwilling guest of Germany. He had won the Military Medal and although subsequently regraded in a lower category volunteered again, went to France in March when he was taken prisoner. He speaks fairly well of his treatment at the hands of 'Jerry'. For a time they were guarded in Belgium by Alsace-Lorrainers, who allowed the women to bring them food. The Prussians took over and were much more rigorous and they worked from three in the morning to 8.30 at night. On one occasion they were marched up and down a ploughed field to make it level for an aeroplane landing. Food was a litre of doubtful looking soup and a third of a loaf a day. The dietary level of the Germans was also low. Some of the prisoners resorted to eating boiled potato peelings, but generally speaking they were kept in fairly good health under the circumstance. Germans often gave him cigarettes and some of them are not bad fellows, he says.

When they were freed they were sent towards Holland but the Dutch guards would not allow them over so they found their way to Ghent where the Belgians treated them in great style. At Brussels they were treated as heroes but the finest reception was when they landed at Dover and sirens sent up deafening noises and the people freely welcomed them.

Several *Chiswick Times* staff have been home on leave. Rifleman E.G. Williams returns to France on Tuesday where he is attached to a POW camp. Private Brown has been with the East Surreys. Lance Corporal Fullegar is a military policemen serving in Ireland. Pioneer Barnes is in hospital with the 'flu'. Recent letters have been received from Gunner Argent, Sapper Bayles, Private Rose and Gunner Wentworth.

27 December 1918. *Chiswick Times*
Germany's Treatment of Prisoners.

Nurse Walsh, attached to the French Red Cross for two years, writes to her parents at Adelaide Road, Richmond.

'I have seen many sad cases of prisoners coming through on their way home. I think the Germans should be given the same rations as the POWs have had. Some are in hospital too ill to travel. Owing to the revolution in Germany many POWs were just turned on to the road. It is believed that about 50 have died from exhaustion. I hope that is not true but it may be, judging from the weak state of many. The idea about what was happening in Germany was when they saw their guards tearing off their iron crosses and army numbers. Some of the POWs wore German hats and French trousers – all so shabby looking like tramps. Dressings had been attached with crinkled paper bandages. I have a piece of bread that appears to be made of sawdust.'

17 January 1919. *Acton Gazette and Express*
Corporal Woodman. POW repatriated.

Of 91, Shakespeare Road, Acton.

He served three years in France, twice wounded, before being taken prisoner near Arras on 28 March 1917. At first reported missing but parents informed he was a POW after two months.

He was put to work on munition dumps and was in a state of semi-starvation under often cruel discipline. Parcels from home saved his life. Long marches were frequent and once at the end of a 50 mile tramp they had to bivouac in an open damp field.

Representing himself as a dock worker he was sent to Geestemunde near the mouth of the Weser and employed in a shipyard where the treatment was better, but he was beaten in the head with a bayonet and imprisoned for 28 days for taking potatoes from a field.

When the armistice was signed they were told by revolutionary marines they were to be free, but were taken to a camp at Parchim, Meckenburg for a month before being shipped to Sweden where he spent Christmas. During the worst part of captivity he was reduced almost to a skeleton. He is now back at home at 91, Shakespeare Road, Acton and has put on weight, yet is still shaken by his privations.

24 January 1919. *Acton Gazette and Express*
Able Bodied Seaman Gordon Hanson. POW experiences.

A report after he arrived home at 40 Hereford Road, Acton.

After being taken prisoner with 600 others he was taken to Doberitz in October 1914 where he worked digging training trenches for German soldiers. Food was sparse but food parcels arrived regularly. There was cruel discipline and punishment was being hung from a pole until some fainted. He saw three or four men shot dead for trivial offences. Starvation deaths were frequent. In May 1915 he was working in coalmines where the food was better.

After a back injury and a spell in hospital, where the treatment was good, he went to Muncheburg where the treatment was fairly decent and he was working on an airfield. He and other prisoners were billeted with civilians and he was paid up to five marks a day.

The Germans were cock-a-hoop over their 1917 victories and they were shown pictures of bombed London. Some of them were employed as dustmen in Berlin. He did not suffer from lack of clothing as others did as he had his dark prisoner's uniform and some clothes came from England.

When the armistice came the German soldiers took their buttons from their caps and gave officers 24 hours to clear out. A sergeant major then took command of the camp. Prisoners struck and were allowed passes into the town but had to be back by 8pm. Visits to Berlin were allowed. He saw something of the street fighting and found the revolutionaries, especially the sailors, very affable. Troops from the front claimed they had won an internal victory.

On December 23rd two English officers took charge of the camp and a party of 300 left on January 7th for Holland. The Americans did wonderful work looking after them at first until the British took over, rigging them up with new clothes. It is a sight seeing them waiting for a bath, about 600 English one side and French, Italians, Russians and Rumanians on the other. One boy was the picture of good health. For four and a half years he had been a cook and an officer's servant.

He arrived in England on Sunday morning where, after two nights at Ripon, he was granted two months leave and he hopes for a discharge.

7 February 1919. *Acton Gazette and Express*
Acton POW's sufferings.

Private J.C. Williams, 2nd Kings Own Yorkshire Regiment, was taken prisoner almost at the war's beginning. He spent 18 months in Russia including three in the firing line. 37 of the 500 who were with him in Russia died from starvation and exposure. One was murdered by a sentry and 385 were admitted to so-called hospitals with frostbite.

21. End of the War

15 November 2018. *Acton Gazette and Express.*
Peace! Acton Celebrations

The news spread on Monday, at the Post Office, the Council Offices, the Fire Station, whispered at first from place to place. Then people gathered at front doors, flags appeared in upper storey windows and the High Street was transformed into a gala. At 10.30am two rockets went up from the Police Station – usually a sign of an air raid and then bugle boys were in the streets blowing the 'All Clear'. More and more flags – on the Council Offices, churches and schools. Church bells rang. In the streets people shook hands and slapped one another on their backs. People ran to get flags.

At one of the few remaining old fashioned houses in the High Street a usually sedate middle-aged gentleman marched up and down his front garden ringing a large dinner bell amid approving cheers from passengers on passing buses.

Children at school, once the news arrived, were given an extra long play interval and there was scant attendance in the afternoon. Many of them joined the celebrations waving flags, beating tin drums and footbaths anticipating the special next day's holiday.

At the Council Offices joy was mingled with sadness that Mr. H. Hodson, the clerk, had lost a son in the last Zeppelin raid and a daughter from the influenza.

Workers left the factories in droves and Munitionettes linked arms to parade the High Street waving Union Jacks and Stars and Stripes in the Vale. Men and girls came down in trams along Horn Lane from the Park Royal factories to join in the excitement.

Yet while this was going on house painters in Stanley Gardens steadily continued touching up window sills. The Public Houses weren't open yet, which was just as well, but there was a rush when opening time came.

Flags were everywhere in the poorer streets, especially in South Acton and Klondyke, where working class patriotism eclipsed the displays of 'villadom.' Every little tenement had little flags in every window and messages were attached to door posts. 'God Bless our Boys.' 'Remember the Fallen.' 'God Bless our Home.' 'For King and Country.' On display were portraits of Kitchener, military and naval leaders and prominent politicians.

Khaki was conspicuous as disabled soldiers paraded doggedly through the drizzle that subdued the celebrations in the evening. Mr. Lewis and Mr. Rudd lead a street march of soldiers recovering from wounds. Some looked exhausted in the drizzle but kept cheerful, looking very damp in the rain. But they stuck it, having stuck worse at the front.

Many laundries and factories shut down for various periods, the workers in many cases being absent, having taken a holiday for themselves.

In contrast to the loud rejoicing in the streets was the quietude of the gathering in Acton Wesleyan Church, where the usual Monday night service of intercession was changed to one of thanksgiving. The Rev. George Hopper prayed that the unity which had enabled the Empire to face the problems of war would be maintained as we grappled with those of the peace.

"Cheers and tears, joy and sorrow mingled today. We cannot realise all that the peace means. The situation is too big to grasp but the hour has struck, the shackles of centuries are broken and thousands of men and women had passed into liberty. We are profoundly grateful to God because it was not arms alone that had wrought this victory.

As I came away from the cemetery this afternoon I heard a man say 'We have smashed them.' I turned to him and said 'My dear friend, we alone have not smashed them; do not forget that God has come to our rescue.'

I want the uppermost thought to be the cause of God and humanity as never before because the perils of peace could be much greater than those of war. The spirit of sacrifice, of devotion, of sympathy, of mutual helpfulness, which has been manifested during the past four years throughout the Empire, should be husbanded in the interests of peace. Our influence must be thrown on the side of order, reconstruction and all that would help solve the problems before us.

There is a war that never ceased – against wrong and vice – that had been shelved because it was felt winning the war was all that mattered, and men had sunk their political, religious and social differences. This was a day when Free Churchmen should give of their best to the State in a spirit of consecration to fresh ideals, aims and purposes.

Let it not be forgotten that a new era dawned at five o'clock this morning, November 11th 1918, the day on which Prussianism fell, on which paganism passed away, and the world's people – God save the people – came into their own. Let us go forth today in a spirit that is larger, brighter and richer.

Might there be no strife between capital and labour, no rekindling of class hatreds and prejudices. We must keep the flag of liberty handed down by our fathers and not let it be smirched. This is a heritage won by other men into the fruit of whose labours they had entered. We must not forget that our children have a much better time before them because of the sacrifice of those dear lads who fought and died for them. The life of each child had been bought by the sacrifice, first by the Son of God, and by the blood of the men who had died on the plains of Flanders and elsewhere."

15 November 1918. *Chiswick Times*
The Dawn of Peace. How the News was received in Chiswick.

Distant maroons sounded the end of the war. Had the end really come? People flocked to doorways. Wounded tommies were the first to realise the tremendous fact. Little processions of singing wounded men began to pass bedecked with flags and national emblems. People were dazed. Words would not come but tears came unbidden to the eyes as men thought of lads who would not be coming back. Mothers and wives felt an unspeakable relief that their menfolk were possibly free from peril.

Once the armistice was realised the atmosphere changed magically. Flags broke out from staffs and windows. Flags of all nations. Bunting burst out on the buses. Milkmen's drays and wagons fluttered with flags. Ladies appeared in the streets with improvised blouses and headgear in the national colours. A group of Belgians dressed in their best with silk toppers formed a circle and sang to one another.

When the news had been confirmed at the Town Hall bells began to ring a joyous peal – at Christ Church Turnham Green, and the more sonorous tones of the old parish church. 'Mafficking' was absent.

Various editions of the papers were eagerly bought and a downpour at night did not stay the demand for 'Peace Editions' with the outline of armistice terms.

At no place was the news received with more enthusiasm than at the schools. Daddy would come back – alas in many cases he never would. They sang the national anthem and flags were passed through the fences into the playgrounds until they were a blaze of colour. One headmaster said 'I think the resumption of business in the circumstances would be a farce. Dismiss!' So the kiddies swelled the throngs of celebrators.

Workers downed tools to join the celebrations and lorries bearing khaki-clad munition work girls arrived.

The footways were filled with good-natured cheering and singing, but always the under-current of soberness. As the night wore on lights, daringly unshaded, shone from windows.

At the Richmond Hippodrome the audience bubbled over the joyousness. At the Chiswick Empire the scene was of indescribable enthusiasm. Cecil E. Bovil, chairman of Chiswick Council, came on the stage and made a short speech – "After four years England and her allies by God's mercy are today completely victorious. Brute force, callous cruelty, deceit and treachery were overthrown. Thousands of mothers are able to lay their heads on their pillows without fear. Thousands of women can be sure of the return of their husbands. Prussian militarism was scotched forever. The one time Emperor of Germany is a fugitive with no place to go. They were going to see he received a just punishment. In our joy let us not forget the thousands of men who had laid down their lives that they at home might be free. Remembering them let us determine that this England should be a different England to what it was before the war. A man's worth hereafter should be his personal character and the purity of his life, and not measured by the depth of his pocket."

15 November 1918. *Chiswick Times*
A letter from Mary Gray. A plea for humility.

'Let those in the Christian faith foster a spirit of humility and compassion, and still the forces of hatred and bitterness that cause sensational rejoicings that mar the closing scenes of this world-wide night. It is easy for most of us to follow where the voices are loudest, but if peace is to be no more than a name, and a league of free nations a reality, we need to guard from surface emotions and heroics and build on something stronger than either. To many of us our hope of inspiration is centered in a church which, in spite of disappointments, is still dearly loved. 'Send us not away fasting, lest we faint by the way.' '

Index

I